# JOHN WILKES BOOTH

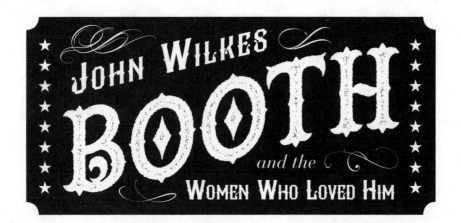

# JOHN WILKES BOOTH

*and the*

## WOMEN WHO LOVED HIM

## E. LAWRENCE ABEL

REGNERY
HISTORY

Regnery History™ is a trademark of Salem Communications Holding Corporation; Regnery® is a registered trademark of Salem Communications Holding Corporation

Cataloging-in-Publication data on file with the Library of Congress

ISBN 978-1-62157-596-2
e-book ISBN 978-1-62157-619-8

Published in the United States by
Regnery History
An Imprint of Regnery Publishing
A Division of Salem Media Group
300 New Jersey Ave NW
Washington, DC 20001
www.RegneryHistory.com

Manufactured in the United States of America

10 9 8 7 6 5 4 3 2 1

Books are available in quantity for promotional or premium use. For information on discounts and terms, please visit our website: www.Regnery.com.

*To Alex, Ari, Elliot, Emmy, and Jack.*

# CONTENTS

THE BOOTH FAMILY      xi

THE WOMEN      xiii

INTRODUCTION      xvii

## PART ONE

| 1 | Sins of the Father | 1 |
|---|---|---|
| 2 | I've Broken My Promise | 11 |
| 3 | Old Sins Cast Long Shadows | 21 |
| 4 | They Idolized Him | 31 |
| 5 | Young and Pretty Maggie Mitchell | 41 |
| 6 | This Harpers Ferry Business | 47 |
| 7 | The Star Sisters: Helen and Lucille Western | 55 |
| 8 | I Cannot Stoop to That Which I Despise | 63 |
| 9 | Almost an Eunuch | 69 |
| 10 | Little Rehearsals: Louise Wooster | 75 |
| 11 | The Southern Marseillaise | 81 |
| 12 | All for Love and Murder: Henrietta Irving | 85 |
| 13 | My Goose Hangs High | 97 |
| 14 | True Grit | 109 |
| 15 | Effie and Alice | 115 |
| 16 | Imagine My Helping That Wounded Soldier | 121 |
| 17 | The Most Beautiful Woman on the American Stage | 127 |
| 18 | Storming About the Country Is Sad Work | 133 |
| 19 | Not a Secesh | 145 |

| | | |
|---|---|---|
| 20 | Isabel Sumner | 151 |
| 21 | A Gang of Misfits | 161 |
| 22 | Lucy Lambert Hale | 175 |
| 23 | Anything That Pleases You: Ella Starr | 185 |
| 24 | Assassination | 193 |
| 25 | I Have Too Great a Soul to Die Like a Criminal | 211 |

### PART TWO

| | | |
|---|---|---|
| 26 | Ella Starr | 223 |
| 27 | Asia and Mary Ann | 227 |
| 28 | "It Cannot Be Denied": Lucy Hale | 243 |
| 29 | Effie Germon | 253 |
| 30 | Alice Gray | 259 |
| 31 | Helen Western | 263 |
| 32 | Fanny Brown | 273 |
| 33 | Henrietta Irving | 279 |
| 34 | Maggie Mitchell | 285 |
| 35 | Ada Gray | 293 |
| 36 | Isabel Sumner | 295 |
| 37 | Louise Wooster | 297 |
| 38 | Clara Morris | 301 |
| 39 | Martha Mills | 309 |

| | |
|---|---|
| EPILOGUE | 317 |
| ACKNOWLEDGMENTS | 327 |
| NOTES | 333 |
| BIBLIOGRAPHY | 405 |
| INDEX | 441 |

John Wilkes Booth *carte de visite*, circa 1863. *Courtesy of Heritage Auctions, www. ha.com.*

# THE BOOTH FAMILY

**Booth, Adelaide Delannoy**

Legal wife of John's father, Junius. She discovered Junius was living a double life, came to America, and made the Booth family's life a living hell.

**Booth, Blanche DeBar**

"June" and Clementina Booth's daughter and an actress.

**Booth, Clementina DeBar**

"June" Booth's first wife and an actress.

**Booth, Edwin Thomas**

John's second oldest brother. Like his father, one of America's foremost Shakespearean actors.

**Booth, Joseph Adrian**

John's youngest brother. Regarded as a failure by his family, he became a doctor later in life.

**Booth, Junius Brutus**
John's father, one of the most famous Shakespearean actors of his day. For twenty years, he deceived his legal wife into thinking he was returning to England while he secretly maintained a second family in America. He was an alcoholic and periodically insane.

**Booth, Junius Brutus Jr. ("June")**
John's oldest brother, an actor and manager. Like his father, he deserted his wife for a younger woman.

**Booth, Mary Ann Holmes**
John's mother, the woman with whom Junius eloped to America while still married. She loved all her children and John the most.

**Booth, Richard**
John's grandfather.

**Booth, Richard Junius**
Adelaide and Junius's son. While touring with his father, he discovered Junius's duplicity.

**Booth, Rosalie Ann**
John's oldest sister. She never married and was her mother's life-long companion and caregiver.

**Clarke, Asia Booth**
John's sister, his confidante, and biographer. She married John Sleeper Clarke.

**Clarke, John Sleeper**
Actor, Asia's husband, and John's brother-in-law.

**Devlin, Mary**
Actress, Edwin's wife, and John's sister-in-law.

# THE WOMEN

**Brown, Fanny**

Said to have been the most beautiful actress on the American stage, Fanny was rumored to be engaged to John. Her photo was one of the five photos in John's pocket when he died.

**Germon, Effie**

Actress—her photo was another one of five photos in John's pocket when he died. She was the only actress to send condolences to John's family.

**Gray, Ada**

Actress—one of John's brief flings.

**Gray, Alice**

Actress—her photo was also among those found in John's pocket when he died.

**Hale, Lucy Lambert**
John's fiancée—her photo was found in John's pocket along with photos of four actresses.

**Irving, Henrietta**
Actress—she tried to kill John in a jealous rage.

**Mills, Martha**
She claimed to have had affair with John and told her children John was their father.

**Mitchell, "Maggie"**
One of the most prominent actresses on the American stage, she had an on-again, off-again relationship with John and was rumored to have been engaged to John.

**Morris, Clara**
Actress—one of the few to write about John.

**Starr, Ella, a.k.a. Ella Turner, a.k.a. Nellie Starr**
Teenage Washington prostitute—she tried to kill herself over John's betrayal.

**Sumner, Isabel**
One of John's affairs, she kept several of his letters.

**Western, Helen**
Actress—her photo was one of the five photos in John's pocket when he died.

**Western, Lucille**
Actress and Helen's sister —she may have had a brief relationship with John.

**Wooster, Louise "Lou" Catherine**
A Montgomery prostitute whom John promised to make a star, she was Birmingham, Alabama's best known madam.

**Wren, Ella**
A Richmond actress rumored to be engaged to John.

# Introduction

When John Wilkes Booth was thirteen, a gypsy, passing through the Maryland countryside near John's boarding school at Cockeysville, offered to read his palm for a few pennies. Johnnie (his boyhood nickname) thought it might be amusing to have his fortune told. He handed over the pennies and stuck out his palm. What the gypsy told him was so unnerving he wrote it down so he wouldn't forget it.

He read and reread the gypsy's prophesy, mulling over what to make of it. Several days later, Johnnie pulled his older sister Asia aside. He had something to show her. They walked to a nearby hollow and sat down, Johnnie leaning his head against Asia's knees. He reached into his pocket and handed her a scrap of paper, by then well-worn from being folded and unfolded many times.

"See here," Johnnie said, pulling the now ragged paper from his pocket, "I've written it, but there was no need to do that, for it is so bad that I shall not soon forget it." "Only a Gypsey's tattle for money," he added as Asia straightened the paper out, "but who shall say there is not truth in it?"

Asia held her breath as she read the first few words of the boyish, penciled scrawl:

> Ah, you've a bad hand; the lines all cris-cras. It's full enough of sorrow—full of trouble—trouble in plenty, everywhere I look. You'll break hearts, they'll be nothing to you. You'll die young, and leave many to mourn you, many to love you too, but you'll be rich, generous and free with your money. You're born under an unlucky star. You've got in your hand a thundering crowd of enemies—not one friend—you'll make a bad end, and have plenty to love you afterwards. You'll have a fast life—short, but a grand one. Now, young sir I've never seen a worse hand, and I wish I hadn't seen it, but every word I've told is true by the signs.

Stuffing the prophecy back into his pocket, John said the gypsy had told him something else as she was gathering her belongings. "I'm glad I'm not a young girl," she'd said, "or I'd follow you through the world for that handsome face."[1]

As the gypsy predicted, John Wilkes Booth had a meteoric career. He was one of the highest paid actors of his time. He was generous and free with his money. He broke many hearts. He died young. And he certainly made a bad end. On April 26, 1865, twelve days after he shot Abraham Lincoln, he was "hunted like a dog through swamps, [and] woods…chased by gunboats till I was forced to return wet, cold, and starving, with every man's hand against me." Refusing to come out of a burning barn where he was surrounded, John was mortally wounded by a bullet that severed his spinal cord.

That the gypsy's predictions were eerily accurate is pure drama. But how much of it is true? The story of the gypsy comes from Asia's remembrances of her brother, penned in the 1870s, in a memoir written to humanize the errant brother she loved. Like many reminiscences, it smacks of elaboration. Is anyone's memory of what someone said or read really reliable after thirty years?

Asia offered another story that "led one to believe that human lives are swayed by the supernatural." Her mother told her that when John was six months old, she had had "a vision" in answer to a "fervent prayer." She was sitting before the fire in their log house with John cradled in her arms. Staring into the fire, she had asked God to reveal the baby's future to her. The flames in the fireplace "leaped up like a wave of blood," she said, and the shape of the country appeared in the flames and then faded into "the boy's own name."

Asia's stories about the gypsy and her mother's vision implied destiny guided her brother's hand when he shot Lincoln. He had no choice. The gods had sealed her brother's fate from the moment of his birth. But John Wilkes Booth's story was not a foreordained Greek tragedy. Like Shakespeare's Macbeth, John Wilkes Booth was a "solid, self-respecting murderer."[2]

He lived in a time of war. Ideologies tore families apart. Fathers, brothers, and sons chose different sides and wore different uniforms. John's sympathies rested with the South. Like many Southerners, he had a deep-seated hatred for the man in the White House who he believed wanted to destroy the Southern way of life—a man he felt had become a despot like Julius Caesar. Someone had to do something. John felt it was his duty to be the South's Brutus.

Historians typically veer in one of two directions regarding the assassination: some make the case that Booth acted on his own; others contend he was a tool of a government conspiracy. Those scenarios leave the basic question still unanswered. In his own time, Lincoln was far from the beloved president time has made him. He was widely despised and had a desk full of death threats. So, why John Wilkes Booth?

Booth family historian Stanley Kimmel pointed the finger at John's family. "I had early come to realize that the motives for the assassination lay far back in the life of John Wilkes Booth," Kimmel writes in the foreword to *The Mad Booths of Maryland*.[3] Kimmel put the Booth family under the proverbial microscope. No one could understand what made John Wilkes Booth tick, he said, without knowing the Booth family history, starting with his father.

"Happy families are all alike," wrote Leo Tolstoy, whereas "every unhappy family is unhappy in its own way."[4] The Booth family was not a happy family. While John's father, Junius, was still married in England, he fell in love with a girl of eighteen (John's future mother) and ran off with her to America, deserting his wife and infant son. He told his wife he would be back in a year or two. He kept up that lie for over twenty years. When his wife eventually discovered Junius's adultery, she came to America and publicly shamed him and his family. At that time in America, a bastard had the same moral social standing as a prostitute, thief, or beggar; the realization they were all tainted with illegitimacy humiliated his children and left them psychologically scarred.[5]

Junius was no model father. His career kept him away from home for nine months of the year. Much of the time, whether at home or on tour, he was drunk. Once he was so desperate for a drink he pawned himself for booze money. At one point a theatre manager locked him in a room before his performance to keep him from drinking. Junius would not be denied. He bribed someone to pour booze into a pipe fitted through the keyhole. Clarence Cobb, who as a boy knew the Booth family well, recalled that Junius "drank enough to float a man-of-war."[6] The night John was born, Junius wasn't even home. He was drunk at the local tavern.[7] When he was at home, he was distant and often suffered periodic lapses of sanity.

Asia was John's older sister by two years and his confidante. Like her older siblings, Junius Jr., Rosalie, and Edwin, she had been humiliated by their father's first wife's screeds about their parents' adultery and the taunts of illegitimacy. Despite living in a family of actors and marrying an actor, Asia was very status-conscious. She shared the opinion of a large segment of America that actresses were a small step above prostitutes. Since John was very close to Asia, her attitudes about actresses influenced his own.

Asia was also the family's historian, but she never mentioned her father's alcoholism—a silence not uncommon among the children of alcoholics. Asia's father was a saint to her. She glossed over all his misdeeds, never mentioning the shame she undoubtedly felt being publicly humiliated as one of the "fruits" of her father's "adulterous intercourse." For Asia, her father's adultery was merely a "boyish mésalliance."[8]

John Wilkes Booth, the ninth of the American Booth family children, was his mother's favorite. Everyone in the family was aware of it, but they didn't envy him. He was their favorite too. He was a pampered child. He grew up a narcissist, a vain and egotistical man whose main ambition in life was fame. In spite of his narcissism, he was immensely liked (up until August 1864 when something changed him). He was "the gentlest man I ever knew..." said an old-time colleague, "universally liked by all his fellow actors and actresses."[9]

John was always considerate of other actors, even the extras, said actor Martin Wright. "Of all the stars that came to play with us [in Cleveland] the one we loved and admired the most was John Wilkes Booth. ...There was never a better fellow or a more perfect gentleman. He was not high and mighty, like most of the stars. Any supernumerary could go to him for advice—and was always sure to get it. Whoever went to him was received with gentle courtesy, and came away an ardent admirer."[10]

He was charismatic. "If you ever came within the range of his personal magnetism and fascinations," recalled a former roommate, "you would involuntarily be bound to him as with hooks of steel."[11] He "cast a spell over most men with whom he came in contact, and I believe all women without exception."[12] A long-time friend, comedian John Mathews, said John was the most winning and captivating man he had ever known. It was an opinion shared by everyone who knew him.

He was a man's man. An excellent horseman. A marksman with pistols. A skilled swordsman. He was athletic but not ruggedly masculine—elegant, not brawny. He was a brilliant talker. He was cultured, eloquent, and good-mannered. He nearly always seemed unruffled and self-assured. His easy-going confidence attracted men and women alike.

To many women, he was a living, breathing aphrodisiac. Five foot seven (average for the 1860s), he weighed about 175 pounds. He had broad shoulders and gently sloping, muscular arms, yet his hands were shapely with delicate tapering fingers. He stood ramrod straight. When he moved, it was with the grace of an athlete. He had ivory pale skin. His hair was thick, curly, and inky black. He had sparkling, coal black eyes—said to be his most captivating feature. Heavy eyelids gave him a touch of mystery. Pearl white teeth accented his smile. Except for a silky trimmed moustache, he was clean-shaven. If there were a *People* magazine in the early 1860s, John Wilkes Booth would have been its "sexiest man in America."

Actress Clara Morris fondly recalled, "It was impossible to see him and not admire him." He was "so young, so bright, so gay."[13] John Mathews once said that if John were a woman, men would have fallen in love with him.[14]

Women packed the audiences wherever he played. He grouched they were not there to appreciate his acting but to gawk at him. When the play was over, they would cram together outside the stage door just to catch a mere glimpse of him up-close. They pawed at him for autographs. He was the first actor on record to have his clothes torn by infatuated women craving something of his as a souvenir to take home.[15]

At restaurants, "slammers of plates and shooters of coffee cups" competed with one another over who would serve him "like doves about a grain basket leaving other travelers to wait upon themselves or go without refreshment." At hotels, maids stole into his room and pulled apart his already made-up bed for the sheer thrill of it and arranged his pillows so that they would be slanted at just the right angle.[16] His friend John McCullough joked John "could be counted on to draw into the house three-hundred chambermaids, three-hundred wet nurses, and a score of widows."[17]

Every day letters poured in from women "who periled their happiness and their reputations by committing to paper words of love and admiration which they could not, apparently, refrain from writing." Other actors receiving similar "mash letters" passed them around and laughed at what they read.[18] John received more than his share of love letters but never shared them. Even if he didn't bother to read them, he snipped away the signatures at the bottom before tossing them. The letters were harmless, he said. "Their sting was in their tail."[19]

Curious to see what they wrote, another actor picked up one of the letters whose signatures John had just removed. "I can read it, can't I, now the signature is gone?" he asked, expecting a nod.

Deadly serious, John replied, "the woman's folly is no excuse for our knavery, put it down please." There was no missing the menace in John's voice. He put it down.[20]

Actresses were as rapturous as his female audiences when they heard he was coming to their theatre. "To play the opposite part to this young genius was the dream of every ambitious young woman of the stage," said actress Rachel Noah, John's leading lady in Cleveland. She remembered how envious the other actresses and ballet girls were after her love scenes with John. From the wings, "She was conscious of a volley of 'oh's' and 'ah's' whenever he embraced me."[21]

A chronic philanderer, John simply could not commit to just one woman until the very end—even then it may have been more manipulation than love. Like many actresses and "well-bred and wealthy ladies, married and unmarried, who did many foolish things for one of his kisses," actress Henrietta Irving found him too easy to love and just as hard to hold on to. One night Henrietta saw John coming out of her sister's room. In a jealous rage, she slashed him then ran off and stabbed herself. "It was impossible to know him and not love him," said actress Clara Morris.[22]

The story of John's plan to kill Lincoln and his eventual capture and death has been told many times. The standard account is that John shot the president in the back of the head on Friday, April 14, 1865, at Ford's Theatre in Washington, D.C., while Lincoln was watching *Our American Cousin* with his wife, Mary, and their two guests. Twelve days later, John was cornered in a barn in Virginia. When he refused to surrender, the barn was set on fire. While still inside, he was shot. He was dragged from the barn alive and died several hours later. A military court later convicted eight of his accomplices. Four of them were hanged; four were sent to prison.

As John lay dying, his pockets were searched. Among his belongings were a pocket diary and photos of five women. Four of those women were stage actresses. The fifth was a photo of a U.S. senator's daughter to whom he was engaged.

John Wilkes Booth was hungry for fame, touchy about politics, and a notorious womanizer. Many books have been written about his politics and his quest for fame, but the stories of those five women and the other women who loved him have been virtually ignored, glossed over as mere footnotes in history. Yet those women were famous women in their own right; they lived their own scandalous lives and were betrayed in love and marriage not just by Booth. They were women who coped with loneliness after affairs gone sour. Women who had once enjoyed fame and wealth but died in abject poverty. Women who became addicted to drugs to escape their turmoil. This book is as much about those women as it is about the assassin who loved callously, hated passionately, and died wretchedly—a man whose last words before he died were "Useless, useless."

# PART ONE

*Character is fate.*
HERACLITUS

# 1

# SINS OF THE FATHER

At an age when most boys were roughhousing with one another, John's father, Junius Brutus Booth, was in an English courtroom being sued for paternity.[1] A neighbor's maid in the Bloomsbury district where the Booth family lived had been fired for her obvious indiscretion and had charged him "with that 'deed of darkness,' which her situation could no longer conceal."[2]

Richard Booth, Junius's lawyer father,[3] was dumbfounded over his son's sexual precociousness. As his son's legal guardian, he was liable for paternity damages and contested the accusation. Donning his black gown and powdered horsehair wig, he grasped his thirteen-year-old's hand and led him into the London court. If the judges saw his son as a boy not yet out of puberty, they might not believe it possible for him to have fathered a child. But the judges were not swayed by Junius's youthful appearance. The girl surely knew the father of her child, they said. Richard was ordered to pay the maid £30 (enough to live on for about a year in 1810) "in expiation of his son's delinquency."

Desperate to find a way to keep Junius too busy to tomcat, Richard apprenticed his son to one profession after another. Junius had no interest in any of them.[4] At sixteen, he was back in court in another paternity suit.[5] This time the complainant was a servant in his father's home. Once again, Richard was ordered to pay child support.[6]

Junius's favorite preoccupation was also responsible for his discovering the profession that would make him famous. The eureka moment came in October 1813 at London's Covent Garden Theatre.[7]

During the day, Covent Garden was a vegetable and flower market. At night, its gardens, pubs, coffee houses, and theatres were London's sex Mecca. "All the prostitutes in the kingdom had picked upon that blessed neighborhood for general rendezvous," said a Londoner who knew what he was talking about.[8] On that October night, Junius was at the Covent Garden Theatre to pick up one of the prostitutes who plied her trade in the theatre's lobby and saloon. Not finding one to his liking—or, more likely, one he could afford—and with nothing else to do, Junius bought a ticket for *Othello*.

Until then, Junius had never heard of *Othello*.[9] But he became instantly star-struck. He was determined to join the glamorous world of the stage.

Like other unknowns, Junius's first acting parts were with amateur theatre groups. Eventually he landed a paying job in a minor role with the Jonas-Penley Company, a small troupe that played in the dock towns in and around London.[10] In August 1814, the Jonas-Penley Company departed for a brief tour in Holland and Belgium. In Belgium, Junius rented a room at the house of widowed hatmaker Madame Agatha Delannoy.

During his three-month stay at Madame Delannoy's, Junius had ample time to become chummy with her four daughters, especially twenty-two-year-old Marie Christine Adelaide. Adelaide (the name she went by) was captivated by the young actor's looks and charisma. She was not particularly attractive, but she was charming and educated. When it was time for Junius's company to go on to his next scheduled engagement, Adelaide told him she was pregnant. Junius said he would marry her.

There was a hitch. Adelaide was Catholic. Junius was Protestant. For a Catholic to wed a Protestant, either Junius would have to convert (which he would not do), or they had to receive a dispensation from the Catholic Church. Adelaide had two choices: she could stay in Brussels and bear the shame of having a child out of wedlock, or she could run off with Junius.[11]

Several weeks after their elopement, probably at Adelaide's urging, Junius wrote to her mother from Ostend on the Belgium coast to make amends. Madame Delannoy wrote back she would give them her blessing if Junius returned to Brussels, married in a Catholic church, and gave up his acting career for a job with more security. In fact, she said she had already lined one up for him.

Calling her "Madame and Dear Friend," Junius wrote back he was delighted she had found him a job. Disingenuously, he said he would like to live in Brussels and did not care that much about money. "I embrace you with all my heart. Also my uncle and my future sisters-in-law," he wrote, adding, "I believe you are angry, but there is no cause for it."[12]

Junius never had any serious intention of taking Madame Delannoy's offer. Two weeks later, he and Adelaide left for England.

Richard was not at all happy to have Junius and his pregnant, foreign lover move in with him.[13] After all the pent-up anger and disappointment drained out of him, Richard let them stay on the condition they find jobs and marry as soon as possible. Adelaide went to work at a millinery. Junius found jobs in theatres in Brighton and other towns outside London.

With the little money they managed to save, Junius and Adelaide wed on May 8, 1815, at a local church. Several days later, Adelaide wrote her mother that she was married and "the happiest of women…getting as fat as a great beast." To assure her mother she was not a "fallen woman," she enclosed a copy of her marriage certificate.[14] Their first child, a girl, was born five months later but died in infancy.

Junius's big break as an actor came by accident in September 1816. Edmund Kean, one of the most raved about actors of his day,[15] was slated to appear in Brighton. When he failed to show up as scheduled, theatre manager Thomas Trotter panicked and called Junius to fill in. Junius hypnotized the audience with his large, piercing, blue-gray eyes; melodious voice; dramatic pauses; and rapid change of facial expressions. When the play ended, the audience enthusiastically applauded the newcomer.

Some wealthy patrons of the Covent Garden Theatre happened to be vacationing in Brighton at the time. When they returned to London, they told friends about the extraordinary newcomer who was just as good as Kean. Curious to see the fledgling actor on stage themselves, they used their influence to have Junius hired for a "trial night" in February 1817.

Sally Booth, the Covent Garden Theatre's leading actress, worried the upstart with the same name as hers would be an embarrassment. During rehearsal, she pulled Junius aside and asked him to tack an "e" on the end of his name. That way no one would think they were related.[16]

Sally Booth needn't have worried. The next day, Junius woke up to learn he was London's newest star.[17] In four years, he had gone from sitting in the Covent Garden Theatre's audience to being its star performer.

An anonymous author was so impressed by Junius that he wrote a book-length biography of the new star.[18]

Relying on his Covent Garden fame, Junius began to demand and receive bigger paydays for his appearances outside London, sometimes earning five times more than his Covent Garden receipts.[19] Despite his being away from London most of the time, he managed to father another child with Adelaide in 1818. Richard Junius Booth was born on January 21, 1819. Junius named him Richard after his father and Junius after himself. Years later, young Richard would turn Junius's life upside down.

As Junius's increasing fame spread beyond England, he began receiving invitations from abroad and left England with Thomas Flynn, his best friend, for an engagement at the English Theatre in Amsterdam.

A few days after Junius's first appearance, the theatre's manager received a note from Prince William of Orange saying he would like to see the young actor he had heard so much about. On the night arranged for the command performance, Junius was nowhere to be found. Panic-stricken, the manager sent Flynn to fetch him. Flynn could not find Junius that night or the next day and stopped searching. Fellow actors speculated Junius been drinking and had fallen into the canal and drowned. A few days later Flynn was playing billiards in a saloon when he heard a familiar voice coming from the backroom. He opened the door to see Junius cavorting with two prostitutes.

Tongue-lashed, Junius became contrite. At a hastily arranged, new command performance of *Macbeth*, he apologized to the prince and begged his forgiveness. He had been "studying Dutch under the tuition of two interesting demoiselles," he explained. They were teaching him the "vernacular of the country," and he had lost all track of time. Amused by Junius's euphemism, the prince nodded acceptance of the apology and sat back to watch the play.[20]

Young Junius Brutus Booth around the time he met Mary Ann Holmes. *Courtesy of Folger Shakespeare Library.*

Junius was back in London in the autumn of 1820, poised to be London's foremost actor and even greater than his rival, Edmund Kean. Strolling to the theatre for rehearsal, he was smitten by an eighteen-year-old girl selling flowers outside the theatre.[21]

Mary Ann Holmes was ten years younger than Adelaide and much prettier. She had soft brown eyes, glossy black curls, full lips, and a pale oval face.[22] Years later, their daughter Asia penciled an "X" next to a day in October 1820 in her father's date book with the following note: "The night mother first saw my father."[23]

Junius was twenty-four at the time, six years older than Mary Ann, and in the prime of life. He had a high, wide forehead, a narrow chin, high cheekbones, an aquiline nose, dark curly hair, muscular arms, and expressive eyes.[24] There was no need to introduce himself. By then he was one of London's most recognizable actors.

Mary Ann Holmes daguerreotype photo. *Courtesy of Library of Congress.*

The 1820s were an era of free love among England's intellectuals. Poet Percy Bysshe Shelley deserted his wife and ran off with sixteen-year-old Mary Godwin, who would later write *Frankenstein*. Shelley's close friend and fellow poet Lord George Gordon Byron was rumored to have had affairs with hundreds of women. Byron's poems were "abjured by married men and read in secret by their wives." Critics railed at his "'cuckoo strain' of adultery."[25] Byron was amused by such comments. "The reading or non-reading of a book," he chuckled, "will never keep down a single petticoat."[26]

Mary Ann was an only child of devout Anglican parents who raised flowers at their plant nursery. They were simple people. Mary Ann could read and write, but there was little to read other than the Bible at home. When Junius gave her a calf-bound set of Byron's collected works, she was thrilled with anticipation of what was on their pages. At night she would take one of the books from under her bed, where she had hidden them, and read it at her window by moonlight along with Junius's passionate letters, telling her she was his "own soul" and he was "your worshipper."[27]

Mary Ann was swept off her feet.

Mary Ann knew Junius was married when she agreed to run off with him. She could not imagine a more exciting life than being with him. There was another reason: she was pregnant. She wouldn't be able to hide her condition from her "very religious and severe" parents much longer.[28]

Junius had a more mundane reason for getting Mary Ann out of London. If his adultery were discovered, the scandal would torpedo his career. Adelaide would sue him for divorce. He was facing not only ignominy but also debtor's prison.

Junius had no qualms about deserting his family, but it was not so for Mary Ann. For a girl raised in a religious home, to run away and live unmarried was much harder. Junius assuaged her guilt by arranging a makeshift wedding at the home of Mrs. Chambers, one of the patrons who had used her influence to get Junius a trial night at the Covent Garden Theatre and who became close friends with him afterwards. Mrs. Chambers was sympathetic to the couple's plight; she had also deserted a spouse for someone else.[29] As part of the make-believe, she had an unofficial marriage license created for the couple.[30] After the private January 1821 wedding, Mary Ann went home to gather her things. Among the few possessions she took with her was the set of Byron's works Junius had given her. Meanwhile, Junius went home to Adelaide. He lied and told her he had lost his audiences and was going to America to revitalize his career and their finances.

Adelaide pleaded to go with him. Junius shook his head. Their son Richard was "too young for the voyage," he said.[31] He promised he would send her £50 or more a year, depending on how successful his venture became. Years later, when Adelaide found out Junius had another family, she demanded more. Much more.

When Mary Ann did not come home that night, her mother became frantic. Going through what was left of Mary Ann's belongings, she found thirty-three letters from Junius (amounting to almost three a day).[32] The only one party to Junius's plans beforehand was his father, Richard. How he reacted can be imagined. A few days later, Richard called on Mary Ann's parents to tell them their daughter had eloped with his son to America.[33]

While on their honeymoon, Junius took time to write to theatre managers in the United States for bookings. When he received a reply from Charles Gilbert, the manager of Richmond's Marshall Theatre, promising a two-week contract starting on July 6, 1821, Junius told Mary Ann to pack their trunks and get ready to leave on the first ship to Virginia.

# 2

# I'VE BROKEN MY PROMISE

On June 30, 1821, the light freighter *Two Brothers* docked at Norfolk, Virginia. Junius and Mary Ann were the only passengers on board. After disembarking, Junius settled Mary Ann and their luggage at a hotel about fifteen miles south of Richmond and then headed for the Marshall Theatre.

From Richmond, Junius embarked on a whirlwind tour, appearing in New York, Baltimore, Charleston, Savannah, Augusta, and New Orleans. Alone in a strange country and with Junius on the road to New Orleans, Mary Ann gave birth to Junius Brutus Jr. on December 22, 1821, in Charleston, South Carolina. Junius did not learn he was a father for a month.[1] A year later, Junius rented a four-room log house in Harford County in Maryland, three miles from the village of Bel Air and about twenty-five miles from Baltimore.

In the 1820s, Baltimore was the country's second largest city. Located at the center of the eastern theatre circuit, it had two theatres of its own, the Front Street Theatre and the Holliday Street Theatre. Living near the city allowed Junius to stop over at his home between tours. Junius's daughter Asia would later write her father settled in rural Harford County rather than in the city to escape the yellow fever epidemic raging in Baltimore.[2] More likely his real motive was to avoid the possibility of running into someone who recognized him from London.

Adultery was no trivial matter in nineteenth-century America. If anyone he knew saw him with Mary Ann and their son Junius Jr., the scandal would end his career.[3] In 1825, when Junius's former rival Edmund Kean appeared at the Park Theatre, he was hissed at and pelted with fruits and nuts and obscenities for an adulterous affair he had had in England. The American public regarded marital fidelity as sacrosanct. A cabin in rural Maryland was far enough away from Baltimore to ensure Junius's secret would not be discovered.

The "Farm," as the family called their cabin, was cozy. Whitewashed on the outside, it had four rooms, a loft, and a kitchen. Servants cooked bread in a round Dutch oven. Food was served on pewter platters with a well-worn silver spoon, a legacy from Junius's silversmith grandfather. The Farm also housed an extensive library of Junius's books.[4]

Soon after moving in, Junius invited his father to come live at his new home. Mary Ann would need someone for protection and help while he was away. Six months later, Richard knocked on Junius's door, toting his books and clothes. There were now four people living in the house— Junius, Mary Ann, Richard, and Junius Jr. A year later there were five. On July 5, 1823, a second child, Rosalie Ann, was born.

Junius liked the solitude of rural Maryland. He decided he would like to try his hand at farming when not on tour and leased a nearby, 150-acre plot for one hundred years (he could not buy land since he was not a citizen). Then he hired some of the local men to move the log house onto his new property.

Since coming to the United States Junius had turned mystic. Animals had souls, he instructed his family. They were not to be killed. Cows were only for milk. No one in the family was allowed to eat meat. When Junius was home, the family followed the rules. When he was away on tour, there was meat on the table.[5]

The Farm was Junius's refuge from his rigorous stage life. In the summers when he was home, he tilled the land, planted fruit trees and a vineyard, and arranged for a stable to be built for horses and a barn for cows. In fall, if he was still at home, he brought his farm-grown vegetables to a nearby, open-air market in Bel Air. On matinee days, when he did not appear before the curtain went up at the Holliday Street Theatre in Baltimore, the manager would send stagehands to his market stall to get him to the theatre, but Junius refused to leave until all his crops were sold. After a number of setbacks, the manager sent someone to buy whatever produce Junius hadn't sold so that he would leave.[6]

In his earlier years, Junius wrote to Mary Ann from his various theatre engagements with instructions for the care of the farm and children. "My love for you," he assured her, "is still undiminished. Take care of your Health & don't be dull or fretting." To his father, he confessed he was sick of acting and would much rather be home.[7] Richard, meanwhile, was often at the local tavern. Junius pleaded with his father to stop drinking. "Madness will be the result if you persist."[8] For Junius to warn his father about drinking and madness was sheer irony. He had started drinking himself and was lapsing into episodic insanity.

Fame had once been Junius's burning ambition. Now his name on a playbill was enough to fill any theatre. He could command a hundred dollars a night, but the intensity he brought to each performance took its toll. Five-hour shows were common. Some theatre managers interpolated songs into Shakespeare's plays. Critics often complained the dramas were just fillers for the songs and musical numbers. One manager inserted thirty songs into Shakespeare's The Tempest.[9]

Theatre in antebellum America was also participatory. If someone in the audience enjoyed a show or a performer, he might climb onto a chair and wave his arms to get the rest of the audience's attention. While the performer remained on stage, the fan would praise him or her.

Most theatregoers did not question songs or long-winded interruptions from the audience, but the interrupted performers would often lose their concentration. Many, like Junius, started drinking to take the edge off after a performance and sometimes to prepare for the strain before going on. In Junius's case, one bottle became two then three. At times he was drunk on stage.

Madness followed, albeit sporadically. One day, Junius was idly chatting with fellow actor Jacob Woodhull in the theatre lobby when Junius's face suddenly blanched. He told Woodhull he felt an urge to cut somebody's throat. That moment, actor Henry Wallack walked by. Had some bystanders not intervened and disarmed him, Junius would have killed Wallack.[10]

By 1827, Junius was hitting the bottle hard and suffering serious mental lapses. At the Tremont Theatre in Boston, Junius nodded to the prompter several times during the play's first two acts to feed him his lines. A little into the third act, he turned to the audience. "Ladies and gentlemen," he blurted, "I really don't know this part." As he was led off the stage, he was overheard pleading, "take me to the lunatic asylum."[11]

At home, life had become a nightmare for Mary Ann. In 1833, a cholera epidemic took the lives of three of their children: five-year-old Mary Ann, four-year-old Frederick, and two-year-old Elizabeth. The five-year-old was the last to succumb. "News of my poor child's decease," Junius said, "tore me from Richmond to prevent its Mother following it to the Tomb...or the Mad-house."[12]

Junius was the one more likely to wind up in the madhouse. Back at home, he dug up his daughter's body, brought it into the house, and placed it in his bed next to Mary Ann. When his favorite horse died, Junius forced a terrorized Mary Ann to wrap herself in a shroud and sit on the horse. While she sat in terrorized silence, Junius walked around her reading a funeral service until concerned neighbors came to her rescue. Subdued, Junius asked them if they wanted a drink.[13] Another time, he built a funeral pyre of chairs and tables and forced Mary Ann to climb on top. He would have set fire to it had Mary Ann not been rescued again by neighbors.[14]

In March 1836, Junius tried to hang himself. When Mary Ann woke in the middle of the night, she found him hanging by the neck. Somehow she managed to get him down and send for medical aid.[15]

Despite his episodic madness, Junius was still fathering children. In 1833, Mary Ann gave birth to their seventh child, a boy they named Edwin Thomas. As usual, Junius was away on tour when his son was born.

Still caring for her younger children at home, Mary Ann delegated her eldest son, fourteen-year-old Junius Jr., "June," to chaperone his father when Junius was away from home. Touring with his father as his dresser, June became as stage-struck as his father had been as a boy.

By 1835, Junius admitted his drinking was "rapidly reducing him to imbecility of mind and to crookedness of passions." It had "kept his wife in misery and fear for the past several years," he told Dr. James Rush, a physician summoned to treat Junius's alcoholism. Rush told Junius his drinking would kill him if he didn't stop. Junius promised he would. Less than four hours later, Dr. Rush found a note from Junius on his door: "Thanks for the advice of being temperate; I've broke my promise, and am again intoxicated."[16]

Mary Ann gave birth to their ninth child in May 1838. They named him John Wilkes. Some historians assume he was named after an English politician and ardent supporter of the American Revolution, but John Wilkes was also a family name. As usual, Junius was not at home at the time of the birth. This time he was not on tour but drunk at the local tavern.[17] Two years later, thirty-eight-year-old Mary Ann gave birth to yet another child, her tenth, a boy they named Joseph Adrian.

With so many people living at the Farm and the assumption that his other family wouldn't discover his secret, Junius rented a home in Baltimore so that his children could go to better schools. Except for summers, they stayed in Baltimore. Six years later, in 1846, Junius bought a two-story, brick house in Baltimore at 62 North Exeter Street. Not long after, the skeleton in Junius's closet would come out of hiding.

Junius was still sending money to Adelaide. Rarely, if ever, was he thinking about their son Richard. Richard, on the other hand, often wondered about his father in America. He was also curious about the country he had heard so much about. In 1842, he wrote to Junius saying he would like to come visit and travel with him around the country. Could Junius send him money for the trip? By then June had gone off on his own. Junius wrote back saying Richard could be his dresser and travel with him during his tours. That way he could keep an eye on him and keep him from finding out about his other family.[18]

Richard tagged along on the tour with his father for three years, never suspecting his father was living a double life. It took ingenuity for Junius to slip away and visit Mary Ann without Richard's awareness. Richard would have gone back to England none the wiser had it not been for an offhand remark from a stagehand who taunted Richard by calling him a bastard. Didn't he know his father's real family was living in Baltimore?[19]

Richard was dumfounded. He wrote his mother, telling her his father had another family. He pleaded for her to come to Baltimore to prove he was not a bastard.

Shocked, Adelaide gathered her things and left for America. Richard did not let on to his father that he had discovered his secret. He made an excuse about tiring of theatre life, found a place to live in Baltimore, and eked out a meager living teaching Latin and Greek while he waited for his mother to arrive.

Junius was oblivious about Richard's leaving. Perhaps it was a load off his conscience to have him gone. Nearing fifty, Junius was looking forward to living a quiet, uneventful life in his new house on North Exeter Street.

Once settled into a room Richard had rented for her, Adelaide lost no time hiring a lawyer. She was going to make Junius pay dearly for making a fool of her.[20] In early March 1847, Junius was in the middle of a rehearsal at the Holliday Street Theatre when Adelaide charged onto the stage, Richard in tow, screaming that the real Mrs. Booth had arrived.

Junius was taken by surprise. He had not seen Adelaide for more than twenty years. Somehow the theater manager coaxed her into having it out with Junius inside his office. Actors and stagehands did not have to put their ears to the door to hear Adelaide screaming for Junius to admit Richard's legitimacy. Junius was heard shouting just as loudly for her to go home. Adelaide left, promising to stay as long as it took to get Junius's last "franc." She vowed to prove in a court of law that Junius's other children were all bastards.[21]

The only way Adelaide could force Junius to make that admission was to sue him for divorce, claiming adultery. But Maryland had a residence requirement: anyone suing for divorce in that state had to reside there for two years. With no money other than what Richard earned as a language teacher at St. Mary's College, Adelaide lived in a second-story apartment and bided her time.[22]

Only known image of Adelaide Delannoy Booth.
*Courtesy of St. Louis Post-Dispatch, August 9, 1891, 12.*

By then, she was fifty-seven and in failing health. She had little money. There was no one besides Richard to help her, and he did not earn enough for both of them. She had to do all the housework herself and had to trudge up and down two flights of stairs for water and firewood.[23] In her spare time, Adelaide haunted the Bel Air market every Saturday where Junius and Mary Ann sold vegetables. Loud enough for everyone to hear, she cursed Junius and shrieked that Mary Ann was a harlot and her children were all bastards. Humiliated in public, Mary Ann did her best to comfort her children who were shunned by former friends.

Junius tried to offer Adelaide money to settle out of court and leave.[24] Adelaide took the money but still demanded Junius publicly recognize Richard as his legitimate son. Junius refused. When the judicial waiting period ended in February 1851, Adelaide filed for divorce, charging adultery.

Junius had no legal defense to contest Adelaide's accusation. She had their marriage license. He was forced to admit he had abandoned her in London and his children with Mary Ann were illegitimate. The divorce decree was granted on April 18, 1851.[25] A month later Junius and Mary Ann officially married on May 10, 1851. It was John's thirteenth birthday.[26]

The divorce was not the end of Junius's and Mary Ann's troubles. Junius was running out of money and still drinking heavily. Drunkenness and bouts of depression kept him in his room when he was supposed to be on stage. With June away in California, Mary Ann had to send either fourteen-year-old Edwin or nine-year-old John to chaperone their father. Edwin, being older, was assigned the unsavory job as his father's babysitter.

Even if John had been the older son, Mary Ann still would have sent Edwin. John was "his mother's darling." She wanted him home.

Aware of his mother's financial straits, Mary Ann's oldest son, June, ventured back to the Farm in May 1852 to persuade his father to come to San Francisco, assuring him he would be able to pay him handsomely as a touring star. In July 1852, Junius, June, and Edwin docked in San Francisco.

Junius Brutus Booth and his thirteen-year-old son Edwin Thomas Booth. Edwin was his father's "dresser." Not only did he look after his father's wardrobe, he also did his best to keep Junius from drinking and arriving at the theatre late. *Courtesy of Folger Shakespeare Library.*

Despite an initial sellout to see the world-renowned actor, June barely made expenses.[27] Junius was so drunk he fell twice on the stage. Nevertheless, Junius demanded and was paid every penny his son June had promised him.[28] Junius left San Francisco in October. Edwin would have left with him, but Edwin had become stage-struck like his brother and father. Junius told Edwin to stay with June and practice his acting skills.

Their father did not make it home. Before leaving San Francisco, Junius had arranged an appearance in New Orleans on his way back. He came down with "consumption of the bowels" after drinking from the Mississippi River and died on November 30, 1852.[29]

Mary Ann had received a telegram in Baltimore that Junius was ill and had left for Cincinnati to help him make the rest of the trip back home. A second telegram that Junius had died never reached her. After recovering from the shock of Junius's unexpected death, Mary Ann had another crisis to deal with. She did not have enough money to ship him home, and Junius had no money on him because he had been robbed. Since Junius had been a Mason, Mary Ann turned to the local fraternal group for help. They collected enough to have him embalmed and shipped in a metal coffin to Baltimore.[30]

Junius was buried in Green Mount Cemetery in Baltimore. Adelaide and Junius's son Richard did not attend the funeral or burial.[31]

Adelaide remained in Baltimore until she died seven years later in 1858 at the age of sixty-six.[32] In 1860, Richard moved back to England, changing his name to Richard Delannoy. He died from typhus in December 1868.

# 3

# Old Sins Cast Long Shadows

**J**ust turning thirteen, his sense of identity still crystallizing, John Wilkes Booth learned he was a bastard. In nineteenth-century America, bastards were non-persons with no kinship or legal right to inherit property. They were restricted from entering licensed professions, not allowed to join social clubs, and barred from participating in civic organizations.[1] Though John had never had any reason to believe his parents were not legally married, he now found that in the eyes of society he was no better than a thief or beggar and his mother was a "fallen woman."[2] The taint was so great that years later, a blackmailer tried to extort money from John's brother Edwin to keep the family shame a secret.[3]

At thirteen, John had to find some way of proving who he was to himself. He scoured the house for his mother's sewing needle, found some India ink, and sat down at the family table. Slowly and painfully, he pricked one hole after another into the crook between his left hand's thumb and forefinger. Then he dabbed the holes with black, India ink, permanently tattooing "J. W. B." into his skin.[4] Almost twenty years later, those initials confirmed that the man dragged from the burning barn at the Garrett farm on April 26, 1865, was John Wilkes Booth.[5]

The humiliation of being bastards affected the Booth children in different ways. June had already left home and had his own scandal to deal with. In 1851, he had abandoned his wife and run off to San Francisco with a younger actress. Rosalie (called "Rose"), John's oldest sister, never married; she remained her mother's constant companion and caretaker until Mary Ann died and then lived with her brother Joseph until her own death in 1889.

Despite her humiliation, Mary Ann is never known to have complained. She confronted her ordeals "with sad and reverent forbearance."[6] Asia dealt with the shame by pretending nothing was amiss at the Booth homestead. Her parents' marriage, she told her friend Jean Anderson, was ideal. "If ever there was perfect love, it was between my father and my mother."[7] In her various paeans to her father, Asia left out his "seasons of abstractions" and never mentioned his drinking, a silence typical of the children of alcoholics.[8]

Edwin was choleric when he read the *New York Evening Post*'s 1858 obituary for Adelaide, describing her as Junius's one-time wife.[9] "Oblige me by contradicting that statement," he wrote the newspaper. "My father was married but once, and then to my mother, who, thank God, still lives."[10] Years later Edwin wrote to his daughter Edwina: "Yr Aunt Asia's memoir of father tells of his first foolish marriage at about 18 to an adventuress of nearly 50 [Adelaide was 24]—she saw the woman once…. I never did."[11] Edwin also denied his father was an alcoholic.[12] Years later he told his daughter Edwina he would have preferred to stay in school rather than being his father's keeper.[13] Like his father, Edwin was also a brooding melancholic and an alcoholic.

Growing up with the shame of illegitimacy was a factor in Edwin and John's sense of unworthiness and craving for fame. Throughout their mature lives, they both strove for respectability, courting social acceptance through their professional aspirations and personal demeanor.[14]

Asia Booth Clarke, John Wilkes Booth's sister, 1884.
*Courtesy of Eleanor Farjeon, ed. The Unlocked Book: A Memoir of John Wilkes Booth by His Sister Asia Booth Clarke. New York: G. P. Putnam's Sons, 1938.*

From the time he was young, all the children knew John Wilkes was their mother's favorite. He was their favorite too. The Booth's neighbor, Mrs. Elijah Rogers, who nursed all the Booth children, "loved the boy dearly." "I knew him from babyhood, and he was always so kind, tenderhearted and good....Many times he has toddled over to our house to get a slice of bread with a thick layer of sugar."[15] Asked if she would give food or shelter to John knowing that he had shot Lincoln, Ann Hall, the black servant who had also taken care of John and the other children at the

Farm, didn't hesitate. "Give him all dat I have to eat, and 'tect him to my last breaf."[16]

John had a "gentle, loving disposition." He was "very boyish" and "full of fun," said Edwin. He would take sleigh rides in July and wear out the sleigh's runners. Everyone smiled and laughed at his pranks. He "would charge through the woods on horseback, spouting heroic speeches," waving a lance a soldier who had fought with Zachary Taylor in the Mexican War had given his father. But no matter what he did, he was "his mother's darling."[17] John was also Rose's "idolized favorite and pet."[18] From the moment of John's birth, "both his parents so idolized and spoiled him that by comparison they seemed indifferent to the older children," writes Stanley Kimmel, the Booth family historian.[19]

With so much love and favoritism, it is hardly surprising that in spite of the family scandal, John developed an exaggerated sense of his place in the world and an ultra-high opinion of himself.

John, Asia, and Edwin's first school was a one-room schoolhouse across the entrance from the Farm. John was not very studious; classmate George Y. Maynadier recalled that John "didn't lack the brains; he lacked the interest."[20] After the family moved to High Street in Baltimore in 1840, Mary Ann enrolled them with private tutors. John "was not quick at acquiring knowledge," said Asia. Yet once he learned something, he never forgot it.[21] After the family moved to North Exeter Street in 1845, John and Edwin enrolled at Bel Air Academy in Bel Air, Maryland. Edwin was there for only a year when his mother sent him off with Junius. John stayed at the Bel Air Academy for three years, from 1846 to 1849. The headmaster recalled he was a handsome boy "in face and figure although slightly bowlegged."[22]

Even as young children, Edwin and other neighborhood boys imagined themselves as actors. Once, Edwin stole the spangles from his father's Shylock costume to create his own costume. When Junius discovered the theft, he assumed John was the culprit and beat him until John admitted that Edwin was the guilty party.[23] It was not the first time Junius beat John or Edwin. Junius was a violent man when crossed.[24] John envied his father's fame, but he never spoke with any love for the tyrant.

In 1849, eleven-year-old John enrolled at the Quaker-run Milton Boarding School in Cockeysville, Maryland, seventeen miles from Baltimore.[25] It was while he was at the Milton School that the gypsy read John's palm and predicted he would have a "fast life—short, but a grand one."[26] John was at the Milton Academy when Adelaide began her lawsuit against Junius.

Cockeysville was not far enough away to keep the gossip about the family disgrace from being heard. The public humiliation left John feeling betrayed. To cope with his shame, John became a bully. He began "to fag the smaller boys cruelly," said a classmate.[27] John also took out his frustration on animals. He tied neighborhood cats together or chased them up onto perilously steep roofs. John's earliest biographer, George Alfred Townsend, said that in those days John was always shooting cats and killed off almost all of them in his neighborhood.[28]

It was not the only time John killed animals. Sitting at a window at the Farm, he shot a dog "for no earthly reason."[29] Another time, John needlessly unloaded three rounds of buckshot into a neighbor's hog that had wandered near the Booth's barn.[30] Asia ignored John's dark side, describing him instead as "very tender of flowers, and of insects and butterflies."

Though generally easygoing, John had a violent streak that came out when he was angered or felt insulted. When an overseer at the Farm, George Hagan, insulted John's mother and sisters, John tore off a tree limb and pummeled Hagan on his head and shoulders when he refused to apologize.[31] "I knocked him down and made him bleed like a butcher," John boasted.[32] The next day Hagan filed a complaint against John for assault.[33] John got off with a simple promise to keep the peace or forfeit a fifty-dollar bond.

In John's third year at the Milton Academy, Edward Gorsuch, the father of one of John's classmates, Tom Gorsuch, was killed—some newspapers said murdered—trying to retrieve runaway slaves who had fled from his farm in 1849 to Pennsylvania, a free state. His friend's father's killing made the incident personal for John. It was the beginning of his sense of identity as a Southerner. Nine years later he wrote that it had been well within Tom Gorsuch's father's rights to reclaim his slaves. "The South has a right according to the constitution to keep and hold slaves. And we have no right under that constitution to interfere with her or her slaves."[34]

John did not have animus toward individual blacks. He liked the family servants, the Halls, and they liked him.[35] During the New York City Draft Riot of 1863, John condemned the "murdering of inoffensive Negroes" and vowed to protect a young Negro boy with his own life if a mob came after him.[36]

Regardless of his *noblesse oblige* toward individual blacks, John Wilkes Booth was a white supremacist. "This country," he would later say, "was formed for the white, not the black man." "Nigs," he said, were better off in slavery. "Instead of looking upon slavery as a sin I hold it to be a happiness for themselves and a social and political blessing for us…True, I have seen the black man whipped but only when he deserved much more than he received." Speaking from personal experience, John said that, whatever cruelty they experienced, he had seen much worse meted out by father to son.[37]

John was fourteen when he enrolled at St. Timothy's Hall, a military-style boarding school, in Catonsville, Maryland, about six miles from Baltimore. Most of the students and John's closest friends at St. Timothy's were from the South. St. Timothy's was where John met Samuel Bland Arnold, one of the conspirators he later enlisted in his plan to abduct President Lincoln in 1865.

John was at St. Timothy's when Junius died. His father had been the family's sole means of support. With him gone, Mary Ann had no income. Besieged with creditors demanding money Junius owed them,[38] she moved back to Tudor Hall—a house he had built near the Farm—with Rosalie and Asia, and she rented the North Exeter Street home in Baltimore for thirty-five dollars a month, much of it going to taxes and mortgage payments.

Their once "bright happy home," said Asia, was now "broken up forever."[39] John and Joseph stayed at St. Timothy's until the term ended in July and then left for Tudor Hall. John's one year at St. Timothy's ended his formal education.

As the oldest male at Tudor Hall, fifteen-year-old John was the man of the house. By then he had become imbued with the South's sense of social status. That meant that family members did not sit at the table with the hired help. John struggled with his sense of equality and "that southern reservation which jealously kept the white laborer from free association with his employer or superior," said Asia, and decided on a compromise. He would eat with them at the same table while his mother and sisters ate their meals elsewhere. Southern ladies, Asia sniffed, did not force themselves to be unduly familiar with "ignorant menials whom they dared not even to call servants."[40]

What John and Asia meant by "ignorant menials" were the Catholic immigrants, mostly Irish and German laborers, who were coming to the United States by the thousands and, in the course of becoming naturalized, were influencing elections. Even though John's own parents were immigrants, neither of them had become naturalized citizens, and they had remained aloof from politics. Actors should not meddle in politics, Junius told his children.[41]

John was a nativist. Only native-born Americans should be allowed to run for political office, he said. That way "great privileges" would not fall into foreign hands.[42] Asia teased him—would he vote for his father if he had become naturalized and run for office? John did not share Asia's feelings for their father. "I'd have cast my vote against him if I'd been of age," he shot back.[43]

Like many native-born (Protestant) Marylanders, John fell in with the new, semi-secret, anti-Catholic American Party, popularly called the Know-Nothing Party. When asked about their activities, members were told to say, "I know nothing."

Know-Nothings believed immigrants were taking over the country and had to be stopped. In 1854, John volunteered to be a steward at a nearby rally for Henry Winter Davis, the Know-Nothing candidate for Congress. On that particular day, John donned a dark, cloth coat with velvet lapels, a pale, buff waistcoat, dove-colored trousers, and a broad, straw hat. Even at sixteen, he was conscious of his appearance. He was "always well dressed," said Asia. He looked "remarkably handsome."[44]

Asia rarely mentioned the family's hard life at Tudor Hall. Looking back on those years, she remembered them as an idyllic time in her life. She and John took early morning rides before sunup "when the dew lay like rain on the grass."[45] They would read aloud to one another. They sang together. John recited Byron's poems and parts of *Julius Caesar* and other tragedies while Asia held the book, correcting him when he missed a line.[46]

To hear Asia tell it, John loved farming and joyfully rose with the sun in his east-facing bedroom, ready to go to work.[47] The truth is John hated farming. He called it "trying to starve respectably by torturing the barren earth."[48] He stayed in bed as long as he could. "I've become a very late riser," he told his friend Bill O'Laughlen.[49] "I have had so much work all day and am so tired," he could hardly find time to write.[50] Visiting Tudor Hall many years later, John's early biographer, George Townsend, said it was the "worst of bad farms, in a bad piece of country."[51]

John was never too tired, however, for girls. Just shy of sixteen, John told Bill O'Laughlen he had his "eye on three girls out here…I hope I'll get enough."[52] He was also aware of his own allure. "You must not think I was blowing when I say I cut quite a dash. I saw pretty girls home from the Fair at ten o'clock at night, some at a distance of four or five miles."[53] A few days later he wrote O'Laughlen he was among thirty-seven couples invited to a "Pick nick," but he didn't mention who he was going with. "Ladies," he said, "have the means of revenge."[54]

# 4

# THEY IDOLIZED HIM

August 15, 1855, was a date John would never forget. It was the night he had his professional stage debut in *Richard III* at Laura Keene's Charles Street Theatre in Baltimore.[1]

The evening was slated as a benefit for John Sleeper Clarke, Edwin's boyhood friend. A day or two earlier, John had called on Clarke to ask if he could find a way for him to appear on stage at the Charles Street Theatre. Clarke promised he would do what he could, but he was not just doing John a favor. Having a son of the great tragedian Junius Booth appear in the cast would lure people to the theatre and drive up profits. To make sure John's appearance would not be missed, Clarke placed three separate advertisements in the *Baltimore Sun* on the same day on two different pages.[2]

When John rode back to Tudor Hall the night after Clarke's benefit, he was brimming. "Well, Mother Bunch [his nickname for Asia], guess what I've done!...I've made my first appearance on any stage, for this night only, and in big capitals."[3]

The Charles Street Theatre was not a first-class theatre. It had no regularly performing stock company and rarely featured well-known talent. It was also summer, the slowest time of the theatrical season.[4] None of that mattered to the seventeen-year-old. He had had his stage debut. He was exultant.

John's mother was less sanguine. She chided that the sole reason he had been taken on was "to gain notoriety and money by the use of his name."[5] Despite his momentary elation, John would remember her admonition and repeat it to Asia when she was thinking about marrying Clarke.

Edwin returned in October 1856, wealthy from a tour in Australia. To help pay off Junius's outstanding debts, Edwin and June had been sending money home to their mother when they could. As neither their mother nor John was up to running the farm, there was no point in their staying on. Edwin decided to move them back to Baltimore. Asia sighed, "the seriousness of life had come, the last happy days of childhood were recollections."[6]

John could not have been happier. He longed to be an actor like his father and his brothers. He had some fond memories of Tudor Hall, but he also remembered how exhausted he had been looking after the farm and how close they had come to starving.[7] None of the family ever lived at Tudor Hall again. The house was put up for rent, and the stock was advertised for sale.[8]

After settling his mother and sisters in Baltimore, Edwin arranged for John to live with Clarke in Philadelphia. By then Clarke was a leading performer at the Arch Street Theatre. Edwin asked his friend to put in a good word about hiring John for the stock company. Clarke agreed to talk to manager William Wheatley on John's behalf. There was another reason he was so agreeable: he was courting John's sister, Asia.[9] Landing John a job could only make Clarke more attractive to the Booth family.

Wheatley did not need much persuading; he had known John's father and may have taken John on as a favor to an old friend. Besides, nineteen-year-old John looked a lot like Junius. Perhaps he had some of his talent.

At that time Philadelphia was the epicenter of the country's theatrical world, boasting three of the nation's most prestigious theatres—the Arch Street Theatre, called the "first temple of drama in America," the Walnut Street Theatre, and the National—as well as an opera house and other smaller theatres.[10]

The Arch Street Theatre troupe was typical of most stock acting companies. Each actor had his or her "line of business," or character type, and was paid accordingly. The typical night's fare was a five-act tragedy followed by a shorter comedy, interspersed with dance numbers and orchestral music. To keep audiences coming back, the play and accompanying pieces changed every night. It was grueling work.

Cast assignments for the next night's venue were posted on a call board after the night's performance ended. Every actor below the leads had to memorize not only his part for every play but also the parts of the senior player immediately above him so that he could fill the role in an emergency. Rehearsals were thorough but not necessarily long. For the lead players, they were often perfunctory so as not to expend their energy. Often they would teach the younger members of the company the basics of timing and entrances and exits.[11] Male actors also practiced choreographed sword fights and took fencing lessons to make their performances more realistic.[12]

John's first professional acting job with the Arch Street Theatre troupe was as a "third walking gentleman," a part that required him to look gentlemanly and only speak a few lines, if any. The salary was eight dollars a week, which was two dollars more than what the "utes" or utility actors were paid. One of those "utes" was Irish-born John McCullough. Broad shouldered with a large head, he looked more like a farmer than an actor.

McCullough would become John's closest friend and a star in his own right. John's last appearance on stage was at a benefit at Ford's Theatre for McCullough.

Remembering his mother's words about being exploited because of his name, John had himself billed as "Mr. J. B. Wilks." He did not want to be admired as an actor "for his father's sake," he told Asia.[13] In later years, John confided to actor Edwin A. Emerson that he had "played under the Wilks name, because his father had told him he would never make it as an actor. John changed his name so as not to tarnish the family name if his father's prediction proved right."[14] In part, John's craving for fame was to prove his father wrong.

For his professional debut, John played a guest at a masquerade ball.[15] There is no record of how he did. The following night he was nervous and blundered through his part. To make matters worse, he showed up late for rehearsals. William S. Fredericks, the Arch Street Theatre's stage manager, railed at him about being late and for not learning his lines. John invented lame excuses for his tardiness. One time he claimed he was late because he had run down Clarke's horse after it had broken out of the stable. In reality, he was late because he had been out all night with another young actor, running down two sisters.[16]

John often murdered his lines, said journalist George Townsend, who witnessed some of John's performances. In an often-repeated story, John was supposed to say, "Madame, I am Petruchio Pandolfo." Instead, he stammered, "Madame, I am Pandolfio Pet. Pedolfio Pat…Pantucio Ped." Then in complete frustration, he blurted, "Dammit! What am I?" The audience and cast roared. Though embarrassed, John laughed too.[17] John protested he had memorized his lines. He had floundered, he said, due to a lack of confidence. It also may have been a lack of sleep.

Once he started earning some money, John left Clarke's home for a boarding house near the theatre. The other boarders were aspiring medical students, artists, and actors. "The most ambitious and the most idle among us," one boarder recalled, "was a young fellow who played inferior parts in the Arch Street Theatre…E. Wilkes [sic]…His whole purpose in life was simply to be known." His "desire for notoriety" was a "devouring passion." Over and over he would say, "I must have fame!"[18]

There was one kind of notoriety John preferred to avoid. One of the female boarders with whom he had become intimate pleaded to go with him when the season at the Arch Street Theatre ended and it was doubtful he would be returning. When John turned her down, she screamed rape. To stall for time, John may have promised to marry her (he would do the same to many more girls). Hush money, probably from Edwin, eventually kept her from pressing charges.[19]

"The handsome Wilkes had the sort of appeal that no woman would resist," writes Stanley Kimmel. "His fascinating dark eyes and melodious voice made them susceptible to his advances." Managing the entire affair with just a few intimate friends knowing, John gained a flattered ego and a false assurance. Like his father who had kept his first wife in the dark for decades about his other family, John considered himself adept at intrigue.[20] It would not be the only time John had a narrow escape from an errant romantic affair.[21]

In late August 1858, Edwin persuaded manager John T. Ford, a friend of the Booth family, to let John play Richmond to Edwin's Richard in *Richard III* at Edwin's benefit performance at the Holliday Street Theatre in Baltimore. To please their mother, who was in the audience that night, Edwin had John billed under his own name. Although playing far above his previous experience, John did well. "Both were superb," said one of the actors. "I shall never forget the fight between Richard and Richmond, in the last act, an encounter which was terrible in its savage realism."[22]

It was realistic because it was not fake. When Edwin had returned from California, he took over as man of the house. John nettled at being slighted in the eyes of his mother and sisters. Edwin, meanwhile, resented that his mother said she was keeping their father's theatrical costumes for John. After years of taking care of Junius's wardrobe and stage jewelry, Edwin felt they were rightly his.[23] The brothers generally managed to keep their rivalry under control. Now and then it came out, but they were never enemies. A. F. Norcross, whose house in Boston both brothers regularly visited when she was a young girl, often saw them together. Edwin adored his brother, she said, and would light up when he greeted him.[24] In Edwin's later years, when he lived alone in his home in Gramercy Park, there were two photos on his bedroom wall. One was his mother's. The other was John's.

What had started out as a novelty—two of the Booth sons on stage together—became a turning point in John's career. John Ford was impressed enough with John's performance that when Edwin asked him to take on his brother at his stock company at the Marshall Theatre in Richmond, Virginia, Ford agreed.[25] In September 1858, twenty-year-old John Wilkes Booth debuted as a stock actor at the same theatre where, thirty-seven years before, his father had had his American stage debut in 1821.[26]

Home to about 37,000 people, Richmond in 1858 was one of America's most elegant cities. The city was the industrial heart of the South, its wealthiest city, and the country's second largest flour milling center. It was also a major slave market where men, women, and children were bought and sold like cattle at Lumpkin's Alley. Four years later, Richmond would become the political capital of the Confederacy. After New Orleans was captured in the war, it became the Confederacy's cultural capital as well.

The Marshall Theatre was the oldest and most prestigious playhouse in the city and Virginia's only full-time theatre.[27] Very aware of Southern sensibilities, Ford avoided hiring performers with Boston accents and actors known to be abolitionists.[28] To increase respectability, Ford also refrained from selling alcohol in his theatres and barred known prostitutes from plying their trade in his theatre lobbies.[29]

Ford hired experienced, reliable actors for his stock company and tried to retain them from season to season. For their part, actors liked performing in Richmond and the South in general. "Social status for actors is nine times greater in the South than in the North," George Townsend commented. "We place actors outside of society and execrate them...the South [takes] them into affable fellowship."[30] Actor John Barron felt the same: "No people ever paid more devoted homage to dramatic art than the citizens of Richmond."[31]

Ford often hired novices like John for minor "lines of business" and promoted them when they proved their ability.[32] As the company's second juvenile,[33] John was paid $11 a week,[34] a sizable increase from the $8 a week he had earned at the Arch Street Theatre.

Although billed as "J. B. Wilkes," no one was in doubt as to his real identity. Chagrinned at being unable to prove himself on his own merits, John wrote to Edwin a week after starting at the Marshall Theatre: "Everyone knows me already, I have heard my name—Booth—called for two nights."[35] "It is no secret in the profession 'Mr. J. B. Wilkes' is John Wilkes Booth, a younger brother of Edwin Booth," the *Louisville Daily Courier* told its readers.[36]

John got on well in Richmond. Years later Asia wrote Richmond was the "idealized city of his love [and] had a deeper hold upon his heart than any feminine beauty."[37] The only thing about Richmond that distressed John was the climate.[38]

He liked the people and was liked in return "by everyone with whom he associated," said George Crutchfield, an acquaintance.[39] Men admired his dignity, his insouciance, and his dashing appearance in what would become his trademark "fur trimmed overcoat."[40] Though a newcomer to Richmond, he "carried himself like a Virginia Gentleman to the manner born."[41]

"With women he was a man of irresistible fascination," commented Edward Alfriend, another acquaintance.[42] Girls "idolized him."[43] He had "beautiful eyes, with great symmetry of features, and an especially fine forehead, and curly black hair…There was a 'peculiar halo of romance' about him."[44]

John Wilkes Booth wearing his trademark fur-collar coat.
*Courtesy of New York Public Library, Billy Rose Collection.*

Soon after coming to Richmond, that "halo of romance" was kindling love letters from infatuated girls from Richmond's prominent families. John had no second thoughts about romantic interludes with actresses. On the other hand, an affair with a girl from one of Richmond's better families could only turn out badly for him when it ended. When John, thinking it would discourage her, didn't answer the letters of one such girl, she became even more determined. She begged him to elope with her, so John turned to Mrs. Isabella Pallen Beale for advice.

Isabella Beale was the wife of Dr. James Beale, one of Richmond's best known doctors.[45] John had gone to see Dr. Beale about some minor illness shortly after coming to Richmond, and they had become friendly. The Beales were avid theatregoers. They had their own box seat at the Marshall Theatre and had seen John's father when he appeared there. Edwin was a frequent guest at their home when he was in Richmond,[46] and John became a regular guest too.

The Beales were also well-connected and knew everyone in Richmond's upper class.[47] They lived with their young daughter Mary in an elegant mansion within walking distance of the Marshall Theatre. Mary adored John and fondly recalled those days: "There was always a warm supper and a warm welcome for my father's guests after the theatre doors were closed."[48]

One night when John was a guest at the Beale's, John asked Mrs. Beale if he could talk to her alone. John told her about the girl who kept sending him letters and wanted to elope with him. What should he do about discouraging her, he asked.

"Meet with her in person," Mrs. Beale advised. "Otherwise she will just keep sending you letters and might do something foolish."

John took her advice. He met the girl at Capitol Square, opposite the Beale home, and managed to persuade her there was no future for them together. The girl tearfully went home "a wiser virgin."[49]

On September 13, 1858, the popular actress Maggie Mitchell began a two-week engagement at the Marshall Theatre. Unlike the Arch Street Theatre, where the lead stock actors were the stars, the Marshall Theatre featured a regular venue of touring stars who entertained for two weeks and then moved on to their next engagement. In the Marshall Theatre system, even the most senior members of the stock company had supporting roles. Stock actors had to learn their parts each day in rapid succession, whereas a star had a round of characters he or she played over and over again.

"It was study! study! study! study! rehearse! rehearse! rehearse! act! act! act!" recalled John Barron of his stock days at the Marshall Theatre. "Almost every night I would leave the theatre after playing two parts and not knowing a line of the two long parts of the next night, and so on through a 40 weeks' season."[50] John wrote Edwin that he should let their mother know he might not be able to write her that week because he had "much to study" to be ready for Miss Mitchell.[51]

# 5

# Young and Pretty Maggie Mitchell

Margaret Julia Mitchell, known throughout her career as "Maggie Mitchell," was just a year older than John when she first appeared at the Marshall Theatre. By then she was already a star—although nothing like the superstar she would be in coming years.

When the 1857 season opened, George Kunkel, the Marshall Theatre's manager, was not a happy man. He had put on "quite a variety of dishes, some truly unsavory."[1] Kunkel's agony ended with Maggie's Richmond debut. Unable to resist, young men smitten with "Maggie's...poses and bewitching glances"[2] were drawn to the Marshall Theatre like flies to honey.

Petite, attractive, and gray-eyed, with flowing, curly, auburn hair, Maggie had a "saucy face" and a "fairy figure." "She is young, pretty, has a good bust, good arms, and 'a knee round as a period,'" beamed an enthralled theatre critic.[3] Several years later, Lincoln's private secretary, John Hay, found her "vivacious," a "dashing young girl, with fine eyes and a pretty mouth."[4] Theatre critics were charmed by her "natural sprightliness," her "effervescing spirit," and her "girlish innocence." All

41

the newspapers raved about her. One even admitted Maggie Mitchell was the "most bewitching little creature we have ever seen upon the stage."[5]

John Wilkes Booth would have agreed. He became one of Maggie's lovers, and later there were rumors they briefly and secretly engaged.[6]

Margaret Julia Mitchell was born on June 2, 1837, in Lower Manhattan, New York, to Anna and Charles Mitchell, Anna's second husband.[7] Both of Maggie's sisters, Mary Anne and Emma, also became actresses, but neither ever came close to achieving Maggie's fame.[8]

A few years after Maggie's parents married, they left Maggie and her siblings with a neighbor and went back to England to visit family. One of the neighbor's boarders was a fledgling actress who took fourteen-year-old Maggie with her to the theatre one day. Maggie was instantly stage-struck. When her parents returned, Maggie announced she was going to be an actress.[9] Serendipitously, on the voyage back from England, her mother had become friends with an old English actor, John Moore, who at the time was the stage manager of Burton's Chambers Street Theatre near City Hall. Seeing that her daughter was set on a stage career, Anna introduced her to Moore and asked him if there was any way he could get Maggie started in the theater. Luckily, Moore happened to be looking for a teenage actress to play the young girl in an upcoming play, *The Soldier's Daughter*.[10]

On June 2, 1851, Maggie made her stage debut. Her self-confidence and perfect performance so impressed Thomas Hamblin, manager of the rival Bowery Theatre, that the next season he hired her at a starting salary of four dollars a week.[11]

Maggie was such a hit at the Bowery Theatre with the "b'hoys" in the cheaper gallery seats that she was called back on stage for her first "curtain call." Hamblin knew a good thing when he saw it and raised her salary to six dollars a week.[12] In her later years, even though she was making hundreds of dollars a night, Maggie recalled she was never more pleased with herself than when Hamblin bumped her wages by two whole dollars.[13]

Sensing her daughter had a bright future ahead of her in the theatre, Anna asked Hamblin for an even bigger raise the next season. When they couldn't come to an agreement, Anna began booking Maggie into other theaters.

In 1853, when she was sixteen, Maggie joined James Robinson's company and played flirtatious soubrettes. John Ellsler was in the audience for one of her performances. He promptly hired her away from Robinson and took her on a tour through Maryland and various western cities. In Chicago, future presidential candidate Stephen Douglas was so smitten with her that he gave her a gold watch.[14]

Maggie's appearance in Cleveland ignited a "Maggie Mitchell craze." Everyone wanted to look like her. Haberdashers couldn't keep up with the demand for hats like the ones Maggie wore on stage. Songwriters composed dances with her name in the title.[15] Playwrights wrote plays for her.[16] Wealthy men named their horses after her.[17]

Maggie's mother did her best to chaperone her daughter, but Maggie was still a teenager. One Saturday night after a show, she slipped away from her mother and spent the rest of the night and all of Sunday with an ardent admirer whom she married. Anna was as distraught as any mother. After tempers cooled, Anna managed to persuade Maggie never to see the man again, believing no permanent harm was done, and later arranged for the marriage to be annulled. After leaving Cleveland she spent the rest of that year and the next hopscotching from theater to theater, "the most charming, irresistible, radiant little Star that shines now in the theatrical galaxy."[18]

In November 1857, Maggie had the first of several appearances at the Marshall Theatre. The *New York Clipper* commented it was not safe for young men to go to the theater when Maggie Mitchell was on stage because her poses and bewitching glances were "a kind of killing" without being actual murder.[19] Rumors also began circulating that one of those "killed" was "a young Clevelander" about to lead Maggie to the altar.[20] A month later the *Baltimore Sun* broke the news that the "young Clevelander" was a man named Paddock.[21] Other papers denied there was any truth to the rumor.[22]

Though they were often seen together, Henry was just one of the men she dazzled. She would soon meet someone just as dazzling as herself.

In 1858, at twenty-one, Maggie was a seasoned entertainer with a reputation as a strict taskmaster. Actor John Barron had met her years before in 1855 at the National Theatre in Washington, D.C. Even then he was "startled when that little elf came on the stage and began to give directions with a vim and exactness that made the old timers ask themselves what had happened."[23]

Maggie preferred short plays at that time in her career. Some nights she staged as many as three a night and appeared in as many as seven different roles, not including the songs, dances, and skits she performed between plays.

For all that to happen, she had to inform the theatre manager well in advance what she was planning to put on so that he could cast each of his stock actors in supporting roles. Soon after receiving their assignments, the actors stayed up nights memorizing their lines and were up before noon to rehearse their parts before the next day's evening plays.

Oftentimes a star did not care for the manager's casting arrangements or the way scenes were blocked and changed them to his or her liking. That meant more rehearsals and more time and effort to cater to the star's directions. The only respite was on Sundays when the theater was closed. Well-trained actors took it all in stride. Second-rate actors chafed. George Berrell was among the latter. Maggie Mitchell was all sweetness and charm on stage, he groused to his diary, but she was an overbearing autocrat at rehearsals—"It would be hard to find a more disagreeable, hateful, fault-finding little cat."[24]

Maggie Mitchell. "Young and Pretty and Has a Good Bust." *Courtesy of New York Public Library, Billy Rose Collection.*

She was a strict disciplinarian, actor John Barron recalled, "but she never required more of the ladies and gentlemen of the company than she herself was willing to do." Before rehearsals were dismissed, she made sure "every member of the cast was letter perfect in the words and business of the two or three plays of the evening. The next day was a repetition of the day before, and so on through the entire engagement."[25]

There is no record of Maggie's first impression of John when she arrived at the Marshall Theatre, but she was as captivated by his looks as every other woman and sent him at least one letter. John's roommate said John "often read me excerpts from letters couched in particularly endearing terms" and laughed that "no one of the writers compared with Miss Mitchell."[26]

Maggie was back again in Richmond for more two-week engage-ments in February, June, and October of 1859. Hundreds packed the theatre each night to see her. The *Richmond Dispatch* told fans to go see Maggie at the Marshall Theatre "If you wish to enjoy...a 'concord of sweet sounds' as they pour forth from the lips of Richmond's favorite."[27]

When not on stage or rehearsing, prominent actors and actresses were often guests at the homes of Richmond's theatre patrons. Maggie and John likely hobnobbed together in Richmond at this time since she had sent him an admiring letter earlier in the year.

Maggie left Richmond at the end of October for her next engage-ment. It would be a year before they saw each other again. In the mean-time, there were other women and a superstardom John craved but could never have imagined.

# 6

# THIS HARPERS FERRY BUSINESS

John was back in Richmond for his second season at the Marshall Theatre when it reopened in September 1859. By then Edwin was planning to marry actress Mary Devlin, and Asia had married John Sleeper Clarke and moved to Philadelphia with him.

Despite Clarke's landing him his first job, John's relationship with Clarke had soured. John remembered his mother telling him Clarke had only arranged John's first stage appearance to capitalize on the Booth name. John suspected Clarke had married Asia for the same reason.[1] Sure enough, when the newspapers announced the wedding, the bride was "Miss Asia Booth, youngest daughter of the distinguished tragedian, the great Junius Brutus Booth."[2]

Asia knew what John had told her was true. In an unguarded moment, she confessed to her friend Jean Anderson she was not in love with Clarke and had married him to please Edwin. Even so, she told Jean that had John objected, she would have put her feelings aside to please him. "My good true husband knows this too."[3] Ironically, Edwin did not attend the wedding, whereas John did.[4] Clarke and Asia soon had two children: Asia Agnes Dorothy, called "Dolly," and Edwin Booth Clarke, nicknamed "Eddie."

Asia Booth Clarke between the ages of twenty-five and thirty. *Courtesy of Eleanor Farjeon, ed. The Unlocked Book: A Memoir of John Wilkes Booth by His Sister Asia Booth Clarke. New York: G. P. Putnam's Sons, 1938.*

The start of the 1859–1860 season at the Marshall Theatre brought some new additions to the stock company. Edwin Adams was the new leading man. Other new additions included Mary White, stage manager Israel B. Phillips, George Wren, and Wren's sisters Eliza and Ella.[5] John's former sister-in-law, Clementina DeBar, recently divorced from his brother June, also joined the cast. Despite the divorce, Clementina had remained on friendly terms with the rest of the family, except Asia, who believed June's concocted story that his and Clementina's daughter, Blanche, was not really June's child.[6]

John's second year at the Marshall Theatre was filled with drama—offstage. On Sunday, October 16, 1859, a shock wave rippled through the South. Abolitionist John Brown crossed into Virginia from Maryland with twenty-one devoted followers intent on fomenting an armed slave rebellion. The insurrectionists cut telegraph wires, took hostages from nearby farms, and seized the U.S. arsenal at Harpers Ferry to arm the local slaves, whom they expected to flock to them when the news of what had happened spread through the countryside.

The insurrection fizzled right from the start. Local militia and the citizenry rallied and forced the invaders to retreat from the armory to a brick fire engine house. By Monday afternoon, they were surrounded with nowhere to escape. The next morning, a company of United States Marines, led by Lieutenant Colonel Robert E. Lee and Lieutenant J. E. B. Stuart, battered down the doors of the fire engine house. In the brief assault, Brown was captured. Brown was tried for inciting a slave rebellion, murder, and treason. He was sentenced to be "swung up" in Charles Town, West Virginia, on December 2, 1859.[7]

The raid ignited the South's worst fears of an armed slave rebellion. The *Charleston Mercury* warned "a repeat of this 'Harpers Ferry' business could turn 'five millions of negroes' loose in the South...it would be worse than a 'Reign of Terror.'" The only solution, the *Charleston Mercury* exhorted, was for the South to sever its political ties to the North. "We must separate, unless we are willing to see our daughters and wives become the victims of a barbarous passion and worse insult."[8]

On Saturday night, November 19, 1859, Virginia Governor Henry Wise received a panicked telegram from Colonel Davis, the officer in command at Charles Town where the hanging was to take place. "Send

500 men immediately," Davis implored, "a large force, armed with pikes and revolvers" was "marching from Wheeling [to rescue] Brown."[9]

Wise quickly rang the bell in the old bell tower in Capitol Square to summon the city's militia groups—the Richmond Grays, the Richmond Blues, the Montgomery Guards, the Young Guards, the Howitzer Corps, and the Virginia Rifles. The tower bell was the purposive signal for the militias to assemble at the train depot at Seventh and Broad Streets, opposite the Marshall Theatre, and prepare for immediate departure for wherever they were needed.

The entire city was in commotion. The *New York Clipper* reported how "not knowing the exact nature of the summons, and supposing actual fighting was going on at Charles Town," the assembling militia and their hasty departure was seen as "a *bona fide* acknowledged and declared war."[10]

Around 8:00 p.m., John Southall, a medical student staying at the Ford Hotel where John Wilkes Booth was also staying, noticed him walking ahead at a brisk pace toward the theatre. Across the street the depot was jammed with thousands of men and excited citizens, cheering the militias leaving for Charles Town. Just as Southall was about to catch up to him, John stopped and stood for a moment, watching the militias boarding the train. Southall believed John made up his mind that instant to go with them.[11]

It may have been a spur-of-the-moment decision, but John had been having second thoughts about his life as an actor for some time. "I think John wishes he had been something else now," his mother mentioned in an earlier letter to John's older brother June, "but he won't acknowledge it."[12] Joining the military is what he wished he had been doing instead. "John is crazy or enthusiastic about going for a soldier," Asia told Jean Anderson. "I think he will get off. It has been his dearest ambition, perhaps it is his true vocation."[13]

Within three hours of the signaling bells, 400 uniformed and armed men prepared to leave Richmond for what the *Richmond Dispatch* called the "seat of war."[14] John saw two of his friends, George Libby and Louis Bossieux, stowing equipment in a train baggage car. John told them he wanted to come with. Libby replied, "No one [is] allowed on the train but men in uniform."[15] Unfazed, John assured them he would buy a uniform the first chance he got. He had such a "winning personality," said Libby, they hoisted him aboard and lent him a coat, a cap, and other items.[16]

George Crutchfield, another of John's friends, was surprised to see him boarding the train. What would George Kunkel, the Marshall Theatre manager, say about his leaving the theatre high and dry. John brushed off the admonition. "I don't know and I don't care," he shot back.[17]

When Edwin received a letter from John saying he had gone off with a Richmond militia, he wrote his fiancée, Mary Devlin, telling her about John's impulsive decision. Mary wrote back "the mad step John has taken" didn't surprise her. "'Tis a great pity he had not more sense but more time will teach him. I hope nothing serious will occur there [Charles Town], for it would frighten your mother so.... foolish boy, what can he be thinking of?"[18]

Not everyone in Charles Town was happy to see the hundreds of young militia men pouring into their city. Merchants worried about vandalism; women worried about their "moral and industrial habits." The *Richmond Dispatch* assured the residents they had nothing to be concerned about—their by-laws forbade militia men from entering saloons or barrooms and using profane or obscene language.[19] Colonel Turner Ashby's Black Horse Militia, camped behind the Richmond Grays, were not familiar with that by-law. George Libby, John, and the other Grays helped themselves to the Black Horse's "runlet of mountain dew [moonshine] which they dispensed liberally."[20]

John Brown did not mind visitors. When an entire militia unit stopped in at the jail, Brown shook hands with each of them.[21] Although he despised abolitionists, John was curious to see Brown himself. The day before Brown's execution, John talked with him briefly.[22] There is no record of the conversation, but John went away feeling an unusual sympathy for the white-haired, scraggly-bearded man.[23]

The Richmond Grays were positioned in a place of honor about thirty to fifty feet from the scaffold. Brown's hands were untied when he walked up to the scaffold. He did not hesitate as he mounted the stairs and looked off in the distance from the platform. To John, it seemed Brown "vainly" expected to be rescued at the last minute. Just before the hood was placed over his head, he shook hands with his executioners and then stood without resisting as his arms were bound behind him and the hood was lowered over his head.

John had seen actors die on stage hundreds of times. Yet seeing John Brown's body plunge through the trap door, jerk upward as the noose tightened, and then writhe in death made John feel faint. Standing next to him, Philip Whitlock saw John grow pale. He could use a good stiff drink, Whitlock heard him mutter.[24]

The Grays returned to Richmond on Sunday, December 4, and were greeted by a large cheering crowd at the depot. The next day the *Richmond Dispatch* editorialized that "not only the city, but the State owed the volunteers a debt of gratitude."[25] John may have thought theatre manager George Kunkel shared the *Richmond Dispatch*'s approval. He didn't. When John showed up at the Marshall Theatre the next day, Kunkel told him he was fired. John had reneged on his commitment, Kunkel said. He had left his fellow actors high and dry. Pack your belongings and leave, Kunkel sputtered.

When the Richmond Greys learned John had been fired for joining the company, a "large contingent" of the militia assembled at the theatre, demanding Kunkel rehire him.[26] Kunkel had no choice. If he stuck to his guns, his audience would have boycotted the Marshall Theatre.

John's service with the Richmond Grays, brief though it was, had a profound influence on him. Booth biographer George Townsend claimed the time John spent with the Virginia militia bonded him to the state.[27] Brown himself left a deep impression on John. "That rugged old hero"

was a brave man, he later told Asia, "the grandest character of the century."[28] Although John admired Brown, he never wavered in his sincere belief that "this country was formed for the white not the black man" and African slavery was "one of the greatest blessings (both for themselves and us) that God ever bestowed upon a favored nation."[29]

"The old man's bold gamble at changing history with a single violent act"[30] had earned him the lasting fame John had always craved. Within a year, thousands of men were singing and marching to "John Brown's Body." That fame had come at a heavy price; Brown had died a criminal's death on the gallows. Facing the certainty of capture five years later, John resolved never to be taken alive rather than suffer the same fate.

Whatever resentment Kunkel or his fellow actors may have had for John's abandoning them, all was forgiven two weeks later when John saved actress Kate Fisher from being burned when her merino dress caught fire after she wandered too close to the stage's gas footlights.[31]

If she had not admired him before, actress Ella Wren now had reason to after witnessing John's bravery. The English-born actress, her sister Eliza, and her brother George had joined the stock company during John's second season.[32] They had started their theatrical careers as a juvenile family team. By the 1850s the team broke up as each of the family members embarked on their own stage careers, Ella as a singing actress.[33]

In the course of their rehearsals and plays together, a romance between John and Ella bloomed. There were rumors of an engagement. Ella's brother, George, had shared a room with John and had no qualms about him as a brother-in-law. "There was no one of my friends that was better liked," he said.[34] When Edwin got wind of the engagement, he buttonholed Ella's other brother Fred and asked him "many questions regarding [his] family, especially of [his] sister, Ella."[35] Respectability was very important to Edwin—no more so than for John. John remembered his sister Asia's feelings about their brother June's daughter Blanche. Asia would be even ruder to Edwin's fiancée, but that was yet to come.

Whatever relationship John and Ella had, it was short-lived. Perhaps the rumored "engagement" was a euphemism for an intimacy that never went beyond the nights they spent together. John never mentioned her in any of his existing letters and Ella never mentioned John.

John's other affairs in Richmond are unknown except for one with a girl known only as Miss Becket. Their relationship appears to have been more than a casual flirtation, but it ended when she fell ill with typhoid fever. Before her death, she had her hair shorn for John to make into a theatrical wig. It was a part of her for him to remember her by. John never spoke of her, but he did have her hair made into a wig. Of all his wigs, it was reputed to be his favorite.[36]

As with all of his romances, John did not lose much sleep getting over Miss Becket; other women easily distracted him. Helen Western and her sister Lucille were on their way to the Marshall Theatre for a two-week engagement beginning April 2, 1860.

# 7

# THE STAR SISTERS: HELEN AND LUCILLE WESTERN

**M**en drooled when Helen Western, with her glossy brunette hair and large, lustrous eyes, "dazzling in their brilliancy," appeared on stage.[1]

John Wilkes Booth knew many beautiful women—many of them intimately—in his life. When John died he had five photographs in his pocket. Four of them were of actresses. One of those actresses was Helen Western.

When Helen and her older sister Pauline Lucille came to Richmond in April 1860, they were still known as the "Star Sisters." Both girls were born in New Orleans. Like many performers of that era, their parents were both entertainers.[2] And like many youngsters from theatrical families, Helen and Lucille (she dropped her first name at an early age) went on stage almost as soon as they could walk. By 1852, they were touring the New England circuit from Boston to Bangor, Maine, with their mother in William B. English's "Dramatic Company" (by then their father had died). Lucille acted the part of a boy, and Helen was the sentimental heroine. By 1856, they were already being called "the old Boston favorites." In 1857,

Bill English married their mother and became his wife's and Helen's and Lucille's manager.[3]

Photos and other items found in John Wilkes Booth's pocket at the time of his death. *Courtesy of Library of Congress.*

Bill English was not oblivious to the stares his tall, dark, graceful, adolescent step-daughters were getting from men in the audience. He had been in the business long enough to know that sex sold. A few years earlier he had leased the National Theatre in Boston to put on an act so risqué for its time, the theatre manager's son beat him with a stick for lowering the "respectability" of his father's theatre.[4]

English became manager of Boston's National Theatre the same year he married their mother and cast the "Star Sisters," English's new name for Helen and Lucille, in a racy melodrama, *The Three Fast Men* or *The Female Robinson Crusoes of America*. The play, featuring them both as men in barely concealing disguises that showed off "the graces of their figures," opened to rave reviews on March 9, 1857.[5] "The most attractive piece ever written," commented the *New York Clipper*. "It is the quintessence of comedy, the par excellence of ingenuity. Although occupying three full hours, it is the only piece on record that entertains an audience so long and so merrily."[6] The *Boston Herald* was similarly enchanted: "There has not been such an excitement to witness a play within the memory of the oldest inhabitant."[7]

English had not anticipated how big a hit he had. Two days after the play opened, the *Boston Herald* reported *The Three Fast Men* had attracted the largest houses in the National Theatre's history. "It is estimated that there were three thousand persons there on Monday evening; every part of the house being packed full.... Miss Lucille personates seven distinct characters. Miss Helen also has quite a number of parts in her hands, and she sings the sweep song capitally."[8]

The storyline involved three young women trying to lure their men, who have gone astray, back to the straight and narrow by disguising themselves as men and behaving in ways that show the errant males their error. Helen and Lucille appeared as sailors, organ grinders, drunkards, gamblers, chimney sweeps, pawnbrokers, rowdies, or some other dissolute characters. Sometimes they appeared in eight different roles.[9] The play ended with a minstrel set in which the male actors sat around in a semi-circle strumming a banjo while Helen and Lucille danced jigs and sang.[10] At one point the mood turned pensive while the musicians played "A Maiden's Prayer." The song was the "hit" tune of the play and became a favorite parlor piano piece of the Civil War Era.[11] At the end of the play, the three fast men married the three devoted women, and everyone lived happily ever after.

Two weeks into the play's run, the *Boston Herald* reported "the house is regularly besieged every evening. Last night the lobbies were crowded to excess."[12] The following week, the *Boston Herald* reported "hundreds unable to get seats."[13]

Lucille initially garnered most of the accolades. Four days into the show's run, the "charming Lucille received bounteous applause." When she appeared in her sixth "protean" character, some women sitting in a private box threw a bouquet of flowers with a small purse attached onto the stage. Inside was fifty dollars in gold. "Miss Lucille," punned the *Boston Herald*, "is winning golden opinions from everybody, and she deserves them."[14]

Helen received her share of attention too. Nearing the end of the play's run, the *Boston Herald* printed a poem to Helen by an anonymous admirer. Her eyes, he wrote, were like "beams of sun," and her cheeks were "like roses in bloom." Her ringlets were as "black as the curtains of night and glossier than the raven in flight" and floated "sunnily down to a bosom of snow."[15]

*The Three Fast Men* played for eighty-seven consecutive nights in Boston, "unprecedented in the annals of theatricals" until then.[16] After another unprecedented three weeks each in Philadelphia and New York, the "Star Sisters" were back at Boston's National Theatre.[17] "Lucille," the *Boston Herald* commented, was "admirable." Helen was "prepossessing ... [she] has a bewitching face and great powers of pleasing."[18] Six months later *The Three Fast Men* played at the National Theatre yet again.[19] Fans were encouraged to stop by Page's store windows to see Cutting & Turner's "elegant photographs of Lucille and Helen, in their protean character."[20]

William Dean Howells, novelist, playwright, and editor of the *Atlantic*, attributed *The Three Fast Men*'s success to what he considered its underlying theme of morality.[21] Less high-minded men in the audience came to leer at Helen and Lucille in revealing clothes. The working class "b'hoys" at New York's seedy Old Broadway Theater didn't scream and whistle at the girls because they were feeling virtuous.[22]

Despite *The Three Fast Men*'s popularity among eastern audiences, theatre critics in the west criticized the girls' scanty costumes and the play's lewdness.[23] The *New Orleans Times-Picayune* did not mince words: "Whatever is low in fun, disgusting in allusion, vulgar in taste, and impure in morals, may be found in the 'Three Fast Men.' Any decent woman would blush to be seen at its representations, and any decent man should be ashamed to countenance it by his presence." In Cincinnati, the play was "suppressed by order of the police." Far from discouraging audiences, the notoriety lured them into the theatres. "It is all very well to say the wretched burlesque they appear in is of a bad and immoral tendency," said another reviewer, but nevertheless, "people go to see the curls and the ankles of two plum and pretty girls—and those who do so, with no intention but that of unreflective enjoyment, will not be disappointed."[24]

Confusing Weston and Western, the *Cincinnati Daily Gazette* claimed Helen and Lucille's moral failings were not surprising since they were sisters of Lizzie Weston Davenport, the adulteress at the center of a public scandal in New York.[25] Helen and Lucille sued the *Cincinnati Daily Gazette* for $10,000 for libel. "This is quite an unique case," the *Pittsburgh Daily Post* editorialized, "one of the first we remember wherein persons have brought suit for being furnished with false relatives."[26] Fans in Boston were riled at the insult to their favorite actresses.[27]

After appearances in Detroit, Cincinnati, Louisville, Chicago, and other major cities in the west, the "Misses Lucille and Helen Western, the young ladies whose rosy cheeks, gaiety of style, etc., made such an excitement among the 'b'hoys,' some months ago," were back at the Bowery Theatre in February 1859.[28]

Three months later, Helen and Lucille leased the National Theatre on their own and cast themselves in "the New Popular Play, *Sickles; or, The Washington Tragedy*." The *Detroit Free Press* reported the play was "a very close and correct dramatization from the facts, and offers with it a good moral in the pure and Puritanical city of Boston."[29] The "facts" involved adultery and murder. In February 1859, New York Congressman (later Major General) Daniel E. Sickles shot D.C. District Attorney Philip Barton Key (son of Francis Scott Key, author of "The Star-Spangled Banner") in cold blood outside Sickles's house in Lafayette Square for having an affair with Sickles's wife, Teresa, for more than a year.[30] In a landmark case, in which Sickles was represented by future Secretary of War Edwin M. Stanton, Sickles was exonerated on grounds of "temporary insanity." It was the first time the insanity defense was successfully used in the United States.[31]

*Sickles* was no show stopper. After a short stage run, Helen and Lucille dropped the play and resumed their stage careers. For the rest of the year they were the headliners in theatres across the United States and Montreal, Canada.[32]

Bored with performing with some semblance of modesty, Helen and
Lucille began dressing even more provocatively in *The Three Fast Men*
and their quips and banter had more sexual innuendo. The *New York
Clipper* commented Lucille and Helen were overdoing it: "We receive
every day awful accounts of their too natural style of acting." The *New
York Clipper* advised them to "dial it back."[33]

Helen Western in a French spy costume. *Courtesy of
New York Public Library, Billy Rose Collection.*

The only ones complaining they were overdoing it were the theatre
critics. St. Louis's theatre critic scowled Helen and Lucille were "poor
actresses, and only to be tolerated before Bowery audiences," but he had
to admit St. Louis's audiences were jamming the theatre every night.[34] A

critic in Wheeling, Virginia, was just as disapproving of the play's "immoral tendency" and just as unpersuasive in discouraging people not to attend.[35]

Meanwhile, sixteen-year-old Lucille had met twenty-nine-year-old James Harrison Mead in St. Louis and was canoodling with the "small and spare framed" ruddy-haired actor.[36] After they married in September 1859, Mead gave up his own acting career and became Lucille's business manager. It was the beginning of the end for the "Star Sisters." Helen and Lucille stayed together for another two years, but Lucille's marriage started a fissure that eventually cracked their act apart. For one thing, the sisters no longer shared the same room. For another, despite being married, Lucille still had a roving eye and was not above flirting with men interested in Helen.

Helen and Lucille's next engagement was at the Marshall Theatre in Richmond.[37] John had been at the Marshall for two years by then. He performed with Helen and Lucille every night except Sundays during their three-week engagement. Like every other male in the cast and in the audience, he was likely smitten with the two sisters, especially Helen, who was coming into her own and no longer simply Lucille's younger sidekick. John was handsome and charismatic, but there is no record of either sister spending time offstage with him. A year later, however, the "Star Sisters" would be at each other's throats over which one of them John preferred to spend his nights with.

# 8

# I Cannot Stoop to That Which I Despise

During the second week of May 1860, John was supposed to accompany Helen and Lucille Western for appearances in Petersburg and Norfolk, but their Norfolk engagement was cancelled when Helen had a relapse from tuberculosis.[1] John would not see Helen again for a year. When they met again, John was on his way to becoming a star himself.

John took advantage of the time off to spend a brief vacation with his mother and Rosalie in Philadelphia. Asia, now married and with a newborn baby, was living in her own house nearby.

One of the souvenirs John brought home was one of the pikes John Brown had intended to use to arm the slaves he expected to join his insurrection.[2] He was proud of the pike because it was given to him by Lewis Washington, a descendant of America's first president. The inscription on the handle read, "Major Washington to J. Wilkes Booth," in large letters.[3]

Most of the family was dismayed that John had broken his theatre contract and joined the militia, but not Asia. She listened attentively to the exploits of the brother she idolized. Basking in her esteem, John let his imagination get the better of him and exaggerated his brief military service. He hadn't just prevented an abolitionist attempt to rescue John Brown. Instead, he boasted he had been "one of the party going to search for and capture" him. Asia admired the picture John handed her of "himself and others in their scout and sentinel dresses."[4]

Booth historian Nora Titone saw resentment of Edwin's success behind John's exaggerations. "As John Wilkes settled into his mother's home in Philadelphia," she wrote, "he would see Edwin's face staring down at him from the drawing room wall" with "a wreath of real laurel, the traditional hero's crown" twisted there by his mother, as well as the scrapbook she kept of many complimentary letters Edwin received from prominent citizens in New York, Boston, and other major cities.[5]

John's exaggerations were typical of the man. It wasn't necessarily resentment but his need for approval, especially from his sister Asia, whose opinion very much mattered to him. Edwin's spectacular rise from journeyman actor to the "most popular tragedian in the United States"[6] was an inspiration, not a cause for jealousy. If Edwin could do it, so could he.

As a stock actor John was earning a paltry salary and was only occasionally mentioned in the papers. As a star like Edwin, he would receive a much higher salary or a percentage of the gross receipts and a regular "benefit" (a tradition in which a star received all the profits for his or her final performance with a company). His name would appear as many as five times in the advertisements, in larger and bolder type than the name of the play, and he would garner most of the attention from theatre critics. The mere fact of being billed as a star prompted audiences and critics to eulogize an actor as such. A stock actor was told what part he was to play, where to stand, when to enter, and when to leave the stage. Stars made those decisions for themselves; they were their own masters. The star was the sun around whom all the planetary stock actors revolved.

As Lincoln said about his bid for the presidency around the same time, the "taste" was in his mouth. John had the taste in his mouth by

February 1860 when he wrote to Edwin about finding him a manager.[7] When the season at the Marshall Theatre ended in May, John decided it was time to move on.

There was just one problem. An actor could not just become a star on his own. He could pay a manager to bill him as a star, but if the aspiring star bombed, it was a costly venture for a manager. Even if John had had that kind of money, pride would have kept him from paying for his own fame. The only other option was to forge a reputation that would convince a manager to take a chance and bill him as a star. It also helped if a fledgling star had connections and a name to trade on. John had both.

John was not the only Booth looking to the future. Mary "Molly" Devlin was a sixteen-year-old stock actress at the Marshall Theatre when she and Edwin first met in November 1856. Mary, the daughter of a poor Irish tailor in New York, debuted as an actress in 1852 when she was not quite twelve. At sixteen, when she signed on with the Marshall Theatre's stock company in 1856, she was a seasoned stock actress. Edwin hadn't given her a second thought when he first met her. Two years later, he began to notice. By then Mary was a confident, hard-working actress. Edwin noticed an innocence and sweetness about her; she was also pretty and unpretentious. When Edwin left for his next engagement at the Holliday Street Theatre in Baltimore, he asked John Ford if she could go with him. Ford agreed, personally believing she was "played out."[8] Edwin, however, believed Mary was leading lady material. Although there were rumors of more than a working relationship between them, Edwin told a friend there was no truth to the rumors but admitted he was attracted to her.[9]

Edwin, however, was ambivalent about women in general and actresses in particular, a product of his dissolute years on his own in California and Australia. He had been a drunkard and a libertine. He had tried to reform but found it impossible.[10] Though less so than John, Edwin was also physically attractive and fawned over by actresses and women in his audiences.[11] "Hundreds of women flung themselves at him," said his manager William Bisham. "They invited him to their houses, they offered to go to his."[12] Edwin thought little of his flings with prostitutes and actresses, but he avoided "pure women," said his lifelong friend Adam Badeau. He "never injured [seduced] a pure woman in his life."[13]

Even though she was an actress, Edwin had begun to have feelings for Mary Devlin. She was, he confided to a friend, "a dear, sweet girl, innocent as a babe." Despite those feelings, Edwin had affairs with other actresses, one of them ending in a venereal disease. With his affection for Mary growing, his affairs began to disgust him.[14] He couldn't get Mary out of his mind. By January 1859, Edwin was calling her "dear Molly" and visiting her family. In April 1859, when Edwin went on a drinking spree, she took care of him until he recovered. When he was away on tour, they wrote to one another. In July 1859, they were engaged.

When Edwin brought Mary home to meet his mother and sisters, Asia would not even see her. Even though her brothers and father were actors, Asia had the same low opinion of actresses most Americans did. For Asia, an actress was a "bold faced woman" who strutted before an audience every night and allowed "men of all kinds to caress and court her in a business way." "That my good and noble boy should throw himself away so lightly is enough to break my heart." "I wanted to love Ned's wife, to let her be my sister," she wrote her confidante, Jean Anderson, "but I cannot stoop to that which I despise."[15]

Asia's attitude toward actresses was not unique. It was commonly assumed that most actresses lived immoral lives on as well as off stage partly because actresses had to travel with male stars or business managers. "With the sole exception of prostitution, to which it was often compared," writes theatre historian Claudia Johnson, no single profession was so loudly and frequently condemned. The catalog of immoral behavior included "'heaving bosoms, lascivious smiles, wanton glances, dubious compliments, indelicate attitudes, kissing' (and a) 'variety of vain and sinful practices' (including falling) 'into the arms of men' on stage" and illicit love scenes backstage.[16]

Many American churches regarded theatres as dens of iniquity and actors and actresses, especially actresses, as the devil's disciples. The Boston Museum was so-called to assuage the guilty feelings of puritanical Bostonians who wanted an excuse to go to the theatre but sought to avoid moral condemnation by first visiting the Museum's "Hall of Curiosities."[17]

While some very famous actresses like Charlotte Cushman and Maggie Mitchell were accepted in genteel society, they were the exceptions. Most were snubbed. Clara Morris, another socially accepted actress, said her mother was "stricken with horror" when Clara told her she was going to be an actress. *Richmond Enquirer* editor William Ritchie's marriage to actress Anna Cora Mowatt in 1854 shocked Richmond's upper crust.[18]

Edwin felt the same misgivings about Mary being an actress as Asia. He told her that before he could marry her, not only would she have to give up her career as an actress, she would also have to live a year away from any contact with the theatre. Mary agreed and went to live in Hoboken, New Jersey, in a house Edwin leased for her and her chaperone, her sister Catherine.[19]

Edwin and Mary Devlin were married in New York on July 7, 1860. John was the only one of the family to attend the small ceremony.[20] Asia's and his mother's absences told John all he needed to know about what they thought about marrying an actress. Asia never did become reconciled to the marriage. When Edwin and Mary left for their honeymoon in Niagara Falls, Asia wrote Jean Anderson she hoped Mary would tumble under the falls or swim in the whirlpool and drown.[21]

After their honeymoon, Edwin and Mary moved into the Fifth Avenue Hotel in New York. They were a happy couple, wrote Lillian Woodman, one of their new friends.[22] On December 9, 1861, Mary gave birth to a girl they named Edwina.

# 9

# ALMOST AN EUNUCH

B lond, goateed, nattily dressed, and sporting diamonds, Matthew W. Canning was in New York in July, hiring stock actors and stars for the 1860–1861 season at theatres he had leased in the Deep South.[1] The previous seasons he had done well and he anticipated having another profitable season. Two of John's friends from the Marshall Theatre, Samuel Knapp Chester and John Albaugh, had already signed on with Canning. When Booth met up with them in New York at the time of Edwin's wedding, they told him Canning was hiring.[2]

John already knew Canning. They had first met in 1857 when John was starting out at the Arch Street Theatre in Philadelphia. Canning was then treasurer of the rival National Theater.[3] Good-natured, though easily "riled" when his patience was tried, Canning was aware John had not been a stellar performer at the Arch. He had mixed feelings about hiring him, especially when John said he was looking for a job as a star, not a stock actor. A stock actor was "a good actor and a poor fool" journalist George Townsend jibed, whereas a star was "an advertisement in tights, who grows rich and corrupts the public taste."[4]

Before leaving on his honeymoon, Edwin had spoken to Canning about giving John a start as a star.[5] Canning was noncommittal. He was in business to make money, not do favors. The *New York Clipper* praised him as "one of those managers who know how to manage."[6] Canning never paid a bill before carefully scrutinizing it.[7]

Regardless of how many tickets they sold, managers took all the risks. They paid for leasing a theatre, for renovations,[8] the salaries for their stock actors and theatre staff, their transportation, any advertising and printing, scenery, wardrobe supplies, gas bills and candles, city taxes, and license fees to playwrights for using their plays. All that was in addition to what they paid the stars.[9]

Managers could only hope to make money by hiring quality stock actors and stars. Reputations filled seats. Managers who agreed to arrange and promote the career of an unproven actor as a star was gambling their time and investment would pay off.[10] Canning was a manager, not a gambler.

John did not have a reputation as a star, but he had a famous name. Canning told Edwin he might hire his brother on the basis of his name, which he knew "would draw me money."[11] Canning told John he would feature him as a "stock star" for six weeks. He would give him star billing and a benefit once a week. He would not give him a star's percentage of the profits.[12]

John agreed except for Canning using his full name. He insisted on being billed as "Mr. John Wilkes," or "J. B. Wilkes." Canning agreed, having already thought of a way to honor his agreement and still use the Booth name to fill seats. He billed John as "Mr. John Wilkes" but added,"brother of Edwin Booth, the eminent young tragedian." Canning's advertisement in Alabama's *Montgomery Advertiser* for his company's upcoming appearance in Montgomery left nothing to speculation: "Perhaps some little explanation might be deemed necessary in regard to Mr. John Wilkes. He is a brother of the eminent young tragedian [Edwin], but to avoid confounding their names, and thereby creating misunderstanding among theatre goers, he has consented to be known simply as John Wilkes."[13]

Prior to opening in Montgomery, Canning leased the Temperance Hall Theatre in Columbus, Georgia, while renovations at the Montgomery Theatre were still going on. Columbus, located on the Chattahoochee River, with a population of about 9,000, was the largest manufacturing town south of Richmond and a major railroad and shipping center in the South. As the city prospered, it became part of a Charleston-Savannah-Columbus-Montgomery-New Orleans theatre circuit. Temperance Hall Theatre, built in 1849, was one of four theatres in the city and its largest.[14]

The troupe opened in Columbus on October 1, 1860, with John as Romeo (the first time he had ever played the part) and Mary Mitchell, Maggie's sister, as the company's leading lady, in the role of Juliet.[15] When John stepped onto the stage, he was enthusiastically applauded.

Canning need not have worried that John did not have a reputation. He did—not as an actor, but as a Southern hero. Everyone with "intense Southern feeling," should applaud Mr. Wilkes, the *Columbus Daily Times* editorialized, for having been among the first to "defend Southern honor and Southern homes" against John Brown's invasion.[16] The following night "there was an unusually large proportion of ladies" in the audience.[17]

Although he played Romeo to Mary's Juliet on stage, there is no hint of John's ever becoming romantically involved with Mary Mitchell offstage. Even had John been interested, an accident short-circuited whatever relationship they might have had. On October 12, during the last week of his appearance in Columbus, John was shot.

Accounts vary about how.[18] Canning said it happened like this: He entered the bedroom he and John shared to take a nap, his gun still in his pocket. ("Everyone carried weapons down in that country, and so did I.") As he was resting, Canning felt John taking the gun out of his pocket, but he was too tired to bother to stop him. John wanted to show off how good a shot he was, Canning continued. He aimed the gun at a mark on a wall and fired. Despite his reputation for being a crack shot, he missed.

Canning claimed he jumped up and tried to grab his gun back, but John held on. He said he wanted another shot, intent on proving his skill. Reluctantly, Canning handed him a second cartridge. The gun was rusted and the cartridge wouldn't fit easily. After managing to load it, John continued scraping away rust from the opened hammer when it snapped down and the gun fired. The ball lodged in Booth's thigh, Canning said. The bullet barely missed the femoral artery and came within inches of turning him into an eunuch. For a variety of reasons, Canning's story is unlikely.[19] The more plausible explanation is that the two men tussled for possession of the gun and Canning accidently shot him.

John spent most of the remaining week of the tour in his hotel room recuperating. He was still in Columbus when the company opened in Montgomery on October 22 to a packed house. The program opened with the company singing "The Star-Spangled Banner."[20] It would be one of the last times the anthem would be heard in Alabama for many years.[21] John caught up with the troupe a few days later but wasn't strong enough to go back on stage until seventeen days after his accident.

Montgomery was a small, quiet town of about 9,000 before the war. Located on a large bend in the Alabama River, it was major depot for tobacco, rice, corn, and cotton (over a million bales were shipped from its wharf in 1860). Destined to be the first capital of the Confederate States of America, it was not a major entertainment center, but its theatre was still on the circuit of various concert artists and minstrel troupes that played the South.[22]

John's six-week contract with Canning ran out on November 3, 1860. He could have gone back north, but he did not have enough money to pay for passage home. In an undated letter written from the Exchange Hotel to a woman he only addressed as "Dear Miss," John thanked her for something she had done for him. He would have liked to remunerate her, he said, but "to use the language of the day...I am very hard up."[23]

The Exchange Hotel where he was staying was Montgomery's most elegant residence. If he didn't have money to leave Montgomery, he wouldn't have had money to pay for a room for an extended stay. The "Dear Miss," likely had given him enough to pay his bill and then some. In the meantime, he filled in his evenings playing without a contract opposite touring stars Canning had hired, and his nights with other "dear misses" and prostitutes.

The first of the touring stars to appear at the Montgomery that season was Kate Bateman. John played Romeo to Kate's Juliet. Kate's father, Hezekiah Bateman, her chaperone and biggest fan, thought John was an outstanding Romeo and brought out the best in his daughter. They were so good together, he talked to John about him touring England with his daughter.[24]

Kate was overjoyed at the prospect of co-starring in England with such "a beautiful creature—you couldn't help admiring him—so amiable, so sweet, so sympathetic."[25]

The tour never came off. A "trifle" ended any further thought about Kate touring with John.[26] The "trifle" was Papa Bateman's learning that John was spending his nights with Louise Wooster, an eighteen-year-old prostitute. When Kate's Montgomery engagement ended, Papa Bateman made sure his daughter never had anything to do with John Booth again. John was just as glad. In the same "Dear Miss" letter, John alluded to his parting of the ways with Kate's father, "Thank God I am not yet a Bateman," he wrote, "and may I never be."[27]

# 18

# LITTLE REHEARSALS: LOUISE WOOSTER

**A** day or two after coming to Montgomery, John was "Lou's" favorite star. "I was truly happy," said the eighteen-year-old prostitute.[1]

Louise Catherine Wooster ("Lou"), was born in Tuscaloosa, Alabama, to a middle-class family of six girls. Her father was an engineer from New York; her mother was a native South Carolinian. Lou's father died a year after the family moved to Mobile, when Lou was seven. Her mother remarried three years later, to a man who squandered whatever money she had and deserted her, leaving her and her daughters destitute. Lou's sister, Margaret, age fourteen, left home and became a prostitute.[2]

Lou's mother died when Lou was fifteen. Her two younger sisters were sent to an "orphan asylum" in Mobile. Lou went to live with a married sister in New Orleans. None too happy about supporting Lou, her husband refused to take his wife's younger sisters in as well. Lou made her way back to Mobile. She forged her older sister's signature on a letter stating her sisters could come and live with her, and took them out of the orphanage.[3]

With no money of their own, the three girls accepted an offer to live with a family friend. The friend seduced Lou and then kicked her out.[4] When Lou became gravely ill with yellow fever, another family friend brought Lou to his home to recuperate. After she recovered, he also seduced her, then took her to a brothel to be rid of her.[5]

With no alternatives, Lou entered "the life," but balked at living a "life of shame in Mobile," where her family was known."[6] With what little belongings she had, Lou left for Montgomery to work at "Big Lize's." "Big Lize" was Eliza Yarbourgh, madam of Montgomery's best known "house of ill repute."[7]

Lou was "young and rather pretty," had a "sweet disposition," and got along well with the other "inmates" at "Big Lize's."[8] She maintained her pride, she said, and her "good old Knickerbocker blood" made her particular about only taking on "the higher class of men that visited our home."[9] That was make-believe. Prostitutes at "Big Lize's" did not have the privilege of choosing their customers. At fifteen, Lou did what she was told.

Girls at "Big Lize's" and most other brothels had short careers. They were usually dead by the age of twenty-five from suicide, syphilis, alcoholism, or morphine overdose,[10] not to mention sexual assault and murder by drunks who shot them.[11]

Condoms were expensive and rarely used. Made from sheep intestines or rubber, they cost $3 to $6 a dozen, about $45 to $90 in today's prices.[12] Sexually transmitted diseases were rampant. Seventy-three thousand men contracted syphilis during the Civil War. Another 109,000 came down with "clap," the common name for gonorrhea.[13] John's own brother Edwin was a "clap" victim.[14] John would eventually come down with syphilis.[15] So did John's good friend and fellow actor, John McCullough. A few years before he died from it, McCullough reminisced how John "was a wonderful companion of poetry, adventure, and disease."[16]

Prostitution was not the sort of life girls chose willingly. "Though the brightest jewel had been plucked from my little crown," Lou vowed to herself she would leave that "life of shame should the opportunity ever be offered."[17]

Lou believed John Booth was that opportunity.

John was her "ideal man, handsome, generous, affectionate and brave." He was her idol. "Oh! How I loved him."[18]

John told her he loved her too. They would never part, he said. He promised he would get her into the theater and teach her how to be a star during their "little rehearsals."[19] John's brother Edwin had seduced a "singing chambermaid" in California with the same line.[20]

John was still "rehearsing" with Louise when Maggie Mitchell arrived in Montgomery on Thursday, November 29, 1860, for a two-week appearance at the Montgomery Theatre.

The next day was Montgomery's annual St. Andrews Society's dinner. Since Maggie's father was born in Scotland, she was part Scottish herself and felt right at home entertaining the gathering at the Post Office Restaurant with songs interspersed between toasts to impending secession, "Robbie Burns," and haggis.[21] John was not Scottish, but Maggie wrangled a personal invitation for him to attend.[22] The following day Maggie also arranged a "Grand Complimentary Benefit By The Citizens of Montgomery" for "Mr. J. Wilkes Booth."[23]

John had vowed he would not use his family surname until he felt he had earned that right. Stepping onto the Montgomery stage that Saturday night on December 1, he felt he had. From then on, he no longer avoided using the name "Booth."[24]

John probably spent Saturday night and all of Sunday with Maggie. On Monday he visited Lou for a "rehearsal." Afterwards he told her he had to leave Montgomery the next day. If he stayed any longer, he said, he would be killed for speaking out against secession.

Montgomery was the home of William Lowndes Yancey, the "Apostle of Secession." When Senator Stephen Douglas, the proponent of popular sovereignty—the principle that people in new territories should decide for themselves if they wanted the territory to be slave or free—stopped in

Montgomery as part of his bid for the presidency in 1860, Yancey's sup-porters pelted him and his wife with rotten eggs.[25] Yancey and the South's "fire eaters" were adamant in their opposition to any restrictions on slav-ery. The only way to maintain their "property" rights in slaves, they insisted, was to secede from the Union and form their own country.

After Lincoln won the national election on November 6, 1860, seces-sion was no longer idle talk. Robert Toombs, a "fire-eating" senator from Georgia, told a Montgomery crowd of over 2,000 at the Montgomery Theatre it was time to end the Union even if it meant civil war.[26]

Despite losing the election, Douglas continued to speak out against the prevailing sentiment in the South for dissolving the Union. It would mean war, he warned, a war that would plunge "the happiest people, the most prosperous country, and the best Government the sun of heaven ever shed his genial rays upon...into the horrors of revolution, anarchy, and bankruptcy."[27]

Douglas's dire warning hit home to John. Long before he became a zealous Southern patriot, he was a staunch Unionist. His father and grandfather had been dedicated to the Union. John agreed with Douglas that war would destroy the country.

Never one to keep his thoughts to himself, John made the mistake of saying them aloud in public to some Montgomery fire-eaters. Did they want to "tear down this great temple of civilization that was the Union, this Monument of our father's greatness," he said to men who had already decided they did. He for one would "not fight for secession or for disunion."[28]

Expressing those thoughts in the Deep South did not endear him to Montgomery's firebrand secessionists. He told Lou he had to leave imme-diately. If he stayed he could be killed or tarred and feathered for what he had said.[29]

Lou begged him to take her with him.

"Impossible!" John told her.

"Then I will never see you again," Lou sobbed. "Something tells me that I will not. Something tells me that this is our final parting."[30]

It was. John left Montgomery for Savannah on December 3 and sailed from there to New York, arriving on December 9. Years later, Lou believed he still loved her.

# 11

# THE SOUTHERN MARSEILLAISE

The Union was in peril. On December 20, 1860, South Carolina adopted an ordinance of secession, declaring its independence from the United States of America. It was no surprise to anyone in the Deep South. Other states were preparing to follow South Carolina's lead, among them Alabama.

The night before South Carolina's announcement, a huge audience at the Montgomery Theatre was in a celebratory mood. When the applause subsided at the end of Maggie Mitchell's act, theatre manager Sam Harris stepped onto the stage. Brimming with pride, he handed Maggie Alabama's new lone star flag, a blue banner with a single star on one side and the figure of Liberty on the other. Liberty held a sword in her right hand; in her left was a flag bearing the single word, "Alabama." Directly above it was Alabama's new mantra: "Independent Now and Forever."[1] Caught up in the audience's enthusiasm, Maggie paraded back and forth across the stage waving the blue silk banner and singing the "Southern Marseillaise," the South's earliest rallying song.[2]

81

Jefferson Davis and Alexander Stephens, the future president and vice president of the Confederacy, were in the audience that night as were "fire eaters" William Lowndes Yancey and Robert Toombs. Never one to show emotion, Davis looked on "like a grey wolf, and with a solemn sort of manner,"[3] as the audience cheered itself hoarse.[4]

North of the Mason-Dixon line, the *Cincinnati Daily Press* howled that Maggie Mitchell "has been chaunting the 'Marseillaise' at the Montgomery Theatre, [and] was presented on Friday night with a 'Lone Star' flag of Alabama."[5] Months later newspapers throughout the North began lambasting her for her disloyalty. Some added that she had also given a "secession speech."[6] A year later those accusations almost torpedoed her career.

After her Montgomery engagement ended in early January, Maggie headed to New Orleans for a two-week appearance at the St. Charles Theatre. At that time New Orleans was one of the country's two major entertainment centers, the other being New York. No entertainer of any stature ignored New Orleans in his or her tour.[7]

Maggie had been a featured star in New Orleans several times before. Her fans had come out in droves. Except for the *New Orleans Times-Picayune*, New Orleans' theatre critics had been routinely bilious in their reviews. The "very susceptible young gentlemen of the dress circle" are enamored with the "pretty little gold fish," the *Daily Creole*'s critic pouted; an "angler" like himself did not find her worth the bait.[8] The *Daily True Delta Tribune*'s critic grumbled she wore too much lipstick and too little clothing. "No wonder the pit applauded her," he went on. "Eve wore a fig leaf. Maggie wore scarcely more."[9]

Maggie was planning to feature *The French Spy* for her upcoming appearance. It was a favorite piece among the attractive actresses of the day because the flimsy costumes they wore in the play were a surefire draw. When she arrived at the St. Charles, she agreed to look at a new play called

*Fanchon, the Cricket*, that orchestra leader Augustus Waldauer told her he had adapted especially with her in mind.[10] Her energy and childlike laughter, he said, would be perfect for the play's impish heroine. Maggie read it over and agreed to put it on during her second week.

*Fanchon* is a melodrama based on a story by French writer Georges Sand, called *La Petite Fadette (The Little Cricket)* which celebrates the virtues of cheeriness and good-naturedness. A sprightly young girl, Fanchon Vivieux, called the "Cricket," lives at the outskirts of a village with her grandmother and has no villagers for friends because the villagers regard her grandmother a witch. Although she has no playmates, Fanchon is not lonely. Her vivid imagination lets her create imaginary companions. The highlight of the play is the "Shadow Dance" in which Fanchon dances with and talks to her own shadow, as if it were a real person.

Maggie Mitchell as Fanchon. *Courtesy of New York Public Library, Billy Rose Division.*

Maggie first appeared as Fanchon on January 23, 1861,[11] and continued acting the part through February. New Orleans' normally ill-disposed critics adored it. The *New Orleans Daily Crescent* gushed Maggie had "far exceeded in interest anything of the kind that has lately been seen on the St. Charles boards."[12]

Maggie was quick to realize *Fanchon*'s potential and bought the rights to the play from Waldauer. She would appear in it an estimated 4000 times. It would make her one of the wealthiest and best-loved actresses in America.[13]

After debuting *Fanchon* in New Orleans, Maggie headed back to Montgomery for a repeat engagement. By then, Alabama had become the fourth state to secede from the Union.[14] Delegates from the other three seceded states were arriving every day in Montgomery to draft a constitution for the new Confederate States of America. On February 9, 1861, three days after her return,[15] the Constitutional Convention met in Montgomery and chose Jefferson Davis as Provisional President of the Confederate States of America. Davis arrived in Montgomery a week later on Saturday, February 16. By then the city was swarming with visitors, politicians and their wives, reporters and "lobby vultures everywhere, ears cocked for a hint of a job."[16]

Diarist Mary Chesnut, wife of James Chesnut, representing South Carolina, didn't care much for Maggie. It wasn't her acting that annoyed her so much as all the attention Maggie was drawing from men. Alabama's fifty-four-year old governor Andrew Moore was particularly attentive. "The old sinner," Mary groused, was "making himself ridiculous" and creating a minor scandal, spending so much time with "the actress woman."[17]

Maggie was supposed to leave Montgomery after her benefit but stayed on, basking in the affection of Montgomery's audiences. On April 11, the day before the batteries at Charleston opened fire on Fort Sumter, she presented a prized silver goblet to the militia unit judged to have been the best at drill and rifle fire.[18] The very next day she boarded a train north. Had she stayed any longer she would have been trapped behind Confederate lines.

# 12

# ALL FOR LOVE AND MURDER: HENRIETTA IRVING

Henrietta Irving loved John Wilkes Booth. When John betrayed that love, she knifed him. Then she tried to kill herself.

Unlike many of the actresses John spent time with offstage, Henrietta was not attractive. In fact, she was rather plain looking. Her most distinctive feature was her long, wavy brunette hair. The most theatre critics could say about her by way of compliment was that she was tall ("commanding height"), had "bright eyes," "aristocratic hands," and had a "finely rounded" or, as one critic put it, a "queenly form."[1] It was a polite way of saying she was stout.

The affair began in Rochester, New York, in January 1861, just weeks after John left Montgomery. The "young American tragedian of great popularity" was appearing for the first time as a star at the Metropolitan Theatre. Henrietta was his co-star. Her sister, Marie, had a lesser supporting role. Although John and Henrietta were both billed as stars, the Booth name was the draw. Evenings were spent on stage at the Metropolitan; nights were spent at the Osburn House hotel where John and the Irving sisters each had rooms.[2]

A "finely rounded" Henrietta Irving. *Courtesy of Lester S. Levy Collection of Sheet Music, Duke University, Durham, North Carolina.*

Their first play together was *Romeo and Juliet*. At twenty-three, John could still have passed for a believable teenage Romeo. At twenty-eight, Henrietta was stretching it. Still, when the play ended, the actors received a warm applause from the audience.[3]

It was only supposed to be a week's engagement for John, but the rest of the week went so well that Wellington Meech, the Metropolitan's manager, kept him on for a second week. Elsewhere audience attendance had fallen off because of the "present disturbed state of the country,"[4] but John and Henrietta were playing to "full and crowded houses."[5] It was the beginning of their near fatal romance.

Henrietta was born in New Bedford, New York in 1833, "of parents in good circumstances."[6] At eighteen, she became stage-struck after visiting New York and made up her mind to be an actress. She moved to New York and paid for acting lessons. When she thought she was ready for a stage career, she bribed Rufus Blake, manager of the Broadway Theatre, $18 to give her an audition. Blake took the money and gave her a tryout, but didn't hire her. Her voice, he said, was too weak for Broadway. "You have youth, beauty and money," he said by way of consolation. "Work hard and in time you will become an actress."[7]

Henrietta was nothing if not determined. Three years later, in September 1855, she had her stage debut at the Walnut Street Theatre in Philadelphia[8] where Charles Walter Couldock[9] was the company's lead stock actor. After the Walnut Street Theatre was taken over the next season by an opera company, Couldock left to go out west. Henrietta asked if he would take her with him. Talk to my wife, Couldock judiciously told her. Mrs. Couldock agreed, provided Henrietta pay her as chaperone, and pay Couldock $100 a month as mentor. Henrietta travelled with Couldock for two seasons. She never begrudged the arrangement.[10]

By 1857 she had come into her own as an actress. During a performance in St. Paul, Minnesota, a "gallant Chippewa Indian named Nam-tam-ab, or Great Blower," was so taken with her that he came on to the stage and presented her with a diamond ring.[11] A short time later, her time with Couldock ended. In the wake of the financial panic of 1857, when many of the country's theaters closed, Couldock left to join Laura Keene's company in New York. Henrietta was on her own.[12] With no other prospects, she signed on as the featured star with William Henderson's stock company in Rock Island, about 200 miles west of Chicago.

Rock Island was too small a community to have a theatre of its own. The "theatre" was the town's City Hall that Henderson rented for $4 a night. There were no reserved seats inside the capacity 600-chair room. Admission was 11 cents, but audiences were enthusiastic enough for Henderson to book the makeshift theatre for six months, with a performance every night except Sunday.[13]

Henrietta bided her time in Rock Island until the financial panic ended the following year. By the summer of 1858, as theatres were back in business, Henrietta headed back to Chicago. In July "Miss Henrietta Irving" appeared in the starring role in the Chicago production of *Aladdin and the Wonderful Lamp*.[14]

After her Chicago engagement, Henrietta toured that part of the country[15] until November 1859 when she headed east for appearances in Troy, New York. By then her sister Marie wanted to try an acting career. In December 1859, Henrietta arranged for Marie to have her debut with the Troy Theatre Company.[16] It was a decision Henrietta would come to regret.

In January 1861, Henrietta headed to Rochester to co-star with John Wilkes Booth. As was common among actors and actresses, John and Henrietta reprised their evening stage roles of Romeo and Juliet at night in their hotel rooms. For John, it was any port in a storm. "Love without esteem," was how journalist George Alfred Townsend described John's feelings for Henrietta.[17] Henrietta believed their affair was much more serious.

John's engagement in Rochester ended on February 2, 1861. He stayed on another week, then left Rochester and checked into Albany's posh six-story Stanwix Hall Hotel, for his upcoming appearance at the Gayety Theatre. Henrietta and her sister Marie stayed in Rochester for another week to finish their own engagement. They were next scheduled at the Gayety, but not until March 18. With little else to do, they left for the Stanwix.

John was scheduled to play Romeo during his first night and Pescara in *The Apostate*, two roles he would play over and over in his career. The advertisement for *The Apostate* was supposed to read "Re-appearance of the Great Tragedian." The printer left the "T" off "Tragedian." Instead, the advertisement ironically read "Re-appearance of the Great ragedian."[18] Two days later, in his role as Pescara, the "Great ragedian" came close to killing himself.

*The Apostate* is about a love triangle that takes place in Spain in the second half of the sixteenth century. At the end, Pescara commits suicide alongside the lady love interest by stabbing himself. During this climactic scene, John's knife was supposed to fall harmlessly on to the stage. Instead, when it hit the floor it opened. When John fell in his death swoon, the knife cut a deep, three-inch gash in his right armpit. Fortunately, a doctor in the audience was able to staunch the bleeding. After he stitched and bandaged the wound, John left for his hotel to recover.[19]

By happenstance, president-elect Lincoln, on his way to Washington for his inauguration, arrived in Albany on February 18, 1861, the same day John had recuperated enough from his wound to go back on stage.

Lincoln's arrival was welcomed by a large parade down Broadway past the Stanwix Hall Hotel on the way to the capitol. Not everyone in the crowd was cheering. Albany and the surrounding county had not voted for Lincoln in the 1860 election and its mayor and state governor were both Democrats.[20] Those supporting Lincoln strung a banner across the street with a simple message: "Welcome to the Capital of the Empire State—No More Compromises."[21] Like everywhere else, Albany sensed the country was on the brink of civil war. "Faces were pale with anticipation of what was about to come …. Blood was at fever heat."[22]

The Delevan hotel where Lincoln was staying was just a short block from the Stanwix. Even if John had had murder in his heart by then, his injured right arm, his firing arm, was taped to his side.

In another of the strange coincidences of history, two of the invited guests at the reception for the Lincolns that night, Clara Harris and her fiancé, Major Henry Rathbone, were also Lincoln's guests the night John murdered Lincoln.

While Harris and Rathbone and Albany's other elites were hobnobbing with Lincoln, John was steaming. Although the war had not yet
started, seven Southern states had seceded after Lincoln, the "black
Republican" was elected. John had become, to use a modern term,
"radicalized" for the Southern cause.

The day Lincoln arrived in Albany, John was overheard at the Stanwix condemning Lincoln for trying to persuade the Southern states that
had seceded to return to the Union. Just a few months earlier in Montgomery, John had been opposed to the dissolution of the country. Over
the Christmas holidays he had begun to think differently. Now that the
South had seceded, he vocally supported secession. When the manager
of the Gayety was informed about John's outspoken views, he asked J.
C. Cuyler, the theater's treasurer, to talk to him about being more discreet. His star's "violent secessionist" talk could hurt ticket sales.

As soon as Cuyler stepped into the hotel the next morning, he could
hear John arguing with two of the other hotel guests. Heading off what
might have turned into a brawl, Cuyler pulled John aside, saying he had
some important business to discuss. Behind closed doors, Cuyler cautioned him. If he did not tone down his inflammatory outbursts, Cuyler
told him he would not only forgo his engagement, he would be made to
leave Albany. And not peaceably.[23]

John chafed. "Is not this a Democratic city?" he challenged.

"Democratic? yes; disunion, no!" Cuyler shot back.[24]

John meant Democrat with a capital "D." Since Albany and the surrounding county had not voted for Lincoln in the 1860 election, John
assumed he was not alone in voicing his feelings about Lincoln.

Chastised, John managed to keep his feelings under control for the
rest of his time in Albany and remained a popular star at the Gayety—so
much so that the manager asked him to stay another week. However,
John had committed himself to appear in Portland, Maine, starting
March 18, at Bill English's Deering House Theatre for the next two
weeks. He promised to return to Albany for another week once his Portland engagement ended. That promise almost cost him his life.

By coincidence or design, Helen and Lucille Western, English's stepdaughters, were John's co-stars in Portland. English was confident that with John and the popular "Star Sisters" on the same stage, all the seats would be filled.

John had not seen either Helen or Lucille since Richmond a year earlier, when he had been merely a stock actor. Now he was the show's headliner. Both sisters were eager to play opposite the virile star.

Bill English knew his audiences. Despite early spring snowstorms, the Deering House Theatre was packed each night to see the flamboyant John Wilkes Booth as Romeo and the "beautiful" and "favorite" seventeen-year-old Helen Western as Juliet. Few would have disagreed with Portland native Nathan Gould that Helen was "one of the handsomest women" ever seen on stage.[25]

John thought so too. Since he was not expected back in Albany for another two weeks, he volunteered to be the lead male actor for Mrs. Mary Ann Farren, the Deering's next star. Evenings were spent with Mrs. Farren; nights with Helen. There was another reason John was not in a hurry to leave Portland. After being with the beautiful Helen Western, John had lost whatever interest he had had in returning to Henrietta.

The two weeks John stayed in Portland coincided with the breakup of the "Star Sisters." No one ever said why they split up. The timing of their breakup was too much of a coincidence not to have involved John. Helen and Lucille had been at each other's throats for a long time, and they did not hide their enmity for one another.

Despite Lucille's being married to James Mead, she was jealous John had chosen Helen over her. It was no contest: "The inspired irregularity of Lucille's face was no match for Helen's perfect and unblemished beauty."[26] There would be other men to fight over, but in the meantime, their career as a sister act was at an end.

The "Unblemished beauty" of Helen Western (left) and the "inspired irregularity" of her sister Lucille Western (right) in later years. *Courtesy of New York Public Library, Billy Rose Collection.*

John was still in Portland on April 12, 1861, when the breaking news about Fort Sumter flashed across the telegraph lines. The aftershock from Charleston's batteries was felt all across the country. A "great eagle scream for war" echoed in every city and hamlet, North and South. In Portland a massive pro-Union demonstration materialized in Market Square outside the Deering House Theatre.

The rally galled John. He was especially irate at the *Portland Advertiser's* enthusiastic support for the demonstration. A week later, he was even more angered hearing about a bloody riot in Baltimore on April 19.

Following the attack on Fort Sumter, Lincoln had called for 75,000 volunteers to quash the insurrection. Every state, including slave states that had not joined the Confederacy, were assigned their specific quotas. Some states, like Tennessee, seceded in response. Border slave states like Maryland were divided in their loyalties. Baltimore, Maryland's largest city, was very Southern in its outlook and had major financial ties with the South, but large numbers of its people were also loyal to the Union.

During the next few days, the city was on edge. Governor Thomas Holliday Hicks tried to muffle the tension by refusing to send any troops out of the state except to defend Washington.

Massachusetts was the first Northern state to send troops to defend Washington. On the morning of April 19, a train carrying the Sixth Massachusetts Regiment pulled into a Baltimore depot on its way to Washington. As the cars passed, a pro-Southern mob surrounded the Northern troops and began shouting insults. As the mob grew, rocks replaced insults, and shots were fired. The beleaguered troops fired back. When order was restored, twenty citizens and four soldiers lay dead on bloodstained Pratt Street.[27]

John was distraught at what he saw as the invasion of his hometown. When he left Portland the next day he was in a foul mood and departed without paying his bills. The *Portland Advertiser* bristled that Mr. Booth lacked "the requisites of a gentleman. He was extremely liberal in his offers and not sparing of promises....to cut the story short, we have not seen the color of the gentleman's money."[28]

When John returned to Albany, the Stars and Stripes were everywhere as a show of support for the Union and a protest against the bombardment of Fort Sumter. As he rode from the train station to the Stanwix Hall Hotel, the foul mood he had been in when he left Portland returned.

John's return engagement at the Gayety with his co-star, Henrietta Irving, opened Monday April 22, 1861. Six days later, Henrietta knifed him.

The attack was reported across the country.[29] The earliest version appeared in the *Cincinnati Daily Enquirer*, Sunday, May 5, 1861: "Miss Henrietta Irving—one of the Irving sisters....entered the room of J. W. Booth....attacked him with a dirk, cutting his face badly. She did not, however, succeed in inflicting a mortal wound. Failing in this she retired to her own room and stabbed herself. Again she failed in her destructive purpose....the cause of this singular proceeding was attributed to jealousy or misunderstanding."[30]

The *Louisville Courier-Journal* added some additional details. It began its story with an eye-catching headline, "All for Love and Murder: Miss Henrietta Irving, well known as an actress in Buffalo, entered the room of J. Wilkes Booth, at Stanwix Hall, Albany, last Friday [incorrectly dating it May 3] and attacked him with a dirk.... she retired to her own room and stabbed herself, not bad enough to 'go dead,' however. The cause was disappointed affection, or some little affair of that sort."[31] Other papers reprinted the *Cincinnati Daily Enquirer*'s report with minor details added for local color.[32]

Modern retellings have added invented spice, such as claiming Henrietta's mind was clouded by "an alcoholic fog" from drinking heavily in John's hotel after that night's performance. When John told her he didn't love her, "despite the fact that their relationship had progressed to carnal knowledge," she lunged at him with a knife.[33]

It was not quite like that. John didn't have a change of heart; he simply had a change of interest. Henrietta was nothing more to John than a plaything, his "temporary mistress." All that week Henrietta had sensed John was two-timing her. When she saw him coming out of her sister Marie's room, she was livid. Seething with jealousy and furious at his betrayal, she ran into her room, grabbed a knife, and burst into his room.

John's face was his fortune. She aimed to disfigure it. John saw the knife coming at his face. He threw up his arm in time to ward off the fatal attack, but still received a gash on his forehead from the upward thrust. Henrietta did not wait to see if he were badly hurt. She ran back to her own room and plunged the knife into her body.[34]

Henrietta did not die from her suicide attempt and she was never charged with attempted murder. Either John did not press charges because he felt remorse at deceiving her, or the police accepted Henrietta's explanation that John had tampered with her affections. For whatever reason, Henrietta was never arrested.

John did nothing to console her. John "took his women as he took his brandy, in long careless draughts, and tossed the empties on a refuse heap."[35] He bandaged his head, packed his costumes in his theatrical trunk, and left for Philadelphia to rest and recuperate at his mother's home. Fortunately for him, the gash was near his hairline and he was able to hide the scar by covering it with his hair.[36]

A few weeks later John was in Baltimore, the "headquarters" for out-of-work actors at the dawn of the war, and ran into Bill Howell, an old friend from his days at the Arch Street Theatre. Howell noticed the scar on John's forehead and asked about it. "It's a wound from a knife inflicted by an infatuated, jealous and angry girl," John said matter-of-factly.[37]

As soon as she was able, Henrietta left for Milwaukee where she had been warmly greeted when she had toured out west. It was far enough away from Albany for her to avoid gossip-hungry newspapers, and a place to recover from her self-inflicted injury and the psychological trauma she suffered.[38] She never spoke of the incident to anyone and there is no mention of John in her autobiography.[39]

# 13

# MY GOOSE
# HANGS HIGH

After chatting with Bill Howell for a while, John asked if he could share Howell's room at his hotel. He was short of funds, he said. He had had to pawn his prized gold-headed cane to get by.[1]

Howell was more than agreeable. Reminiscing about the time he spent with John in Baltimore, Howell waxed nostalgic. He had not liked John when he first met him, he said, but after you came to know him, "you would scale the mountain's peak, breast the ocean's billows or pour out your heart's blood to serve him….You could not resist his captivating manners, his genial smile and his personal magnetism.…his heart and soul beamed out of his eyes…[he] was that sort of man that if you ever came within the range of his personal magnetism and fascination you would involuntarily be bound to him as with hooks of steel."[2]

Howell was one of the fortunate actors who still had a job. Theatres across the country had closed. With men leaving home by the thousands to join the army, and anxiety about the war dampening enthusiasm for entertainment, the theatres were empty. A short time after John left Albany, the Gayety closed and was reconverted into stores. Theatres in the South were faring no better. All over the country, actors and actresses found themselves without a job.

John spent his days writing to managers to arrange play dates for the upcoming season, playing billiards, and drinking with other actors who, like him, were hibernating until times got better. Most of the time he hung out at a hotel that was a favorite with out-of-work actors. The hotel had two bars. Actors who had not been long out of work hung out at the more fashionable bar upstairs where drinks were 15 cents. When their money began to run out, they loitered at the downstairs bar where drinks were 10 cents each.[3]

Evenings John would sit in the audience at the Holliday Street Theatre taking in the plays and waiting for Howell. After returning to their hotel room they talked for hours about their prospects. Howell recalled how John "would crayon out for me his hopes and desires in a way that was irresistibly fascinating."[4]

They also naturally talked about the war. Maryland was militarily and politically tense. Less than a week after the bloody riot in Baltimore that left four soldiers and twelve citizens dead, Union forces occupied Baltimore and imposed martial law, and Lincoln suspended *habeas corpus*, meaning that anyone considered a Southern sympathizer faced imprisonment without trial. There was zero tolerance for dissent. Any pro-Southern statement or show of support meant immediate arrest and detention at Fort McHenry, where Baltimore's mayor, chief of police, the entire city council, and other officials were already incarcerated. Thousands of Marylanders slipped across the Potomac River into Virginia and became part of the Confederate army's "Maryland Line." John and Howell toyed with the idea of stealing off to Harford County, where John had grown up, to raise a company to join up with the "Maryland Line" or some other regiment. After federal troops occupied Baltimore, they decided it was no use.[5]

When John was not writing to managers for engagements, playing billiards, or drinking, he was out looking for female companionship. Walking with Howell during one of their morning strolls, John noticed a strikingly beautiful girl through a millinery store window on nearby Gay Street.

Ask your friend at the *Baltimore Sun* to find out who she is, he said. Howell's contact told him Miss W (he never disclosed her identity) came from one of Baltimore's best families. That piqued John's interest. Respectability, like fame, was important to him.

 Learning she sang in the choir at the Methodist church, John saw an opportunity to meet her. He borrowed money from his long-time friend, Stu Robson, and redeemed the gold-headed cane he had pawned, so that he could impress Miss W. John was not a churchgoer, but he was sitting in a pew alongside Bill Howell on Sunday, waiting for the choir to come out and sing. After the service was over the two men stood in the vestibule trying not to stand out. But it was a neighborhood church. They were noticed.

When Miss W. came down the choir stairs, John thought it was his chance to meet her. "To our chagrin," said Howell, "three or four young fellows who had made themselves obnoxious to us while we were waiting, hastened to gather around Miss W. like a body guard and went off down the street tittering."

The next morning John received an anonymous letter. "Your impertinent attention to and constant following of Miss W. have been observed by a number of her gentlemen friends," the letter read. "In case you persist in trying to force yourself into the lady's presence," said the letter writer, her friends "will give you what you richly deserve."

John handed the letter to Howell and asked his opinion. Howell saw John was nettled and it would be best to make light of it. Those fellows were miserable plug uglies (a notorious Baltimore street gang), he said, not worth John's notice. The comment mollified John. He put Miss W. out of his mind. There would always be other Miss Ws.

John craved fame, but he wanted it on his terms. Unable to afford an agent or business manager, he was managing his own career, setting up engagements and negotiating terms. Less than a year out as a star, he was already receiving offers from theatre managers. E. L. Davenport, manager of Boston's Howard Atheneum, offered him a booking in

November. John turned it down. "He thinks me a novice crazy to play in Boston and that he will get me for nothing. Which to tell the truth is nearly as much as he has offered me," he told Joe Simmonds, a cashier at the Merchants Bank in Boston who he had met that summer and with whom he had become close friends.[6]

As much as an engagement in Boston (the "Athens of America") would have been a big step up from the smaller theatres he had appeared in, John was not going to be taken advantage of by managers who thought they could hire him on the cheap because he was just starting out.

John had a scheme to make Davenport come up with more money: he would manufacture a bidding war. John urged Simmonds to talk to some of the people connected with the Boston Museum (the Atheneum's main rival) and tell them that Davenport "wants me bad" but they were wrangling over payment.[7]

The plan didn't work—either Davenport didn't bite, or Simmonds didn't follow through. Either way, John embarked on his own whirlwind tour that brought him the fame he coveted. "The genius of Booth the senior has descended in no small measure to the son," said the *Providence Daily Post*; "he has extraordinary physiognomical power" (*Buffalo Daily Courier*); "fully sustained all that has previously been said of his superior qualities as an actor" (*Detroit Free Press*); "rarely so spell-bound by the delineations of any actor" (*Cincinnati Daily Commercial*); "the most original actor we have seen in a great many years" (*Louisville Daily Democrat*); "possessed with genius in the highest degree" (*Indianapolis Daily Journal*).[8]

Not all his time was spent on stage. Part of his time in Buffalo he was under arrest at a police station. Walking by a Buffalo store displaying captured Confederate trophies, John impulsively broke the store's plate glass window, was arrested, and fined fifty dollars.[9]

Despite John's "patriotic froth,"[10] and Asia's belief that soldiering was "perhaps his true vocation,"[11] John never enlisted in the Confederate army.

According to Colonel Richard Johnson, with whom John had become friends, John's fear of blood kept him from combat. Johnson said that he had asked John to go with him to a funeral home to pay his respects to Johnson's deceased friend. "I would have gone in with you, but the sight of human blood is terrible to me," John allegedly said, "the sight of blood drives me wild."[12] It was an improbable excuse. John had seen blood many times and it had not driven him "wild." He'd had a nose bleed during a performance of *Romeo and Juliet* and not lost his equanimity. He'd merely turned his back to the audience to keep them from seeing the blood running from his nose. Another time he smeared blood on his own face to enhance his fighting scene in *Richard III*.[13]

John once told Asia his "soul, life, and possessions are for the South."

"Why not go fight for her, then?" she snapped. "Every Marylander worthy of the name is fighting her battles." As soon as it was out of her mouth, Asia regretted saying it.

John was silent for a while. Then he explained he had not enlisted because he believed he could do so much more as an undercover agent. "My brains are worth twenty men, my money worth an hundred." His profession as an actor and his name were his passport, he said. It let him travel wherever he wanted. "My beloved precious money—oh, never beloved till now!—is the means, one of the means, by which I serve the South....Not that the South cared a bad cent about me, a mere peregrinating play-actor," he groused.[14]

It was narcissism in the extreme, pure and simple. No one ever considered John brainy. There is no record of his donating any money to any Southern cause. As for his name allowing him to travel wherever he wanted, after he left the South he never returned. His travel in the North was unhindered.

The other reason he gave for not enlisting was simpler and more straightforward. He'd promised his mother he would "keep out of the quarrel, if possible."[15]

John's mother was a widow with no income beyond rents from the farm and the money John was sending her. Her eldest son June was in

California. Edwin was about to leave for England. Her youngest son, Joe, was floundering. Asia was married with her own family. Beyond her dependence on him, everyone in the family knew John was her favorite, their mother's "darling."[16]

"The love and sympathy between him and his mother were very close, very strong," said actress Ann Hartley Gilbert, "no matter how far apart they were, she seemed to know, in some mysterious way, when anything was wrong with him. If he were ill or unfit to play, he would often receive a letter of sympathy, counsel, and warning, written when she could not possibly have received any news from him. He has told me this, himself."[17] Among John's last words just before he died, as he lay gasping for breath, was "mother."

Mary Ann had a mother's talent for instilling guilt in her favorite son. "I am all alone today," she wrote him, a month before the assassination. "I am going to dinner by myself. Why are you not here to chat and keep me company? No, you are looking and saying soft things to one that don't love you half as well as your old mother does...It's natural it should be so, I know...I cannot expect to have you always." A week later, Mary Ann wrote that she was lonely and feared for his safety when he mentioned he was thinking about enlisting. "I never yet doubted your love and devotion to me—in fact I always gave you praise for being the fondest of all my boys, but since you leave me to grief I must doubt it. I am no Roman mother. I love my dear ones, before country or anything else."[18]

Regardless of all his other faults, John was devoted to his mother. He kept the promise she had forced on him, but he brooded over it throughout the war.[19] It was during one of those brooding moments that he broke the glass window in Buffalo displaying captured Confederate trophies.[20]

The New Year of 1862 began with two weeks at Ben DeBar's theatre in St. Louis, a block away from the Planters' House hotel where he stayed during his engagement. John felt at ease with DeBar.[21] Like him, DeBar did not hide his Southern sympathies. On more than one occasion the provost marshal cautioned DeBar about catering to "rebel tastes" at his theatre.[22]

Like Maryland, Missouri was divided in its loyalties. On May 10, 1861, Maggie Mitchell had been onstage at DeBar's in *Fanchon* when gunfire from a minor skirmish nearby panicked the actors and audience. The next day Maggie packed her bags and left Missouri for the relative safety of New York and other eastern cities.

Federal troops ended the brief show of resistance in St. Louis and restored order, but audiences were slow in coming back. In August, the city was placed under martial law. "All dance houses, theatres, concerts, negro minstrels, or any other places of public resort, of like character," were ordered closed at 10:30 p.m. Any disturbance of the peace would not be tolerated.[23]

Unable to keep his pro-Southern feelings to himself, John was arrested in St. Louis for disorderly conduct when he was overheard saying he wished "the whole damned government would go to hell." To gain his release he had to swear allegiance to the Union and pay a $500 fine.[24]

McVicker's Theater in Chicago was the next stop on John's tour. All the pent-up feelings about not fighting in the war came out on stage during his swordfights. John's role as Pescara in *The Apostate* so riveted audiences, three of St. Louis's newspapers requested repeat performances.[25] The *Evening Journal* summed up John's tour in Chicago with a rave review. "Mr. Booth has but few equals upon the tragic stage, which is saying much of a young man not twenty-two years of age," but ended its encomium on a sober note. "He may be the head and front of the American stage, or he may add another to the list of victims of a fatal appetite, upon whose breakers so many bright lights of his profession have perished."[26]

Basking in the praise he had received in Chicago and throughout his western tour, John returned to his native Baltimore more confident in

himself than ever. For his opening at the Holliday Street Theatre he had
the playbills print his appearance with the heading:

> I have no Brother, am like no Brother
> I am—myself alone.[27]

It was a clear declaration that he was his own man, not a facsimile
of his brother Edwin or his father. Baltimore's theatre critics were as
effusive in their praise as those in the West.[28]

What the papers did not report is John's almost killing actor Jim
Herne in a fight over a woman.

Twenty-three-year-old James A. Herne (he changed his name from
James Ahearn) was as handsome, rugged, spirited, and just as much a
carouser and skirt-chaser as John.[29] Herne's big break as an actor came
in 1861 just after America went to war with itself. John T. Ford, manager
of the Holliday Street Theatre in Baltimore and the Atheneum in Washington, was having trouble keeping stock actors going into the army or
leaving for other theatres, and offered Herne a job.

For the next three years Herne shuttled back and forth between
Ford's Holliday and Atheneum theatres, eventually becoming the
company's leading male. He was still one of the Holliday Street Theatre's stock actors when he met John, the Holliday's star. The two men
liked each other and became friends—until they got into an argument
over a woman. In a violent burst of temper, John almost killed Herne.[30]
The argument likely occurred on the night of February 20, 1862. Up
until then Herne was listed in the cast with John. After February 20,
his name was no longer included in the advertisements for John's
appearances.[31]

On March 3, Maggie Mitchell opened in Baltimore at the Front Street
Theatre.[32] John appeared there a week later for a benefit on behalf of

George Kunkel, his former manager at the Richmond Theatre. There is no mention of how much time they spent together.

John finally got the booking he had longed for at the Boston Museum. Although he was confident in himself, "he felt timid" about appearing before "coldly critical" Boston audiences.[33]

Despite his determination to be judged on his own merits, the audience's first thought was how he matched up to Edwin.[34] The *Boston Post* wrote:

> Shut your eyes, and listen, you will think Edwin is before you; many of the tones are so like his; but now open your eyes, and you will see a *better* Edwin standing before you.
>
> His face has the real Booth Cut, the gleaming eye, the thin lips curling downward, the marked angle of the jaw, the delicate aquiline of the nose. The head seems not quite so large as his brother's but more statuesque, more Byronic; and the forehead, when he takes the stage hat off, seems always, even in repose, as full and square, and beautiful as the brow of Brutus.
>
> He is taller, and more closely knit in muscle and frame than his brother, with shoulders square and the broad chest more like his father's. His whole movement speaks of energy and animation, rather than grace and melody...the intensity the Old Booth had to the extent of frenzy ... he has given to his son, John Wilkes, in a far greater measure than to Edwin...We have never seen such [stage] fighting, behind the foot-lights, since old Booth died.[35]

Kate Reignolds, John's leading lady at the Boston Museum, vividly remembered how John completely immersed himself in his characters.

And how frightened she was when he did. "How he threw me about! Once [he] even knocked me down, picking me up again with a regret as quick as his dramatic impulse had been vehement." On one of the nights when they were in the last act of *Romeo and Juliet*, the buttons on John's cuff caught in Reignolds's hair. Trying to tear them out, John shook her, stepped on her dress and tore it apart. When the curtain came down at the end of the play, Romeo had a sprained thumb, Juliet's hair was on his sleeve and she was in rags, her two white satin shoes lying in the corner of the stage![36]

Women in the audience were sexually aroused at the way John rough-handled Reignolds. "The stage door was always blocked with silly women waiting to catch a glimpse, as he passed," Reignolds grumbled. "It is my earnest belief that if ever there was an irresponsible person, it was this sad-faced, handsome boy."[37] At matinee performances (when respectable women could attend unaccompanied by men),[38] they would surround the exit door. So eager were they to see him and to touch him that stage manager Edwin F. Keach had to come out and restrain them.[39]

By the end of the season in June, John had performed 162 times in eleven cities. Reviews had almost always been positive. Theatres had been filled to capacity. His popularity was at its height. His income had soared "to figures only dreamed of by others in the profession."[40] Women jammed the exit to the stage door after each performance. His *cartes de visite* sold by the hundreds.

"Dear Miss," John wrote to a fan pleading for one of his *cartes de visite*, "I have come to the conclusion that a noncompliance with your request would be a crime, especially if my not refusing will afford you the pleasure you mention."[41]

The *carte de visite* was an inexpensive pocket size (two-and-a-half by four inches) portrait or full-length image of an individual or group of people, who had their pictures taken in a studio. During the Civil War, they were a way for soldiers and their families to keep the images of their loved ones fresh in their minds. They were also a major commercial enterprise for photographers who advertised them in newspapers and for theatre managers who sold images of favorite actors and actresses by the thousands to fans.[42] An actor or actress whose *carte de visite* was being offered for sale was a sure sign of their stardom.

Richard Marshall Johnson, a St. Louis criminal lawyer and a drinking buddy of John's, wrote him about a sad experience with a girl to whom he had given John's *carte de visite* as a gift. The girl thanked him and said she wanted one with his autograph. Johnson promised that the next time John visited the city he would bring John to her house and he would personally give her an autographed *carte*. "Today she sleeps in Bellefontaine Cemetery having died shortly after I gave her the picture," he wrote John. "When I visit her family and see her album," Johnson continued, "I see the name of J. Wilkes Booth written at the bottom of your photograph and think of the unfulfilled promise that she should know you.... She was a woman of rare and beautiful excellence."[43]

Along with the fan mail there were offers from theatre managers from all over the country. He could pick and choose his appearances, the plays, and the salary and benefits he expected.[44] In August he wrote the manager of the Metropolitan Theatre in Indianapolis that his time until after March was filled except for two separate weeks. If he wanted him, it would be for half the take after the manager's eighty dollars, and half of everything at benefits.[45]

At the start of the next season John was making over $650 a week, and sometimes as much as $900 a week. "My goose does indeed hang high (long may she wave)," he beamed.[46]

# 14

# TRUE GRIT

A t the start of 1863 John was at the top of his game. Even Edwin had to admit his brother was a star. In late January, Edwin and Mary were living outside of Boston in Dorchester, near enough to be in the audience at the Boston Museum to see John in *The Apostate*. It was the first time Edwin had seen John act since the Marshall Theatre. "He played Pescara—a bloody villain of the deepest red...my brother presented him—not undone, but rare enough for the most fastidious 'beef eater'...he is full of true grit," said Edwin, "I am delighted with him."[1]

Mary Devlin had a more distanced take on John's performance. The audience liked him, but he "lacked character," she opined, "he can't transform himself." His combat scenes were "strictly gladiatorial." The audience was more delighted with the muscles in his arms than his acting.[2]

A month later, Mary Devlin was dead.

She had come down with a cold in early February when she had gone to see John at the Boston Museum. The cold turned into pneumonia, fatally complicated by the venereal infection she had contracted from

Edwin, a consequence of his libertine days.[3] Edwin arrived from New York too late to be at Mary's bedside when she passed.

When he received a telegram from Edwin about Mary, John cancelled his scheduled opening at the Arch Street Theatre in Philadelphia to attend her funeral.

A week later John opened at the Arch Street Theatre on March 2, 1863. He was anxious to prove he was no longer the stripling who forgot his character's name at the same theatre four years earlier.[4] He was also happy to be in Philadelphia where he could visit Asia at her house on Race Street and play with her two toddlers, Dolly and Eddie. John "lays on the floor and rolls over with them like a child," Asia wrote Jean Anderson. He "laughs outrageously at me for having babies—to think that our Asia should be a mother."[5]

Asia was pregnant with her third child when John was visiting. Her two babies were the dearest little playthings imaginable, she wrote Jean, but confided she was "sorry to be in such a strait again. Don't be in a hurry to turn a lover into a husband," she moped.[6] John hoped Asia would name her new baby, if a boy, after him. Adrienne Clarke, a girl, was born May 23, 1863.

John was beginning to think of new ways to make money. Deciding one such way was to invest in real estate, he sent Joe Simmonds, his friend at the Merchants Bank in Boston, a draft for $1,500. The money was for a down payment in bidding for shares of the Boston Power Water Company, a company selling development property on Commonwealth Avenue. Simmonds was able to get the property for him for a little more than $8,000.[7]

John's next booking was at the Holliday Street Theatre in Baltimore with Alice Gray as his leading lady. John would see Alice again and would carry her photo in his pocket when he died. Initially, however, there wasn't any romance between them. After Baltimore John headed to Grover's Theatre in Washington. The advertisement for his opening on April 11, 1863, hailed him as "the pride of the American people—the youngest tragedian in the world—a star of the first magnitude—son of the great Junius Brutus Booth—brother and artistic rival of Edwin Booth."[8] The accolades of the previous months continued. The *Washington National Intelligencer* called his performance in *Richard III* "inspired: He played not from the stage, but from the soul and his soul is inspired with genius."[9]

British actor Charles Wyndham, one of John's supporting cast, also saw the genius in him. Like many others, he was especially struck by John's looks.

> Picture to yourself Adonis, with high forehead, ascetic face corrected by rather full lips, sweeping black hair, a figure of perfect youthful proportions and the most wonderful black eyes in the world. Such was John Wilkes Booth....He was the idol of women. They would rave of him, his voice, his hair, his eyes. Small wonder, for he was fascinating.[10]

None of the newspapers mentioned it, but a growth in John's neck had grown so large it was not only painful but also beginning to show above the collar line of his theatrical costumes. John's manager, Matthew Canning, said the growth "made a bad impression." Canning made an appointment for John with Dr. Frederick May, a prominent Washington surgeon.[11]

Booth wanted it removed, said Dr. May, but was concerned the operation would prevent him from fulfilling his engagement. May reassured John if he "would be careful not to make any violent efforts," it would not be a problem.

"Then do it," John said.

"Young man, this is no trifling matter," Dr. May replied. "You will have to come back when I have an assistant here."

"Cut it out right now," John demanded, "Canning…will be your assistant." John was in no mood for argument. He sat down on a chair, leaned his head back, and exposed his neck.

"Now cut away," he said.

Canning came close to fainting at the first cut. "Black blood gushed out," said Canning. It seemed as if Dr. May took John's neck partly off. "Booth did not move," said Canning, "but his skin turned as white as the wall."

Just as Dr. May was complimenting Canning about his being a remarkable assistant for holding up at the sight of so much blood, Canning's stomach "gave way." His legs buckled, and he crumpled onto to the floor. Fainting from blood loss, John tumbled out of his chair and onto the floor beside him. After Canning regained consciousness, Dr. May chided him that he wasn't as much of an assistant as he had thought.[12]

Days later, after both men had recovered, John joked that the bullet that had lain in his body from the time Canning shot him in Columbus years before had "worked [itself] up from somewhere in the muscles [of his thigh] to his throat."[13]

John was very sensitive about the tumor. He did not want anyone to know the scar on his neck was due to an ailment. He asked Dr. May to say he had removed a bullet instead of a tumor if anyone asked.

The next day, when John wrote to his friend Joe, he kept up the deception. "Am far from well," he said. "Have a hole in my neck you could run your fist in. The doctor had a hunt for my bullet."[14] He told David Herold, one of the conspirators he later enlisted in his plot to kill Lincoln, the same lie when they first met.[15]

John was back in Dr. May's office a few weeks later to have the wound re-stitched. He had ignored Dr. May's admonition to avoid physical contact. His leading lady had embraced him with such force, he told Dr. May, that she had popped the wound open again.[16]

When he recalled John's visit years later, Dr. May identified the actress who had embraced him so hard as Charlotte Cushman, but it wasn't Charlotte Cushman. She was not in Washington at the time.

The actress who squeezed him so hard was either Effie Germon or Alice Gray. After his engagement at the Grover's Theatre was over, John had leased the Washington Theatre for two weeks starting April 27, 1863, and had hired both Effie and Alice as his leading ladies for the makeshift company he managed to cobble together. (The Washington Theatre didn't have a permanent manager or stock company. Instead it was leased by various managers for short-term engagements.) Effie had been his leading lady at Grover's Theatre; Alice had been his leading lady at the Holliday Street Theatre just prior to coming to Washington. John had both their photos in his pocket when he died.

# 15

# EFFIE AND ALICE

"**D**ashing, laughing, laughter-making," Effie Germon was eighteen, "in the bloom of youth and beauty." "Her face was fresh and girlish, with hair combed down over her temples and ears." Theatre critics called her "Pretty Effie Germon."[1]

Born in Augusta, Georgia, in 1845, Euphemia "Effie" Germon was related to the Jeffersons, one of the oldest theatrical families in America.[2] Like her mother, Jane Anderson Germon,[3] Effie began her acting career when she was very young. In July 1857, at twelve, she made her debut at the Holliday Street Theater in a little-known play, *Sketches of India*, as Sally Scraggs.[4] The following season she landed a job with Laura Keene's company in New York as Augusta in the first American performance of *Our American Cousin*. Keene felt the diminutive actress (she weighed only 90 pounds at the time)[5] was too young for the part and didn't keep her on. Weeks later Effie was hired on as a stock actress with Edwin Booth and John Sleeper Clarke at the Walnut Street Theatre in Philadelphia.

At fourteen Effie was still too young to play Augusta convincingly, but she wasn't too young to fall in love with handsome, seventeen-year-old, virtuoso violinist, Carlo Patti.

It was a truly whirlwind romance. Three months after Carlo came to Philadelphia, Effie and Carlo ran off to Providence, Rhode Island, to get married. The famous violinist was too young to marry, the *Providence Evening Press* complained. "The young rogue can't be more than twenty."[6] No one seemed to care that Effie was even younger. Like so many teenage marriages, it was doomed from the start. Carlo had the proverbial roving eye. The couple soon separated and later divorced.

By 1862, seventeen-year-old Effie Germon had made a stage career for herself as a "soubrette," a mischievous, flirtatious coquette. It was a role that came naturally to her "genuine sense of humor" and "sparkl(ing) wit,"[7] and one that that kept "the 'Johnnies' busy"[8] in Montreal when she played there. The "Johnnies" were the not-so-secret agents of the

Effie Germon at age twenty-six, six years after her affair with John Wilkes Booth. *Courtesy of Library of Congress.*

Confederate government who had set up headquarters in the Canadian city.[9] When that engagement ended, Effie left for Grover's Theatre in Washington to co-star with the "eminent young American tragedian, J. Wilkes Booth."[10] After their appearances at Grover's Theatre ended, John asked Effie to be his leading lady for a new venture he was undertaking at the Washington Theatre. She agreed.

Effie was not the only leading lady John invited to join his troupe. He also hired Alice Gray.[11] Since a company only needed one leading lady, John had something more in mind than just filling acting slots when he hired them both.

None of John's contemporaries ever mentioned any romantic relationship between John and Alice or Effie. There are no known letters they exchanged. There is nothing to indicate they were romantically involved at all. Nothing at all—except that Alice's and Effie's photos were in his pocket when he died.

There is another reason Alice Gray is in the history books. She was the last actress to appear with John at his final performance on March 18, 1865, at Ford's Theatre, a month before John shot Lincoln. The play was *The Apostate*. John played one of his signature roles, Duke Pescara. Alice was Florinda, the love interest.[12]

Alice Dehan, who later took the stage name Alice Gray, was born in 1835 in upstate New York, outside Buffalo, to Irish immigrants Patrick and Ann Dehan.[13] A short time after Alice's father died in late 1849, Alice and her mother and brother moved to Boston.[14]

Like many young women whose mothers were left with no support, Alice had to go to work to help out. Luckily, she found a job in the theatre. In June 1849, at age fourteen, she had her first acting role under the name Alice Gray in *Old Job and Jacob Gray* at the Boston Museum.[15] She would appear in that same play in various age-appropriate roles for the next seven years.[16]

Alice had not just picked her stage name out of a hat. "Alice Gray" was the name of the girl every man longed for and could not have in a popular ballad of that time. The song's refrain, "My heart, my heart is breaking / For the love of Alice Grey," invariably appeared alongside Alice's name whenever she was mentioned in the newspapers.[17]

After leaving Boston, Alice took a job as the lead stock actress at the Metropolitan Theatre in Buffalo.[18] The next season she was at the Bowery Theatre in New York. Despite her favorable reviews, the country was still in recession, and the Bowery closed. In May, Alice was back in Buffalo at the Metropolitan Theatre. It was not an auspicious reappearance.

Alice was unaware manager Tom Carr's wife was jealous her husband was paying too much attention to the young actress. She began plotting sabotage. When Alice opened as Lady Teazle in *School for Scandal*, she was barraged with loud and persistent hissing from the audience. Alice didn't know what was wrong. She stood on stage and appealed to the hissing public to let the play go on, but the hissing continued. There was nothing else to do except bring down the curtain.[19]

The *New York Clipper*'s correspondent thought it was genuine dissatisfaction with the young actress.[20] Two weeks later the *New York Clipper* apologized. Alice had not been hissed because of "any want of merit." "'We say nothing' about rumors of jealousy," the newspaper added, implying more than if it had.[21]

Alice knew there was no point in her staying. Carr agreed to release her from her contract. By coincidence John's sister-in-law, Clementina DeBar Booth, was her replacement.[22]

Two weeks later, Alice landed a job for a few weeks as a stock actress with Edward Eddy (Henrietta's future husband) at the Broadway Theatre then went on to play at the Washington Theatre. Although she had only been on Broadway for a few weeks, the advertisement for the Washington's opening night boasted Alice had just come "from the Broadway Theatre, N.Y.," enhancing her and the theatre's status.[23]

Reviews were mixed. As the leading lady to superstar Barry Sullivan in *The Gamester*, she was praised for the "truly womanly conception" of her part and a "natural pathos rarely equaled."[24] In *King Lear*, she was "nothing great."[25]

The next season Alice was in Charleston, South Carolina, as leading lady with C. F. Marchant's stock company. "She possesses all the requisites for a fine actress; youth, beauty, and talent," the *New York Clipper* told its readers. Unable to keep from punning on the popular ballad, the newspaper added, "many a Southern 'heart is breaking for the love of Alice Grey'" every time it mentioned her name.[26]

While she was breaking hearts, Alice came down with yellow fever, a disease that plagued the South.[27] After a two-month convalescence she felt well enough to go back to work. A local critic praised her "fine histrionic talent, delicate womanly perception, correct and clear enunciation, lady-like carriage, graceful person, winning countenance, and speaking eye."[28]

Alice Gray. *Courtesy of U.S. National Park Service.*

In summer 1860, John Ford hired Alice as the leading female stock actress for his Holliday Street Theatre company. It was Ford's intention, the *Baltimore Daily Exchange* told its readers, to open the new Holliday Street Theatre season with the young and beautiful Miss Alice Gray as leading woman, reputed to be "possessed of more than ordinary professional talent."[29] Alice did not disappoint. The *Baltimore Sun* praised Alice for her "quite unexpected grace [and] talent" for which she was applauded by the audience. "She is a brilliant accession [to the Theatre]."[30]

Alice was the leading lady at the Holliday Street Theatre again when John opened in March 1863 in *Richard III* with John as Richard and Alice as Queen Elizabeth.[31]

John was impressed (and perhaps libidinous) enough to hire her along with Effie Germon a month later as one of his leading ladies for his brief venture as manager of the Washington Theatre.

The critic for the *Washington National Intelligencer* did not say anything about Effie's performance. What "particularly impressed" him was Alice's "beauty and spirit"[32] and John's "strong passionate" role in *The Robbers*, a performance that "would not soon be forgotten by anyone" in the audience.[33]

Among those who would not forget was twenty-two-year-old Lucy Hale, the daughter of New Hampshire Senator John Parker Hale. She was impressed enough that she sent him a bouquet of flowers.[34] Lucy would see a lot more of John; it was a passing appreciation for now. John said goodbye to Alice and Effie and left for his next engagement in Chicago.

# 16

# Imagine My Helping That Wounded Soldier

**W**hile guns were blasting away at Gettysburg, Pennsylvania, on July 1, 1863, John Wilkes Booth was on stage as Hamlet at the Academy of Music in Cleveland, asking himself, "To be or not to be?"

Gettysburg was not the Confederacy's only catastrophic setback that week. In the west, Vicksburg, the Confederacy's last major stronghold on the Mississippi River, surrendered on July 4 to General Ulysses S. Grant's Army of Tennessee.

The combined defeats at Gettysburg and Vicksburg were major turning points in the war. The Confederacy would not consider invading the North again. Gettysburg was a major morale builder for the North and General Lee was no longer regarded as invincible. Vicksburg's capture strategically severed the Confederacy in two. Texas, Arkansas, and western Louisiana were cut off from reinforcements and manufacturing materiel from the east. The east was cut off from beef from Texas and salt from western Louisiana.

There were also diplomatic repercussions. Southern hopes that European powers would officially recognize the Confederacy's independence were shattered. Prospects for a Europe-negotiated peace settlement were dashed. The war would drag on for two more years, but the spirit went out of the Confederacy with those two defeats.

These setbacks and Lincoln's Emancipation Proclamation undoubtedly troubled John. The Proclamation declared that slaves in the states still in rebellion against the Union were free as of January 1, 1863. Although the Proclamation had no means of enforcement as long as those states were still in rebellion, abolitionists and black people, slave and free, celebrated what Lincoln would later call in his Gettysburg Address "a new birth of freedom." The Confederate setbacks at Gettysburg and Vicksburg had brought that birth of freedom closer to reality.

John arrived in New York to spend the summer of 1863 with Edwin and the rest of his family, except for Asia who was still in Philadelphia. It was not a happy reunion.

Edwin was still grieving over Mary. Less than two weeks after burying her, Edwin wrote his friend Adam Badeau, "My heart is crushed, dried up, and desolate.... All is dark; I know not where to turn."[1] Now a single parent to one-year-old Edwina, Edwin needed someone to look after his daughter while he was away at work. His first thought was his mother and Rosalie. For them to take care of Edwina, he would need a home. In May 1863 he closed his house in Dorchester, Massachusetts, and leased a house on East Seventeenth Street for six months until he could find one to buy. He found one in June on East Nineteenth Street in New York and made plans to move there in the fall. Until then, Edwin, Edwina, his mother and sister Rosalie, and his younger brother Joe, June—recently returned from California—and John were all living in the house on East Seventeenth Street.[2]

Having his family with him eased the burden of looking after Edwina, but not his despair. Edwin called on a well-known spiritualist of the time, Laura Edmonds, to summon Mary's spirit from the dead. Burdened with grief, he convinced himself that Mary was communicating with him.[3] Edwin even initiated séances of his own at his house with his friend Adam Badeau and John and the rest of the family.[4]

While John was staying at Edwin's house, the city was rocked by what would be called the New York City Draft Riot.

The riot was a spontaneous reaction to the Conscription Act Congress passed on March 3, 1863, and signed by Lincoln to enlist another 300,000 men to make up for the thousands of dead and wounded. Reports of the carnage at Gettysburg were appalling. General George G. Meade's Army of the Potomac River had turned back the invasion, but 23,000 men had been killed, wounded, or were missing (Confederate losses came to an even higher 28,000).

New York was a deeply conflicted city. It was pro-Union, but its manufacturing industry was heavily dependent on Southern cotton. The city belonged as much to the North as to the South. Although the state voted for Lincoln in 1860, it elected a Democrat as governor, and New York City voted Democrat in favor of Stephen Douglas. Fernando Wood, the city's Democratic mayor at the start of the war, had advocated the city's proclaiming itself an independent port so that the Union would not interfere with its trading with the Confederacy.

Conscription infuriated large numbers of poverty-stricken Irish immigrants who were Democrat and pro-slavery. Already heavily prejudiced, they were also hostile toward free blacks who were competing with them for low paying jobs. The Emancipation Proclamation had fueled concerns about even greater competition from the anticipated hordes of former slaves who would be streaming north. As long as the South was retaining its sovereignty, the Emancipation Proclamation was an empty gesture. For the Irish and other immigrants, being ordered to leave their homes and families to fight to liberate those former slaves whose freedom would drive down wages or take their jobs was grating.

Especially galling was a provision in the Conscription Act that any-one who could afford to hire a substitute or pay the government $300 could avoid enlistment. It was a sizable sum in those days, one far beyond the means of families living in slums.

The first draft lottery was held on Saturday, July 11, 1863. On Mon-day, protesters stormed the offices where the draft was held and destroyed everything inside. From there, the protest turned into a full-fledged riot. As the fury took hold, the rioters went after black people and black busi-nesses. Several black men were lynched amid cheers for Jefferson Davis. Others were beaten and killed. Black children in an orphan asylum on Fifth Avenue were barely evacuated before their building was torched. Rioters were rumored to be searching house to house, burning the homes of white people who sheltered blacks. Despite the cancellation of the draft lottery on July 14, the riot continued for two more days.

Whatever generalized feelings John had about the war and whatever prejudices he had toward black people, those feelings did not extend to individuals. It was that kind of contradiction that accounts for John's risking his life to rescue Adam Badeau—an officer on General Ulysses Grant's staff—and Badeau's black servant from the mob.

Badeau, a close friend of Edwin's, had been injured in the Union assault on Confederate-held Port Hudson in Louisiana. With his leg immobilized, Badeau was recuperating at the home of a relative in the heart of the riot-torn city. Although Edwin had invited him to stay at his house, Badeau had not wanted to impose himself on his grieving friend and had gone instead to stay with relatives.

Although Badeau was not in uniform, if the house he was living in were broken into, the rioters would not have taken long to realize he was a Union officer, and he and his black servant would have been beaten and killed. Despite the personal risk, John ventured into the maw of the riot and brought Badeau and his black servant back to Edwin's house.

When the carriage pulled up in front of the house on Seventeenth Street, Edwin came out and he and John lifted Badeau out and carried him up the stairs to Edwin's room. Badeau's black servant was hidden in the cellar to avoid his being seen. Edwin and John took turns bringing him food and water and cleaning and bandaging Badeau's wound. When Badeau wrote about the incident years later, he was amazed John had taken care of "a soldier wounded for the cause he should have hated."[5] Except for John's feelings about Lincoln, hating the cause did not necessarily mean hating those who supported it. John was not oblivious to the irony. "Imagine my helping that wounded soldier," he chuckled when he told Asia about it.[6]

John spent the rest of the summer at Edwin's playing with Edwina, talking with his mother and brothers, and writing to theatre owners and managers to set up engagements for the next season. Nights were spent at the city's "public and private house[s] of prostitution." He was particularly fond of Sally Andrews, the landlady of a house at 67 West Twenty-Fifth Street—fond enough for rumors about their being lovers to exist.[7]

In September, he opened his new season with a fortnight appearance at the Howard Athenaeum with veteran co-star Mrs. Julia Bennet Barrow. After his Boston engagement he embarked on a two-week whirlwind tour of New England with Mrs. Barrow and "the most beautiful woman on the American stage."

# 17

# THE MOST BEAUTIFUL WOMAN ON THE AMERICAN STAGE

**D**uring World War II every GI drooled over Betty Grable. During the Civil War, Billy Yank drooled over Fanny Brown.

Slightly less than middle height for that era, Fanny had coal black eyes, dark curly hair, a fair and delicate complexion, a soft smile, a pleasing voice, and a "rounded and glorious form."[1] T. Allston Brown, editor of the *New York Clipper*, the newspaper of the stars and wannabees, personally knew or knew about every actor and actress in the business. In Allston Brown's opinion, no actress came close to Fanny's matchless beauty.[2] Captain Noble D. Preston, Tenth New York Cavalry, was among the hundreds if not thousands of civilians and soldiers who fell asleep every night with Fanny's picture tucked away in a pocket.[3]

The average age of the Civil War soldier was twenty-six.[4] Many were between eighteen and twenty-one. They were mostly farm boys and men who had rarely been more than a hundred miles from home. Long-time friends from the same town often joined the same regiment. None of them were prepared for the rigidity, routine, and tedium of camp life. Most of the time they were drilling, marching, gathering wood, or

127

standing picket duty and coping with the boredom of it all. To while away the time waiting for orders, they played dominoes, cards, dice, checkers, and chess. They read books and, even better, letters from home from mothers and fathers and the wives and girls they left behind.

Fanny Brown. "The Most Beautiful Woman On The American Stage." *Courtesy of New York Public Library, Billy Rose Division.*

For fifteen or twenty-five cents, men and teenage boys who had no one to dream about at home sent away for *cartes de visite* of "the mysteries and delights of naked female beauty"[5] or less racy photos of the actresses they had seen on stage or in newspapers, to fantasize over them.[6] Four of the five photos in John's pocket when he died were actresses. Three of those four were rather ordinary headshots. The other was a full-length photograph of (fully-clothed) Fanny Brown, "the most beautiful and bewitching [woman] that ever graced the American stage."[7]

Fanny was born in Cincinnati in 1837 to itinerant circus performers. She made her stage debut in 1843 at the age of six as an extra in *Cinderella* at the Boston Museum on Tremont Street.[8] Her salary was two dollars a week, paid to her mother. At sixteen, "pretty Fanny Brown" was cast as "little Eva" in *Uncle Tom's Cabin*.[9] A year later she was the "circus-rider's child" in a dramatic version of Charles Dickens's *Hard Times*. For the real-life daughter of a circus-rider mother, it was art imitating life. It wasn't a very prominent part, the *Boston Herald*'s critic said, but Fanny had made it "conspicuous by her fine rendition,"[10] undoubtedly coached by her mother.

Just before her final year at the Boston Museum, fans turned out for a benefit for the eighteen-year-old girl who had "grown up in the Museum."[11] At her curtain call she was showered with bouquets of flowers. One of those bouquets had a diamond ring with ten jewels attached. It was, the *Boston Herald* said, "a deserving tribute to the merits and industry of this favorite young actress."[12]

The next season, Fanny was the star attraction at the recently remodeled Burton's New Theatre on Broadway. The "unsightly boxes in the second tier" had been removed, new chandeliers dangled from the ceiling, the walls were painted, and a new green cloth curtain replaced the old drapery. A new company had also been formed with "celebrated artistes," among them "Miss Fanny Brown, from the Boston Museum."[13] Not long after settling in at Burton's New Theatre, Fanny met Fred Buckley, one of the famed, minstrel Buckley's Serenaders performing down the street from Burton's New Theatre at the New Hall Theatre.[14]

Fred Buckley (1833–1864) was also a child star. At eight, he was a violin virtuoso nicknamed "Little Ole Bull" and "Master Ole Bull"[15] after a famed Norwegian violinist. Like John Wilkes Booth, Fred Buckley was "undisputably [sic] handsome," received love letters daily, and had many affairs.[16]

Four months after they met, nineteen-year-old Fanny and Fred were married in January 1857.[17] Fanny spent the next four years living with her mother in Boston and taking care of her newborn son while Fred was away on tour.[18] Three years into the marriage, they divorced.[19]

With Fred no longer sending her money and her own meager funds running out, Fanny left her toddler in her mother's care and went back to work. Boston's one-time favorite child actress is "no longer 'Little Fanny,'" commented a Boston theatre critic.[20] When she appeared at the Varieties Theatre in New Orleans the following season, theatre critics saw the beauty, not the talent. She has a "sweet and pleasant face" and "did her best...perhaps that's enough," they reckoned.[21]

In October 1861, Fanny was at the Winter Garden in New York, starring in John Sleeper Clarke's production of *The Octoroon*.[22] Nights were spent mingling with New York's "Bohemian" writers, artists, musicians, and entertainers at Ada Clare's house on West Forty-Second Street. The men at Ada's were "clever and distinguished," and the women were "beautiful and brilliant," but none of the women were "as beautiful as Fanny Brown."[23] Fanny is "one of the most fascinating actresses it has ever been our lot to see,"[24] opined the *National Republican*.

In January 1863, Fanny was slated to appear at the Drury Theatre in Pittsburgh in the title role of *Pocahontas*. The theatre critic was ecstatic over her upcoming appearance. Pittsburgh, he wrote, had a "new aspirant for fame in the histrionic world," a "dashing beauty...in the person of Miss Fanny Brown."[25]

When Fanny did not show on time, Bill Henderson, the Drury Theatre's manager, sent her a telegram asking where she was. Fanny's manager answered that Fanny's mother had died.[26] It was true, but it was not the reason Fanny didn't show. When Fanny told John Sleeper Clarke she would be leaving, he had offered her an extended stay at the Winter Garden. Fanny was having too good a time hobnobbing with New York's elite to leave for the "Burgh."[27] She also needed to go back to Boston to make arrangements for someone to take care of her son now that her mother had died. It was while Fanny was in Boston that she met John Wilkes Booth.

John had just finished an engagement at the Howard Atheneum in September 1863 with veteran actress Mrs. Julia Bennett Barrow. In between engagements, they had put together a "Booth-Barrow Combination," a small core company to tour New England's lesser theatres until their next scheduled booking at the Academy of Music in Brooklyn.

Next to fame, John's "chief passion was [still] for women,"[28] and Fanny Brown was beautiful. John invited her to be part of his company. Fanny was just as passionate about handsome men. She accepted.

The "Combination" scheduled performances in six towns with two or three nights at each. Critics in each town expected the dramatic entertainment coming their way would be "the finest and best ever produced here."[29] While John came in for most of the press coverage, Fanny wasn't totally ignored. The company, the *Springfield Republican* reported, included "the beautiful Fanny Brown, from the Winter Garden, New York."[30]

Three days later John and Fanny were in Providence at the Academy of Music. John opened with *Richard III*. This time Fanny had more press coverage. "The Pretty Miss Brown, as Lady Anne," said the *Providence Daily Journal*'s critic, "drew largely upon the interest of the audience."[31] It was their love scenes and John's performance in *The Lady of Lyons*, however, that got the most attention. Booth, the *Providence Daily Journal* added, "need fear no rivals in artificial love making."[32]

The *Hartford Courant* reported the same sanitized review of John and Fanny's love scenes when they appeared in the same play in that city. "There is so much art in love-making that the skill of an actor must be remarkable to portray faithfully all the warmth, passion and 'dignity' which is mandatory to give enchantment to the mimicry."[33] What the *Providence Daily Journal* and *Hartford Courant* did not know was that for John, it was not so much stage skill as offstage practice.

Although John and Fanny were booked into separate rooms during their tour for appearance's sake, their rooms were next to one another with adjoining doors.[34] In November 1863, there were rumors that "J. Wilkes Booth will shortly lead to the hymeneal altar the beautiful and fascinating Fanny Brown."

Enigmatically, the short notice in the *New York Clipper* about the rumored wedding ended with "Where's Dolly?"[35] While rumors were floating around about John getting married, he was also seeing a woman known only as Dolly.[36]

By the time the *New York Clipper* got around to the story, the whirlwind affair was over. In early November Fanny was in Philadelphia at the New Chestnut Street Theatre,[37] and John was in Washington, D.C., at Ford's Theatre for the start of a two-week engagement.[38] When John died two years later, Fanny's full-length photo was in his pocket.

# 18

# STORMING ABOUT THE COUNTRY IS SAD WORK

The vagabond life of a touring star was grueling. Touring stars were freelance performers. Unlike stock actors, touring stars were not attached to any theatre. They played for a limited engagement in plays they chose to perform and in parts they chose for themselves. When the engagement ended, they or their manager packed their trunks and moved on to the next theatre.

John was tiring of opening in a different city each week on a Monday, rehearsing different plays during the day, playing to an audience at night, taking a benefit on Friday, ending on Saturday, and then travelling on Sunday to another city for his next opening. If he had a two-week engagement, the routine would be repeated except for the Sunday interlude. With matinees, a star could appear in twenty plays during a fortnight engagement.[1] "Storming about the country is sad work," Edwin told his friend Larry Barrett. "Successful as he is, my brother [John] is sick of it."[2]

It was especially grueling for a physical actor like John who threw himself into every role and was accident-prone to boot. In February 1861, he almost killed himself in Albany during the final act of *The Apostate* when he fell onto a prop dagger and cut a three-inch gash in his armpit.[3] In Portland, Maine, in *The Corsican Brothers*, he was supposed to slide across the stage on a plank while holding a rapier in the air. The plank hadn't been properly greased. Instead of sliding smoothly, it stuttered across the stage, jolting John's head back and forth. The audience howled watching him being "unwillingly jerked along."[4] In Columbus, Georgia, he was shot in the thigh.[5] In Cleveland, he was almost blinded when he was cut just above one of his eyes during a sword fight.[6] In *Richard III* he took turns driving his opponent over the floodlights into the audience and going over the floodlights himself during their swordfight.[7] "When he fought, it was no stage fight," said actress Kate Reignolds, one of his leading ladies. At night he would try to palliate his bruises by soaking them "in steak or oysters."[8]

John was not just tiring of travelling; he was also having serious misgivings about acting. During one of his melancholy moods, he complained that actors were nothing more than "mummers, of the quality of skimmed milk. They know little, think less, and understand next to nothing."[9] He began to think about alternatives to acting besides real estate.

In 1859, discovery of large deposits of oil near Franklin, Pennsylvania, had touched off a frenzy like the California gold rush of the late 1840s. Kerosene made from petroleum oil had "revolutionized home lighting."[10] Compared to $2 per gallon (about $200 per gallon in today's prices[11]) for "spermaceti" oil from the sperm whale people used to light lamps, kerosene from oil cost only 58 cents a gallon.[12] It was not only nearly four times cheaper, it was also easy to produce, smelled better, and didn't spoil on the shelf like whale oil. There was money to be made cashing in on the newly discovered oil fields. John wanted a piece of it.

While he was at the Academy of Music in Cleveland in November 1863, John asked John Ellsler, the Academy's manager and a friend, what he thought about investing in the Pennsylvania oil fields. Ellsler was just as excited at the prospect of sudden wealth. They got together with two other of Ellsler's friends, Thomas Mears and George Paunell, and formed a partnership to buy leases to drill near Franklin. They called their venture the Dramatic Oil Company.[13]

In mid-December, John, Ellsler, and Mears took the train to Franklin and leased drilling rights on property south of Franklin in Venago County.[14] They then left Mears to get the project started while John and Ellsler fulfilled their theatre commitments for the season. If all went well, they would return in June 1864 to start drilling. Days later John left for Leavenworth, Kansas. It was the farthest he had ever travelled and an engagement he would come to regret.

Leavenworth was a small outpost that provisioned nearby Fort Leavenworth and travelers heading west on the Oregon Trail.[15] The town was not on any theatrical circuit and was not easy to get to. There was no obvious reason for John to have sought a booking there other than an opportunity to make some money before his next engagement.

From Franklin, he boarded a train that took him to Ohio where he changed trains for Chicago. From there he took another train to Hannibal and then another train to St. Joseph, Missouri. From St. Joseph, he took a train to Weston where he boarded a steamboat to take him across the Missouri River to the town of Leavenworth, four miles from Fort Leavenworth.[16] On December 22, 1863, he opened for the first of nine performances at Leavenworth's Union Theatre. He was still in Leavenworth when a brutal cold snap hit the Midwest.

On January 1, 1864, on one of the coldest days in the Midwest in recent memory, one of John's ears was frostbitten after walking in the bitter cold to say goodbye to some friends staying at Fort Leavenworth, four miles away. Before returning to Leavenworth, John handed his pocket flask to a black man named Leav, whom he had hired to carry the flask and other items. Somehow Leav lost the flask on the way back. John could have found liquor in Leavenworth, but he had a special attachment to that "treasured flask." Despite the cold, he headed back.

Coming up to the Fort, he later described how he inwardly groaned seeing a wagon "crushing my best friend" (his flask) just in time to "kiss him in his last moments by pressing the snow to my lips over which he had spilled his noble blood."[17]

Downhearted, John rode back to Leavenworth in time to catch the boat that would take him back across the Missouri River to Weston. From there he could make connections with trains that would get him to St. Louis for his next engagement at Ben DeBar's Theatre on January 4, 1864. After helping to cut the ice on the river so that the boat could dock, John arrived in Weston in time to board the train for the thirty-mile trip to St. Joseph where he booked a room at the Pacific House Hotel and went to bed "a dead man."[18]

John woke the next day expecting to catch the train from St. Joseph east to St. Louis. The weather was of a different mind. A major snowstorm had battered the Midwest overnight, leaving more than two feet of snow on the ground. Trains buried under snow were unable to move. "Here I am snowed in again," he wrote the friend he had visited in Fort Leavenworth, "and God knows when I shall be able to get away."[19] John telegraphed Ben DeBar not to expect him for several days. The days dragged on. January 4 came and went and John was still stuck in St. Joseph along with everyone else in the city.

"Our people are in a terrible fix," the St. Joseph Morning Herald reported. "The snow has effectually shut us out from 'all the world and the rest of mankind' and there is no prospect of relief. Yesterday the white flakes came down thicker and faster than ever."[20]

With nothing else to do and "down to my last cent," John arranged to give a dramatic reading at Corby's Hall on January 5,[21] for which he received $150.[22] He was asked to give another reading the next day. Though short of money, he declined. It was so cold inside (the temperature was down to nine degrees below zero in the morning[23]) that the constant foot stamping and moving around to keep warm made such a racket he could hardly hear himself. The St. Joseph Morning Herald lamented on how "full grown men…on such an occasion of last night could stamp like elephants and move chairs like anvils, plainly they were 'stupid dolts.'"[24]

Three days later the storm was still battering the Midwest. "This is a big storm," the St. Joseph Morning Herald agonized on January 8. "In the memory of man, no such cold weather, and no such a fall of snow has been known as we are now suffering."[25] A traveler who had made it to St. Joseph by sleigh from Breckenridge said he had seen trains covered with as much as thirty feet of snow and figured it would be more than ten days before they could move.[26]

John could not wait that long. He was losing a lot of money by missing his play date in St. Louis. If he could get to Breckenridge, he could catch the train still running to Macon and from there go on to St. Louis. With the $150 he had earned for his reading, he hired a four-horse sleigh for $100. On January 9, he set off for Breckenridge sixty miles away.[27]

John opened at DeBar's Theatre on January 12, 1864, "worn out, dejected and as melancholy as the dull, gray sky above."[28] "It was hard enough to get to Leavenworth, but coming back was a hundred times worse. Four days and nights in the largest snow drifts I ever saw…I never knew what hardship was till then."[29] When the conductor stopped the train on account of the deep snow, John put a gun to the conductor's head and threatened to kill him if he didn't keep going.[30]

After five nights of his scheduled two-week run at DeBar's Theatre, John left for a three-city engagement at George Wood's Theatre at a $300 a week guaranteed payment. John arrived in Louisville on Sunday, January 17, 1864, and opened at Wood's Theatre two days later on Monday.

Kitty Blanchard, a young dancer at Wood's Theatre at the time, had never met John. He was, she recalled, a "good actor, 'extremely' handsome. Good-natured. Very dissipated. A great lover of horses."[31]

Ada Gray was John's leading lady at Wood's Theatre. It was her first season in Louisville where she had become an audience favorite.[32] She also became John's favorite—for the time being.

Little is known about Ada physically other than she was described as "large of stature." Being tall was a handicap for an actress. When she "towered way above her leading man," it made love scenes, "to say the least, unsatisfactory and undramatic."[33]

Ada Gray. John Wilkes Booth's love interest in Nashville, Tennessee, "towered way above her leading man." *Courtesy of The Players Foundation for Theatre Education, New York.*

Ada was born in Cambridge, Massachusetts, in 1845 and made her debut at fifteen at the Boston Museum as an extra. She had impressed the manager enough that he promoted her to a "utility" spot. A Rochester

theater manager happened to be in the audience at one of her performances and offered her a job as a "walking Lady" at his theater. Ada
continued to impress and was offered bigger parts, rising to second billing and eventually to leading lady at Ben DeBar's Theatre in St. Louis
before moving on to George Wood's theater in Louisville.[34]

   Although five foot seven, John was too self-possessed to be embarrassed beside the taller actress or to have any hesitation about romancing
her at night. When he left Louisville for Nashville he asked George Wood
to let him take Ada with him as his leading lady. Whatever relationship
they had in Louisville soured soon after they came to Nashville.

   In the hotel room next to theirs, Sara Jane Full Hill heard what
sounded like a drunken brawl. She opened her door to see if there
was anyone outside who might lend a hand and buttonholed a chaplain passing by. Not to bother, said the chaplain. It was John Wilkes
Booth in the adjoining room and his leading lady "who was also his
mistress."[35]

   The two apparently made up because John's reviews showed no sign
of ill feeling. The *Nashville Daily Union* reported John fulfilled all
expectations and his Nashville appearances would not be forgotten.[36]
Mrs. Hill would not forget his Petruchio in *Taming of the Shrew* when
John sent fake hams flying over the stage during the banquet scene. One
of the fake hams bloodied an orchestra musician when it hit him in the
nose. Another landed in the lap of a woman sitting up front.

   Mrs. Hill thought Mr. Booth had to have been drunk to have acted
so recklessly. "He was a very handsome dark man, but my impression of
him," she recalled, "was that he was of a wild and undisciplined nature
and inclined to dissipation, that he liked to pose, and was theatrical."[37]

   John never shared the stage with Ada again. Nor is there any record
of their ever seeing one another again. Ada was just a passing fancy,
someone to idle away the time with when he was not out cavorting with
his new friend, Tennessee's Military Governor Andrew Johnson, or with
one of Nashville's 1,500 known prostitutes.[38] Before Johnson left for
Washington on February 8, 1864, he and John were seen together escorting two sisters around Nashville.[39] John later may have capitalized on

Johnson's lechery to pin down his whereabouts on the night of the assassination.

John's health began to deteriorate noticeably after Nashville. He was scheduled to open with *Richard III* on February 15, 1864, at Wood's Theatre in Cincinnati. Instead he opted for the less demanding role of Othello. Even then, a local newspaper commented that he seemed "indisposed."[40] Tuesday night he was visibly ill on stage. Wednesday he was too sick to go on at all. One newspaper commented that Mr. Booth "should have been in the care of a physician."[41] Another newspaper reported John "was so ill, his physician positively prohibited him from leaving his room."[42]

Thursday he rallied and was back on stage, although it was clear he had not fully recovered.[43] By Friday, he was reported to be whole again.[44] Just before leaving for his next engagement in New Orleans, John wrote to Richard Montgomery Field, the Boston Museum's new manager, that he had been "very sick here, but am all right again" and would be in Boston for their agreed engagement beginning April 25.[45]

John arrived in New Orleans on March 10 and opened at the St. Charles Theatre four days later. The *New Orleans Times-Picayune*'s critic was the first to pick up on John's nagging hoarseness, commenting that it had worsened to the point that "his playing suffers in proportion;"[46] his performances were disappointing.[47] A few days later on March 25, the *New Orleans Times-Picayune* commented again about John's hoarseness.[48] The next day he was so ill he wasn't able to go on. The St. Charles Theatre's manager alerted theatregoers that the night's performance was cancelled "in consequence of the severe and continued cold under which Mr. Booth has been laboring for several days [and] he is compelled to take a short respite from his engagement."[49] Resting in his room, John wrote Field at the Boston Museum he had been too sick to respond to Field's last letter.[50] John was still too sick to appear on Sunday. By Monday he felt well enough to go back on stage, although it was "still evident," the *Times-Democrat* noted, that "the gentleman is still afflicted by hoarseness."[51]

The *New Orleans Times-Picayune*, which had been rough on John, was conciliatory about his last performance on April 3 before he left for Boston. "He would have been much more of a success," it conceded, "had he not during his entire stay labored under the disadvantage of a hoarseness."[52] The *Times-Democrat*, which had always been friendly, likewise commented on how John had soldiered on during his three-week engagement while laboring "under a violent hoarseness." Most actors would have cancelled their entire booking, but he was determined "to disappoint neither management nor public."[53]

John's hoarseness was nothing more than a periodic strain of the actor's trade, writes John's biographer Michael Kauffman. While some critics noted John's voice problems in their reviews, Kauffman comments that other critics watching the same performance did not mention it. Though John was hoarse from "time to time, the problem was not chronic," says Kauffman. It only cropped up after a long journey and usually in severe weather. "Knowledgeable critics took such things into account."[54] Kauffman points out that Edwin and June (and many other actors) also experienced bouts of hoarseness.[55] However, their spells were few and far between compared to John's, whose hoarseness persisted even after he left New Orleans.

It's also possible, Kauffman notes, John's hoarseness could have been caused by being run down from all the difficult travel and severe weather on his way back from Leavenworth and in New Orleans.[56] John was undoubtedly weakened from all that travelling and the terrible weather. His hoarseness could have been symptomatic of bronchitis, an inflammation of the lining of the airways. Had it been bronchitis, he would have been coughing all the way through his performances. None of the newspapers mentioned any coughing. More likely his recurrent hoarseness was symptomatic of something much more serious—like syphilis.

Although John's engagement at the St. Charles Theatre ended on April 4, he stayed on in New Orleans, for whatever reason, for another week before leaving for Boston. That last week in New Orleans involved his singing "The Bonny Blue Flag," the second most popular patriotic Confederate song after "Dixie."[57]

According to Ed Curtis, half-brother of John's New Orleans landlord, John and some friends were walking along the street after they had just finished playing billiards when one of them dared John to sing the popular song. General Benjamin "Beast" Butler, New Orleans's Union military commander, had forbidden anyone from singing, whistling, or playing the tune, declaring it treasonous. To show he meant business, he fined Armand Blackmar, New Orleans's first music publisher, five hundred dollars and raided the stores of every music seller in the city, confiscating and burning every copy of the song.[58]

John was well aware of what it meant to sing "The Bonny Blue Flag" in public. Without a second thought, he began chanting its opening lines, "We are a band of brothers, and native to the soil," loud enough for anyone to hear. The men with him were dumbfounded at John's deliberate offense and scattered as he continued singing, "fighting for the property [slaves] we gained by honest toil."

In less than a minute he was surrounded by Union soldiers brandishing pistols. John remained unperturbed. He claimed he was a visitor to the city and had only just heard it on the streets. It was a catchy tune. He had not known it was illegal to sing it.

Anyone else would have been arrested after giving such a lame excuse, said Curtis. "But Booth could do pretty much as he pleased. He had a way about him which could not be resisted, the way which permits a man to overstep the boundaries of the law and do things for which other people would be punished."[59] Had he been arrested, he would have been sent to Ship Island, the prison off the coast of New Orleans, for the rest of the war.

John left New Orleans *en route* to Boston on April 9. It was another long journey starting by boat up the Mississippi River to Cairo, Illinois, or St. Louis, Missouri. From there it was a week-long trip by train to Boston. He arrived in Boston on April 16[60] and checked into Amelia Fisher's boarding house on Bullfinch Place, a popular hostel for actors. There was a reason John settled in at Amelia's rather than the more luxurious Parker House Hotel. Maggie Mitchell was boarding at Amelia's.[61]

# 19

# NOT A SECESH

ince leaving Montgomery before the war, Maggie had had a rough time. Word about her singing the "Southern Marseillaise" had incensed many in the North. Newspapers demanded she say something about her disloyalty and about parading on stage with Alabama's secessionist flag. Denunciations intensified and were multiplied. Singing and parading with a secessionist flag spiraled into stomping on the Stars and Stripes. Northern newspapers demanded she explain her actions.[1] Vilifications of the "little petticoated rebel"[2] boiled over in December 1861 when Maggie appeared in Pittsburg, a city feverish with patriotism.

Days before Maggie's arrival, Captain Walter Braun, a dedicated boozer and habitual rabble rouser, became incensed his city was welcoming a "Secesh" (Northern slang for a secessionist). Ranting that a turncoat was in their midst, he cajoled several of his fellow tipplers to go to the theatre, demand Maggie explain her disloyalty, and, if they didn't get a satisfactory answer, burn down the theatre. Hearing rumors of a pending riot, Mayor George Wilson alerted theatre manager Bill

Henderson and said he would post police in the aisles, but he warned Henderson they might not be able to control the situation.

As soon as Maggie appeared on stage, Braun and his minions started hissing from their seats in the front balcony row. Police immediately converged on Braun and hauled him off to Mayor Wilson's office. Wilson fined Braun for creating a disturbance, thinking that would cool him off, and then let him go. As soon as he was free, Braun headed back to the theatre, arriving just as the play ended.

As the curtain fell there was no applause or curtain call. After suffering through the audience's palpable hostility, Maggie was relieved to be done for the night. Moments after reaching her dressing room, however, she heard shouts for her to "come out!" Henderson hurried to her door and told her he would stand with her on stage to answer the audience. As soon as she stepped back out on the stage, Braun bellowed, "Explanation! An explanation is what we want."

"You'll get it," Henderson answered. But Maggie was too agitated to reply. Henderson led her back off stage, promising the explanation they demanded. When he reappeared, he told the rabble-rousers they'd been misinformed. Maggie and two other well-known members of Henderson's company, who had played with her in New Orleans, denied she had torn down an American flag and trampled it onstage. If Braun had seen her pulling down a flag and trampling on it, it would not have been the Stars and Stripes, it would have been the red, white, and blue French flag in *The French Spy*. Doubtless, that was what a drunken Braun must have seen if he had really been there at all.

The audience had no difficulty believing Henderson. They all knew Braun was a loudmouth drunk. Humiliated, Braun beat a hasty retreat from the theatre amid a loud chorus of jeers and hisses. After the ruckus, a number of newsmen met with Henderson in his office. By taking on Braun about the flag accusation, one of the newsmen pointed out, he had sidestepped the allegation about Maggie singing the secessionist "Southern Marseillaise." He had defused the accusation of her hauling down the American flag, but he had not denied her alleged singing the "Marseillaise."[3]

The *Cincinnati Daily Enquirer* had a blithe reaction to the brouhaha, saying Captain Braun "was voted an ass for his pains."[4]

Maggie thought the scandal was over when she left Pittsburg, but there was more to come. In its March 8, 1862, issue, the *New York Clipper* reported it had received a copy of the playbill from the Montgomery Theatre for December 14, 1860. There in big block letters was the announcement that Maggie Mitchell would "chaunt the Southern Marseillaise Hymn! Assisted by the entire company.... Here we have it in black and white."[5]

After it printed proof of Maggie's singing the "Marseillaise," the *New York Clipper* reported it had received an anonymous letter from someone calling himself "Non-Professional," accusing her of a litany of traitorous misdeeds. She had "chaunted" the song, he said, not only in Montgomery but also in other Southern cities, she had trampled the American flag, she had been on the rostrum at the state house in Montgomery when Jefferson Davis was inaugurated as Provisional President of the Confederacy, and she was still supporting the South because she had two brothers in the Confederate army.

Maggie was forced to admit she sang the "Southern Marseillaise" in Montgomery. She apologized in the *New York Clipper* for her misdeed, but she denied singing it in any other city and denied all the other allegations. She did have a brother living in Memphis but didn't know if he was in the Confederate army and doubted it. He was deaf and couldn't serve even if he had wanted to.[6]

The *New York Clipper* accepted her apology and asked "Non-Professional" to send proof of the other allegations. When none came, the *Brooklyn Daily Eagle*, always partisan toward Maggie ("in no city is she more admired and respected than in Brooklyn"[7]), gloated that Maggie had been vindicated. "Maggie Mitchell Not 'Secesh,'" it trumpeted.[8]

The accusations were settled for good in May 1862 after the *New York Clipper* published a letter from actor R. Y. McClannin, stating he felt obliged to "speak out like a man" about "Non-Professional's" lies. McClannin said he had been one of the actors at the St. Charles Theater

in New Orleans when Maggie was in *The French Spy*. Maggie's trampling the Stars and Stripes was nonsense, he said. It "could only have
originated in the noodle of 'Non Professional' as no sensible manager
would have allowed it." McClannin added he had known Maggie for
many years and had no doubt of her loyalty to the Union. Other than
the newspapers and a few misanthropes like Captain Braun and Non-
Professional, who were possibly one and the same, the accusations of
Maggie's disloyalty waned in the ensuing months.

By September 1862, John Hay, Lincoln's personal secretary, seems
not to have heard any talk of Maggie's disloyalty and was as taken as
everyone else by her onstage acting when she appeared at Ford's Theatre.
"[In] Miss Maggie Mitchell, whose name has been for a few years well
known to theatre goers, as that of a bright, vivacious, and dashing, young
girl, with fine eyes and a pretty mouth, great aplomb, and a perfect
knowledge of stage business…we see the promise of a better day for
American comedy."[9]

The theater critic for *De Bow's Review* was just as effusive. Maggie,
he said, was drawing crowded houses and turning "the heads of half the
spoony shoulder-straps (i.e., officers) in Washington. Nightly the stage
is flooded with bouquets, and frequently with more substantial evidences
of admiration until the green houses of Washington and the pockets of
her admirers are about equally empty."[10]

One of those "spoony shoulder-strapped officers," General James
A. Garfield, future U.S. president, saw Maggie several times at Ford's
Theatre. "The little woman" had a strong hold on her audience, he said.[11]
President Lincoln and his wife were just as impressed and sent her an
invitation to have tea at the White House. Had there been any believable
blather about Maggie's trampling on the flag, Lincoln would have been
crucified in the papers for sipping tea with a "petticoated rebel."[12]

When Maggie opened at the Boston Theatre on May 16, 1864, for
her own four-week engagement starting with *Fanchon*,[13] John was at the

nearby Boston Museum. Although they were competing for audiences, when the curtain came down, the two spent their nights together at Amelia Fisher's boarding house.[14]

Sunday nights John and Maggie had tea together with Maggie's mother, who was still accompanying her on her tours. Other times, they went out riding together. "He rode with ease and grace....I was often out with him on horseback," she said.[15]

Maggie never hid her feelings about John. After the assassination she was asked by a reporter what she thought about him.

"He was a delightful companion," she answered.

"Was he handsome?" the reporter asked.

"Oh, very. Indeed," she answered without a moment's hesitation.[16]

# 28

# ISABEL SUMNER

John Wilkes Booth "was licentious as men, and particularly as actors go, but he was not a seducer," said John's earliest biographer, journalist George Townsend, hedging his bet with "as far as I can learn." Townsend was not naïve. He was aware of John's reputation, but he'd heard of an incident where John had tried to act honorably. It involved a young girl who had become enamored of John and kept sending him flowers, love notes, photographs of herself, "and all the accessories of intrigue."[1]

John was used to that kind of attention. He usually ignored it, but the girl was persistent. He finally agreed to see her, anticipating a quick intimacy. She was "so young, so fresh, and so beautiful," he felt remorse taking advantage of her, writes Townsend. He tried to discourage her from what she had come for. He had no affection for her, he said. "Go home, and beware of actors, they are to be seen, not to be known."

"That only made the girl more determined," says Townsend, "and one more soul went to the isles of Cyprus [the legendary home of prostitutes]."[2]

Female historians Joyce Knibb and Patricia Mehrtens smile know-
ingly at Townsend's saying John hesitated at "debauching" young
innocent girls who flirted with him.[3] The only time he had shown
"restraint" was when he was just starting out his career in Richmond
and turned away an infatuated girl—and that was because she came
from a prominent family. Seducing a respectable white woman in the
South was a violation of the South's code of honor and demanded
vengeance, often in the form of a duel. John was not afraid of a duel,
but a scandal would end his career in Richmond. He did not have the
same qualms about getting involved with Northern women. He had
shown no such restraint in Philadelphia with a girl boarding at his
rooming house nor, for instance, about a liaison with sixteen-year-old
Isabel Sumner, a girl he met in Boston when he was not out drinking
tea or riding with Maggie Mitchell.

Isabella (she preferred Isabel) was born in 1847 in Boston, the oldest
of a family of four girls. Their father, Charles Henry Sumner, was a
prosperous Boston grocer with a home at 916 Beacon Street. Although
he had the same surname as Massachusetts's well-known Senator Charles
Sumner, they weren't related. Isabel's mother was Sally Tileston.

Bumping into Charles Sumner sometime near the end of John's four-
week Boston tour, poet Julia Ward Howe, whose "Battle Hymn of the
Republic" would become one of the best tunes of the Civil War, asked
him if had yet seen John at the Boston Museum. "He's a man of fine
talents and noble hopes in his profession."

"Why, n-no madam," Sumner sniffed, "I long since ceased to take
any interest in individuals." Slightly annoyed at Sumner's hubris, Mrs.
Howe snapped that Sumner had made great progress. "God has not yet
gone so far—at least according to the last accounts!"[4]

Isabel likely met John in May 1864. Possibly she was one of the many
girls and women who waited at the stage door after a play to catch a

glimpse of John when he left the theatre.[5] Isabel was a petite brunette with lively blue eyes and a pretty oval face. Somehow she managed to get his attention. They saw one another for several days until John left Boston to spend a week in New York at Edwin's, visiting his mother and Rosalie.

Teenage Isabel Sumner. "How shall I write you, as lover, friend or brother?" *Courtesy of John Rhodehamel and Louise Taper, eds. "Right or Wrong, God Judge Me": The Writings of John Wilkes Booth. Urbana, IL: University of Illinois Press, 1997.*

When they said their goodbyes, they promised to write to one another. John had made that promise to other women many times before. This time he kept it. Ten days later Isabel received the first of six known letters he sent her.

His first letter, dated June 7, 1864, is not at all in keeping with John's reputation as a Casanova. Instead, it shows him vulnerable and unsure of himself.

"Dear Miss Isabel," he headed his letter and asked, "How shall I write you; as lover, friend, or brother?"

Friend or brother implied their relationship was only platonic. Lover implied much more. Until he heard back from her, John told her, he would have to be satisfied with "Dearest Friend." He tells her he wants to protect her from the "wiles of this bad world" and keep her "good and pure."[6] It was the same lodestone of "purity" that had drawn his brother Edwin to Mary Devlin.

Like a lovesick schoolboy, John asked, "Do you think the least little bit of me," then begged Isabel to forgive him for asking. "I know the world, and had begun to hate it," he wrote and went on to tell her what would make any teenage girl or grown woman giddy hearing from the most sought-after man in America: "[When] I saw you. Things seemed changed."[7]

John ended that letter asking Isabel to keep all his letters to herself and not to show them to even her closest friends. He might write some foolish things, he said, and didn't want anyone else to read what he had written. John had been as discreet about the letters from other women that he'd received. He expected the same from Isabel but felt he had to say so. On the off-chance that his letters might be intercepted, he sent them to general delivery at the Boston post office instead of her home address.[8]

One of the "foolish things," he said, he didn't want anyone else to read was his telling her "I love you." He would be embarrassed, he said, if some stranger read it. Self-absorbed as always, he told her to "never trifle with anothers [sic] heart"[9] with no sense of the irony of what he was saying.

John left New York for Pennsylvania on June 8 to start developing the oil fields he had invested in. He would be gone about three weeks, he told Isabel. He hoped she would write to him. When he didn't receive a reply after two weeks, he sent a second letter. "Have you forgotten me so soon?...Do not forget me...I should hate to be forgotten so soon."[10]

When John returned to New York on July 14, there were several letters from Isabel. Thinking about her kept him awake all night. At 2:30 a.m. he dashed off a quick note telling her how happy he was to get her letters. Absence, he said, had made his heart grow fonder. "I had no idea how much I care for you till the last week or so." In his first letter he said he was reluctant to say he loved her. After anxiously waiting to hear from her, he no longer cared. He wanted to let her know "I love you."[11]

When Isabel didn't write back, John fretted she had been offended by his openness. After ten days without a return letter, he wrote asking if he had said anything that upset her. If he had, he apologized profusely. He was sorry for allowing "my fancy to play so free." He couldn't write anymore. His fear of losing her, he said, "seems to paralyze my hand." If she didn't want to hear from him again, he wrote, he wouldn't trouble her anymore, but he would never stop thinking of her as "something *pure and sacred*." Then he added he wasn't going to wait for an answer. He was coming to Boston.[12]

Two days later John registered at the Parker House. Conspiracy theorists contend he was there to meet with Confederate agents.[13] If so, John would have had to have planned that meeting months in advance. He had just written Isabel two days earlier he was coming to Boston after previously writing her several letters about how much he loved her. If those letters were a cover, he would have had to anticipate he was being watched and that his letters were being read, despite his telling Isabel not to show them to anyone and his addressing them to her at general delivery at the Boston post office.

Because the names of four of the guests at the hotel are untraceable, conspiracy advocates maintain they were Confederate aliases.[14] John's letter to Isabel makes it clear he was in Boston to see Isabel, not some elusive Confederate spies. If those unidentified guests were Confederate agents, their registering at the Parker House at the same time as John was a mere coincidence.[15]

How long John stayed in Boston, how much time he spent with Isabel (without Isabel's parents knowing anything about it), or what they said to one another, can only be guessed. John was acting like a lovesick teenager. Before saying goodbye, he gave Isabel a pearl and diamond ring and had it inscribed "J. W .B. to I. S."[16] A gift like that would have sent any girl's head spinning. Isabel assured him she was still his "friend."

Promising he would soon see her again, John left Boston at the end of July 1864 for a brief visit with his mother and sister Rosalie at Edwin's in New York, then he left by train with Edwin and his brother-in-law John Sleeper Clarke to visit with Asia in Philadelphia. The talk at the beginning of the trip was innocuous until it got around to the war. John and Clarke had once been friends, but they'd had a falling-out. John believed Clarke had married Asia for her family name. Though he never let on, John may also have harbored some resentment for Clarke's stealing some of Asia's affections.

Edwin and Clarke were more than aware of John's views about the war. They had tried to steer away from any talk about politics, but talking politics was hard to avoid with a war going on. The conversation was calm at first. Then turned angry. When Clarke mentioned some news about the South's recent setbacks, John's face hardened and he began drumming his fingers on the seat. Clarke didn't read the menace in his face. He made the mistake of insulting Confederate President Jefferson Davis. John's short-fused temper exploded. He lunged at Clarke, grabbed him by the neck, and shook him side to side, like a dog shaking a toy between his teeth. Seeing what was happening, other passengers shouted for John to stop and tried to break his hold on the hapless Clarke. After John's rage exhausted itself, he hurled the terrified Clarke back onto his seat. Standing malignantly over him, his face visibly "twisted with rage, he snarled, 'If you value your life, never speak in that way to me again of a man and a cause I hold sacred.'"[17]

After what must have been an unpleasant stay at Asia and Clarke's home, John made up his mind he had to do something in support of the Southern war effort. In early August 8, 1864, he left Philadelphia for Barnum's Hotel at the southwest corner of Calvert and Fayette Streets in Baltimore. The Barnum was one of the largest and swankiest hotels in America, capable of housing six hundred guests. Once settled in, John sent word to two boyhood friends, Samuel Bland Arnold and Michael O'Laughlen, to meet him there.

Samuel Arnold was thirty years old, four years older than John, five foot eight, about the same height as John, with thick dark hair, a moustache, and a slight beard. The last time he'd seen John was in 1852 when they were schoolmates at St. Timothy's Hall.

Michael O'Laughlen was twenty-four, two years older than John. He was five foot five, had black hair and black eyes, and sported a bushy moustache and a thin goatee below his lower lip. O'Laughlen also hadn't seen John since they were boys when he lived across from the Booth home on North Exeter Street in Baltimore.

Arnold and O'Laughlen had both served in the Confederate army and both had been discharged, Arnold for sickness, O'Laughlen for disability. Both men had taken the loyalty oath to the Union, but their loyalties were still with the South. Both were also bored with their lives. Arnold was unemployed with nothing to do except look after his mother and work as a laborer on his brother's farm. O'Laughlen worked in the family feed business.

John greeted them as old friends, offering drinks and cigars. Neither man had any idea why John had asked them to his hotel, but they were curious and excited to be with the now-famous actor. As Arnold and O'Laughlen relaxed and grew comfortable, John brought the conversation around to the war and a plan he had recently formulated to capture Lincoln on his way to his summer residence. After taking him prisoner, he was going to bring him to Richmond where the government could barter his freedom for the release of Confederate POWs. John used the word "capture," not "kidnap." "Kidnapping" was tawdry. "Capture" had a military ring to it. They would be heroes, he told them. John was as persuasive as ever. Arnold and O'Laughlen agreed to help.

As the two men were leaving, John said he had to wind up his business dealings in New York and would soon get back to them. John's "business dealings" were a secret tryst with Isabel, who was coming to New York to see him. The old proverb about plans going astray was only too true in John's plan. Days after returning to New York, John came down with a severe infection in his right arm that landed him in bed for several weeks.[18]

The infection was erysipelas. Also known as "St. Anthony's fire" (named after the healing Christian saint appealed to for a cure) and "holy fire," erysipelas is a bright red rash symptomatic of a serious, sometimes fatal, streptococcus infection that causes high fever, chills, vomiting, headache, and lassitude. Erysipelas can occur on its own, but it is also known to be symptomatic of syphilis.[19] The infection would keep him bedridden for three weeks.

John Wilkes was "quite sick," "suffering from a diseased arm" Asia wrote a friend. "He fainted from the acute pain, and Junius carried him and laid him upon his bed."[20]

While he was laid up in bed, John wrote to Isabel, who by then had come to New York hoping to see him, that he had come down with "eryeocippolis."[21] Isabel sent him flowers and a get-well letter. John sent her a return letter apologizing for "not being able to see you" because he was too sick to leave the house.[22]

When she received his note saying he couldn't see her, Isabel wrote back she would come to him. John wrote back his doctor had just cut a two-inch gash in his arm to relieve his symptoms; he wouldn't be up until the next day at the earliest.[23] Isabel sensed that John did not want to see her at all. Disillusioned, Isabel returned to Boston.

For an unmarried sixteen-year-old to have traveled on her own, likely lying to her parents about where she was going, who she was seeing, and who she was staying with, was scandalous for those times. For Isabel to come to New York, John would have had to have booked a room for her at a hotel ahead of time. Their relationship had passed being platonic.

Despite what must have been heartbreaking unrequited love, Isabel remained faithful to John in one way: after John assassinated Lincoln, other women who had a romantic relationship with him, as well as mere acquaintances, burned his letters or got rid of any gifts he gave them,[24] but Isabel kept John's letters and the pearl ring he gave her with its inscribed "J. W. B. to I. S."

Isabel was undoubtedly in love with John. Was he ever in love with Isabel? His obsession with her was out of character with the John Wilkes Booth womanizer of history. What did this matinee idol, fawned over by women drooling with lust, see in a chaste sixteen-year-old school girl?

One answer is that Isabel was not like the other women he knew. John was close to his sister Asia. Her good opinion meant a lot to him. They were more than just brother and sister. Only two years apart, they were the best of friends. They had weathered their father's odd, often frightening delusions. They had been humiliated and called bastards and been shunned by former friends when neighbors learned their parents were not legally married. They had confided their innermost thoughts to one another. When a gypsy told John he would be famous and die an early death, the only one he told was Asia.[25]

John knew how Asia felt about Edwin's late wife Mary Devlin. Mary had been an actress and was Irish. To Asia, that meant she wasn't respectable. Like John, Asia never got over her humiliation of being illegitimate. Having an actress like Mary in the family, a woman with no respectability in middle-class society, was almost as humiliating. John intuited that Asia would have approved of Isabel. Isabel was "pure." She also wasn't Irish. That meant John could court her with no second thoughts that Asia would turn on her like she had turned on Mary Devlin.

The greater mystery is why John stopped seeing or writing to Isabel. His erysipelas infection eventually healed. He could have pursued Isabel again. John was impulsive, passionate, charming, like the Romeo he impersonated onstage—but he was also unable to commit to any lasting relationship.

John's affair with Isabel fits right into psychologist Bryn C. Collins's casebook description of the Romeos she has treated.[26]

Week one: Romeo (John) meets someone (Isabel) and finds himself swept off his feet (June 7, 1864: "How, shall I write you; as lover, friend, or brother. I think so much of you... ").

Week two: He soon begins to feel he does not know how he could have survived without her (June 17, 1864: "I should hate to be forgotten so soon.").

Week Three: He can't stop thinking of her. He can't work because he can't concentrate. He just wants to spend time with her (July 24, 1864: "it's impossible for me to rivet my mind to a single line of study, or in fact, to anything else.").

Week Four: Sorry, I can't see you (August 26, 1864: "You cannot imagine how sorry I was in not being able to see you.").

Then, "suddenly it's gone. Everything stops. There's no fight. There's no discussion... Romeo simply disappears." John never sees Isabel again. He does not write to her and does not even think about her anymore.

Collins did not have John Wilkes Booth's infatuation with Isabel in mind when she narrated that typical scenario, but the parallels are uncanny. Romeos are the way they are, writes Collins, because they cannot feel subtle emotions. They see everything on a grand scale. They expect everyone to feel the same. Romeos are unable to limit themselves to one affair, says Collins, no matter what they promise. Once they lose the excitement of the romance, the affair is over and they move on to the next one.

All that was certainly true of John Booth. But something else, involving a grandiose belief he could change the course of the war, had changed his feelings about Isabel around that time.

# 21

# A Gang of Misfits

**W**hat were the Confederacy's prospects in July 1864? To some they seemed good.[1] In May and June of 1864, the Confederacy had handed the Union major defeats at the Battles of the Wilderness (May 5–7, 1864) and Cold Harbor (May 31–June 12, 1864). The Confederate government sensed that the loss of thousands of lives, war weariness, and the despair that no end was in sight would bring pressure on Lincoln to end the war and offer a peace plan. If Lincoln conceded Southern independence, the fighting would end. But as major a defeat as Wilderness and Cold Harbor were for the North, the Confederacy was bleeding a steady death.[2]

With its much larger population, the Union could replace its dead, wounded, and imprisoned fighting men; the South could not. In April 1864, General Ulysses Grant, knowing that the North could sustain its losses whereas the South couldn't, suspended prisoner swaps. Grant acknowledged it was hard on the men in captivity, but if he continued allowing exchanges, the war would go on until all of the South was exterminated.[3] Lincoln was not about to concede something he had resolutely resisted. In Grant he had a commander who was just as resolute.

In July 1864, Lincoln issued a public statement about his willingness to offer liberal terms to the South to end the war.[4] But there were conditions. The South had to return to the Union, abandon slavery, and halt further military action.[5] When John read Lincoln's proposal in the *New York Tribune*, he became convinced Lincoln was determined to subjugate the South. He began to think it was up to him to prevent that from happening.

The plan John came up with was to abduct Lincoln on the way to his summer home and take him to Richmond where the government could barter his return for the release of Confederate POWs. It was not an original plan.[6] Major Joseph Walker Taylor, a nephew of former President Zachary Taylor, had proposed the exact same plan in the summer of 1862, but Confederate President Jefferson Davis refused to condone it. Shaking his head, Davis told Taylor that Lincoln would not let himself be taken prisoner without a fight and would be killed in the attempt. He refused to sanction what would be construed as having given his consent to assassination. Besides, said Davis, what value would he be to the Confederacy as a prisoner? If Lincoln were captured and brought to Richmond, Davis said he would have to treat him like the magistrate of the North.[7]

Had John sought official support from the Confederate government when he decided to "capture" Lincoln in August 1864, it would never have been approved. A presidential election was coming up in the North in a few months. Many, including Lincoln himself, believed he would not be re-elected. Contrary to the public esteem for Lincoln after his death, during his presidency he was unpopular, not only in the South but also in the North where he was held in contempt by a large segment of the population. He had only won the presidency in 1860 with less than

40 percent of the votes because the divided Democrats had fielded two separate candidates.

During his presidency, Lincoln had suspended many constitutional rights. Without consulting Congress he suspended habeas corpus, the right to protest or challenge imprisonment, and he had instituted conscription, an executive order that triggered riots in New York, Philadelphia, and other cities and towns in the east. His Emancipation Proclamation was especially reviled by thousands of families whose men were being drafted to fight for a cause they did not believe worth dying for. Even those in his own Republican Party had turned against him.[8]

Lincoln's anticipated Democrat opponent in the upcoming election was the former commander of the Army of the Potomac River, George McClellan. The Democrats were strongly in favor of a negotiated peace. Lincoln, well aware of his unpopularity and the anti-war sentiment across the North, did not expect to be re-elected.

The Confederate government was keeping close tabs on the upcoming election. There was no reason to kidnap Lincoln. It would have been political folly to abduct Lincoln when waiting a few months would end his presidency. With McClellan as president there would be a negotiated peace that included independence. Besides, kidnapping Lincoln would harden the North's resolve and might sway the election to the Republicans in Congress who would have to approve a peace deal. England and France would certainly turn against the South for abducting the equivalent of a monarch.

The exhilaration among the Democrats and the Confederate government turned to despair three days after McClellan's nomination. On September 3, 1864, Lincoln received a momentous telegram from General William Tecumseh Sherman: "Atlanta is Ours and Fairly Won." Overnight public opinion in the North turned 180 degrees in Lincoln's favor. Lincoln's re-election was now a certainty.

With Lincoln no longer a lame duck and the Confederate army's diminishing strength, the Confederate government was now receptive to the once dismissed idea of capturing Lincoln. Carrying out that plan would require military or organizational experience. No one in the Confederate Secret Service would have put John Wilkes Booth, a man with no military training, in charge of such a major undertaking when they had someone like Captain Thomas Nelson Conrad, a military man who had been tried and tested.

When Conrad broached his plan to capture Lincoln, he was listened to in high places. Unlike John, who was acting on his own, Conrad received approval from the very top of the Confederate government. With letters from President Jefferson Davis to Secretary of War James Seddon and Secretary of State Judah Benjamin authorizing his mission, Conrad was provided with $400 in gold to cover expenses. Letters were also sent directing Lieutenant Colonel John S. Mosby and Lieutenant Charles H. Cawood, operating in Maryland and Virginia, to aid and facilitate his mission.[9]

Unlike John, Conrad and his spies hid out in a house in Lafayette Square across from the White House and shadowed the president to make sure he would be alone on evening trips to his summer home. On the day set for the abduction in late September, Conrad was set to spring the trap. But the abduction never came off. Conrad had to abort it because Lincoln was no longer alone on his way to his summer home. He had a cavalry guard escorting him. Someone had leaked Conrad's plan. John was completely unaware the Confederate government had backed another kidnapping mission. As he himself said, he was, "a Confederate at present doing duty upon his own responsibility."[10]

On October 18, 1864, John registered at the posh St. Lawrence Hotel in Montreal.[11] The St. Lawrence was "Little Richmond," the not-so-secret headquarters of Confederate agents in Canada.[12] John expected his reputation would guarantee his being heard. Although John was often seen near some of those Confederate agents, the only Confederates he is known to have had more than a passing conversation with were Patrick Martin and George Sanders.[13]

Martin was a former Baltimore liquor dealer turned blockade runner. John initially contacted him to ship his wardrobe to the South. When he learned Martin knew many Confederate sympathizers in rural Maryland,[14] he confided his plan to kidnap Lincoln and take him through Maryland and Virginia to Richmond. Martin was supportive and offered to give John a letter of introduction to two Confederate loyalists, Drs. Samuel Mudd and William Queen. Both men lived near Bryantown and would be able to help him once he got Lincoln into rural Maryland.

George Sanders also had no official standing in the Confederate government but operated in Canada as if he did. Sanders possessed a charisma that won him many friends, but behind his radiant blue eyes and charming smile was a man who put personal gain before patriotism. Even those who liked him never trusted him—and for good reason. His achievements always fell short of what he promised.[15]

Sanders may have chatted with John, but he didn't do anything to aid John in his kidnapping plan. Beverley Tucker, a senior Confederate agent staying at the St. Lawrence, claimed Sanders never mentioned John Wilkes Booth. After the war ended, Tucker told the *New York Times* that prior to Lincoln's assassination, he had never heard of John Wilkes Booth.[16]

The day after Lincoln's re-election, John checked into the National Hotel in Washington. Two days later, he took a stagecoach out to Bryantown to meet Drs. Queen and Mudd. John wasn't sure how much he could trust Dr. Queen, so he told him the reason he had come out there was to buy some land and horses and to learn something about the neighborhood. The next day Dr. Queen introduced him to Dr. Mudd. John showed Dr. Mudd the same introductory letter from Martin he'd shown Dr. Queen. Now feeling more confident about disclosing his real reason for having travelled to that part of the state, he told them about his abduction plan and queried them about the roads to the Potomac River. Queen and Mudd were sympathetic and introduced him to other Confederate loyalists in the area. His preparations over, John returned to New York where he came down with another bacterial infection.

This time it took the form of painful, swollen carbuncles (large abscesses). "John's neck [is] bad with boils," John's brother June wrote in his diary.[17] Carbuncles are another of the myriad symptoms that can occur as an isolated infection or as a symptom of a serious lingering infection.[18] Despite the pain, John appeared for the first and only time on stage at the Winter Garden with his two brothers in *Julius Caesar*. The occasion was a fundraiser for money to erect a statue of Shakespeare in Central Park in honor of the playwright's 300th birthday.

Unbeknownst to John, George Sanders had been planning a sabotage operation involving setting fire to New York City's hotels. By happenstance, one of those hotels was next door to the Winter Garden where John and his brothers were performing that night.

During the second act, the play came to a sudden and dramatic halt when firemen charged into the theatre believing the fire next door had spread to the theatre. Edwin stood calmly on stage and assured the audience it was only smoke from a fire next door and that it had been put out. Reassured by his calm demeanor, the audience returned to its seats. The fires at the other hotels were also extinguished with minimal damage.[19]

On Sunday morning, John, June, Edwin, and their mother were sitting around the breakfast table at Edwin's home. Small talk eventually turned to the fire. Edwin called the arsonists cowards. John defended them. The fire, he said, was justifiable as "an act of war."

Edwin lost his normally controlled temper. He swore he would not tolerate any such talk in his home from a "rank secessionist." He demanded John "cease his treasonable language" or leave.[20]

John was not about to be told what he could or could not say. Despite feeling ill from the pain in his neck, he packed his bag and left for Asia's home where he knew he would be welcome. June felt John was too ill to travel alone and left with him.

As soon as they arrived at Asia's, she got John into bed and sent for a doctor who lanced a large boil festering on John's neck.[21] The boil was sore, but in and of itself it would not have confined him to bed. The boil was symptomatic of the more serious infection lingering in his body. It kept him in bed for several days.

While recuperating, John had a lot of time to think about his life. He had lost money in his oil venture, his beloved South was on the verge of defeat, he was fretting that he would not be able to return to his stage career because of his vocal problems, and he was anxious about his recurring illnesses.

Nothing seemed to be going his way. Outwardly he kept up a brave façade. Inwardly he was tormented and had been since the late summer of 1864 when all these problems hit him at once. "You seem so different from your usual self," Joe Simmonds, John's banker friend, told him.[22]

John's only solace was his plan to capture Lincoln. If he could pull it off, he would be hailed as a hero in the South and have the lasting fame that meant so much to him.

Before leaving Asia's, John reached into his jacket and handed her a large envelope. The packet had a single word on it: "Asia." "Lock this up in your safe for me," he said. "I may come back for it but if anything should happen—to me—open the packet alone and send the letters as directed, and the money and papers give to their owners."[23]

Asia didn't think that John's giving her something to hold on to for safekeeping was that ominous. "It was not unusual to speak thus of possible accidents," she said, "for in these reckless times the travel was rough and incessant, and a traveling actor's life is one of exposure to danger."[24]

Before leaving, John kissed his sister goodbye and left. Moments later he came back into the room.

"Let me see you lock up the packet," he said.

Asia was puzzled, but she did as he asked. John watched as she placed the packet in an iron safe. After they came back into the room, as Asia was sitting down on the sofa, John came and knelt down at Asia's feet and laid his head in her lap. "Then as we rose together, he kissed me very tenderly."

"Try to be happy," he said as he turned away.[25]

The envelope, opened after the assassination, contained U.S. bonds worth $4,000, transfer of his oil properties to June and Rosalie, and two letters. One of those letters was addressed "To Whom It May Concern." The other was to his mother.

John's "To Whom It May Concern" letter contained his manifesto, his reasons for kidnapping Lincoln. He had titled it "To Whom It May Concern" as a jab at Lincoln, who had used that address in his July 1864 letter to the *New York Tribune*.[26]

Assuming his letter was being read after he had abducted Lincoln, John said he had taken him prisoner to prevent the South's demise. "This country was formed for the white not the black man."[27] Lincoln, he said, was bent on total annihilation of not just slavery but the entire South.[28]

In the letter to his mother, John poured out his disillusionment and depression. "I have cursed my willful idleness, and begun to deem myself a coward and to despise my own existence," he told her, unburdening the guilt he felt about not fighting for "the cause I love. The cause of the South…should I meet the worst, dear Mother, in struggling for such holy rights, I can say 'Gods' [sic] will be done'…should the last bolt strike your son, dear Mother, bear it patiently…at best life is but short, and not at all times happy."[29]

On December 23, 1864, while Dr. Mudd was in Washington ostensibly shopping for the holidays, he introduced John Wilkes Booth to John Surratt Jr., the third man to join his band of conspirators. Surratt was twenty years old and living with his mother, Mary Surratt, at her three-story, brick boarding house at 541 H Street in Washington.[30] During the war, Mary Surratt's tavern in Maryland was a known safe house for Confederate spies and couriers.[31] Surratt would be a valuable asset. He had been a trusted Confederate courier since 1863, and he knew the Virginia terrain over which the kidnappers would have to travel to get to Richmond.

The day after meeting Surratt, John left for Edwin's to spend Christmas with his family. While in New York, he had drinks with Samuel Knapp Chester, an old actor friend, and tried to recruit him in his abduction plot.[32]

Chester balked at the idea.[33] He protested he wanted no part of the scheme. John was not used to being turned down. His frustration turned to anger. Even so, he persisted. As Chester turned to leave, John warned him that if he breathed a word about what he had just told him, he would be hunted down and killed.[34]

Two days later, John met with Arnold and O'Laughlen in Baltimore and left a trunk with them containing Spencer rifles and other guns, ammunition, knives, handcuffs, and canteens. Buy a horse and carriage, he told them, and bring the weapons to Washington. John's kidnapping plan was beginning to pick up steam.

In January 1865, John Surratt recruited the next man on the team, twenty-six-year-old, German-born George Atzerodt from Port Tobacco, one of the towns in the Confederate "underground." Atzerodt was a part-time painter and boatman who was making some extra cash ferrying Confederate spies across the Potomac River to and from Port Tobacco. After Atzerodt agreed, Surratt bought a larger boat for Atzerodt to ferry Lincoln and his captors across the river.[35]

To fill in the time until the roads were travelable, Arnold and O'Laughlen rented a room at 420 D Street, paid for by John, scouted out the city and the roads to the bridges into Maryland, and, when they were not reconnoitering, spent their time drinking at Ruhlman's Hotel on Pennsylvania Avenue.[36]

In January, John agreed to co-star with Avonia Jones in *Romeo and Juliet* for her farewell benefit at Grover's Theatre. The *Washington*

*National Intelligencer* raved at his performance ("his death-scene was the most remarkable and fearfully natural that we have seen for years upon the stage") but also noted that John "suffered from huskiness of voice."[37] John had not performed for more than six months. It was more than enough time for his voice to have recovered had the problem been temporary. John's chronic hoarseness, his erysipelas, the infections in his neck, and his later physical problems were becoming more and more indicative of an underlying serious ailment.[38]

John recruited two other men into the conspiracy that month. Twenty-three-year-old David Herold, an unemployed pharmacy clerk, whom John had met a year earlier, was easily persuaded to join. Herold wasn't considered very bright by Dr. Samuel McKim, at whose pharmacy Herold had once worked.[39] Despite his mental shortcomings, Herold was familiar with Maryland's backroads and the people in the area.

The other new recruit was Lewis Thornton Powell. Six-foot-tall Powell was muscled and menacing. He had been wounded and captured at Gettysburg, escaped from prison, and had briefly served in Colonel John Singleton Mosby's Partisan Rangers, which he deserted. A violent man, he was known as "Terrible Lewis Powell." On one occasion he was arrested in Baltimore for beating a black maid for not cleaning his room and talking back to him. Throwing her on the ground, he stomped on her and punched her in the head, almost killing her.[40]

William Doster, Powell's lawyer, said Powell's "mind seemed of the lowest order, very little above the brute, and his moral faculties were equally low." Doster believed Powell was *non compos mentis*, someone not in control of his own mind.[41]

Like the others, Powell was taken in by John. Three or four days before his execution, Powell told Dr. Abram Gillette, his spiritual advisor, that he had been encouraged with "dreams of glory and the lasting gratitude of the Southern people."[42] Powell was a man who could be counted on to do what he was told and who would fight his way out of a scrape. John couldn't have hoped for a better recruit.

On March 14, 1865, John summoned his gang of misfits to meet him at Gautier's restaurant at the corner of Twelfth and Pennsylvania. None of them had anything in common other than their Southern sympathies and their susceptibility to John's charismatic magnetism and his money.

Gautier's restaurant was one of Washington's best restaurants. It had a separate large dining room and smaller rooms for private parties.[43] As John's gang lounged drinking beer and sipping oysters in one of Gautier's private rooms, John told them the plan to capture Lincoln was set for the following night, March 15, at Ford's Theatre while Lincoln was in the presidential box. John was excited. March 15 was the Ides of March, the day Julius Caesar was assassinated.

John gave each man his assignment. Michael O'Laughlen would extinguish the gas lights, darkening the theatre. Under cover of darkness, John and Powell would dash into the presidential box, handcuff Lincoln, and lower him over the railing onto the stage. Sam Arnold would then whisk Lincoln out of the theatre and away from Washington to George Atzerodt, who would be waiting to take their prisoner across the Potomac River into Virginia. Once on the other side, John Surratt would be waiting with fresh horses to get them to Richmond.[44]

The plan was ludicrous. Arnold told him so. Michael O'Laughlen agreed. Even if they managed to get Lincoln out of the theatre, Arnold said, Washington was crawling with soldiers and police. The abductors would have to run a gauntlet of federal checkpoints. Then they would have to elude patrols up and down every main and back road in Maryland, Virginia, and at every known point on the Potomac River where they could cross from Maryland to Virginia. The bridges were all guarded. They would be stopped by the sentinel.

"Shoot the sentinel," John barked.

Arnold answered that if he did, it would alert every soldier in the area. "I want the shadow of a chance for escape and success."

John was infuriated. "You find fault with everything concerned about it," he retorted.

"No," Arnold replied. "I want a chance and I intend to have it. You can be the leader of the party, but not my executioner."

"Do you know that you are liable to be shot? Remember your oath," John shot back.

"If you feel inclined to shoot me, you have no further to go [but] I shall defend myself," Arnold answered.

Powell and Herold said nothing. They went along with whatever John asked without question.

John still had enough presence of mind to realize there was no convincing Arnold or O'Laughlen. After some conciliatory words, tempers cooled. Nevertheless, Arnold and O'Laughlen were both fed up. If John didn't come up with a better plan by the end of the week, Arnold and O'Laughlen said they were going back to Baltimore.[45]

Two days later around noon, John summoned his gang for one more try at Lincoln. He'd heard Lincoln was going to be the guest of honor at a matinee performance for convalescing veterans at the Campbell General Hospital, several miles from the White House. They could stop him on the way back, overpower and handcuff him, and use his own carriage to carry him through Maryland to the Potomac River.

Just to make sure the rumor about Lincoln's appearance at the hospital was true, John rode out there. As nonchalantly as he could, he asked actor E. L. Davenport when Lincoln was expected and swallowed hard when the actor told him he was mistaken. Lincoln wasn't expected there at all.

Had John read the newspaper, he would have known that Lincoln was scheduled to take part in a ceremony at the National Hotel to present a captured Confederate flag to an Indiana regiment. Ironically, the ceremony was taking place at the very same hotel where John was staying.

By the end of the day, everyone was discouraged. Arnold, O'Laughlen, and Powell left for Baltimore. Herold, Surratt, and Atzerodt stayed in Washington for a little longer. John stayed in Washington for another day to appear in *The Apostate* on March 18, 1865, at a benefit at Ford's Theatre for his friend John McCullough.[46]

Despite all the disappointments, John's mind was still focused on his plan. He checked into the Barnum Hotel in Baltimore on March 25 in the early morning and sent a note to Sam Arnold to meet him. By the time Arnold arrived, John had become impatient and had checked out and was on his way to Washington. Before leaving, however, asking for Arnold, John left him a note to give the capture plan one more chance.

Arnold made what would turn out to be a fatal mistake. He answered John in a letter written on March 27, now dubbed the "Sam Letter," that would later incriminate him in Lincoln's assassination. In it, Arnold advised John that before he made any more plans he should "go and see how it will be taken at R___d."[47] By "it" Arnold was referring to John's abduction plan. After the assassination, the government maintained "it" referred to the assassination, implicating him as an accessory before the fact.

On April 2, 1865, the Confederate government abandoned Richmond. Whatever lingering plans John still had about capturing Lincoln were no longer feasible. Even if he could kidnap Lincoln, there was nowhere to take him.

John was in New York at Edwin's when he learned about Richmond. While lost in thought, his brother June asked him about his oil speculations. Snapped out of his reverie, John replied his investments had not turned out as profitably as he hoped.[48] No matter, he said, oil speculation wasn't important to him anymore. June was surprised. John was always going on about making a fortune in oil. What had happened to change his mind? he asked.

Out of the blue, John told June he was "in love with a lady in Washington and that was worth more to him than all the money he could make."[49] All the while John was scheming to kidnap the president of the United States, he was still chasing women.

Three days later, on April 5, 1865, John boarded a steamer for Newport, Rhode Island, and registered at the Aquidneck House. He signed the register "J. W. Booth & Lady, Boston."[50] The Lady was never identified. Presumably she was the "lady in Washington" he spoke about to June, but the "Boston" beside her name suggests otherwise.

Two days after Union forces entered Richmond, crushing his plan, John was apparently not so dismayed that it kept him from the clandestine rendezvous with "a Lady."

The next few days were spent in Boston with the mysterious lady. On April 7 he returned to New York alone. Later that day he ran into Samuel Chester and asked him to meet for dinner.

Now that John had given up any idea of abducting Lincoln, he was no longer embittered toward Chester for his refusing to be an accomplice in the kidnapping plot. Despite their not parting before on the best of terms, Chester agreed to meet him at the House of Lords restaurant on Houston Street in lower Broadway.

As they were eating Welsh rabbit and drinking beer, Chester could not help noticing John kept kissing a ring on his finger. Chester asked about it.[51]

"Just a little affair I'm engaged in," John answered dismissively.

Chester let it go for the moment, but his curiosity was piqued. Women crowded the back doors of the theatre just to get a glimpse of this man and deluged him with letters. John, however, was not known for giving his heart to anyone.

After dinner, as they were strolling along the street to the theatre, Chester momentarily stopped and turned to John. "Tell me the story of the ring," he asked again.

This time John was more forthcoming. "I'm engaged to be married to a young lady at Washington."[52]

Chester was dumbfounded. John was notorious for his womanizing. But never had he asked any of the women he had been involved with to marry him!

When Chester later related their conversation at the conspiracy trial, he told the court John had told him who the woman was. Chester "would not like to compromise the lady by giving her name, he said, but [she] is of a very respectable family."[53]

The "respectable" lady was Lucy Lambert Hale.

# 22

# LUCY LAMBERT HALE

I f opposites attract, John Wilkes Booth and Lucy Lambert Hale were made for each other. John was an ardent racist; Lucy was an abolitionist. John was trim; Lucy was stout. John was an Adonis; Lucy was a plain Jane.

Their affair began in 1862. Two days before Valentine's Day, John and June were both staying at their brother Edwin's house in New York. Neither was able to sleep. John could not stop thinking about Lucy, a girl he had seen from a distance in Washington a few days earlier. June was sleepless because John kept waking him up to pester him for advice about a valentine letter to Lucy. He finished at 3:30 a.m. June went upstairs to bed. John stayed downstairs on the sofa. He wanted to be up early enough to put his love note in the morning's mail.[1]

This was still an era when men did not speak to women of high social status without a formal introduction. Valentine's Day was an opportunity for a man to write a letter to a woman to whom he had not been introduced, to make her aware of his feelings without breaching social etiquette. Despite his overwhelming self-confidence with most women,

John was anxious that this girl not feel affronted by attentions from an actor.

The letter arrived in time. Lucy Hale opened it, looked at the bottom to see who it was from, and was puzzled. The letter was signed "A Stranger." Lucy read on:

> My dear Miss Hale,
>
> Were it not for the *License* which a time-honored observance of *this day* allows, I had not written you this poor note... You resemble in a most remarkable degree a lady, very dear to me, now dead and your close resemblance to her surprised me the first time I saw you.
>
> This must be my apology for any apparent rudeness ... To see *you* has indeed afforded me a melancholy pleasure. If you can conceive of such, and should we never meet nor I see you again believe me, I shall always associate *you* in my memory, with her, who was very beautiful, and whose face, like your own I trust, was a faithful index of gentleness and amiability.
>
> With a Thousand kind wishes for your future happiness I am, to you,
>
> A Stranger.
>
> St. Valentine's Day
>
> 1862.[2]

Despite his womanizing, in early 1862 John was not yet the famous star he was soon to become. Most of the women—girls would be more accurate—he had an interest in were teenage actresses. John was confident among his own. Among women unconnected to the theater, especially "society" women, he was careful to observe the etiquette of the day. Lucy's father was a United States senator from New Hampshire. A United States senator's daughter was used to being in the company of sons of prominent political and social American dignitaries. John was an actor, a profession in very low standing among the elite.

Signing the note "A Stranger" was not as enigmatic as it might seem. At the time John was preparing for the lead in an upcoming lengthy play in Baltimore later that month. The play was called *The Stranger*.[3]

Nevertheless, it was a peculiar valentine. Someone less narcissistic might have phrased it differently. It was hardly romantic to tell a woman she reminded him of a dead girl he had once loved. But perhaps the most puzzling question is who was it Lucy reminded John of?

Most likely it was the "Miss Becket" whom John had fallen in love with during his early stock days at Richmond's Marshall Theatre. Their affair ended tragically when she fell ill with typhoid fever. Before her death, she had had her hair shorn for John to make into a theatrical wig for him to remember her by. Like other actors, John had many wigs; hers was his favorite.[4]

What was it about Lucy that attracted John Wilkes Booth, the handsomest man in America?

She was certainly not a knockout. Descriptions of Lucy as pretty with clear skin and a stunning figure are fanciful.[5] Characterizing her as one of Washington's beauties is fictional romanticism on the part of authors who seem to have never looked at her photo.[6] The picture of Lucy that John had in his pocket when he died is matronly, to put it kindly. The few other photos of Lucy are no more flattering.[7] The only physical descriptions of Lucy by contemporaries are that she had dark hair, grey blue eyes, and was "rather stout."[8] Hardly descriptions of a girl who turned the head of someone like John.

If not her looks, what then?

Lucy possessed a charisma and a personality not unlike John's. John Hay, Lincoln's private secretary, was in love with her. Hay had known her from their school days and told her he didn't know anyone "of equal charm or equal power of gaining hearts, and equal disdain of the hearts you gain." He loved and admired her. He didn't understand her and never hoped to, he said, because if he did, she would lose some of her "indefinable fascination." Her "magnetic vitality fills every place [she] left with haunting fancies and dreams."[9]

A "rather stout" Lucy Lambert Hale. *Courtesy of James O. Hall Research Center, Surratt House Museum, Clinton, Maryland.*

Lucy Lambert Hale (Lambert was her mother's maiden name) was the younger of the Hales' two daughters. Their older daughter, Elizabeth, was born in 1835. Lucy was born six years later in 1841 in Dover, New Hampshire.

Lucy was a young girl of twelve at boarding school in Hanover, New Hampshire, when she began turning heads. Her first known flirtation was with William Chandler, a Concord boy, future United States senator, and secretary of the Navy. Chandler sent her adolescent love letters from Harvard University in the form of poems when he was a freshman.[10]

Bill Chandler was not the only one of Lucy's admirers who would later make his mark in American history. In 1858, when she was seventeen, Lucy had a brief flirtation with eighteen-year-old Oliver Wendell Homes Jr., a future Supreme Court Justice. They met when they were both vacationing in Maine with their families. As soon as Holmes got back to Harvard, where he was a freshman, he started writing to Lucy at her boarding school in Hanover, and she wrote back.

In one of his letters, Oliver confessed he had a "slightly jealous disposition." "Give my respect to all the young ladies at Dover and thereabouts," he said, but "to none of the 'male species.'" Oliver signed it "Your aff. Friend." In a P.S., he said he appreciated her perfuming her letter and its meaning, assuring her he would take the first chance to follow its invitation."[11] The perfume was called "Kiss-Me-Quick." Lucy pretended to be offended by Oliver's inference.

One of her letters hinted he wasn't the only one writing her, and in Oliver's next letter he demanded, "How many young gentlemen do you keep going at once on an average?"[12] His suspicions were right. In late 1860, a Harvard student, known only by his initials, W. P. K., was begging Lucy "in the name of one whose destiny is in your hands, do not discontinue our new born correspondence in its very commencement."

Lucy had told W. P. K. not to write anymore because he had become too ardent and said he loved her. "In case we do not have a civil war," he said he would be at Harvard for another term and would be more than happy to visit her in New Hampshire and pleaded for her to reconsider and write to him again.[13]

Lucy still kept Oliver dangling. After his father returned from a trip to Hanover, Oliver asked if he had seen Lucy. Holmes Sr. said he had and that when he'd asked her about the students at her school, she had only pointed out the men. He feared, he said, that Lucy was a flirt. Oliver already knew that. In his next letter he went back to addressing her formally as "Dear Miss Hale."[14]

Shortly thereafter, Lucy persuaded her father to let her transfer to a boarding school in Boston. Her being closer to Harvard would be entertaining.

Another of the heads Lucy was turning belonged to Frederick Anderson, Robert Lincoln's roommate at Harvard. Anderson had met Lucy sometime in March or April 1864, and she had asked him for a photo of himself. Anderson apologized for sending an older photo. Anderson then reminded her he had some of her jewelry that she had asked him to hold on to when they were at some unstated reception. At the bottom of Anderson's letter, Robert penned a short note to Lucy inviting her to their Class day. He had no objection to her coming, he said, if she promised to be good and not allow any freshman to be presented to her.[15]

Lucy's family were staunch abolitionists. John Parker Hale had served in the United States Congress from 1843 to 1845 and in the United States Senate from 1847 to 1853 and 1855 to 1865. When Hale lost his election bid for another term, he petitioned Lincoln for an appointment as United States minister to Spain.

After his valentine letter to Lucy in 1862, John forgot about her. The next time Lucy saw John was a year later when she watched him on stage in Washington and sent him a bouquet of congratulatory flowers. After that "Miss Hale was always at the play with a bouquet and smiles for him."[16]

The Hale family had rooms at the National Hotel in Washington and had been living there since 1861. Since John was also staying at the National Hotel, they had ample opportunities to be together. On one particular night they were both at one of the hotel's "hops." "The hotel was a blaze of light," a guest recollected. No matter where he went, every woman could not help gaping at the "tall, dark" Adonis, secretly wishing they were the girl clinging to his arm. "There were some who caviled at her choice [because John was an actor]...the young girl's sweet face seemed excuse for any infatuation."[17]

By March 1865 Lucy was committed to John. There was never any announcement or formal engagement. Lucy never mentioned it publicly. She didn't tell her father. If she had, he likely would have tried to break up their relationship. When Lucy asked her father for an extra ticket for Lincoln's second inauguration, she didn't tell him who it was for. Senator Hale, the strong advocate for abolition, had no idea the ticket was for a defender of slavery.[18]

Was John in love with Lucy or just using her to get close to Lincoln? John could and did have his pick of virtually any woman. His "beauty of person and face, fascinating manners, and thrilling voice, made him a 'darling' among the susceptible sex."[19]

What attracted John to Lucy was what John Hay saw in her—an "indefinable fascination" and a "magnetic vitality." She had another asset in Booth's mind that had nothing to do with looks or personality. She had respectability. Marriage to a senator's daughter would have increased John's own respectability and social status.

Whatever else was going through his mind, John began thinking about marriage. A few days after the inauguration, he wrote to his mother confiding his feelings for Lucy and that he was going to ask her to marry him.

John's mother already knew about his feelings for Lucy. She had always had a sixth sense about her favorite son.[20] Besides, Mary Ann wrote back, his secret was no secret at all. His brother Edwin already knew all about it. A friend of Edwin's had told him John was "paying great attention to a fine young lady in Washington." "You have so often been dead in love," his mother wrote, "and this may prove like the others." Knowing him better than anyone else, she urged him not to be "like a child with a new toy, [who] only craves the possession of it."

Then came the big question: "Would her father give his consent?" Mary Ann Booth, married to an actor, mother of three actors, was well aware of the low opinion most people had about the acting profession. "You know in my partial eyes you are a fit match for any woman, no matter who she may be—but some fathers have higher notions."[21]

A few days after receiving his mother's letter, John asked Lucy to marry him. She said she would. They agreed to keep their engagement secret and exchanged rings. A week before the assassination, dining with Samuel Chester in New York, John told him that the ring on his finger was from a woman to whom he had just become engaged.

Lucy's cousin, John Parker Hale Wentworth, was also in on the secret. The day after the inauguration, Wentworth and Lucy were in John's room at the National Hotel. No one knows what they spoke of, but John and Lucy each wrote some verses on the back of an unused envelope. John's poem read:

> Now, in this hour, that we part,
> I will ask to be forgotten never.
> But in thy pure and guiltless heart
> Consider me thy friend dear Ever
> J. Wilkes Booth

The verses on the other side read:

> "For of all sad words from
> Tongue or pen.
> The saddest are these—
> It might have been."
> March 5th 1865
> In John's room.[22]

The verse in quotes is from "Maud Muller," a poem written in 1856 by John Greenleaf Whitter. Unlike the other, it wasn't signed. Handwriting analysis later proved it was written by Lucy.[23] Women of Lucy's social standing weren't supposed to visit gentlemen in their room. Lucy was not conventional. And she was in love.

Some historians speculate the two lovers wrote those poems about parting because they were broken-hearted over Lucy's leaving for Spain with her father, the United States' newly appointed minister to that country. Since Hale didn't receive approval until just before the assassination, that speculation of romantic tearful goodbyes is anachronistic. The poems were not to one another. They were to Lucy's cousin and John's roommate at the hotel, John Wentworth. Wentworth had come to Washington for the inauguration. Now that it was over, he was leaving for southern California as an Indian Affairs Agent. The poems were a goodbye to Wentworth.[24]

John had also confided to his brother June he was "in love with a lady in Washington"[25] and was going to marry her.[26] He also told Asia. A few weeks after John's death, Asia wrote Jean Anderson that "their marriage (John's and Lucy's) was to have been in a year, when she promised to return from Spain for him, either with her father or without him."[27]

The one thing that could always be counted on with John when it came to women was that he couldn't be counted on at all. All the while John was courting Lucy, he was plotting to kidnap Lincoln and take him to Richmond. Success would have barred his return to Washington and marriage to Lucy. It is unlikely Lucy would have left her family and gone to live with John in the South. Skeptics have good reason to doubt how genuine John's feelings for Lucy were. A skeptic might also point out that besides Lucy's photo, John had photos of four other women in his pocket when he died. Would a man in love and engaged to be married carry pictures of other women alongside his fiancée's photo?

Moreover, the night before he made the fateful decision to murder Abraham Lincoln, John probably spent the night with prostitute Ella Starr.

Whatever feelings, genuine or otherwise, he had for Lucy and all the other women in his life, John's first love was always John. Everyone else and everything else came second.

## 23

# ANYTHING THAT PLEASES YOU: ELLA STARR

A fter Confederate General Robert E. Lee surrendered his army to General Ulysses Grant on April 9, 1865, the war was essentially over. John was depressed and drinking even more heavily than usual, sometimes quaffing a quart of brandy in less than two hours.[1] John's friend John Deery thought his drinking was more than just a spree. Deery sensed John was tormented by some inner stress.

The day after Lee's surrender, John bumped into Henry Phillips, one of the stock actors at Ford's Theatre. Phillips was on his way to Jesse Birch's saloon with some friends. He invited John to come along. John nodded. "Anything to drive away the blues," John said.[2]

"What gives you the blues?" Phillips asked.

"This news [Lee's surrender] is enough to give any man of right feelings the blues," John answered. Phillips and the men with him didn't say anything. After John left, Phillips turned to his companions. "He is a rank rebel," he grumbled.[3]

The next day John's emotions swung from blue to raging red. Standing outside the White House with Lewis Powell and David Herold and thousands of others, John waited to hear Lincoln speak about his plans for the future. When Lincoln told the crowd he was considering giving the vote to black soldiers who had fought for the Union, John became livid.

"By God, I'll run him through. That's the last speech he will ever make," he muttered.[4]

John could not change the outcome of the war. There was no longer any point to abducting Lincoln. But if Lincoln were dead, there would no longer be talk about turning the country over to the black man.

The day after Lincoln's speech, on the afternoon of Thursday, April 13, John was on his way to pick up his mail at Ford's Theatre when he bumped into actor Edward Emerson. John was visibly agitated. In the course of their conversation John swore that "somebody ought to kill the old scoundrel."[5]

Emerson was startled at John's outburst. He told him he didn't want to hear such talk and was leaving. John's temper was too far gone for him to stop. In one quick motion he snatched Emerson's cane from his hand and slammed it down on Emerson's shoulder, breaking the cane in pieces.[6]

At that instant John made up his mind that the "somebody" who ought to kill Lincoln was John Wilkes Booth. And he thought he knew how.

With the idea of killing Lincoln now rattling inside his head, he hastened over to Grover's Theatre five blocks away on Pennsylvania Avenue. Grover's and Ford's were Washington's two main theatres. John had played in both and was on personal terms with both their managers. He had heard that C. Dwight Hess (most acquaintances called him C. D.), part owner and manager of Grover's Theatre, was planning a spectacular illumination, in addition to *Aladdin and the Wonderful Lamp*, the play for Friday night. Lincoln had been a regular guest at both Ford's Theatre and Grover's Theatre. Lincoln preferred Grover's Theatre and often invited Leonard Grover to sit in the box with him. John thought it likely Hess would be sending Lincoln complimentary tickets for the show.[7]

John's mind was racing. It would be a golden opportunity to kill the scoundrel, his chance to avenge the South. He would be remembered forever for killing a tyrant. He would be Brutus to Lincoln's Caesar. And he would kill him in a theater. It would be the consummate act of his career.

Acting on his hunch, John made his way to Grover's Theatre. Nonchalantly, he asked Hess if he was planning to invite Lincoln to see the illumination on Friday night. Hess said he had in fact intended to send Lincoln an invitation but forgot. He thanked John for reminding him and sent the invitation right off.[8]

At long last John felt that fate was on his side. He would kill Lincoln at Grover's Theatre while he was sitting in the presidential box.

After leaving Hess, John went upstairs to Deery & Simpson's Billiard Saloon. He chatted with John Deery, an old friend, then said something that surprised Deery. John asked him to buy him a ticket for Friday night in a seat next to the presidential box. Deery was puzzled. John could have had a ticket for free from Hess. Why did he want to buy one? John said something about wanting to pay for it himself and handed him some money, saying he would pick up the ticket later.[9]

John was too excited to sleep that night. Around 2:00 a.m. he wrote a cryptic letter to his mother telling her "everything is dull; that is, has been until last night," apologizing for its brevity with "am in haste."[10]

The letter wasn't written from his room at the National Hotel. Walter Burton, the proprietor and night clerk at the National Hotel, said the bed in John's room had not been slept in that night.[11] Although engaged to Lucy Hale, John most likely spent the night with his favorite prostitute, Ella Starr.

At nineteen, Ella Starr, a.k.a. Nellie Starr or Ella Turner, was "a rather pretty, light haired little woman."[12] Jim Ferguson, owner of the Greenback saloon and restaurant next to Ford's Theater where John often ate with Ella on occasion, said Ella was one of the most beautiful women he had ever seen. It was obvious that John was very fond of her, said Ferguson, and she was as "fierce as a tigress in her devotion" to him.[13]

Like John, Ella was a bastard. Her mother, Ellen Flynn, had married John Starr in Baltimore in 1831. He died four years later, leaving her destitute with two children, John and Mary Jane. With no means of support, she did what many other women with two dependents and no family did—she became a prostitute. Ella was born in 1844 or 1845, fathered by one of her mother's visitors. Ellen had no idea who the father was and gave Ella her dead husband's name.

In 1852, when she was about seventeen, Ella's sister Mary Jane married Henry Treakle, a "very respectable typo" (a printer). After their marriage Mary Jane moved from Baltimore to Petersburg, Virginia, with her new husband and brought Ella to live with them.[14] Her brother's whereabouts at that time are unknown.

Mary Jane's "matrimonial knot" came undone a short time after she married. Whether they divorced or simply separated isn't known. Like her mother, Mary Jane had no money and took up the only profession open to her. She spent a brief time in Richmond and then moved to Washington to work at her mother's brothel. By this time Mother Starr was the prosperous madam of a bawdy house in Washington where the "Cyprians," "Daughters of Eve," "Fallen Angels," "Painted Jezebels," and "Women of the Town" practiced the world's oldest profession.[15]

Prostitution had always been rampant in Washington, but nothing like it was during the war. By 1862, "women of the town," gaudily dressed in gaily feathered hats, satin dresses, and jewelry, openly promenaded or rode with officers in their carriages along Pennsylvania Avenue and dined with them in restaurants next to the city's respectable citizens. One army officer was said to have attended a minstrel show at the Old Fellow's Hall with a harlot on each arm.[16]

At the height of the Civil War sex trade, Major William Doster, Washington's provost marshal, tallied more than 450 bawdy houses of all types in the city. The better-known houses had names like "The

Haystack," "The Ironclad," "The Oven," "The Wolf's Den," "The Devil's Own," and "The Blue Goose," or "Madam Wilton's Private Residence for Ladies." With thousands of off-duty soldiers, bureaucrats, politicians, office seekers, professionals of every sort, gamblers, and laborers, Washington was a magnet for prostitutes from towns and cities along the East Coast and Midwest. Ambitious madams from New York, Philadelphia, Baltimore, and as far away as Chicago and St. Louis closed their houses and headed for Washington with their best girls. Any place and every place was a potential sex mart. Bawdy houses were surrounded by saloons, groceries, local businesses, and private boarding houses. Prostitutes in the better class bawdy houses lived where they worked. Those in lesser houses lived in the same boarding houses as other working men and women and often plied their trade in their rooms, or at hotels, private homes, the back rooms of gambling dens, music halls, saloons, or in parks and alleyways.

Mother Starr's three-story bordello at 62 Ohio Avenue was one of Washington's more fashionable bawdy houses in "Hooker's Division," in present-day Federal Triangle.[17] It was called "Hooker's Division" because it was where General Joe Hooker's troops were stationed when he was in charge of defending the city.[18] It was just a coincidence that the general had the same surname as the slang term for prostitute. Prostitutes were already known as "hookers" when Joe Hooker was in short pants.[19] During his evening buggy rides with Mary, Lincoln would have seen the comings and goings at many of the brothels and saloons in "Hooker's Division" and heard their "inmates," many of whom had strong secessionist leanings, cheering for Jeff Davis and shouting Stonewall Jackson would soon be there blowing the city to hell.[20]

After Mary Jane took over her mother's brothel, the house became known as Mollie Turner's, the name Mary Jane began calling herself to avoid being found if someone were looking for her. Ella also adopted the Turner surname. A year or two later Mary Jane married John C. Burns, a pimp, about whom nothing else is known, but she never took his name.

Mollie's bawdy house was one of John's favorites. It was an exclusive house with just three "inmates"—Mary Jane (Mollie), Ella, and Fannie Henderson, as well as its own cook. According to Washington's provost marshal's listing of all the city's brothels, Mollie's was a class 1 brothel (ratings ranged from class 1 to "very low").[21] Upscale brothels like Mollie Turner's were left alone by the police because of the embarrassment that might occur if a senator or other important dignitary were among the "johns" taken into custody during a raid. Besides, police officers and detectives were also among their clients.

John Deery recalled a particular time that he and John were regulars at Mollie Turner's. Deery was there to see Mollie, the "young landlady," while John was there to be with "her rather cold younger sister" who he said was "slavishly devoted to him."[22] Several years later Deery repeated the story, saying that his lady of the night was Mollie Turner. He didn't recall her sister's name.[23]

Although Ella was a "working girl," John, like many army officers and politicians who caroused in public with their favorite prostitutes, occasionally took Ella out to eat at restaurants like Jim Ferguson's and sometimes took her with him when he went out of town. As usual with John, he never confined his attentions to only one woman. By February 1865, he was seeing less of Ella and paying more attention to Senator John Hale's daughter, Lucy.

Desperate to see him again, Ella sent him a note:

My Darling Boy,
    Please call this evening as soon as you receive this note &
I'll not detain you five minutes—for god's sake come.
    Yours Truly
    E. S.

If you will not come send a note.[24]

Another letter, this one signed only "N" for Nellie and dated Friday 6:00 p.m. implored him to "Please try and come down tomorrow as soon after two as possible? You can dine privately with me [dine was under-lined]. So do not mind your dinner. Be very good [very underlined] until I see you. Anything that pleases you will be acceptable."[25] There is no indication that John answered her note or called on her until April 13, 1865, the night before he assassinated Lincoln.

There was another note from yet another prostitute that John never saw. It was sent from New York and dated that same day, April 13, 1865, but was postmarked April 19. It carried the signature "Etta" and stated that she had received John's letter dated April 12 saying he would be in the city on the sixteenth. Etta wrote that she sympathized with John and had also had the blues since the fall of Richmond "and like you, feel like doing something desperate." Etta said that due to a misunderstanding, her landlady had told her to leave, and she was now living in a hotel and had used up all the money John had given her when they last met. She needed him to send more, she said, now that she was keeping herself "secluded as a nun…as you desired…which is not agreeable to me as you have found ere this, but anything to oblige you darling…Don't let anything discourage you."[26]

After the assassination, Colonel John A. Foster, at the Judge Advo-cate's Office, believed if he could find out who the mysterious "Etta" was, it would lead him to other links in the conspiracy. He sent a copy of the letter to Police Superintendent John Kennedy in New York asking him to search all the brothels in New York to find "Etta."

"After eighteen hours constant search [of] every public and private house of prostitution of a class such as Booth could visit," Kennedy wrote back he hadn't been able to locate anyone named Etta. John was a frequent visitor at many New York brothels and was said to be fond of Sally Andrews, the landlady of No. 67 West Street. Kennedy also learned from another prostitute, Anne Horton, at No. 3 Clark Street, that she had had a close relationship with John, but he had broken it off. She had tried to win him back but hadn't seen him for three months or more.

Neither Anne Horton nor Sally Andrews fit the case of "Etta," Ken-nedy reported back. He was convinced the letter was a hoax. He had not been able to find any instance of a boarder who had had a misunderstanding with her landlady and had not found anyone registering in the hotel where Etta said she was staying. "A letter written Thursday 13th, not posted until Wednesday 19th tells its own story," said Kennedy, "especially when the tenor of it, and other circumstances have already made it fishy."[27]

If the Etta letter were a hoax, as it seems, it begs the question of who concocted it and why. The author must have been someone from New York who was aware of John's affairs with at least two New York prostitutes. The mystery of the Etta letter has never been solved.

# 24

# ASSASSINATION

April 14, 1865, was a holy day in Christendom—Good Friday, the
anniversary of Jesus Christ's crucifixion. It had now been five days
since Robert E. Lee surrendered the Army of Northern Virginia,
the Confederacy's main military force, to Union Lieutenant General
Ulysses S. Grant. Confederate General Joe Johnston still had a sizable
army in the Carolinas, and there were still pockets of Confederates in
arms elsewhere, but the bloody fratricidal war that had torn the country
apart for four years was virtually over.

President Abraham Lincoln woke around 7:00 a.m., dressed, and
shambled down the hall to work in his office before he breakfasted. Sitting at his table that morning, Lincoln donned his specs and wrote a note
to General Grant. Grant and his wife, Julia, had arrived in Washington
the day before and were staying at the Willard Hotel on Pennsylvania
Avenue, about two blocks from the White House. Willard's was not
Washington's largest hotel, but it was its most posh. While both North-
erners and Southerners lodged there, they used different doors so as not
to run into one another.[1] When they arrived, Grant received an invitation

to ride with Lincoln and his wife later that evening to watch the city's
"grand illumination." Mary pointedly omitted Julia from the invitation;
a few weeks earlier they had had a falling-out. Sometime during their
ride through the city, Lincoln invited Grant and his wife to go with him
and Mary to the theatre the following night.

Mary Lincoln received two invitations to go to the theatre on April
14. The earlier invitation was from C. D. Hess, manager of Grover's
Theatre, to see *Aladdin and the Wonderful Lamp* and the special illuminations he was planning for Friday.[2] The second invitation, from Dick
Ford at Ford's Theatre, arrived at the White House sometime during
breakfast.

Mary asked Lincoln if he would mind going to Ford's Theatre instead
of Grover's Theatre to see *Our American Cousin,* a comedy about Asa
Trenchard, a good-natured rube from Vermont who visits England to
claim a family estate. Laura Keene, playing Asa's kissing cousin (although
she was forty at the time), was the star of the show. She owned the rights
to the play and had performed in it more than a thousand times. This
was to be her last performance in Washington. Lincoln said he didn't
care and would go to Ford's Theatre if that was what Mary preferred.

After breakfast, Mary sent a note to Dick Ford saying she and Lincoln and the Grants would be happy to accept his invitation. Another
note went to Hess thanking him for his invitation. They would not be
attending, but their son Tad and his chaperone were happy to go in their
stead.

Harry Ford, Dick's brother and the theatre's treasurer, was ecstatic.
Good Friday was one of the worst box office nights of the year, and he
had expected most theatregoers would be at the "illumination" at rival
Grover's Theatre that night. The president's presence would boost ticket
sales. Even better, Mrs. Lincoln said that General Grant and his wife
would be accompanying them. The two most famous people in America
at his theatre would bring the gawkers out. Harry lost no time blocking
off the presidential box seats on the cardboard seating plan posted in the
ticket window. In the margin he wrote, "President and his party will be

at the theatre tonight." Then he dashed off a note to the newspapers announcing their attendance in time for the afternoon edition.

That same morning, John breakfasted unusually early at his hotel with Lucy Hale,[3] then he strolled over to Booker and Stewart's barbershop on E Street around 9:00 a.m. to get a shave and haircut. On the way he met David Herold, Michael O'Laughlen, and two other men. John had sent word to his gang to meet him there but didn't say why.

John was always vain about his personal appearance. "In his leisure, he liked to stand in front of the Theatre [Ford's], twirling his mustache and frankly exhibiting himself," said Joseph Hazelton, Ford's Theatre's program boy.[4] It was especially important to look dashing that day. History would remember him not just for what he did but how he looked when he did it.

Charlie Wood had been a barber in Baltimore before moving to Washington and had cut John's hair when he was a boy. Wood had just returned from cutting Secretary of State William H. Seward's hair at his home. Seward was bedridden, having been injured in a carriage accident several days before. John slid into Wood's chair. Wood lathered and shaved his face and sculpted his distinctive horseshoe mustache. That done, he sprinkled John's black, curly hair with tonic and trimmed it. Wood recalled that John seemed to be in an upbeat mood.[5]

Telling his accomplices to wait in the barbershop for a while, John hastened over to Grover's Theatre to make sure Lincoln was coming that night. Outside the theatre Helen Moss and her sister-in-law Julia Hess, the manager's wife, were chatting. Both looked downcast. What was wrong, he asked? Helen Moss told him a messenger from the White House had just left a note that the Lincolns wouldn't be there that night.[6]

John was crestfallen. He couldn't believe what Helen Moss had just told him. He burst into Hess's office to make sure.

Helen Moss wasn't wrong. Lincoln would not be there that night. John was downhearted. Fate was again conspiring against him. Outside Grover's Theatre, John got into a heated argument about the war with George Wren and a number of other actors loitering about after that morning's rehearsal. Wren thought John had been drinking. It wasn't liquor that was roiling John; it was frustration.[7]

John trudged back to the barbershop, told his gang to go about their business, and drifted back to his hotel. When he came in, Henry Merrick, the hotel clerk, thought John looked unusually pale.[8]

Disheartened, his dream of lasting fame now dashed forever, John brooded in his room until before noon then strolled over to Ford's Theatre, five blocks away, to collect his mail. Providing a mailing address was one of the courtesies Ford's Theatre provided for actors. Spotting the dapper actor coming down the street, carrying his gold-handled cane and faultlessly dressed in a loose hanging cape and his gray Inverness overcoat with a chinchilla collar and deep sleeves, Harry Ford remarked to a man standing beside him, "Here comes the handsomest man in America."[9]

As he was picking up his letters at the box office, John noticed the diagram of the theatre's floorplan through the ticket window and Harry Ford's penciled comment in the margin that Lincoln and his party would be at the theatre that night.[10]

"Is the old scoundrel going to be here tonight?" he asked Harry.

Ford told him he shouldn't talk that way about the president. And yes, Lincoln was coming to see the show that evening along with General Grant and his wife. In fact, stagehands were at that very moment removing the partition between boxes seven and eight on the second floor "Dress Circle" to create a single, larger presidential box for the Lincolns and their guests.

John's mind was spinning. As he sat down on the front steps to read his mail, he realized here was the golden opportunity he'd been hoping for. Even better, it was a chance to kill not just Lincoln but Grant as well.

Lost in thought, he left the theatre and walked toward Pennsylvania Avenue. On the way he bumped into an old friend, John F. Coyle, editor of the *Washington National Intelligencer*. As the two men shook hands,

John casually asked Coyle, "What would be the result if someone would put Lincoln and the cabinet out of the way?"

"We don't have any Brutuses in these days," Coyle chuckled.

John chuckled in return, said goodbye, and went on his way.[11]

As he continued walking, John realized he might be able to decapitate the whole federal government by also eliminating Vice President Andrew Johnson and Secretary of State William H. Seward as well. The ensuing chaos would give the South a chance to regroup and survive.[12] As long as General Joe Johnston was still viable in North Carolina, John believed the Confederacy was not doomed. He left word for what remained of his gang to meet him at 8:00 p.m. in Lewis Powell's room at the Herndon House.

An hour or two later John returned to Ford's Theatre to reconnoiter the upstairs presidential box. John Maddox, Ford's Theatre property manager, saw him approaching and invited him to go next door for drinks at Peter Taltavull's Star Saloon. John declined at first, saying he had a pain in his heart. Then he abruptly changed his mind.[13] Later that same day, Bill Ferguson would also ask him to go with him for drinks. Again, John declined at first, claiming "a touch of pleurisy"[14] was giving him chest pain. Then, as before, he changed his mind.

After drinking with Maddox, John returned to Ford's Theatre, broke off a wooden piece from one of the musician's stands in the orchestra, and went up the stairs to the presidential box. If anyone saw him, they didn't think anything of his being there. He was just one of the actors and a friend of the manager's.

John was very familiar with the layout of the presidential box. He had sat in the box himself to watch plays at Ford's Theatre when it was not otherwise occupied.

The entrance to the presidential box was through a ten-foot-long by four-foot-wide vestibule. John knew that when the door to the vestibule was locked, no one would be able to enter the box. But the lock on the door had been broken for some time. Once inside the vestibule, he whittled a notch in the wall behind the door and jammed in the wooden bar to make sure it would keep the door from opening once he was inside. John planned to escape by jumping over the balustrade at the front of the box. It was nine feet above the stage,[15] but he had made those kinds of leaps before.

Satisfied, he removed the bar, scooped up the scrapings from the floor, and placed the bar behind the door. Walking briskly, John headed over to the Kirkwood House where Vice President Andrew Johnson was staying. Hours earlier, John had told George Atzerodt to register at the same hotel.

John had had a passing acquaintance with Johnson when Johnson was governor of Tennessee. They had even kept two sisters as mistresses and been seen carousing together. He asked the clerk at the front desk if Johnson was in. Was John calling on Johnson just to make sure he was still at the Kirkwood House? Possibly it was also to ask Johnson for a pass to cross military lines so that he could make his escape without being unduly questioned at checkpoints. He would tell Johnson he wanted to lease a theatre in the South. Whatever his reasons, before leaving John left a note for Johnson: "Don't wish to disturb you; are you at home?"[16] It was a meaningless message. The clerk had just told him Johnson wasn't "at home." It is just one more enigma about the assassination that keeps historians scratching their heads.

Next he went to Mary Surratt's boarding house on H Street. Once John Surratt, Mary's son, became an integral member of John's gang, John had become a regular visitor at the Surratt's. In no time at all, he had become quite friendly with Mary, a homely widow of about forty-five. Rich or poor, young or old, homely or beautiful, there was no woman John failed to charm. Louis Weichmann, a boarder at Mary Surratt's boarding house, thought Mary and her daughter Ann were rivals for John's attention. Mary called John "my Pet." In a letter he wrote to his cousin Belle Seaman, John Surratt described how excited his mother and sister Anna became when John Booth came to the house.

You wouldn't believe, John wrote, the "scamperings...such brushing and fixing."[17]

In March, when John was still plotting to kidnap Lincoln, he sent John Surratt, Atzerodt, and Herold to Mary Surratt's tavern in Surrattsville to cache two Spencer carbines, ammunition, and supplies for when they would be needed. The afternoon of the assassination, he asked Mary to take a parcel for him to her tavern for someone to pick up later that night.

No woman said no to John. Mary Surratt was no exception. John's photograph with the word "Booth" written in pencil on the back of it was among the things she had hidden in her room when she was later taken into custody. Whether Mary knew there were binoculars inside the package, or what John was planning, is another detail historians still argue about. As she handed the package to John Lloyd, the man to whom she had rented the tavern, she told him to have it and the "shooting irons" ready later that night.[18]

When General Grant returned from his ride with Lincoln and Mary on Thursday night to see the city-wide illuminations, he told his wife Julia that Lincoln had invited them to go to the theatre on Friday. Still smarting from an earlier quarrel with Mary, Julia didn't want anything to do with Mary. Lincoln was Grant's superior, but Julia was his wife. Grant had been married long enough to know his priorities. He told Lincoln the day he hadn't known Julia had already made plans to visit their daughter in New Jersey and they would be leaving on the four o'clock train.[19]

When Lincoln informed Mary that the Grants would not be going with them, Mary sent a last-minute invitation to Clara H. Harris and her fiancé Major Henry Reed Rathbone, asking them if they'd like to go. Clara Harris was the daughter of New York Senator Ira Harris, a Lincoln family friend. She and Rathbone had both been guests at

Lincoln's reception in Albany, New York, in 1861 on his way to his inauguration. Clara and Rathbone were both happy to go with the Lincolns the night of the fourteenth.

After leaving Mary Surratt's, John reserved a horse for the day at James Pumphrey's stable on C Street. Around 3:00 p.m., Jim Ferguson saw John on his horse talking to John Mathews, one of Ford's Theatre's stock actors. Mathews was an old friend of John's. They had known each other since they were boys growing up in Baltimore. They had had a falling-out when John tried to recruit Mathews for his kidnapping plan and Mathews refused, but John had gotten over his anger and had visited with him in his room at the Petersen House, across the street from Ford's Theatre. Ironically, it was the same room to which Lincoln would be taken after he was shot. The bed on which John rested when he visited Mathews was the same bed on which Lincoln would die.[20]

While they were talking, Mathews looked up and noticed Grant and his driver riding by in an open carriage on their way to the train station.

"Why, Johnny," he motioned to John, "there goes Grant. I thought he was to be coming to the theater this evening with the President."

John was just as surprised. "Where?" he exclaimed.

Mathews pointed to the barouche hurrying by. John stared for a second, squeezed Mathews's hand in a farewell shake, and spurred his horse into a gallop to overtake the barouche.[21] Passing the carriage, John wheeled his horse back in the opposite direction to make sure it was Grant speeding by. Seeing him leaving, John must have thought that once again his plans would come to naught. If Grant were not going to be at the theatre that night, Lincoln might likewise have changed his mind.

Gloomily John trotted back to Ford's Theatre and stabled his horse at a small private stable he had leased behind the theater. Anxious for any word about Lincoln, he trekked over to Peter Taltavull's Star Saloon next door to Ford's Theatre. He had to find out if Lincoln had also cancelled. Not hearing anything about a cancellation, he inwardly drew a breath of relief. Grant had got away. He still had Lincoln.

Around 5:00 p.m., Lincoln and Mary took their usual buggy ride together through the city, escorted by two cavalrymen. Mary had not seen him so lighthearted in years. He even seemed "playful" to her.

"Dear Husband," she leaned toward him, "You almost startle me with your great cheerfulness."

"Well I may feel so Mary," Lincoln answered, "I consider this day, the war has come to a close."[22]

They talked about what they would do after his term in office was over. He had saved some money, he said, but not enough to support them. "We will go back to Illinois, and I will open a law-office at Springfield or Chicago and practice law, and least do enough to help give us a livelihood."[23]

After he left Peter Taltavull's Star Saloon, John returned to his room at the National Hotel, changed into a black wool overcoat, black inner jacket, dark riding breeches, and knee-high black leather boots, donned his black slouch hat, and loaded his derringer.

John's derringer was a muzzle-loaded, .44 caliber, single-shot weapon. Less than four inches long, it only weighed a half pound and fit easily inside his coat pocket. A revolver could fire up to six times without having to reload, but a single shot was all he would need when he entered the presidential box. As far as John knew, Lincoln and his wife would be the only ones in the box. John slipped the gun into one of his coat pockets and a Bowie knife into another. The knife was just in case someone tried to interfere with his escape. Its blade had "Liberty" and "America" and "The Land of the Free" stamped into it.

John did not leave much else in the hotel. Charging through rural Maryland and Virginia, he would have little use or room for the personal belongings he left behind. Whether it was deliberate or merely carelessness, he didn't bother destroying the letter Samuel Arnold had written him a month before, warning him to check with Richmond before going ahead with kidnapping Lincoln. There was also another mysterious letter in the trunk from an unidentified woman, pleading for him not to go ahead with his dangerous plan.[24]

Around 7:00 p.m., John came down from his room and tossed his keys to George Bunker, the night clerk at the National Hotel. Just before he left he asked Bunker if he was going to the theatre that night. Before he could answer, John added, "You should. There will be some fine acting there tonight!"[25]

A half hour later, John dropped in at Peter Taltavull's Star Saloon again and had a drink with Ford's Theatre's orchestra leader Bill Withers. As they were talking about actors they knew, Withers joked that John would never be as great as his father. "An inscrutable smile flitted across his face," said Withers. "When I leave the stage," John replied, "I will be the most talked about man in America." Withers didn't give it much thought at the time. Later he remembered it with a shock.[26]

John rendezvoused with Atzerodt, Paine, and Herold in Powell's room at the Herndon House around 8:00 p.m.[27] They had no prior inkling of what he was planning. He would kill Lincoln, Powell was assigned to kill Secretary of State Seward, Atzerodt was assigned to kill Vice President Johnson, and Herold was to show Powell the way to Seward's house. John told them to time their assassinations for about 10:15 p.m. to coincide with his killing Lincoln.

At 7:00 p.m., William Crook, Lincoln's usual body guard at the White House was still at his post. He was supposed to be relieved at 4:00 p.m. When his relief, John Parker, arrived, Crook told him there would be two others in the president's coach that night. He suggested Parker get to the theatre about fifteen minutes ahead of the presidential party.

The Lincolns left the White House around 8:15 p.m. It was a chilly night. A damp heavy fog clogged the air. The streets were still rutted and muddy from the Spring thaw. The Lincolns' coachman drove them to Fifteenth and H Streets and picked up Clara Harris and her fiancé, Major Henry Rathbone. Parker met them when they arrived at the theatre a little after 9:00 p.m.

A large gas lamp in front of the theatre lit the entrance. The Lincolns and their guests stepped onto a wide wooden platform so that they wouldn't muddy their shoes.

Usher James O'Brien led the party up the winding staircase to the second-floor dress circle. Lincoln tried to slip into the presidential box unnoticed. As he edged along the outer wall to the vestibule, his six-foot-four-inch height, long black wool coat, and stovepipe hat were instantly recognizable. Everyone rose and cheered.

Lincoln bowed in acknowledgment and continued into the box. As he and the others passed through the vestibule, no one noticed the notch in the wall or the bar on the floor behind the door. They walked to the end of the vestibule and through the door to box eight, into the expanded presidential box. Parker followed. His duties were to escort the president to and from wherever he went, not remain the rest of the time with him. Parker left after the Lincolns and their guests were seated.[28]

Lincoln gravitated to a velvet-covered rocker at the left-hand corner of the box behind one of the two yellow curtains at either end of the box. A gas-lit chandelier hanging from the ceiling provided dim light inside. Except to the actors on stage and people in the audience opposite the presidential box on the floor below, Lincoln was hidden from sight unless he leaned forward over the railing. Mary sat in a chair next to him. Clara Harris sat on the far side of the box and Major Rathbone sat behind her with his back to the door John planned to enter.

At 10:00 p.m. Powell and Herold reined in their horses outside Secretary of State Seward's house facing Lafayette Park. Seward was in bed, suffering from a concussion and broken bones after being thrown from his carriage. Powell forced his way into the house and managed to slash the bedridden Seward in the face with a knife and injure one of Seward's sons before being stopped by other members of the household.[29] Powell fought them off and bolted for the front door. Blind with rage, he stabbed a messenger who had just arrived and ran out of the house, looking for Davy Herold. Herold was not there. He had heard the screams from inside the house, panicked, and run off, leaving Powell, who was unfamiliar with Washington, on his own.

Everyone Powell injured at Seward's house would recover.

Around the same time that Powell was knocking on the door of the Seward house, George Atzerodt was at the Kirkwood House to kill Vice President Johnson. Neither Powell nor Atzerodt would have known where to find their quarry if John hadn't told them where they would be and when they would be there.

Seward's whereabouts were no problem. John knew Seward would be at home from reading the news about his accident. Just to be sure, he had seduced the Seward's chambermaid, Margaret Coleman, to pump her for information about which room was Seward's.[30]

John had made sure of Johnson's whereabouts by stopping at the hotel earlier that day and verifying that he was still there. The note John left for Johnson, later presented at the conspiracy trial—"I do not wish to disturb you, are you at home?"—has long perplexed historians. Why would John have written such a note if the desk clerk told him Johnson wasn't in? Just as perplexing is a version of the note—not presented at the trial—that the *New York Tribune* published on April 16, 1865: "I do not wish to disturb you, but would be glad to have an interview."

Did John come back for that interview and briefly meet with Johnson?[31] If so, that second message and their meeting may have been suppressed so as not to implicate Johnson in the assassination.[32] In return for the favor of a pass, John could have offered Johnson his favorite company. "Paying for political string pulling with sexual favors, has long been a second currency in Washington."[33]

John was well aware of Johnson's weakness for women. They had caroused together in Nashville before Johnson became vice president with Johnson's mistress and her sister.[34] John would not have to look very hard for someone to be with Johnson that night. Ella Starr was so much in love with him she had told him she would do "anything that pleases you."[35] If he told her he owed Johnson a favor and asked her to entertain him for the night, she would have gone along, guaranteeing that Johnson would be in his room when Azterodt came by. And by the way, could she make sure the door to his room was open?

None of that is known for certain. But it accounts for what later happened. What is known is that when Atzerodt made his way to the hotel, the door to Johnson's room was ajar, but he lost his nerve and fled, closing the door.

About a half hour later, former Wisconsin Governor Leonard Farwell pounded on Johnson's door. He had raced to the Kirkwood House from Ford's Theatre with the news that Lincoln had just been shot. Farwell waited for Johnson to open the door, but Johnson didn't answer. Farwell pounded again and yelled to Johnson, "If you are in this room, I must see you!"[36] Finally, Johnson opened the door.

Johnson may not have answered the door right away if Ella was with him.

John had acted in *Our American Cousin* twelve times, not including rehearsals. He knew all the lines by heart. He also knew the joke that would send the audience laughing so loud that the bark of a gunshot would be muffled.

Around 9:30 p.m., John left Peter Taltavull's Star Saloon and walked around to the back of the theatre to the stable where he left his horse. He saddled the mare, put on his spurs, walked the horse over to the back entrance of Ford's Theatre, and shouted for stagehand Ned Spangler to come hold the horse for him. Spangler told John he couldn't, as he was needed inside to change scenery. He called to "Peanut John," the boy selling peanuts in the theater, to come out and handed him the reins, saying John would soon come back for the horse.

Around ten o'clock in the evening, John entered the theatre, nodded to John Buckingham, the doorkeeper, listened in the lobby for a few moments to what the actors on stage were saying, and left. He came and went several more times before going upstairs to the Dress Circle. Buckingham later claimed he heard John humming to himself on his way up.[37]

Just as the Lincolns had about an hour earlier, John walked along the rear wall toward the other side of the theatre. Picking his way around the people who had moved their chairs into the aisle to better see the stage, he made his way toward the vestibule and the presidential box. Several people noticed him. Some said they saw him hand someone sitting outside the vestibule a card before entering. If he did, that person has never been identified.

Once inside the vestibule, John slid the wooden bar into the notch he had made earlier so that no one would be able to intrude. Then he squinted through a hole he had made that afternoon in the door to box seven. Although the gaslight inside had been turned down, John could still see Lincoln silhouetted in a rocking chair on the far left and Mary beside him. Clara Harris and Major Rathbone were out of his line of vision.

John nudged the door to box eight ajar and listened. It was nearing the moment when actress Helen Muzzy, as the scheming Mrs. Mountchessington, berates bumpkin Trenchard, played by Harry Hawk, for not knowing "the manners of good society." John waited for Harry Hawk to deliver his gut-busting comeback line:

"Don't know the manners of good society, eh? Well, I guess I know enough to turn you inside out, old gal-you sockdologizing old man-trap!" Today no one laughs when by rare chance someone says sock-dologizing, but in John's day it was a euphemism for an emasculating woman.

John eased the door open a second or two before the fateful line to fire at the crescendo of laughter. But he missed his cue and fired just as the laughter began to fade. Everyone in the audience heard the shot; no one knew what to think. The actors and stagehands knew there wasn't any gunshot in the play. Something was wrong.

John's timing was off because he hadn't expected anyone else to be in the box other than Lincoln and Mary. When he eased the door open, expecting to creep up behind Lincoln, he saw a man in the sofa sitting with his back to him. He was momentarily flummoxed. Who else was in the room? Caught off guard, he hesitated. Instead of firing within inches of Lincoln's head, John fired from just inside the door, about five feet from Lincoln, seconds later than intended.

At the very moment John fired, Lincoln was leaning over the balustrade and looking down to the left at someone in the audience.[38] There had been no time to aim. Even if he had, from a distance of five feet, a derringer is an inaccurate weapon because of the gun's recoil. In Columbus, Georgia, before he was shot in the thigh, he had missed a mark in the wall five feet away firing a derringer.

Leaning over the rail, Lincoln's head was a very small target. If John had been aiming at Lincoln's head, he likely would have missed because of the gun's recoil. Lincoln's back was a much larger target for a man hurrying his shot. Instead of hitting Lincoln in the back, the recoil jerked the derringer upward, sending the bullet slamming into the back of Lincoln's head. It entered behind his left ear at 450 feet per second, ploughed seven inches into his brain, and rendered him senseless.[39]

Jim Ferguson, the only one in the audience looking up at the presidential box at the moment of the assassination, saw Lincoln leaning over the bannister seconds before the shot. Ferguson could not see into the box because of the dim light inside, but he saw the "flash of a pistol." The flash, he said, didn't come from behind Lincoln. It came from "right back in the box."[40]

Rathbone didn't see the shot. He heard it from behind him. Startled, he jumped up and turned toward the assassin. A dense cloud of gun smoke momentarily obstructed his view of the assassin, but not completely. Rathbone lunged at the gunman.

John flung his now useless gun away and pivoted toward his attacker, slashing him with his dagger. Rathbone instinctively raised his arm to ward off the blow. The knife cut through Rathbone's jacket, slicing into his arm between his elbow and shoulder, barely missing the brachial artery.

John dashed to the balustrade. The nine-foot jump onto the stage was formidable, but John had made similar leaps before. This time he was distracted. Out of the corner of his eye he saw Rathbone coming at him. As he leaped one of his spurs caught in the flag draping the balustrade, and he crashed off balance onto the stage, breaking the fibula bone in his leg above the ankle. Picking himself up, still defiant, he shouted, "Sic Semper Tyrannis" ("Thus Always To Tyrants," Virginia's state motto), and ran offstage, brandishing his knife to ward off anyone who tried to stop him.

Harry Hawk, alone on stage, was directly in John's path. "I did simply what any other man would have done," he later related to his father, "I ran."[41]

It took a few moments for the audience to realize what had happened. "There will never be anything like it on earth," actress Helen Truman recalled. "The shouts, groans, curses, smashing of seats, screams of women, shuffling of feet and cries of terror created a pandemonium that throughout all the ages will stand out in my memory as the hell of hells."[42]

Call boy Billy Ferguson was just gathering some books that he was supposed to place on a desk for the next scene when he heard the shot. Moments later he heard John crashing onto the stage. He ran into the passageway and was standing next to Laura Keene as John sped by between them, shoving them apart. John passed so close to Ferguson he could feel John's breath on his face.[43]

Orchestra leader William Withers was standing further back in the three-foot-wide passageway with actress Jeannie Gourlay when John came toward them, screaming for them to get out of the way. Gourlay was too slow. John pushed her back with one arm and slashed out at Withers, cutting a gash through the left side of Withers's coat, but not deep enough to wound him. The hapless Withers was too frightened to get out of the way. John slashed again, this time cutting him in the shoulder and neck. "Damn you," John grunted and shoved Withers sprawling to the floor.[44]

With no one else in the way John sped toward the unlocked rear door into Baptist Alley. Without a word, he struck Peanut John, who was holding his horse's reins, with the butt of his knife to get him out of the way then kicked him when the boy didn't move fast enough. Despite his broken leg, he mounted his horse and galloped off through Washington toward the Navy Yard Bridge. John was confident that he would be safe once he was across the Anacostia River into Maryland and Prince George's County. Only one man in that county had voted for Lincoln in the 1860 election.[45]

Ordered by an army sentry to halt and explain what he was doing out after the 9:00 p.m. curfew, John kept calm. Though he was feeling the pain in his leg, he managed not to grimace. With all the aplomb he could muster, he said he had been in Washington on an errand and was just finishing his business. He hadn't known about the curfew he said. Without thinking, he told the sentry his name was John Wilkes Booth and that he was heading for Beantown in southern Maryland. It was a fatal mistake. His pursuers would now be able to track him.

Ten minutes later David Herold crossed the same bridge. Despite everyone's opinion of him as being "dull," Herold didn't give the sentry his real name or state where he was going. Instead he said his name was Smith and he was heading for White Plains, Maryland.

Herold was the only other member of the gang to make it out of Washington. Powell and Atzerodt were later arrested. John Surratt was in Elmira, New York, on another mission and escaped to Canada before he could be apprehended.[46] Mary Surratt and Ned Spangler, who were suspected of helping John escape, were taken into custody and later charged as conspirators, as were Arnold and O'Laughlen.

The conspirators were not the only ones to be arrested. Everyone else at Ford's Theatre, actors as well as stagehands, was suspected of collusion in the assassination and arrested. Even though he was nowhere near Washington at the time, John T. Ford was also arrested and thrown in jail, as were his brothers Harry and Dick Ford. Laura Keene and Harry Hawk were arrested, given bail and passes to leave Washington, and then rearrested in Harrisburg. Carpenter Edmund Spangler was arrested, tried, and sentenced to hard labor on the flimsiest suspicion of complicity.

25

# I Have Too Great a Soul to Die Like a Criminal

**W**hen David Herold caught up with John, the two fugitives headed southeast to Surrattsville (now Clinton, Maryland). Riding hard, at midnight they reined in at Mary Surratt's tavern, ten miles from Washington, to pick up the guns and field glasses hidden there. Mary Surratt's telling Lloyd to have the "shooting irons" ready when John came for them later that night would go far to convict her as one of John's accomplices.[1]

In pain from his broken leg, John stayed saddled while Herold pounded on the door and retrieved the ammunition, guns, and field glasses—as well as a bottle of whiskey—from Lloyd. Herold handed one of the carbines up to John. John shook his head. He needed both hands to hold on to his spirited horse. They each took a long swallow from the whiskey bottle and headed out. As they were leaving, Herold boasted to Lloyd, "I will tell you some news. I am pretty certain we have assassinated the President and Secretary Seward."[2]

The two fugitives headed for Port Tobacco, intending to cross from there into Virginia, but the pain in John's leg had become excruciating.

211

Instead, John remembered Dr. Mudd and turned south to his home, far out of the way.

It was a fatal decision. Had John continued on to Port Tobacco some thirty miles further, he would have reached it by sunrise and crossed the Potomac River into Virginia long before their pursuers could have caught up to him. A day or two later, John would have been deep in the South where he could expect help as he and Herold made their way to Mexico.

Four hours later, around 4:00 a.m. on Saturday, John and Herold rode up at Dr. Mudd's house. Mudd cut John's boot from his leg, slipped off his stocking, and felt along the leg. John's fibula, one of the bones in his leg, was fractured about two inches above his ankle. In Mudd's judgment, "it was as slight a breaking as it could possibly be." After applying a makeshift splint, he told one of his servants to make a crutch. John and Herold stayed the night. In the morning John shaved off his mustache, breakfasted, and rested while Mudd left for Bryantown to procure a buggy for his injured patient. He was unable to find one but undoubtedly heard the news of the assassination. He was relieved when the two men said they were leaving. If they were taken prisoner at his home, he would be arrested as one of the conspirators. John paid him twenty-five dollars and set off for the Potomac River, about twenty miles away.[3]

When Dr. Mudd was later questioned he claimed he had not recognized the fugitive. The military tribunal didn't believe him. Dr. Mudd had met with John on at least three occasions. He was found guilty of aiding and abetting John but not of being personally involved in the assassination, and he was sentenced to life with hard labor at Fort Jefferson in the Dry Tortugas, seventy miles off Key West. He missed being hanged by one vote.[4]

Several miles after leaving Dr. Mudd's, the fugitives lost their way near the Zekiah Swamp. Around nine o'clock that night, they encountered Oswald Swann, a black tobacco farmer, who gave them food and whiskey and guided them to Rich Hill, the home of Samuel Cox, four miles from the Potomac River.

Cox was a wealthy land owner and a prominent member of the Confederate underground in southern Maryland. The two men had not met before, but by then Cox had heard the news that John Wilkes Booth had killed Lincoln. Cox knew he would be risking arrest if John were caught at his house. Federal troops had been seen combing the area, looking for the fugitives. Cox gave them some food but refused to let them stay in his house. He told his overseer, Franklin Robey, to take them to a gully in the woods about a mile away. Later that morning he sent Robey to relocate them to another spot in a dense pine thicket another half mile away on his neighbor's property. If John were caught, the neighbor, not Cox, would be arrested.[5] Cox then summoned Thomas Jones, about three miles away. Jones was a Confederate courier and did not shy away from helping the fugitives. While he made arrangements for getting the fugitives across the Potomac River, he brought them food, blankets, and newspapers.[6]

Far from the hero he imagined he would be for killing Lincoln, John was shocked to read in the newspapers that he was a pariah. Shivering under a blanket in the woods for the next five days, waiting for Jones to get them across the river, John put his thoughts down in a red leather pocket diary:

> I am here in despair...hunted like a dog...wet, cold and starving...every mans [sic] hand against me...And why? For doing what Brutus was honored for, [for] what made [William] Tell a hero....[I] am looked upon as a common cutthroat. My action was purer than either of theirs...I hoped for no gain...I struck for my country and that alone...I struck boldly, and not as the papers say. I can never repent it, though we hated to kill...I cannot repent it...our country owed all her trouble to him, and God simply made me the instrument of his punishment.[7]

After several mishaps, on April 23, 1865, the fugitives crossed the Potomac River into Virginia and made their way to Port Conway where

they met William Storke Jett and two other Confederate soldiers, Major
M. B. Ruggles and Lieutenant A. R. Bainbridge. The three men, former
members of Colonel John Singleton Mosby's cavalry, were waiting to
take the ferry across the Rappahannock River to Port Royal.

Herold introduced himself as David E. Boyd and John as his brother,
James William Boyd. James, he said, had been wounded in the leg while
escaping from prison where they had been held for some time.[8] Jett and
the others became suspicious Herold was hiding something. Never one
to keep a secret, Herold soon bragged, "we are the assassinators of the
President...Yonder is J. Wilkes Booth, the man who killed the President."[9]

While they were talking, John hobbled over to the group on his
rough-hewn crutch. He was no longer the handsomest man in America.
He was wearing his now seedy, black slouch hat, dark clothes, a cavalry
boot on one foot, and a black stocking on the other, inside a shoe cut
away at the top. His injured leg was noticeably swollen. His face was
haggard. He was bearded, not having shaved for several days. His eyes
were sunken, but they still had their peculiar bright glow.

"I suppose you have been told who I am?" he asked. Ruggles nodded.
Shifting his weight onto his crutch, John yanked his gun from his belt.

"I am worth $100,000 to the man who captures me," he said. There
was no emotion in his voice.[10] The three men replied they didn't sanction
his killing Lincoln, but "were not men to take 'blood money.'"

John put his gun back in his belt. Ruggles hoisted John onto his
horse, and they all crossed the river. After landing, Jett led them a short
way to the home of William Peyton, a Port Royal friend of his. Peyton
wasn't home but his daughter was. Jett asked her to take care of the
wounded man travelling with him until the day after tomorrow when he
would return for him. Miss Peyton agreed at first, but on seeing the
seedy, unshaven man she changed her mind. She protested the impropri-
ety of keeping a man in the house with her alone. She suggested Jett take
him to the Garrett house down the road.

Richard H. Garrett's farmhouse was a large wooden framed building with broad porches on every side. It rested on a little hill with rolling
fields spread out in every direction. Jett introduced himself as a local boy.

He had a wounded Confederate soldier with him, he said, by the name of John W. Boyd, who was on his way home and needed to rest because of his wound. Could Garrett take care of him for a day or two until Jett would return for him?

The Garretts hadn't heard about the assassination and took Jett at his word. Jett went on to Bowling Green while Ruggles and Bainbridge continued on their journey home. Before they left, John told Ruggles and Bainbridge that whatever happened, he would not be taken alive.[11]

Colonel Everton Conger, Lieutenant Luther Baker, and a twenty-six-man detachment from the Sixteenth New York Cavalry led by Lieutenant Edward P. Doherty were in hot pursuit of the fugitives. They had tracked them down to Port Conway where they were informed that Willie Jett and some Confederates had escorted two other men, one with a crutch, across the river not very long before and that Jett was going to see his girlfriend in Bowling Green, fifteen miles away.

After crossing over to Port Royal, Conger and his men sped down the road to Bowling Green. Without knowing it, they passed right by John and Herold at the Garrett farm. Jett was taken prisoner without a fight. Threatened with hanging, Jett told Conger John was at the Garrett farm. Conger ordered him to show them the way.[12]

The Garretts still didn't know the real identity of their guests, but Garrett's oldest son, Jack, was beginning to suspect they were not who they said they were. The second night of their stay, Jack told them they had to sleep in the barn instead of the house. Fearing the two strangers might steal their horses in the early morning, he locked them in.[13]

Around 2:00 a.m. on April 26, 1865, the federals were outside the Garrett farm. Doherty's men were exhausted. They had been chasing John for two days without sleep and with very little food. Energized at the prospect of finally capturing Booth, not to mention the reward money, they took down the outside fence and surrounded the house.

Once the men were in place, Conger pounded on the Garrett's front door. The first one out was Richard Garrett. Conger demanded to know where the two visitors were. Garrett dissembled, first claiming they were gone and rambling about how they had come without his consent and that he hadn't wanted them to stay. Conger ordered one of the cavalrymen to bring a lariat rope and threatened to hang Garrett if he didn't tell him where they'd gone. One of Garrett's sons hurriedly intervened for his father and told them the men Conger was looking for were in the barn.

With Doherty's cavalrymen positioned around the barn, Baker ordered John and Herold to come out. John clung to the remote possibility that the men outside were in fact Southerners. "For whom do you take me?" John shouted through the door.

"It doesn't make any difference," Baker shouted back. "Come out!"

John shouted back he would come out if they were friends, but not if they were foes.

Conger was growing impatient. "If you don't come out," he shouted, "I'll burn the building."

"If you will withdraw your men in line one hundred yards from the door, I will come out and fight you," he challenged.

Baker would have none of it. They had not come to fight, he shouted back; they'd come to take him prisoner.

Peering through the slats outside, David Herold saw the soldiers piling hay against the barn. He told John he wanted to give himself up. John called him a damned coward. "Surrender if you want, but I will fight and die like a man."

"There's a man in here [who] wants to come out," John shouted to his captors.

"You had better follow his example and come out!" Conger shouted back.

"No. I have not made up my mind," John answered. Then, as if it was all a stage drama, John again challenged his captors to fight outside. Conger replied that they were there to take John prisoner.

At that point, Herold shouted he was coming out. As soon as he exited the barn, he was seized and tied to a tree.

Conger ordered the troopers to put more hay against the barn. "We will fire the barn in two minutes if you do not come out," he shouted.

"Well, my brave boys," John shouted back, "prepare a stretcher for me."

Conger set the hay on fire. "It blazed very rapidly," Conger later recalled, "lit right up at once."

John did not have many choices. No matter what, he would not allow himself to be taken alive, paraded through Washington, and made to sit shackled in silence, enduring insults, a trial with an inevitable verdict, and inevitable death by hanging.

John had not forgotten the sad spectacle of John Brown's hanging. Brown had died bravely. John respected that. But he had died a shameful death. John had watched the condemned man climb the platform, his hands bound behind him, the hood drawn over his head and the noose looped around his neck. He had seen the body drop through the floor, spasmodically jerk, then dangle until the rope was cut.

John would not let that happen to him. "I have too great a soul to die like a criminal," he had written in his diary.[14] He would not shame his family with a criminal's death—especially his mother. He knew intuitively what she would want. In fact, his mother confessed a hope he would kill himself and spare the family the disgrace of his being hanged as a criminal.[15]

Burning to death was too horrible an option. Brutus had fallen on his own sword rather than be taken alive. Could he do anything less?

Conger peered through a crack between the wooden beams as the flames engulfed the barn. Seeing John start for the door at the other side of the barn, he ran around the outside. Just as Conger was halfway around, he heard the blast of a pistol.[16]

The shot struck John in the neck, severing his spinal cord and paralyzing him. No one knows for sure who fired the shot.[17] John vowed never to be taken alive. The only way to be sure that would never happen was to take his own life.[18] Most historians, however, believe Sergeant Thomas P. "Boston" Corbett's claim that he shot Booth. Although ordered to take him alive, Corbett, a self-castrated religious zealot, said he shot Booth through a large crack in the barn because he believed Booth was about to shoot one of the civilian detectives attached to his unit. "Providence," Corbett said, "directed my hand."[19]

Fatally wounded, unable to move, John was dragged from the burning barn onto the Garrett porch begging, "Kill me! Kill me!"

Baker replied he would do no such thing and sent for a doctor. Seventy-one-year-old Dr. Charles Urquhart from nearby Port Royal arrived within the hour. Urquhart did not need more than a few minutes to conclude the wound was fatal. He gave John an hour to live and went home.

While John was close to death on the Garrett porch, Everton Conger went through his pockets. Inside was a compass, a small pipe, shavings to make a fire with, a file, a spur, a stick pin inscribed "Dan Bryant to J.W.B.," a candle, a money order from a Canadian bank, about one hundred dollars in U.S. currency, a pocket diary, and five photos.

Conger glanced at the five photos (of Alice Gray, Helen Western, Fanny Brown, Effie Germon, and Lucy Hale) tucked into John's diary but didn't give them more than a passing look. He put them back inside the diary and rode off with John's possessions to hand them over to Lafayette C. Baker, head of the War Department's National Detective Police. Baker in turn brought the diary and photos to Secretary of War Stanton.

Stanton rarely if ever went to the theatre. He would not have recognized the photos of the four actresses. But he might have recognized the photo of the daughter of a prominent senator who had just been appointed minister to Spain. He sequestered the diary and photos in the War Department. Stanton was not about to enhance the assassin's reputation by linking him to a prominent family, especially the family of a senator.

Stanton handed the diary and the photos over to Judge Advocate General Joseph Holt with an order not to introduce the diary or mention the photos at the conspiracy trial. The diary never came to light until two years later at the impeachment trial of President Andrew Johnson. When it was examined, forty-three pages were missing, adding fuel to the unquenchable conspiracy-theory fire.[20] It would be another ten years before anyone bothered to try to identify the five women in the photos.

John lingered on in agony for three more hours, pleading to be killed. Close to death he gasped, "Tell...my mother...I died...for...my...country."[21]

Unable to move, John asked that his paralyzed hands be lifted to his face. With glazed eyes, he tried to focus on the palms from which the gypsy had long ago predicted he would come to an untimely end. "Useless, useless," he muttered.[22]

At around 7:15 a.m., on April 26, 1865, John Wilkes Booth died.

Lieutenant Doherty took the saddle blanket from his horse, ordered Mrs. Garrett to bring him a darning needle, and sewed John's body inside. They hoisted it onto a wagon, and Lieutenant Baker brought the body to the USS *Montauk* at the Washington Navy Yard where several people who had known John identified the body.

Dr. John Frederick May, the doctor who had operated on John's neck to remove a tumor in 1863, was one of those examining the body. Dr. May's first impression was that the corpse bore no resemblance to the man he had treated. He asked that the body be turned over so that he could get a better look at the dead man's neck. Seeing the scar where he had operated, he nodded. It was Booth, he said, but "his appearance is so much altered...looks older...more freckled." Years later, May stated that the right leg was the one broken, not the left. May's comments about the body and the contradiction about the injured leg would add to a popular urban legend that John had escaped and that the man who died at the Garrett farm was an imposter.

To frustrate any possibility of John's resting place becoming a shrine for the South, Stanton ordered his body buried in secret in an unmarked grave in Washington's Old Arsenal Penitentiary. It remained there until 1869 when President Andrew Johnson granted Edwin permission to remove it for reburial in the Booth family plot in Green Mount Cemetery in Baltimore.

# PART TWO

[They] loved not wisely, but too well.

*OTHELLO*, ACT 5, SCENE 2 (MODIFIED)

# 26

# ELLA STARR

The "inmates" at Ella Starr's brothel[1] were having a late breakfast the morning of Saturday, April 15, 1865, when someone breathlessly dashed into their house with the news John Wilkes Booth had murdered President Lincoln.

They all knew John. He was a regular "visitor." And they all knew Ella was in love with him. After they got over their momentary shock, they looked around for Ella. It was almost 11:00 a.m. Ella wasn't up yet. They had to tell her the startling news.

Ella already knew what had happened. The night of the shooting, Ella may conceivably have been in Vice President Andrew Johnson's hotel suite at John's bidding. Listening at the bedroom door, Ella would have overheard Leonard Farwell telling Johnson that Lincoln had been shot.

Later that night or sometime in the early morning, Ella was shocked to learn that John had been identified as the assassin and that Secretary of State Seward had been attacked. John's sending her to Johnson that night would have been an act of betrayal and made her unwittingly party to murder.

Ella was heartbroken. John had been the one bright spot in her taw-dry life. Now that was over. All she wanted to do was die.

Locking her door, she put a picture of John under her pillow, poured chloroform into a cloth, and breathed deep, intending to kill herself. (Chloroform was used by insomniacs to help them sleep.)

The next morning, guessing Ella was still asleep, the other girls dashed upstairs and pounded on her door. After pounding several times and yelling her name and getting no response, they barged in.

Ella was on her bed. They nudged her and called her name, but she didn't move. Panicked, they sent for several doctors. The doctors smelled the lingering chloroform and immediately realized what had happened. Fortunately, they were able to revive her. When she regained conscious-ness, Ella told them she wished they hadn't saved her.

"The Mistress of Booth Attempts Suicide," was the *Washington Evening Star*'s page two headline.[2] Two days later, detectives raided her house. They arrested Ella and all the "inmates, from the mistress to the cook, eight in all" and hauled them off to police headquarters as possible accomplices.[3]

By then Ella had gotten over John's duplicity and was smart enough to distance herself from being implicated in John's treachery. During her interrogation, she said her name was Nellie Starr. She was a prostitute, nineteen or twenty—she didn't know which—unmarried, and had known John Wilkes Booth as a customer for several years at the house where she worked.

She hadn't seen him, she claimed, for two weeks—although it is likely John had spent the night of the thirteenth with her. She said she didn't recollect how he was dressed the last time she saw him. She seemed to remember he had on dark clothes and a slouch hat. She said she hadn't been on good terms with him for some time (also a lie). No, she had never heard him say anything unfavorable about President Lincoln. No, she didn't know any of the people associated with him. She signed the state-ment with two of her aliases, Nellie Starr and Ella Starr. Fannie Harri-son, one of the other girls at the brothel, signed her statement as a witness.[4]

The authorities suspected she was lying. She likely would not have tried to kill herself had she not been on good terms with the assassin. They also had the note she'd written him in February calling him "my darling boy" and pleading with him to see her.[5]

William Doster, Lewis Powell, and George Atzerodt's lawyer had her held in the witness room for two days[6] but never asked her to testify. Her "sort of evidence," he later said, "was not very much to the point."[7]

Ella's whereabouts aren't known after the conspiracy trial. She is listed in tax rolls for 1867 and 1868 as the owner of property adjacent to the brothel.[8] Most likely she remained in Washington until her mother sold the bawdy house on Ohio Street in 1868. After that there is no trace of her until 1883 when her name came up in news items about her sister, Molly, who was contesting her half-brother John W. Starr's will.[9] In reporting the fight over inheritance, a Chicago newspaper said Molly had a sister, once "the wife of John Wilkes Booth," who was "now living elegantly and respectably in New York."[10]

Ella's name cropped up again in 1901 in an interview with actor Harry Hawk. Hawk was recalling the night of the assassination when John ran toward him brandishing his knife, just after shooting Lincoln. Hawk said he'd taken off like anyone in his place seeing a man coming at him with a knife. Now, fifty years later, Hawk said he'd had another reason to run—he thought John was after him for introducing a friend of his named Wilson to Ella Starr. Wilson had become infatuated with Ella, and she was taking advantage of him. Hawk said he couldn't stand Ella's making a dupe out of his friend. To wean him off of Ella, he told him about her relationship with John. Hawk said Ella didn't take kindly to losing a generous customer and made up a story about Hawk. When John came at him waving his knife just after assassinating Lincoln, Hawk thought he had "taken some cranky notion to avenge her publicly."[11]

Ella's name came up one more time in an article in the *Richmond Dispatch* about the rumor that someone other than John had died in the Garrett barn. His mistress, Ella Starr, it said, was still alive, "the wife of an honest mechanic."[12]

# 27

# ASIA AND MARY ANN

Asia shrieked. Lying in bed, five months pregnant with twins, she stared dumbfounded at the *Philadelphia Inquirer*'s April 15 bold, front-page headline:

MURDER OF PRESIDENT LINCOLN!
His Assassination Last Night While at Ford's Theatre, in Washington!
J. WILKES BOOTH THE SUPPOSED MURDERER

Startled by the hysterical scream coming from his bedroom, her husband John Clarke's first thought was that Asia or one of the children was hurt. Rushing into the bedroom he was relieved to see Asia sitting up in bed holding the morning *Philadelphia Inquirer*. What was wrong? Clarke blurted. Asia didn't say anything. She merely held up the paper.[1]

She couldn't believe what she'd just read. How could the brother she idolized have done what he was accused of? She knew he was devoted

227

to the South. But this? Everyone in the Booth family knew their lives would never be the same.

Edwin was in Boston in his room at the Parker House on the night of April 14, 1865, entertaining some guests. Around half past twelve he rose with a glass of champagne in his hands to give a toast. He was just about to speak when there was a knock on the door. A boy came in, asked for Mr. Booth, and handed him a telegram. Edwin excused himself for a moment while he opened the envelope and read the brief message. In an instant, his face turned white.

"My God!" he uttered. Sinking onto a nearby chair, he put his head on a table next to the chair and wept. Someone picked up the telegram and read it to the room: "John Wilkes Booth has shot Abraham Lincoln at Ford's Theatre."[2]

Later a detective searched Edwin's trunks and correspondence for any incriminating evidence. Finding none, the *Boston Evening Transcript* published a letter from the detective exonerating Edwin of any "knowledge that such an act was contemplated."[3]

What could anyone with "the once honored and now despised name expect?" Edwin rhetorically asked Adam Badeau. How could someone "so lovable and in whom all in the family found a source of joy in his boyish and fighting nature have done such a thing....two days ago [I was] one of the happiest men alive. Now what am I?...I am half-crazy now...Poor Mother! I go to New York today—expecting to find her either dead or dying [from shock]."[4]

June was in Cincinnati at Pike's Opera House the night of the assassination. "This morn news came of the death of the President & John's deed last night in Washington," he wrote in his diary. "The excitement was so great that I remained in the Hotel till the night of Monday the 17th."[5] Late that night he left for Asia's, arriving the next day.

After Asia and Clarke got over their initial shock, they remembered the package John had left with them a few months earlier. Clarke dashed over to the safe where Asia had put it. Beside bonds and a deed were two letters, the one to his mother and the other his "To Whom It May Concern" manifesto, laying out his reasons at the time he wrote it for kidnapping Lincoln.[6]

Clarke sat on the letters for two days, wondering what to do with them. Since neither letter implicated him or Asia, he believed publicizing them would show the public they had had nothing to do with John's heinous act. John's "To Whom It May Concern" letter clearly stated he was acting on his own. There was no mention of anyone in the family. Clarke decided to show them to a journalist at the *Philadelphia Inquirer* on April 19. Together they called on United States Provost Marshal William Millward, asking permission to have them printed in the *Philadelphia Inquirer*. Millward read them and agreed to only allow the "To Whom It May Concern" letter to be published. The letter to John's mother, he felt, might garner sympathy for the assassin.

John's "To Whom It May Concern" letter was never introduced as evidence in the conspiracy trial.[7] When Secretary of War Stanton read its reprinted text in the *Washington Evening Star*, he was livid. Stanton felt the letter would not only exonerate the Confederate government from complicity in the assassination, it also might result in some people feeling sympathy for the assassin and could diminish the animus toward the other conspirators. With that in mind, Stanton dashed off an angry note to Millward, demanding an explanation for his allowing the letter to be printed. Millward answered that rather than creating sympathy for the assassin, in his opinion, it was proof positive of a conspiracy.[8]

After the letter appeared in the newspapers, government agents swooped down on Asia and Clarke's house and turned it upside down looking for incriminating evidence. Anything associated with John's name was confiscated—photographs, letters, and anything else that belonged to him. Even a little picture of him hanging over the babies' cribs in the nursery was confiscated. After they left, other agents, "enraged and furious," searched and ransacked the house. All Asia's mail was opened before being handed over to her. The servants were asked to spy on her.

"North, East and West the papers teemed with the most preposterous adventures." One newspaper reported, "on hearing the news [about John] Mrs. J. S. Clarke had gone mad, and was at present confined at the Asylum at West Philadelphia…The tongue of every man and woman was free to revile and insult us. Every man's hand was against us; if we had friends they consoled with us in secret; none ventured near."[9]

Asia's sole visitor was a Claud Burroughs, who told her he was an actor that Edwin had sent "on a secret mission" for papers she had hidden on her person. In fact Burroughs was a detective trying to fool her into giving up whatever she might in fact have concealed when the house was searched.[10]

Recalling those trying days, Asia wrote, "Those who have passed through such an ordeal—if there are any such—may be quick to forgive, slow to resent; they never relearn to trust in human nature, they never resume their old place in the world and they forget only in death."[11]

One of the men posted at her house, charged with following her from room to room, was gentle and polite, unlike the others. Against orders he offered to bring his wife with him to stay with Asia. Asia thanked the man for the offer but declined. Privately she said she would "rather have been watched by ten men who could keep quiet, than one chattering female."[12]

Mary Ann was living at Edwin's house in New York when she heard the news. Two weeks before the assassination, she had written John that she had "never yet doubted your love & devotion to me—in fact I always gave you praise for being the fondest of all my boys."[13]

After they got over their shock at the "ghastly intelligence" in the morning paper, authors Thomas Baily Aldrich and his wife, Edwin's neighbors, first thought was how it would affect "the poor mother who idolized her wayward and misguided boy." After a hurried breakfast they rushed over to Edwin's. Mary Ann and Rosalie were sitting in silence, stricken and stunned with grief.

Outside newsboys kept passing by shouting, "The President's death, and the arrest of John Wilkes Booth." Mary Ann moaned, "O God, if this be true, let him shoot himself, let him not live to be hung! Spare him, spare us, spare the name that dreadful disgrace!"[14]

Edwin had telegraphed from Boston and would soon be home. The next day the Aldriches and a small group of Edwin's friends were at his house on Sunday when he stepped from his carriage, looking "spectral as if the grave had given up its dead."[15]

The nightmare for Edwin and the rest of the family had begun. Every day letters, notes, and messages arrived at the house warning Edwin the name Booth should be exterminated and anyone bearing it should be killed. There were threats about his house being burned. The family's only hope was that John wouldn't live to be hung, that he would at least spare them that last disgrace.

Ten days later Clarke telegraphed Mary Ann in New York that Asia was "seriously ill." Could Mary Ann come at once? On April 26, on the way to the ferry, Thomas Aldrich and Lout Thompson, another one of Edwin's friends, heard a newsboy shouting, "Death of John Wilkes Booth. Capture of his companion."

Thompson closed the windows, and he and Aldrich did their best to talk loud enough to drown out the doleful news. At the station, they told Mary Ann that John was dead and handed her a newspaper. Mary Ann read the story of John's capture and death and his next to final words, "Tell my mother that I die for my country."[16]

While Mary Ann was reading about John's death, T. J. Hemphill, acting manager at the Walnut Street Theatre, knocked on Asia's door at home. He needed to see her, he told the servant who answered. Pale and visibly nervous, the old man held on to the center table for balance and wouldn't look directly at her. Asia knew.

She collapsed on the sofa, turned her face to the wall, and silently thanked God the end had come. Chocking back sobs, Hemphill turned around and left.[17]

Asia's and the rest of the family's troubles were only beginning. The entire family came under suspicion of complicity in the assassination. June and Clarke were both arrested at Clarke's home and jailed at the Old Capitol Prison where they were held without charges for several weeks.

A letter June had written to John, advising him to get out of the oil business and not be so vocal about his politics, had put him under a cloud. The "oil business" was considered code for the plot to murder Lincoln. Clarke had made the mistake in believing John's letters would exonerate him. Instead, John's leaving them at the Clarke home was regarded as complicity. The letters implied June and Clarke had known what John was planning—John would never have left those letters there had they not been involved. June and Clarke were locked in bare rooms with just a bag of straw and blankets. The only "convenience" was a slop bucket and a pitcher.

Asia would also have been arrested and taken to prison had she not been pregnant. The doctor who had nursed her through her various illnesses had to send a telegram to Washington confirming her "condition." She was allowed to stay in her home. A male detective stayed in the house to make sure she didn't run off. (In August, Asia gave birth to twins, Lillian Theresa and Creston Joseph. Asia hadn't known she was carrying twins. When she found she was pregnant, she'd planned to name her baby John Wilkes Booth Clarke, if a boy. That was now impossible. Lillian died a year later.)

Edwin was the only one allowed his freedom. He was then at the height of his career, a national icon, having just completed his hundredth continuous performance of *Hamlet* just three weeks before the assassination. As soon as Edwin could, he left for Philadelphia to be with Asia and his mother. "I can give you no idea of the desolation which has fallen upon us," Asia wrote Jean Anderson. "The sorrow of his death is very bitter. The disgrace is far heavier."[18]

The only consoling letter Asia received was from one of John's former lovers, Effie Germon. Dated May 3, 1965, Effie wrote: "Although a perfect stranger to you, I take the liberty of offering my sympathy and aid to you in your great sorrow and sickness." Effie lived not far from Asia's house in Philadelphia and offered to help in any way she could. She would have offered earlier, she said, had she not been ill herself. Asia treasured that letter "as precious gold."[19]

Mary Ann tried to be strong for Asia's sake, but she was "crushed by her sorrows," Edwin wrote his friend, Emma Cary. "She feels her woe greater than she shows."[20]

Edwin had moved in with his sister and mother to help out as best he could while Clarke was languishing in jail. There was another reason to stay at Asia's. Edwin had become engaged to Blanche Hanel, a woman from a wealthy Philadelphia family. Unsurprisingly, Asia did not like her, calling her a "fashionable flirt" and a "stickler for decorum."[21]

Shortly afterward, the engagement was off. Blanche's father objected to any connection to the Booth name.[22]

Clarke was released from prison on May 26; June was held until June 23. Edwin's being treated with kid gloves grated Clarke. He was as innocent as Edwin but had been shabbily treated. A festering resentment soured him on Edwin and all the Booths, including his wife. "Look at me," he ranted to Asia, "I was dragged to jail by the neck—literally dragged to prison—and Edwin goes scot free, gets all the fame."[23] Clarke told Asia he wanted a divorce. His life, he said, was ruined because of the Booths.

John's warning when Asia told him she was marrying Clarke popped up inside her brain. "Bear in mind," John had told her, "you are only a professional stepping-stone."[24] Clarke had no grounds for a divorce, and Asia refused to give him one.

Still fuming with resentment, Clarke realized there was a way to get back at Edwin—he would stage *Our American Cousin* at the Winter

Garden, which he and Edwin jointly owned. The play was indelibly associated in the mind of Americans with John Wilkes Booth and would remind everyone Edwin was the brother of the assassin.

But the rights to perform the play anywhere were owned by Laura Keene, and Clarke did not have her permission. Clarke had even been sued by Keene seven years earlier for putting on the play at the Arch Street Theatre in Philadelphia and been ordered by the court to pay Keene a licensing fee. Clarke didn't care. He was determined to humiliate Edwin. Clarke staged it anyway and Keene sued him again. Keene lambasted him in the newspapers for "the bad taste of seeking to deprive me of the use of this play." Your effrontery, she wrote, was "only equaled by your ever appearing in a comedy which ought to have only a memory of shame and sorrow for you and every member of your family."[25] Ironically, Laura Keene's lawyer was a Mr. W. D. Booth. Relations between Clarke and Edwin were quite frosty after that. Edwin severed his partnership with Clarke at the Winter Garden, although they still remained partners at the Walnut Street Theatre.[26]

Life for Asia was dismal. Her husband was feuding with her brother. Her mother was in deep despair, and her daughter Lillian had died almost a year to the day of the assassination. "I think I am getting like poor mother," she wrote Jean Anderson, "hardened to sorrow."[27]

A year later, Clarke left for England with their son Eddie to take an engagement as actor and manager of one of London's theatres. Asia remained in Philadelphia waiting for him to decide if he wanted to move there permanently. In February the following year, she wrote Jean Anderson that Clarke did want to make their home in London. Dutifully, she told Jean, "I must submit."[28] In March of 1868, Asia was settled in at "My cozy English home" outside northwest London.[29]

Mary Ann was not so hardened to sorrow that she didn't agonize over John's body not receiving a proper burial. Edwin tried to obtain permission from Secretary of War Stanton to retrieve his body from Washington's Old Arsenal Penitentiary for reburial in the family cemetery. Stanton didn't even respond to his request.

Edwin next petitioned General Grant.

> I appeal to you—on behalf of my heart-broken Mother—that she may receive the remains of her son. You can understand what a consolation it would be to an aged parent to have the privilege of visiting the grave of her child, and I feel assured that you will, even in the midst of your most pressing duties, feel a touch of sympathy for her—one of the greatest sufferers living.[30]

"His mother, being very aged, [Mrs. Booth] craves the dead body so as to inter it before she dies," the *New York Times* reported.[31] The request, it informed its readers, had been denied.

Failing to get permission from Stanton or Grant, Edwin appealed to John H. Weaver, sexton at one of Baltimore's churches and a Baltimore undertaker, to see if he could persuade President Andrew Johnson to release John's body. Perhaps, he thought, Johnson might listen to a clergyman.

Johnson was in his office being interviewed by the associate editor of the *New York World* when one of his secretaries handed him a card. Ordinarily Johnson would have ignored it but told the secretary to bring Weaver in. The "slim, solemn, mournfully quiet" undertaker, dressed every inch like someone ought to in his profession, was the soul of politeness and decorum. He explained why he had come, reiterated Edwin's plea to rebury John's body in Baltimore, and assured Johnson it would be removed with no fanfare. The request came at an opportune time. Johnson was about to end his presidency and by then had become embittered toward both Stanton and Grant. Three days later, Johnson released the body. Edwin entrusted the Booth's family friend John T. Ford to make the final arrangements to ship John's body to Baltimore after its exhumation.[32]

The same afternoon that Johnson released John's body, Weaver and some others unearthed the pine casket. Once cleared of the dirt, the name "John Wilkes Booth" was visible in black, inch-long capital letters on the pine lid.

Four soldiers carried the box to a red express wagon and covered it with a blanket to hide what was underneath. Everything and everyone in place, the driver shook the reins and the little, stubby sorrel trotted off.[33]

At the Washington undertaker's store at the back entrance on Baptist Alley where John had made his escape, John's youngest brother Joseph, now a doctor, was waiting to identify the body. John's body had been wrapped in a blanket, which was now badly decayed. After four years, John's head had become detached from his body. Although now hardly recognizable, Joseph nodded it was John. John Ford was at the train station when Joseph arrived in Baltimore late that night, February 15, 1869, with John's remains. Ford telegraphed Edwin in New York, "successful and in our possession here."[34]

Two days later, John Ford broke off rehearsals at his Holliday Street Theatre and told everyone to take the day off. Speaking softly to Blanche Chapman, his goddaughter, he told her to get her sister Ella and come quietly with him. "Keep your eyes open and your mouths closed," he muttered.[35]

Blanche and Ella followed him over to a room at the back of Weaver's funeral parlor behind the Holliday Street Theatre where years before John had been a featured star. John's brothers Edwin and Joseph, his sister Rosalie, June's wife, John's mother Mary Ann, the Booth's now elderly neighbor Mrs. Elijah Rogers, and a few other family friends were gathered around the coffin. The sides of the coffin were decayed. Patches of clay from the Old Arsenal Penitentiary burial site still adhered to it.

Despite the secrecy about the transference of the body, rumors about its being at Weaver's spread, and curiosity seekers began gathering outside, hoping to get a glimpse of John's remains. William Burton, one of Ford's stock actors, sensed it had to have been something important for Ford to cancel that day's rehearsal. Burton buttonholed another actor,

Frank Rose, and whispered to follow him. The two men hopped the fence around the undertaker's shop and managed to slip in the back door. No one seemed to notice them.

At some unspoken signal, Edwin, John Ford, and undertaker John Weaver moved to the head of the coffin. Junius stayed at the side. Weaver and his assistant removed the screws in the lid and raised the cover. "We want to make sure that there is no mistake about this," said Ford as he and the undertaker unwrapped the blanket around the body. Blanche almost fainted at the sight of the remains.[36]

The face that had once been the handsomest in America was now just a detached head with hair still clinging to it. The locks were damp and matted and had no real color. "It was not so black and shiney as it was long ago," Mrs. Rogers thought to herself.[37] Though Blanche had heard that hair grew after death, she was still surprised that the hair had grown almost to shoulder length.

The flesh on the rest of the body had disintegrated, leaving blackened bones inside a rotted, rough, brown coat, black pants, and vest. A riding boot, split open at the top, was still on the left foot that John had broken when he jumped onto the stage at Ford's Theatre.

If it's John's body, there will be a gold-plugged tooth on the right side of his jaw, next to the eyetooth, Edwin murmured. Weaver lifted the head from the box and passed it to the family dentist. The gold-plugged tooth was where Edwin said it would be.[38] The dentist then handed the head to anyone else who wanted to see the tooth.[39] No one spoke as the skull was passed around.

William Burton broke the silence. "That boot looks like a pair John used to wear when we went skating," he said to no one in particular. "If it is there will be a hole in the heel made by the screw of the skate," meaning a hole in the boot where the skating blade was attached. Weaver removed the boot and examined it. Inside the heel was a hole, just as Burton said there would be.[40]

Before the lid was replaced, Annie Ford clipped a lock of John's hair then handed the scissors to Blanche Chapman. Blanche looked at Mary Ann, asking if she could cut some too. Mary Ann nodded. Blanche bent over, gathered one of "those glorious ringlets" in her hand, and cut it off. She saved some of the locks for herself and sent a few strands to Maggie Mitchell, who everyone in the theatre knew had been John's one-time lover and rumored one-time fiancée.[41]

The following day, February 18, 1869, John's body was taken to Green Mount Cemetery outside Baltimore and placed in a receiving vault until the ground was soft enough for a grave to be dug. Days before the interment, on June 26, Mary Ann had asked her former Bel Air neighbor, Mrs. Elijah Rogers, to "get the children" out of the ground at the old farm and bring the remains to the cemetery so that they could be interred with John.

The pall-bearers, all of them men from the theatre who had known John, carried his coffin from the vault to its gravesite. His family, "Aunty Rogers," and about fifty others stood in silence as John's body was interred in the Booth family plot. "I loved the boy dearly," Rogers tearfully recalled. "I knew him from babyhood, and he was always so kind, tender-hearted, and good."[42] Dressed in deep mourning dress, Mary Ann was visibly overcome,[43] but at least "the bereaved mother has the melancholy satisfaction of placing her leaf of evergreen on the sod above the grave of her wayward son."[44]

After John's body was lowered into the grave, the remains of Mary Ann's other deceased children, in one box together, were laid on top of John's coffin, and the grave was filled.[45] The family, "much stricken with the sorrow of the occasion, had the deep and heartfelt sympathies of all present."[46]

"Oh Poor John," a tearful Aunty Rogers later recalled, "Sorryful for such A hansom boy he was to let the enemy of souls Cheat him out of so much pleasure, as he could have done so much good in this world for he was A gentleman. Dear boy, good boy...poor fellow. I hope the lord had mercy on his soul."[47]

There were no demonstrations at the funeral. Everything was quiet and dignified. Several of the women put flowers on the grave. Edwin arranged for his father's remains and monument to be moved from Baltimore Cemetery to Green Mount Cemetery. On one of the sides of the monument a new inscription was added: "To the memory of the children of Junius Brutus and Mary Ann Booth. John Wilkes, Frederick, Elizabeth, Mary Ann, Henry Byron."

Asia was happy during her first years in England.[48] However, by 1870 her marriage was falling apart, she was lonely, and she hated living in England.[49] To pass the time she began writing a memoir of her brother John, which she hid from Clarke—who meanwhile was seldom home and kept a mistress.[50] "It is marvelous how he hates me—the mother of nine babies," Asia wrote, "but I am a Booth—that is sufficient."[51]

One day her ten-year-old son, Creston, came home crying. Some American boys had asked him whether he was related to the Booth who had murdered President Lincoln. Creston had no idea what they were talking about. Asia couldn't bring herself to explain, but Clarke had no hesitation in telling his son about the hated family, and "for the first time [the boy] learned the story that had brought consuming and ineffaceable sorrow to his parents."[52]

Another major tragedy came in 1881 when Asia's oldest son, Edwin ("Eddie") Booth Clarke, drowned at sea.[53] Eddie had been Asia and Clarke's favorite.[54]

In 1888, in an attempt to find relief from her rheumatism, Asia was vacationing in Bournemouth, a seaside resort on the south coast of England, when she took ill. A cable urged Clarke and their son Creston, who were in the United States, to hurry back to England. They arrived a few days before she died on May 6. She was fifty-two. Per her request, Asia was buried in the family lot at Green Mount Cemetery.

Unbeknownst to Clarke, before her death Asia had entrusted her memoir about John to her daughter, Dolly, telling her to take it to Mr. Farjeon, one of Asia's few family friends, and to ask him "to publish it sometime if he sees fit."[55] When the Farjeons read Asia's memoir, they agreed its immediate publication was not possible. Apart from the fact that the assassination was still a vivid memory in many people's minds, some of the people Asia wrote about, including Edwin, were still alive. Although Edwin had outlived the shame of his brother's assassination, he would not want those memories stirred up again. So they laid Asia's 132-page memoir aside until everyone mentioned in it was no longer living.

Almost sixty years later, Eleanor Farjeon, the Farjeons' daughter, approached G. P. Putnam's Sons with the manuscript; Putnam's immediately recognized the memoir's uniqueness and published it in 1938. Farjeon decided to title it *The Unlocked Book: A Memoir of John Wilkes Booth by His Sister Asia Booth Clarke*[56] and added her own foreword. The memoir, Farjeon wrote, "shows him [John] as a person." It was Asia's hope, she said, that her memoir would make the name of John Wilkes Booth less hated.[57]

For historian Henry Steel Commager, it didn't. Commager rejected Asia's fawning paean to the brother she loved. "John Wilkes Booth, like other criminals, has had a great deal more attention than he merits and the attention has often been sentimental and romantic."[58] Historian Allan Nevins called the memoir a "curious, pathetic, bitter little memoir...written with a tortured pen."[59]

In England, an ocean away from the still-smoldering animosity toward John, the *Scotsman* magazine was more congenial, although it also considered it "pathetic." "To his sister Asia, John Wilkes was during his lifetime a hero; after his death a martyr...It is easy to see why the attention of the writer was concentrated on the period when her brother was happiest and most lovable."[60]

In 1996 Asia's memoir was republished as *John Wilkes Booth: A Sister's Memoir* with an introduction and scholarly background by Professor Terry Alford.[61] Reviews of the 1996 edition had an entirely different tone. The memoir is "a very valuable portrait of the Civil War and Reconstruction period," wrote one reviewer. "As a teaching tool it will recall not only the historical moment of Lincoln's death but also much of the context in which it happened."[62] "John Wilkes Booth, the assassin, emerges as a man—a more total likeness than we have known before," wrote another reviewer.[63]

In late January 1884, Mary Ann fell and fractured her hip.[64] Six months later Edwin wrote "poor mother" wasn't getting any better. "I fear her fate is fixed—never to walk again, & poor Rose! How patient & long-suffering her life has been. Their case is pitiable & I wish I could relieve it."[65]

Mary Ann Holmes Booth, John Wilkes Booth's mother, in her old age. *Courtesy of Folger Shakespeare Library.*

Mary Ann had not had a happy life. Her love for her husband Junius had been a "rock to break her heart upon."[66] The "failure" of her "brighter dreams and hopes" had embittered her heart and divested her life of all romance and sentiment.[67] "I am not a great advocate for marriages," she told her granddaughter Edwina.[68]

After Asia and her other children left home, Mary Ann lived much of her life in hotel rooms and apartments with her daughter Rosalie. She often felt alone. John's death crippled her spirit. "Mother is very much broken, I think," Edwin wrote six months after the assassination. "Poor soul! She seems to have still a lingering hope in her heart that all this will prove to be a dream."[69] Her thoughts tormented her. "She bears up bravely and conceals the pain she feels," said Edwin.[70]

In later life, Mary Ann was consumed by worrying about Edwin and her surviving children. Her face was kind, wrote a journalist for the *Trenton Evening Times* who watched her from his building, but "sometimes full of sadness, as if her soul had had bitter days to bear." Only "when she talks to her birds" did a "sweet smile light up that face."[71]

Mary Ann Holmes Booth died in New York at Joseph's home on October 22, 1885, from pneumonia and heart failure after catching a cold. She was eighty-three.[72] Edwin had his mother embalmed and interred in the family grave in Green Mount Cemetery.[73] "She looked about forty and very beautiful," he told Lawrence Barrett, "as I remember her in my boyhood."[74]

# 28

# "It Cannot Be Denied": Lucy Hale

**D**ays after the assassination, sensational rumors about John's engagement to a senator's daughter spread like wildfire, despite Lucy Hale's father's and friends' denials and efforts to keep her name out of the papers. It was simply too juicy a story for reporters to ignore.

In Cincinnati, where John's brother June was appearing at Pike's Opera House, reporters confronted him at the Burnet House where he was staying. June couldn't hold out against all the badgering and admitted the rumors were true. Days before the assassination, he said, John had sent him a letter saying he was engaged to Miss Hale but there was opposition to their marriage.[1]

A day later, the denials came fast and furious. The *Boston Daily Advertiser* printed a letter from a "gentleman" from Boston "who is entirely competent to give an opinion" about Lucy's engagement. The "gentleman" identified only as "C" vehemently denied there had been any such engagement:

In your paper of this morning, you gave a dispatch from Cincinnati, stating that 'J. Wilkes Booth was to have been married soon to a daughter of Senator Hale.' There is no truth in
that statement, nor the slightest foundation for it; and I would
request thet [sic] in justice to Senator Hale and his family, you
will give this same publicity you have the statement.[2]

The *Springfield Republican* editorialized that John Wilkes Booth
"wasn't the kind of a man that any young lady of character would have
noticed, much less married."[3] There was "no truth whatever in the
report," the *Cincinnati Daily Enquirer* asserted. The only relationship
between the two was a "ball-room acquaintance." The *New York Tribune* called John's impending marriage to Lucy "the most impertinent
bit of gossip that has lately crept into some of the journals."[4]

Despite the denials, the rumor mill was now churning full blast. An
unidentified woman was said to have been allowed to board the *Montauk* with other VIPs and had cut a lock of the assassin's hair as a
memento. No one doubted the mystery woman was Lucy. Years later, a
variation on that rumor had Lucy grieving for John and having a premonition that someone else was lying dead on board the *Montauk*.
Unable to go aboard herself, she purportedly prevailed upon Maggie
Mitchell, the most famous woman of the day, to go to the *Montauk* and
bring something that would prove or disprove it was in fact John. According to this new variation of the story, Maggie, who had herself been
intimately associated with John, was said to have managed to clip a lock
of the dead man's hair and to have known immediately it wasn't him.[5]

Later, disregarding its previous confidence that the rumors were
false, the *Springfield Republican* admitted John and Lucy had in fact
been engaged: "It cannot be denied, we are afraid, that John Wilkes
Booth, the assassin, was engaged to be married to a daughter of Senator
Hale. He has been very much of a beau among the ladies of the National
Hotel at Washington the past winter."[6]

Relying on a private source, the *Dayton Daily Empire* reported the
rumor was true:

There is positive evidence of its truth [the engagement]; but this evidence is in private letters, which cannot be denied; [the *Daily Empire's* source] adds that Booth was very intimate with the wives and daughters of prominent Republican Senators and Representatives at the National Hotel last winter. They must have known that he was not only a secessionist, but a gamester and a whoremonger. Such was his general reputation, and because he was handsome and could spout Shakespeare by the hour, these ladies permitted intimacies that have carried them with the infamous assassin into the newspapers. All I can say is—served them right—good enough for them. When our women, married and unmarried, are so coarse, so reckless and so wicked that they like to dally with temptation, that they rather enjoy intimacies with scoundrels, let them take the consequences. They are none the worse for being found out.[7]

The *Boston Traveller* editorialized that the names of the women who had had anything to do with the assassin should not be protected, condemning his engagements to "sundry daughters and sisters of prominent politicians." It continued:

It is notorious that ladies of social distinction placed themselves freely in his way, sought introductions to him, invited him to the parlors at the National and other hotels, and considered it quite the thing to indulge in a conversation, a flirtation or a dance with the handsome rake. Not innocent girls only but married ladies also, are those whose names are now bandied about Washington in infamous connection with the name of this vile assassin. Why should it not be told of? The reputation is the legitimate penalty of the association. It is shameful that lewd fellows of every degree, bold, garrulous libertines, who can dress well and talk gossipy nonsense and quote Shakespeare as Wilkes Booth did, have a welcome

entrance into the fashionable circles of this country. In Booth's
case there is no excuse of ignorance. His disloyal principles
and his loose morals were alike notorious. And those who
knowing this, courted his seductive society, are suffering the
disgrace of it, as they ought to.[8]

Even those who did not personally know Lucy did what they could
to keep her name from surfacing. At the conspiracy trial, Sam Chester
reiterated his conversation with John in New York when John told him
he was engaged to be married to a young lady from Washington, but
Chester said he would not like to "compromise the lady by giving her
name" since she came from "a very respectable family."[9] Chester was
never pressed to disclose the mystery woman's name.

Detectives tried unsuccessfully to identify the "lady" that John had
checked into the Aquidneck House in Newport with on April 5. No stone
was left unturned—except for Lucy. Lucy was never questioned.

One reason Lucy's name never appeared in the news coverage was
a prevailing sense of propriety where women of high social standing were
concerned, as is evident in Chester's testimony.[10] Benjamin Perley Poore,
who transcribed the trial proceedings, later commented that the name
of the "estimable young lady, whose photograph was found in his [John's]
pocket-book after his death was honorably kept a secret [during the
trial]."[11]

Booth biographer Terry Alford conjectures Lucy was never questioned because her father met privately with Andrew Johnson after he
was sworn in as the new president and convinced him that his daughter
Lucy knew nothing about John's murderous plans. It is improbable such
a discussion occurred. Even less probable is that Johnson agreed. Hale
and Johnson had been at loggerheads over political issues for a long time,
and Hale had publicly railed against Johnson in the past.[12]

To put a lid on the scandal, Lucy's father squirrelled her away as
soon as his appointment as minister to Spain was approved. Several days
later Edwin told Asia he received "a heart broken letter from the poor
little girl to whom he [John] had promised so much happiness."[13] Asia

in turn wrote to her friend Jean Anderson that John and Lucy were "devoted lovers" and were to be married when she returned from Spain, with or without her father's approval.[14] Edwin had not named the "poor little girl." Asia just assumed it was Lucy. But Edwin would hardly have described Lucy as a "poor little girl." More likely he meant Ella Starr, whose attempted suicide had been widely reported. Lucy never once mentioned or alluded to John in the diary she kept during her time in Europe and never mentioned him in any of her correspondence.[15]

When Lucy returned to the United States in 1870, five years after the assassination, her return went relatively unnoticed. She was now twenty-eight with no more ambition than to take care of her ailing father at their home in Dover. He died three years later.[16] Hale's death reawakened the scandal, and for the first time the papers reported that Lucy's photo had been among the five photos in John's pocket when he died.[17]

Mrs. Lucy Hale Chandler after giving up "the romantic ideal of her youth." *Courtesy of Anonymous. New Hampshire Women: A Collection of Portraits and Biographical Sketches of Daughters and Residents of the Granite State. Concord, NH: New Hampshire Publishing Co., 1895.*

Less than a year later, Lucy married widower William Chandler—her long-time admirer and now a well-known politician and publisher—in a private ceremony at her family home in Dover. "Miss Hale, now past 30," the *Chicago Daily Tribune* wrote in its Social World column, "has at last given up the romantic ideal of her youth [meaning John Wilkes Booth], to marry W. E. Chandler! 'So runs the world.'"[18]

Gossip about Lucy's affair with John should have gone dormant after she married the staid Chandler. But four years later, in June 1878, the *Chicago Daily Inter-Ocean* touched off a bombshell: "We publish this morning an extraordinary story connecting the names of Robert Lincoln and J. Wilkes Booth as lovers of Miss Bessie Hale, and assigning a new motive for Booth's action in regard to President Lincoln."

Then came a series of sensational headlines:

Booth and Bob Lincoln

Were J. Wilkes Booth and Robert Lincoln Rivals In Their Love Making

A Virginian's Story of Booth's Insane Jealousy of Young Lincoln

He Hated the President Because He Loved his Country, And Hated the Son Because He Loved Bessie Hale

The Night Before the Assassination—Booth's Threats Against the Lincolns

The Revenge of a Rebel and a Jealous Lover[19]

The *Brooklyn Daily Eagle* had a shorter, equally attention-getting headline: "A new version of the crime with a Love Story Thrown in."[20]

According to the *Chicago Daily Inter-Ocean*, investigative journalist Alexander Hunter had learned about the love triangle from a Mrs.

Temple who claimed to have been one of a circle of friends of the Hales' and John's at the National Hotel. "Booth," she allegedly told Hunter, had "the most jealous temperament I ever knew; he was insane, sometimes, it seemed to me, and when Bessie [she called Lucy "Bessie"] accepted any attention from any other man, Booth would act like a patient just out of Bedlam."

Mrs. Temple asserted that John Wilkes Booth was the most ardent of Lucy's admirers except for Robert Lincoln, who was madly in love with her. Her parents pressed her to marry Robert, and she would have given in, said Mrs. Temple, but for "Booth, who, with his charm of personal manner, and intellect, carried the day and won her heart."

According to Mrs. Temple, John had dinner with her and the Hale family several hours before the assassination. John was his usual entertaining self, but when it was over, Temple said, he bowed to leave and abruptly came back to the table, took Lucy's hand, "gazed with one long lingering look in her face," and left. When Lucy heard about the assassination, Temple said, she came into her room in a "fearful state of excitement." Temple claimed Lucy then wrote a letter to John telling him she would "marry him even at the foot of the scaffold."

"Bessie" never recovered from the shock, said Temple. Asked what she thought Lucy's future would be like, Mrs. Temple reflected that in her opinion it would be "'a dead woman's life.'"[21]

The *Chicago Daily Inter-Ocean* newspaper told readers that Mrs. Temple's story "deals, we are assured, only with facts." Other papers were skeptical. "This story varies from others on the same subject," said the *Rockford Daily Register*, "chiefly, in being sillier and less probable."[22]

Robert didn't wait to be asked for his reaction to the story. Reading the article in the *Chicago Daily Inter-Ocean*, the normally placid Robert Lincoln was livid. He was a successful Chicago lawyer with many important clients and was married to Senator James Harlan's daughter. He preferred to stay out of the public limelight. In this instance he felt he had to publicly deny there was any truth in the story and dashed off an angry note to the editor of the *Chicago Daily Tribune* categorically refuting the whole story.

Robert said he had never known any such person as Mrs. Temple. He also vowed he had never even seen John Wilkes Booth in his life. During the time mentioned in the story, Robert said he had been in Washington for no more than two or three days and had only returned the morning of April 14, 1865.[23]

The same day that Robert's denial appeared in the *Chicago Daily Tribune*, the *New York Herald* published the Hunter article and Robert's reply saying it proved what "a gorgeous and pyrotechnic liar" Hunter was.[24] Throughout the country, other newspapers followed suit. The *Philadelphia Inquirer* sought out actor John Mathews, one of John's former friends, for his comment. Mathews was adamant the story could never have happened. "Wilkes Booth was not a man to act toward a rival in any such manner," Mathews insisted. "He wasn't a man who would have whispered idle threats about another man. He would have clobbered Robert with everyone watching."[25]

If Lucy was ever asked about the Temple article, she declined to answer. Her husband Chandler was likewise never questioned by the sensationalist media.

Several days after the story appeared, the *New York Tribune* tracked down Alexander Hunter in Virginia where he was a member of the state legislature.[26] Confronted with the many contradictions in his story, Hunter said Mrs. Temple was a made-up name but nevertheless a real person who'd been a "trusted friend" of President Lincoln's, "as well known in Washington as the President's wife." He had given her the fictional name of Mrs. Temple because identifying her would have been an "unwarranted liberty," and he wouldn't disclose it without her permission.[27] The *New York Tribune* shot back that Hunter hadn't been as concerned about taking the same "unwarranted liberty" with Lucy's reputation.

Despite its total fantasy, the story was too juicy not to become part of the John Wilkes Booth legend. Lucy was never called Bessie. Lucy's sister's name was Elizabeth and was affectionately called "Lizzie." "Bessie" is a diminutive for Elizabeth, but never Lucy. Nevertheless, some historians, professional and amateur, still refer to Lucy by that name, a legacy of the Temple article. Hunter's anecdote about Lucy telling Mrs. Temple she would marry John even at the foot of a scaffold has also become part of the John Wilkes Booth legend.[28]

Lucy's marriage to a career politician kept her busy. They had their first and only child, John Parker Hale Chandler, in 1885 when Lucy was forty-four, relatively old for a first-time mother. Most of Lucy's married life was spent shuttling between her home in Concord, New Hampshire, and Washington, D.C., fulfilling her role as a "spirited and gracious helpmate and hostess."[29]

Lucy died in 1915, at seventy-four. None of the newspapers reporting her death mentioned her relationship with John Wilkes Booth, but some friends of the family said she never got over her infatuation with the assassin.[30] William Chandler died two years later in 1917. He was buried next to his first wife, Ann Caroline, who died thirty years earlier in 1871.

Chandler's family continued to deny the rumors about Lucy's engagement to John long after both their deaths. In 1944, Leon B. Richardson, Chandler's biographer, said he had asked Admiral Lloyd Chandler, William Chandler's son by his first wife, about the rumors. The admiral, Richardson stated, was intensely hostile to his stepmother and did not believe there was any truth to Lucy's engagement to John first because Lucy was in no way romantic or likely to be moved by infatuation, and secondly because his father was too straight-laced to have married a woman with a tainted past. The rumor, he insisted, was "malignant and entirely unfounded."

Richardson said that from all he had learned, Lucy was "a thoroughly unpleasant woman."[31]

# 29

# EFFIE GERMON

**W**hile John was making his escape from Ford's Theatre, Effie Germon was on stage at Grover's Theatre five blocks away, singing "Sherman Has Marched to the Sea."[1] George Wren was waiting in the wings about to go on when manager C. D. Hess came running over "with a face like death." "Lincoln has just been shot in his box at Ford's," Hess blurted. Without thinking, Wren's first reaction was "John Booth did it."[2]

Inside the theatre, the audience panicked. Everyone rushed toward the doors, assuming the Confederates were attacking the city. Someone else shouted it was a ruse concocted by pickpockets to get people crashing into each other so that they wouldn't feel their wallets being lifted as they rushed out the doors. Reassured, they headed back to their seats only to be told seconds later that it was true.

Like everyone else, Effie scrambled to leave the theatre. Unlike the actors and actresses at Ford's Theatre, she wasn't detained or suspected of involvement in the assassination. Since the theaters were all closed afterwards, there was nothing for her to do but leave for her home at

254 JOHN WILKES BOOTH

1129 Race Street in Philadelphia where she was living at the time with her mother. By coincidence, her house was about a block away from John's sister's Asia's home at 1021 Race Street.

Effie could not have known John had her photo in his pocket when he died, but her memories of John were still vivid, and she felt she had to send Asia some words of consolation and an offer to help if needed.[3] Other than Effie, none of John's acting friends contacted his family to express their condolences. Asia said she treasured that small token of kindness.[4]

By 1866, Effie was a celebrated actress in her own right. Two song-writers named dance tunes after her, expecting that name recognition would boost sales.[5] Sculptor Constantino Brumid used her image as the model for Columbia, the maiden sitting to Washington's left in his painting *The Apotheosis of Washington* (1865) in the rotunda of the Capitol.[6]

Effie decided to stay in Philadelphia at the Walnut Street Theater, at that time jointly managed by John's brother Edwin and Asia's husband John Sleeper Clarke.[7] The *Spirit of the Times* said she was "a decided improvement on the soubrettes of the present day with whom we have been afflicted, and combined with a beautiful face and figure, has a sweet, clear voice, which adds materially to her attractions."[8] She stayed until 1869 when she left for New York as the star at Wallack's Lyceum Theater and married minstrel Nelson "Nelse" Seymour. The "doll-faced actress's" rollicking performances drew sell-out audiences.[9]

Effie landed in the middle of a minor international ruckus when a young man, identified only as a "certain scion of English nobility," became infatuated with her. Night after night he sent her expensive gifts, including priceless heirloom jewels. The impetuous "scion's" family pressured the British government to get them back. Effie could not have been more surprised when England's minister to Washington rapped on her door to negotiate for their return. Effie agreed to give back the heirlooms in return for their value, dollar for dollar, in other gems.[10]

Effie and Seymour had been living together for a year when Seymour read in a newspaper that Carlo Patti, Effie's former husband, was returning to the United States from France with his new wife, opera singer Nully Pierls.[11] Despite Effie's having divorced Carlo, his coming to New York unsettled Seymour and he divorced Effie.

A few years later, Effie married again. Her third husband was a musician, known to history only as "Mr. Smith." Smith died less than a year later, but they were married long enough for Effie to have her first child, a boy about whom nothing is known except for her naming him Harold.[12] Effie's fourth husband was minstrel Charles F. Gibbons. Like many theatrical couples, they were seldom together. While Effie remained in New York, Gibbons travelled the country and worked for many years in San Francisco before returning to New York.[13]

Effie Germon "beyond the boundaries of her bodice" before going on the Banting diet. *Courtesy of New York Public Library, Billy Rose Division.*

Now in her late forties, Effie had "grown beyond the boundaries of her bodice."[14] Her weight (the news media called it "superfluidity of the flesh") was becoming a career crisis. She decided to try and lose weight on the "Banting diet,"[15] a new, low-carb fad, and her attempted weight loss drew national attention.

After relating the success story of Fanny Davenport (another portly actress), the *New York Daily Times* reported how Effie Germon, "the charming soubrette of Wallack's theatre," was doing on the Banting system. She suffered from hunger and thirst and often felt weak. Instead of losing weight, Effie put on more pounds. "Stouter and stouter did I grow on that till I was obliged to give it up, so that of late I do nothing but take all the exercise I can, and that seems to keep me about the same weight from year to year."[16] In all likelihood, Effie had been cheating.

Now "thoroughly matronly," Effie resigned herself to her weight and its inevitable typecasting. As the "corpulent grandmother" in *Our Baby*, Effie was "faithful to reality."[17]

Effie Germon at age sixty. "I feel as young as I did at thirty," but "I know my time has passed." *Courtesy of New York Public Library, Billy Rose Division.*

Despite her matronly appearance, Effie was still a vibrant woman, but her marriages were less so. Husband number four, Charles Gibbons, died in 1881.[18] Marriage to husband number five, actor Albert Roberts, lasted three years. Her sixth and last marriage was to a man named Fiske. It is unknown how long that lasted.[19]

In 1905, at sixty years of age and retired, Effie told an interviewer, "They say I'm too short for grandes dames, and of course I know my time has passed for soubrettes, although I feel as young as I did at thirty." She would have liked to continue working, she said, but no one would hire her.[20] Her last appearance on stage was in 1907 with Ethel Barrymore.

Effie spent her remaining years at the Actor's Fund Home on Staten Island until her death in 1914 at age sixty-eight. Although she had once been a very wealthy woman, she had lost (or been cheated out of) her wealth and died penniless.[21]

# 38

# ALICE GRAY

Had it not been for her ambition, Alice Gray would have been arrested along with Ford's Theatre's other actors and actresses in the aftermath of the assassination.

A month before, on March 18, 1865, she had been John's leading lady at Ford's Theatre when he volunteered to come out of retirement to appear in a benefit for his friend, John McCullough. In the week before the assassination she was still at Ford's Theatre but had been increasingly absent.[1] John Ford knew she was pursuing her "New York ambitions" and began grooming Jeannie Gourlay as her replacement. On the night of the assassination, Alice was still away on one of her "absences," and Jeannie Gourlay stepped in as her replacement in *Our American Cousin*. Unlike the rest of the cast at Ford's Theatre, Alice was never arrested.

There is no trace of her for the next few months until July 22, 1865, when she began appearing at P. T. Barnum's Academy of Music in New York.[2] Two months later she was at Barnum's Winter Garden Theatre as leading lady, filling in for Rose Etyinge, who had fallen ill just before opening night. Alice hadn't had much time to rehearse her part and at times fumbled her lines. "Otherwise," the *New York Clipper* commented, "she is a very acceptable leading stock actress."[3]

The next few years were spent barnstorming in and around Ohio. From December through January 1866, the "beautiful and brilliant artiste Miss Alice Gray" was the headliner at Turner's Opera House in Dayton.[4] At Wood's Theatre in Cincinnati she "riveted the audience;" in Columbus she was lauded as a spellbinding actress "of rare beauty and grace."[5] In the off season she placed an ad in the *New York Clipper* that "responsible managers" could reach her for the coming fall and winter seasons at her home in Cincinnati.[6]

In New York, George Wood at the Old Broadway Theatre hired Alice as his leading stock actress for the 1866–1867 season.[7] Two weeks after it opened, the *New York Herald*'s critic noted that Alice was playing to overflow audiences. He commented, "If not already enthroned [she] will undoubtedly become a favorite in New York."[8]

The following season Alice was at the Holliday Street Theatre in Baltimore along with Effie Germon, playing opposite Edwin.[9] Being together again must have brought back reminiscences of their time with John. After Edwin's engagement ended in October, Alice and Effie were hired as leading ladies at the Walnut Street Theatre in Philadelphia for the rest of the season.[10]

Most of the next season was spent in New Orleans as lead stock actress at the Varieties Theatre. A few months after she started there she was almost hit in the face by an apple that someone in the gallery threw at the performers for fun.[11] When the season ended in late April, Alice left for Cincinnati for a brief appearance at the National Theatre opposite headliner Charles Pope.[12]

Pope felt he had good chemistry with Alice and hired her as his leading lady when he took over as manager of the Mobile (Alabama) Theatre in January 1870.[13] The *Mobile Register* was especially complimentary to Alice who "grows nightly upon Mobile audiences and gave us last night a truly womanly presentation of the womanly part of Clara Douglas in *Money*."[14] The chemistry continued when they both appeared next in New Orleans at the St. Charles Theatre.[15]

At the end of the season, the Orleans Dramatic Relief Association and Shakespeare Club gave Alice a farewell benefit, which the *New Orleans Times-Picayune* said she richly deserved: "Few of the actresses who have visited New Orleans have gained more warm friends than Miss Grey [sic]," said the *New Orleans Times-Picayune*, adding "her unvarying modesty and grace of deportment have won for her that admiration which is worth far more to a true woman than the brief triumphs won by unblushing mediocrity though unladylike actions or indelicate expressions."[16]

When Pope agreed to be manager of the new Opera House in Kansas City in 1871, he hired Alice as his leading lady. The Opera House was a commercial flop.[17] Alice did not see much future in staying and left in April. A month later Pope also resigned and left.

By the late 1880s, Alice Gray was past her prime and had to settle for unheralded minor roles with small companies. Her final years as an actress were spent with the oddly named "Held by the Enemy Company." In 1887, she married William L. Lawson in Haverhill, Massachusetts.[18] Other than his name, nothing is known about him. On the way to Bridgeport from New York in October 1890, she was not feeling well. Nevertheless, she went on stage that night. The next day she was taken to the hospital where she died of "apoplexy."[19]

Her obituary in the *Cincinnati Commercial Tribune* commented that Alice had been an "exemplary Catholic, and had made more than one fortune but had died poor as a result of her prodigality and generosity to those in and out of the profession."[20]

# 31

# HELEN WESTERN

Helen and Lucille Western each went their own way after their spat over John in April 1861. Lucille became a dramatic actress. Helen went in for light comedy and capitalized on her looks. In August 1861, she opened at the Holliday Street Theatre in Baltimore.[1] The *Baltimore Daily Exchange* told its readers, "Miss Helen Western, the pretty and talented actress, whose New York fame follows her here...ranks, young as she is [at seventeen], among the first in her line of light comedy, and promises soon to be at the very head of her profession."[2]

Helen stayed six weeks at the Holliday Street Theatre before moving on to Washington in September where she was booked into the National Theater. A month later she was back at the Holliday Street Theatre "turning topsy turvey the heads of the bucks of the 'monument city.'"[3]

One of the "topsy turvey" heads Helen turned was Bill Hoblitzell's, a wealthy Baltimore engineer.[4] In love with Helen from the moment he saw her, Hoblitzell followed Helen when she went up north for her next engagement and proposed to her in Troy, New York. Hoblitzell knew his family would never approve of his marrying an actress, so they eloped and left for Paris in November 1861.⁵ A year later, Helen gave birth to a girl she named "Sallie Lawrence Hoblitzell."⁶

Helen was not the simple-minded beauty she was made out to be by disapproving theatre critics. Though only eighteen years old and a young mother, she put together a travelling company, set Hoblitzell to work as her publicity agent, and toured England, Ireland, and Scotland for the next two years.

Theater reviewers in England and elsewhere were just as taken with her beauty as American critics. There were also those who were just as disapproving. In London and Hull, "her admirable and clever" appearance garnered enthusiastic reviews. The applause she received testified to the audience's deep satisfaction.⁷ Liverpool's theatre critic, on the other hand, was frigid. Although he conceded she was "remarkably beautiful," he said she was "stupid." The same critic later praised Edwin Booth, who appeared after Helen, as "a great actor," but Edwin "couldn't draw expenses" whereas Helen "made money."⁸

At the end of her two-year tour, Helen left for home with two-year-old Sallie and without Hoblitzell. During their time abroad, Hoblitzell and Helen had become estranged, and Hoblitzell had gotten himself into at least one serious confrontation with theatre managers. Hoblitzell hadn't realized what being married to an itinerant star would be like. He tired of following Helen around as her manager and returned to the United States without her or his daughter.

Helen had originally made arrangements to appear in Montreal. On her way back she changed her mind and headed instead for her mother's home in Malden, a small town north of Boston. As soon as she settled Sallie with her mother, Helen filed papers to divorce Hoblitzell and booked herself in Baltimore then Alexandria then Toronto.⁹

Helen was the star attraction at the Broadway Theatre from July to August 1864 where she filled every seat in the theatre with men willing to "'pay any price' to gawk at her in her barely concealing costumes."¹⁰ A titillated *New York Times* critic had little to say about the plays she appeared in and a lot to say about how she looked. "When we state that Miss HELEN WESTERN is a well looking lady, with a free and unembarrassed presence in the fairest of garments, we have said all that is necessary."[11]

Helen Western, circa 1864. *Courtesy of New York Public Library, Billy Rose Division.*

A growing number of theatre critics, however, began lambasting Helen's "naked school" of acting and complained about her "stripping class" of plays that stretched the bounds of immorality. The *New York Post* complained her style of acting and lack of refinement was "sometimes really offensive" and "disgusted the respectable portion of the audience."[12]

The *New York Clipper*, the theatre trade's newspaper, which had previously commented on Helen's and Lucille's raunchy antics as the "Star Sisters," defended Helen:

> Let Miss Western go ahead, and play the pieces that please
> her patrons most.... Shakespeare is not her forte, and the
> people would cut her if she attempted anything of that sort.

Her line is the sensational and people go to see as such of a
pretty woman as they can for the money, and as Miss Western
is one of the pretty kind, the lovers of the beauties of animated
nature go to see and hear her.[13]

One of those lovers of beauty was John Wilkes Booth. John was
staying at his brother Edwin's home in New York for the summer and
undoubtedly kept up with who was starring at the local theatres. During
Helen's last week at the Broadway Theatre, the theater management
handed everyone in the audience her photo as a souvenir.[14] That photo
was likely the one he had in his pocket when he died. Despite his many
other affairs, for John the brief time they spent together was an affair to
remember.

In March 1865, Helen was robbed and then fell in love again. She
was at the Chestnut Street Theatre in Philadelphia when a thief broke
into her room and made off with some of her most valuable stage dresses,
worth about $2,500.[15] A few days after the break-in, she met Jim Herne,
the male lead at the nearby Walnut Street Theater's stock company. Less
than a year before his involvement with Helen, Herne had been romancing Helen's married sister, Lucille. Herne would eventually marry Helen
but would abandon her and go back to Lucille.

Herne met and fell in love with Lucille when she was the headliner
at the Holliday Street Theatre, but she was married to James Mead, and
Herne eventually withdrew.[16] Herne stayed on at the Holliday Street
Theatre until his contract ended in August 1864 then left for Philadelphia. Although he was still carrying the proverbial torch for Lucille, it
didn't keep him from taking up with her sister Helen when she appeared
at the nearby Chestnut Street Theater in March 1865.

For Helen, an affair with Herne may at first have been her way of
getting back at Lucille, whose liaison with Herne was common theatre

gossip. Whatever the reason, as her feelings for the handsome Irish actor deepened, she began missing the scheduled eleven o'clock rehearsals. When Helen didn't show up for yet another rehearsal, her manager, James Guest, began pacing. Dripping with sweat, he "puffed about, and waddled up and down in front of the theatre his fat cheeks hanging down below his ears like a couple of hams from a pair of butcher's hooks."

Exasperated, Guest asked the actors milling about on stage, "Where's Jim Herne? Find him and perhaps we'll know where Miss Western is."

"I seen 'im half an hour ago," said one of the theater's stagehands.

"Where?" Guest nervously asked.

"Why, sir, he was driving down Chestnut Street in an open carriage."

"Who was with him?"

"Helen Western, sir."

"Helen fury!" Guest blasted. "That means a rehearsal of catfish and waffles at the Wissachickon [hotel] and none here!"[17]

Helen was in Boston at the Howard Atheneum for her next scheduled appearance when the news about the assassination flashed across the country. Though it doubtless jolted her, there is no record of her reaction to the news nor to John's death. One can only imagine how she would have reacted had she found out that John had her picture in his pocket when he died.

Helen drew the usual packed male audiences at the Howard Atheneum. Mayflower, the Boston theater critic, wisecracked that she was "playing with all her ancient vigor and abandon. She is a favorite with the Howard audiences, who have an eye for beauty, and Helen is comely to look upon—-a good deal" and was especially a hit with the "physiologically curious." "There was no denying," Mayflower added, no doubt enjoying his pun, that "Miss Western *outstrips* [Mayflower's italics] all her contemporaries."[18]

In July 1865 Helen was booked at the Theatre Royal in Montreal. The Royal was a popular venue for American actors in the 1860s during the summers, but there was another reason Helen arranged a booking there—Jim Herne was in Montreal.

Sibling rivalry aside, Helen's feelings for Herne were genuine. Three weeks after she arrived in Montreal, she and Herne were married in what columnist Amy Leslie would later describe as "one of the most tragic romances of the American stage."[19] Although Herne was Helen's husband, he was still in love with Lucille.

In September, Helen was back in Boston at the Howard Atheneum "displaying her symmetrical shape." Mayflower, one of Helen's most ardent admirers among Boston's theater critics, noticed a woman who had just come from a meeting of the "friends of physical culture." The woman "had so far overcome her natural scruplings of modesty," said Mayflower, "as to discard the ordinary garments of her sex and to appear in a costume altogether novel and striking." But compared to Helen Western, the woman's lower extremities were "what a pipe-stem is to a watermelon."[20] By 1866 Helen was dressing even more provocatively. Her appearance in *The French Spy* was "naked and vulgar" with the "wantonness of a Bacchanal." In the *Pet of the Petticoats*, "she perpetrates gags which are really indecent."[21]

The "bacchanals" were not all on stage. Herne was a drunkard and Helen succumbed to his dissipation. In November, they were in Biddeford, Maine, for a one-night performance. When no one came on stage, the audience hooted and hollered. Helen and Herne heard them from their room in the back of the theater but paid no attention. They were dead drunk.

Tired of waiting and hissing, the grumbling audience left. The furniture dealer from whom Herne had rented tables and chairs for their dressing room came backstage to claim his property and forced his way into Helen's room. Inside, empty bottles were strewn all over the floor. A barely costumed Helen, in her role as a fairy nymph that night, was lounging on a sofa. Herne and several other actors were sprawled in chairs. Everyone was juiced. Defiantly standing on wobbly legs, Helen and Herne rose to confront the intruder.

In the brief tussle that ensued, the furniture man scratched Helen's face. Plastered as she was, she managed to deck him and sent him sprawling. Sensing blood dripping from her face, she became frightened and fell into Herne's arms. Just as he was about to fall into a chair with her on top of him, he stammered, "I'll, hic, protect you to the last, hic!" and collapsed. The *New York Clipper* reported the debacle as "A Gay Old Time" without further comment.[22] It would not be the last time Herne's boozing would keep his leading lady from performing.

Helen's next fracas occurred in February 1867 at the Chestnut Street Theatre in Chicago. Reverend Dr. Hatfield, a clergyman well known to Chicago's citizenry for raiding and closing down theatres he considered immoral, burst into the Chestnut Street Theatre with a police escort during *The French Spy* and shut down the "salacious" play.[23] The grand-standing raid had no lasting impact. The next night Helen was back on stage as provocative as before.

A few months later Helen received an offer from Tom Maguire in San Francisco she could not refuse. In return for a fifty-night engagement at his Opera House, Maguire promised her "very liberal terms," payable "in gold."[24]

Helen and Herne arrived in San Francisco in late April 1867.[25] McGuire had playbills printed that titillated theater-goers with "a fresh sensation and a fresh topic for conversation."[26] Colored photographs of Helen were posted in window store fronts and remained up for months.[27] A life-sized oil portrait, displayed in a store window, by an artist, Fortunato Arriola, made him a celebrated local artist.[28]

Helen was showered with bouquets of flowers from the audience at her opening on April 29. The theatre critic for the *Daily Alta California* gushed that "her movements are graceful, her voice is powerful, and some of her attitudes are grande."[29] California's other theatre critics were far less enthusiastic, praising the "Western shape" while disparaging the "Western acting."[30] Helen's performance of Nancy Sykes in *Oliver Twist* "was rather a Bowery g'hal than a creature of low life in London."[31] The critics were also appalled at Helen's scanty costumes. "Helen Western outstrips anybody ever seen at the San Francisco theatres," said one columnist. "The Monkey was clothed in comparison."[32]

Back east, Helen retreated to their farm in Massachusetts and wrote the *San Francisco Chronicle* that she was "completely disgusted with the people of California."[33]

By then Helen and Herne's marriage had come apart.[34] Like Lucille's husband, Herne had sapped his wife's money. When Herne learned that Lucille's marriage had also come apart[35] and that Lucille had accepted an engagement in San Francisco while waiting for her divorce, Herne made up his mind. He left Helen and headed back to California.[36]

After Herne left, Helen hired Charles Wing as her new business agent and tried to resume her career, but by then she was seriously ill.

In early November 1868, while on stage in Pittsburgh, she felt an excruciating pain inside her abdomen and had to leave in the midst of her performance.[37] After a few days' rest, she felt well enough to travel to Washington for her scheduled appearance at Wall's Opera House. Wing booked her into the Kirkwood House,[38] the same hotel Vice President Andrew Johnson had been staying at when Lincoln was shot.

Helen barely managed to get through her first night. "The performance was given but not enjoyed by the audience," the *New York Clipper* reported, adding that Miss Western was "laboring under quite a severe illness."[39] Wall's Opera House remained dark for the next two nights while Helen recuperated in her room. By the third day Helen felt strong enough to return. Just before start time Wing sent word Helen was still in too much pain to go on stage. Minutes before the curtain was to go up, the theatre manager came on stage to inform the audience two of the theater's stock actresses would play her scheduled parts.[40]

The next night Helen mustered her remaining strength and went on stage despite still feeling ill. Halfway through the first play of the night her voice turned husky, she slurred her words, and she became so unsteady on her feet she fell onto the stage several times. Many in the audience thought she was drunk and hissed and jeered as the curtain abruptly came down.[41]

With Helen gravely ill and languishing in her room, there was no money coming in, but Wing was still running up heavy bills for "extras" like wines, liquor, etc.[42] At the height of her career, Helen was estimated to have been worth $100,000, the equivalent of a million in today's dollars. Much of it had been drained away by her various managers, including Herne. Helen had also been very charitable to other actors who had fallen on hard times.[43] Now her money was almost all gone. Wing pawned some of Helen's wardrobe to pay their hotel bill and promised the manager they would check out the next day.

When it came time to depart Helen had taken a turn for the worse. The manager agreed to let Helen stay but insisted she would have to move to a smaller room (by coincidence she was staying in the same suite as Andrew Johnson the night of the assassination[44]) because it had been rented to a congressman and his wife.[45]

Helen was wrapped in warm clothing and blankets, seated in a chair, and carried to her new room.[46] A doctor, called in to examine her, did not hold out hope for improvement.[47] On the morning of December 11, 1868, just before she died, Helen was heard to mutter, "This is becoming serious."[48]

She was just twenty-three. Her cause of death was reported as "congestion of the bowels."[49]

Wing had Helen's body clothed in a pearl colored silk dress, one of her remaining stage costumes he hadn't pawned,[50] and arranged with an undertaker to have her body shipped by train back to Boston. When the undertaker demanded payment in advance, Wing bartered Helen's remaining possessions as payment[51] and paid off his bill at the Kirkwood House with the rest. Somehow he managed to scrape enough money together to accompany Helen's remains back to Boston.

Helen was interred in Mount Auburn Cemetery outside Boston.[52] Lucille told a friend that she had had a premonition Helen was going to die a month before she passed.[53] Neither Lucille nor Herne came to Helen's funeral.

Although they had started out as a sister act, Helen and Lucille had been opposites from the beginning. Helen was a lighthearted and playful actress; Lucille was what theatre critics liked to call a "legitimate" actress, which meant either Shakespeare or melodramas. But in one respect Helen and Lucille were no different from one another: they both fell victim to Jim Herne's charm and both suffered for it.

In the spring of 1869, Herne was offered a job as manager of the Grand Opera House in New York. He and Lucille came back east by train from California, stopping off at various towns along the way to earn some extra money. In Salt Lake City, the manager of the local theater had to cancel their shows twice—once because Herne was too drunk to go on stage, and once because Lucille "was so beastly drunk" she could hardly speak her lines. The *Utah Daily Reporter* bemoaned that the night's aptly titled potboiler, *The Foul Play*, was a "foul play indeed."[54]

Despite Lucille's considerable earnings, Herne was spending her money as fast as she was making it. To cope she turned to morphine, a drug legal in America until the early twentieth century.[55] By 1873 Lucille was seriously ill. A year later Herne left her and returned to California.

Lucille became a recluse after Herne left.[56] On January 11, 1877, a few minutes into her performance, the theater manager lowered the curtain. Lucille was so weak she could not speak above a whisper. She was helped back to her room where she lapsed into a coma and died. She had just turned thirty-four. Just before becoming unconscious she muttered, "Rest at last."[57] Herne did not attend her funeral.[58]

Although they had not spoken to one another for more than twenty years, with the exception of one appearance to raise money for their destitute mother, the "Star Sisters" were reunited in death, buried in Mount Auburn Cemetery in Boston beside one another and alongside their step-father, William English, who had launched their career. Looking at the markers in Mount Auburn Cemetery where Helen and Lucille are buried, no one would know they were sisters. The name on Helen's tombstone is "Helen Western Herne." Lucille is buried under the name "Pauline Mead."

# 32

# FANNY BROWN

om Maguire was looking to hire an actress. With a fortune made
from his San Francisco saloon and gambling house, he'd expanded
into show business and was owner of the 2,000-seat Jenny Lind
Theatre. To manage it, he hired John's eldest brother, June Booth.[1]
Maguire knew that a sure way to pack a theatre was to put sex on stage,
at least as much as sensibilities at the time allowed. In 1863 he had hired
Adah Isaacs Menken, an actress who scandalized New York's critics and
delighted its audiences as Prince Ivan in *Mazeppa*, riding offstage wearing a revealing, flesh-colored body stocking. Sticking to his strategy of
hiring the flashiest performers money could buy, Maguire sent his agent,
Sheridan Corbyn, to New York in September 1864 to hire Fanny Brown,
the most beautiful woman on the American stage, "at a good salary,
payable in gold."[2]

Despite great expectations, Fanny was a disappointment. The *Boston
Post*'s critic told readers back home Fanny's "beauty seems to eclipse her
acting."[3] Another critic was more blunt: "We can scarcely chronicle a
success for the lady. It was simply a mistake."[4] Fanny had not been the

273

draw Maguire expected. A quarrel over money turned ugly. Fanny accused Corbyn of calling her "a fiend under the mask of a woman" and threatening to "break every bone in her body."[5]

After Corbyn fired her, Fanny sued him for breach of contract. The *New York Times*'s correspondent couldn't resist quipping, "she is great in breeches you know."[6]

Fanny's next job was at the rival Metropolitan Theatre where she reprised Adah Menken's role in *Mazeppa*. The *San Francisco Chronicle* was particularly impressed with her swordsmanship. Fanny "would distinguish herself as a light cavalry officer in Sherman's army...She possesses a rare fighting talent that ought not to be wasted."[7] During their New England tour the year before, John Wilkes Booth had taught her how to use a sword.

Audiences were not as enthusiastic. Fanny moved on to Worrell's Olympic Theatre where she played a tambourine and sang "with much gusto 'I'd Choose to be a Baby,'" a song written by Fred Buckley, Fanny's ex-husband. The *New York Clipper* quipped that Fanny singing the baby business in his family nursery "wouldn't be at all undesirable."[8]

The "baby business" may not have been that far from Fanny's mind. By then she had fallen in love. In 1866 she married William Lawrence, a circus acrobat who called himself "Signor Felix Carlo,"[9] and accompanied him and his troupe on a brief tour to Portland, Oregon, and other venues in the Northwest.[10]

After their Northwest tour Fanny sailed for Australia with Carlo, who had signed on with John Wilson's Circus Company.[11] While Carlo was performing with the circus, Fanny reprised her role as Mazeppa at the Theatre Royal in Melbourne, "the first appearance in this quarter of the Globe of the Lady Equestriene and actress Miss Fanny Brown, Who will enact the role of Mazeppa, making the fearful assent to the back of the wild horse."[12] After Melbourne, Fanny took her act to New Zealand, whose audiences were just as enthralled as Melbourne's to witness "this great spectacle."[13]

Fanny and Carlo were back in San Francisco in 1868. While Carlo was making arrangements to tour South America with the Chiarini Circus,

Fanny agreed to star in a parody of *Antony and Cleopatra*. But even for Fanny the play was too lewd. She backed out "to avoid mouthing disgusting passages." Two other actresses backed out for the same reason.[14]

In 1879 Carlo died from kidney failure while they were touring in Jamaica.[15] Broken-hearted, Fanny gave up performing, moved back to Boston, and bought a house on Washington Street. Several years later in 1885, she returned to San Francisco for a brief reappearance at Maguire's Opera House. Although well into her fifties by then, she was still being advertised as the "beautiful actress."[16]

A chubby Fanny Brown in her late forties. *Courtesy of New York Public Library, Billy Rose Division.*

Living in quiet retirement in Boston, Fanny had no idea someone in the government had become obsessed with her. Among the artifacts taken from John's body and stored in the judge advocate general's (JAG) office were the five tinted *cartes de visite* he'd kept in his pocket. The women in the photos were presumed to be actresses but were initially mistakenly identified. By the 1890s, four of the women in the photos in John's pocket had been identified, albeit incorrectly for a time. Eventually they were correctly identified as Helen Western, Alice Gray, Effie Germon, and Lucy Hale. The identity of the woman in the remaining photo of Fanny Brown was still unknown. It also differed from the other four in that their images were all profiles whereas Fanny's photo was a full-body image of her dressed in a gown and looking directly at the camera. Determined to track down her identity, a clerk in the JAG office secretly and unlawfully took the photo to the nearby studio of J. J. Faber where he had it duplicated with the label "The Mysterious Beauty" inscribed below it and circulated copies in hopes that someone might identify the last of John Wilkes Booth's photos.

Fanny Brown. "The Mysterious Beauty." Fanny's
*carte de visite* was found on John Wilkes Booth's
body when he died. *Courtesy of U.S. National Park Service.*

The photo was eventually identified, but it isn't known when or by whom. All that is known is that years later John Simonton, the custodian of the JAG office, sent a copy to author Francis Wilson for a book he was writing about John Wilkes Booth. Simonton told Wilson the photo had been recognized as Fanny Brown and that the caption, "The Mysterious Beauty," "had been effaced from the original."[17]

In 1892, Fanny inherited a large amount of money from a friend of her mother and used some of it to build the Hotel Biner on Washington Street in Boston.[18]

Although getting on in years, Fanny missed the stage. At age sixty she boarded a train for Los Angeles for one last appearance at the Orpheum Theatre.[19] She died six months later in 1891 at her home in Boston,[20] one of the few women in John's life who did not die in poverty or misery.

# 33

# HENRIETTA IRVING

Nothing good ever came of knowing John Wilkes Booth. With one or two exceptions, every actress he was involved with experienced marital strife, heartbreak, substance abuse, or destitution.

Henrietta Irving, the star-crossed lover who tried to disfigure him in a jealous rage and then turned the knife on herself, took a long time to recover from her near fatal suicide. Either her injuries were very serious, or she was so traumatized she just needed to get as far away as she could to recover her health and sanity. So she moved to Milwaukee.[1] What she did for the next two years is a historical blank.

The first indications that she had recovered are advertisements in late 1863 in several New York papers for Henrietta's appearances at the Park Theatre in Brooklyn and the Olympic Theatre on Broadway.[2] The *Boston Post*'s theatre critic was impressed. "New York," he told his readers, had "a new actress, a Miss Henrietta Irving, a handsome, graceful and self-possessed young lady, with the most efficient black eyes, and a pleasant voice."[3]

The *New York Tribune*'s critic praised Henrietta for bucking the current trend of actresses dressing up in expensive costumes. An actress "may be as empty [headed] as you please," the *New York Tribune* sniffed, provided she appears radiant. Other actresses, it urged, should follow Henrietta's example.[4] Henrietta was such a favorite at the Olympic Theatre that its musical director, Thomas Baker, wrote a polka he named after her which featured Henrietta's full-length portrait on the cover.[5]

At the end of 1864, Henrietta signed on at the St. Charles Theatre in New Orleans[6] where thirty-two-year-old Edward Eddy was actor and manager.[7] Meeting Eddy was destined to be a turning point in her life; at the time it was just another engagement.

Six feet tall, handsome, with a powerful voice, Eddy had been a favorite melodrama star at the boisterous Bowery Theatre in New York for many years before coming to New Orleans. When Henrietta first met Eddy, he was happily married to Mary Matthews, a retired actress, and had taken her and their son with him to New Orleans. A week later, tragedy struck. Eddy's wife fell ill and died.[8] Eddy was inconsolable. When Eddy returned to New York to bury his wife, Henrietta moved over to the Varieties Theatre.[9]

If Henrietta thought she had put the past behind her, she was mistaken. After the assassination, newspapers all over the country dredged up her almost murdering Lincoln's killer in Albany four years previously.[10] Oddly, none of the newspapers interviewed her about her relationship with John. Whatever her reaction was when she heard her former lover had shot President Lincoln, she kept it to herself.

Later that year Eddy was back in New Orleans at the St. Charles Theatre, acting once again with Henrietta. Eddy was lonely. So was Henrietta. Never a star who traded on her looks and no longer youthful, she was as much in need of someone to be with as he was. Their professional relationship turned into more than camaraderie. In April 1867, they married.[11]

By the 1870s, Eddy was past his prime and in failing health.[12] Henrietta was also losing her appeal.[13] By 1875, Eddy was struggling to find work. In November he and Henrietta left for Kingston, Jamaica, where they were booked for an extended engagement. Five days after their arrival, Eddy developed a fever. On the morning of December 16 he suffered a stroke. His last words were "My God! What is the matter with me?"[14]

Despite receiving $25,000 for his New York house at auction in 1872, Eddy had squandered it all.[15] Henrietta had not saved much either. Suddenly widowed, Henrietta was "without funds." She managed to borrow enough money to bring Eddy's remains back to the United States, expecting that Eddy's Masonic lodge would remunerate her since Eddy was a thirty-third-degree Mason. Although they buried him with full Masonic pageantry,[16] the lodge refused to reimburse her because Eddy had not paid his dues.[17]

Eddy's death and her financial distress were too much to cope with, and Henrietta fell ill. With nowhere else to turn, she appealed to the *New York Sun* newspaper for help. She had been confined in bed for weeks, she said, "by illness brought on by grief and want. I am without the common necessaries of life—fire, wood or medicine. God help me if this my appeal to you should fail." Her illness was being made worse, she said, by constant letters from Jamaica demanding repayment of the loans she had incurred, including one for the shroud in which Eddy was buried. "I am heart-broken."[18]

The *New York Sun* was moved by her plea and sent a journalist to visit her. Entering her room, he was startled to see a large Newfoundland dog sitting by her bed, "looking as though he knew that his mistress was in trouble." Henrietta was thin, pale, very weak, and nervous from long illness.

Henrietta rose from her bed to hand him the bills and dunning letters from the people in Kingston demanding repayment. Inability to pay them back, she said, was keeping her sick. Eddy had left her nothing and she had no savings of her own. She did not have to say how grief-stricken and discouraged she was, said the reporter; it was all in her face.[19]

Reading about Henrietta's plight, *Pomeroy's Democrat*, a Chicago newspaper, editorialized there was something sad about the acting profession:

> Forty-nine out of every fifty actors, actresses or professional people live the most unhappy lives. They are nervous, restless, rambling and desultory. Year after year they are knocked around from pillar to post, mussed, squeezed, tumbled, seduced, forsaken, deserted, as a luscious orange is picked, squeezed sucked dry and the skin at last thrown in the gut-ter...It is not the person, so much as the vagabond life actors and actresses lead that cause their grief—having no homes, always on the move, thrown into all manner of temptations. While we like to see a play or performance, we had rather bury a child than see it embark in such a hazardous calling, that is, if it was a child we loved.[20]

Henrietta Irving toward the end of her career. *Courtesy of New York Public Library, Billy Rose Division.*

Henrietta eventually recovered, and with help from friends she repaid her debts and was able to resume her career.[21] But offers in New York were few and far between. In 1880 she agreed to hire on as the leading actress in Helena, Montana, at the Sawtell Theatre and at theatres in the outlying towns around Helena.[22]

When the company closed its season in Helena, Henrietta formed her own touring stock company out west.[23] When that venture flopped, she headed back east and toured with various stock companies.[24] By 1888 she was suffering from uterine fibroids (growths in the uterus that cause excessive menstrual bleeding and associated weakness), for which the only treatment at that time was an abdominal hysterectomy, "one of the most critical operations known to surgery."

Henrietta was still broke. She couldn't afford the operation unless the Actor's Fund helped out. She had used money the Actor's Fund had already sent to pay past debts for board. Before that she had sold her theatrical dresses. Please look into my case, she pleaded with the Actor's Fund's manager. "I do not think you can find a more deserving one. I have always been faithful to my duties and endeavored to the last to help myself without the assistance of others."[25]

Henrietta never got money for the operation. She continued to suffer but had to keep working. In 1891, a *New York Dramatic Mirror* journalist recalled how in her younger days Henrietta had been "a young and dashing actress" and sighed that now she was relegated to playing "a chastened and refined representative of old women's parts."[26]

At sixty-two, Henrietta was drained, ill, and destitute. Her last seven years were spent as a patient of the Home for Incurables in Fordham, New York, paid for by the Actor's Fund.[27] She died November 29, 1905. Her death certificate listed uterine fibroids and cerebral apoplexy as the cause of death.[28]

# 34

# MAGGIE MITCHELL

he night that Lincoln was shot, Maggie was in Louisville at a boarding house with her mother, her sister Mary, Mary's husband, John Albaugh, and Kitty Blanchard. In the middle of the night, Kitty was awakened by a gong at the front door rung so fast and furiously her first thought was fire. She hopped out of bed, wondering what the commotion was about. Just then the door was pushed open, and "Miss Mitchell appeared in the dark passage, as white as a sheet and trembling like a leaf."

Stammering, she blurted, "President Lincoln—tonight—Washington—shot—news just come—don't known the details or who did it. Johnnie [John Albaugh] has gone to the telegraph office to find out and get the next dispatch."[1]

Minutes later, Mary and the others assembled in Maggie's room, huddling together to wait until Albaugh returned. An hour or so later, he came into the room and dropped into a chair. No one said anything, waiting for Albaugh to tell them what he had heard. Maggie broke the silence.

"Tell me what happened!" she exclaimed

Albaugh's face was white.

"Tell me," she repeated.

Albaugh looked up at her and in a hoarse whisper said two words: "John Booth." Maggie was so shaken she cancelled her scheduled engagement in Louisville.[2]

Almost twenty years later, Maggie Mitchell claimed to have dreamed—on the very night of the assassination—that she was standing on the stage at Ford's Theatre when John Booth assassinated Lincoln.[3] It was what psychologists call "false memory." She felt so close to John that years later she imagined she was there, if only in a dream. Many people are positive that they have envisioned some eventful occurrence at the time it was happening, even though they are thousands of miles away. The mind often juggles its memories.[4]

Imagining being at Ford's Theatre was not as strange as it might have been for someone else. Maggie had been the featured star at Ford's Theater many times and knew its layout. She knew where Lincoln would have been sitting when he was shot and knew John would have had to cross the stage to escape through the back door.

Moreover, her relationship with John made it easy to place him in one of her dreams. John Wilkes Booth was not some matinee idol she had once seen on stage. She had personally arranged for his benefit in Montgomery before the war and had wrangled an invitation for him to attend the St. Andrews banquet there. They had acted on stage together, stayed at the same boarding house, and gone riding together.

Those who knew Maggie were aware of her feelings about John Wilkes Booth. "It was such as a woman's life was worth in those days to have had an intimate friendship and acquaintance with him, but I braved all this and secured the lock of his hair," she confessed to the same journalist she told about her dream. "No one ever had more beautiful hair than he," she mused. "'Twas the loveliest hair in the world."[5]

By May of 1867, Maggie had been working nonstop and decided to go on vacation with her mother on what was being billed as a "Mediterranean Excursion to Europe and the Holy Land." All the accommodations were guaranteed to be first class. The trip's organizer, Charles C. Duncan, boasted that only passengers of high moral standing would be taken on board. To eliminate any undesirables, potential passengers were told they had to submit their requests in writing and their applications would be vetted by a special committee. In reality the only vetting that was done was by Duncan himself. The only criterion for respectability was payment of $1,250 per passenger with a down payment of ten percent at acceptance.[6]

Duncan was an early proponent of celebrity endorsements, although in his case he didn't bother to ask permission to use the names he put in his advertisements. Almost as soon as the list of "stars" was publicized, most of them bailed out. The first to cancel was the clergyman and former abolitionist Henry Ward Beecher. Upset at Duncan's using his name to lure passengers on board, Beecher remembered he had a previous commitment.[7] General William T. Sherman bowed out for similar reasons, claiming he was needed to protect his beloved country against the Indians. Mark Twain was overjoyed Sherman bowed out. Duncan had furnished Sherman's room like a palace. With Sherman gone, Twain was next in line for what he said was a "promotion" to Sherman's room.[8]

Maggie was the next to back out. Before she signed on, amateur performers had been booked for the entertainment aboard ship. When Maggie joined, Duncan told reporters Maggie would like nothing better than to entertain the passengers. When she learned what Duncan had been promising in her name, she balked. All she had wanted was a quiet, uneventful vacation voyage. Even though she had paid the ten percent deposit for herself and her mother, she forfeited it and booked another trip to Europe on a less publicized ship.[9] The only celebrity to stay with the announced voyage was Mark Twain, who later wrote about the trip in *The Innocents Abroad*.

At thirty-six, Maggie was beginning to feel lonely. In October 1868, she married Henry Paddock.[10]

When the newspapers found out about their marriage, they delved into Henry's past. A hatmaker by trade, he was said to be "better educated than most commercial men" and quick-witted. He had moved to New York after Maggie left him in Cleveland, was twenty-three when the war broke out, had served three years in the Ninth New York Regiment, and had been honorably discharged after being wounded in the head. After he recovered from his wound he relocated to Toledo and went back into the hatmaking business. Whenever the time and opportunity allowed, he continued courting Maggie.[11]

Two years after marrying Henry, Maggie gave birth to a girl she named Fanchon, after the character in the play that had made her famous. There had been complications during the birth. The newspapers reported Maggie had become paralyzed and was not expected to recover. A few days later she rallied. By July the papers were reporting she was no longer in danger.

Four months later, Maggie was back on stage with Henry as her new business manager—not that she needed anyone to manage her money. Maggie had begun investing her earnings as early as 1863 when she bought shares in Ford's Theater.[12] Stage appearances were garnering her as much as $10,000 a month. She was also earning money as a celebrity endorser for a skin beauty product, *L'Email de Paris*.[13] With all that money pouring in, Maggie bought real estate in New York and New Jersey.

Besides a large home near Fifth Avenue in New York, Maggie paid $200,000 for a summer home in fashionable Long Branch, New Jersey. She furnished it with paintings, statuary, rare and costly books, and Japanese artifacts. She called it Cricket Lodge, after the character that had made her rich and famous.[14] Summers were spent at Long Branch with family, including her brother's two children, whom she had adopted in 1878 after her brother and his wife died in Memphis of yellow fever.[15]

Now into her fifties, Maggie began putting her energy into other business and real estate ventures. In 1888 Maggie announced she was planning to build a theatre on a site she owned in Harlem. The news took a number of New York investors by surprise, especially a syndicate of prominent land speculators—among them theatre manager and composer Oscar Hammerstein—who were buying up property in Harlem's still largely uninhabited farm land.

Hammerstein and his syndicate believed they could entice New Yorkers moving further uptown to their Harlem development by building a theatre that featured the leading stars of the day. To secure the property they needed, they unfortunately hired Harlem real estate developer and con man, twenty-year-old, self-proclaimed millionaire Allen H. Wood, authorizing him to pay upwards of $250,000 for Maggie's Harlem property.

Maggie was an astute businesswoman and a lot wilier than the Hammerstein syndicate. She found out about their plan and hired an architect to draw up plans of her own for a theatre.[16] She had no intention of constructing a theatre of her own, but if the Hammerstein syndicate believed she was, she could demand a higher price for her property. Leaving them to stew, Maggie sailed for Germany to see her daughter who was in school there, leaving her new business manager and new leading man, Charles Abbott, to negotiate the sale of her property if it came to that.

Acting on Maggie's behalf, Abbott accepted Wood's offer of $110,000 for lots Maggie owned at the corner of Seventh and 124th Streets. Wood gave him a down payment and a promise to pay the rest from the mortgage he was arranging.[17] Wood started construction on the new theater before his mortgage deal was finalized but ran out of money to pay his contractors. The property reverted back to Maggie. She immediately put it back up for sale. With the walls Wood had partially erected it was now worth more than what Maggie had originally sold it for.[18]

It was not all smooth sailing for Maggie. The reason Charles Abbott and not Maggie's husband, Henry Paddock, was looking after her business interests is that by then Maggie had divorced Henry.

Maggie and Henry had been married for fifteen years. There was not "a happier or kindlier couple in the world," the *Washington Post* told its readers.[19] A year later their marriage was on the rocks. While sorting through their mail Maggie chanced to come across an envelope addressed to Henry. Thinking it was a business letter, she opened it. It was a love letter to Henry from a woman in Syracuse named Minnie Moore. When Henry came home she fired him as her manager and told him to move out.[20]

Maggie filed divorce proceedings a year later in 1888 but was persuaded by friends and family to forgive Henry and try for a reconciliation. The reconciliation didn't last. Maggie filed for divorce again, offering Henry what she thought was an equitable settlement.

Maggie was worth about half a million dollars (about twelve million in today's dollars) at the time. Henry felt he was entitled to more than what she had offered. Unless Maggie gave him a much larger payoff, he said he would contest the divorce. He also countersued for the money he said Maggie owed him as her manager for the last fifteen years.[21]

Maggie wasn't someone to toy with. She threatened to countersue on grounds of adultery and said he wouldn't get anything. Despite the Minnie Moore letter, Paddock denied he had been unfaithful. Maggie's lawyers called Minnie Moore as a witness. She testified under oath she had been intimate with Henry and hadn't known he was a married man. Minnie's mother also testified that she was aware of Minnie's affair with Henry. She said she also hadn't known he was married. Henry was dead in the water. The divorce was granted in April 1889.[22] Maggie didn't have to pay him anything.

Newspapers following the trial reported Maggie "gets cleverly clear of the fellow by process of law." Asked why it had taken her a year to

Maggie Mitchell, age fifty-six, at the time of her divorce. *Courtesy of New York Public Library, Billy Rose Division.*

divorce Henry after she had learned about his infidelity, Maggie said it was because she was not in the habit of airing her personal affairs in public and was "adverse to any whiff of public scandal."[23]

Two months later, in June 1889, Maggie secretly married Charles Abbott at her Long Branch home. Maggie was fifty-three; Abbott was thirty-five. Like the stars of today, Maggie was followed around by the paparazzi of that era. By chance one of them happened to look at the register at the hotel in Brockton, Massachusetts, where she was staying and noticed Abbott, who was still acting as her leading man, signed the register as "Charles Abbott, wife, and maid." The hitherto secret marriage made front page news in the *Chicago Daily Tribune*.[24]

Maggie often said she wouldn't know what to do with herself if she quit acting but did retire in 1892. For the remainder of her life she alternated her time between her home in Long Branch and her home in New York.

In August 1917, Maggie fell ill and was confined to her home. On March 18, 1918, she lapsed into a coma. Four days later, at the age of eighty-one, she died.

Newspapers across the country noted her passing in articles ranging from a half to a full column in length. In its final tribute to her, the *New York Clipper* eulogized that "she left a niche which has never been filled, and possibly never will be."[25]

In 1907, Maggie's daughter, Fanchon Paddock, married a wealthy Pittsburgh businessman named Harry P. Mashey. The "P" in Mashey's middle name, like the "P" in Julian Mitchell's name, was for "Paddock," but they were not related. One summer when Harry was visiting his parents in Long Branch, he was curious about the neighbor who had the same last name as his middle name. Harry arranged to meet Fanchon and found they had other things in common besides their same names.[26] A short time later they became engaged.[27]

# 35

# ADA GRAY

A da Gray, the actress John had had a brief affair with in Nashville, went on to have a brilliant career afterwards but also died destitute and alone.

In 1865 Ada took a job in Albany as leading lady at the Trible Opera House. In 1872 she married Charles S. Watkins, her manager, and spent the next two years as a homemaker. Boredom set in and after two years she resumed her stage career (with Watkins still her manager).[1] Two years later, she was a major star on Broadway, billed as the "Celebrated Tragedienne."[2] For the next twenty years she appeared across the country, almost exclusively in *East Lynne*, nearly two thousand times in all.[3] *East Lynne*, a cynic wrote, "kept women crying in the best theaters of the country for more than a dozen years."[4]

Some theater critics had seen the play so many times they'd become inured to its appeal. *East Lynne* was "better suited to such communities as Peoria than Washington," said one of the more unmoved journalists,[5] reflecting what by then was the characterization of Peoria as the bellwether city of American taste. At one time, "will it play in Peoria" was the watchword for middle America's theatrical sensibilities.

During her tours in the west two actors joined her company who would later become famous—not because of their acting ability. One was William Jennings Bryan, four-time presidential candidate, who acted under the name "Mr. Jennings."[6] Years later, long after Bryan had given up show business for politics, Ada said she was shocked to see him as a presidential candidate. "It was a big jump," she said.[7]

The other was twenty-one-year-old D. W. Griffith, destined to become the preeminent director of the emerging silent movie industry.[8] Griffith would only stay one season with Ada when he joined her company in 1896, acting in Ada's vintage *East Lynne* and other less well-known plays during her farewell tour.

The company played in small towns in Indiana during the winter months to initially favorable reviews. As the winter became colder, so did the audiences. Trade journals reported attendance had started out as "good" and gradually faded to "moderate," "poor," and then "extremely poor."[9] Ada might have toughed it out, but by then her health had also given out.

Just before her death at age fifty-seven, Ada was living alone in a little cottage, a penniless, helpless invalid.[10] The little money she had saved had disappeared, and she was forced to make do as best she could with what little she had left.

"For more than forty years of her life she had known little else but tears and heartaches in her role in *East Lynne*," the *Washington Post* told its readers, "it was her misfortune in her closing years to bring those tribulations from the stage into her real life. Failing health forced her to give up her career."[11]

Ada died in August 1902 in New York in the Home for Incurables in Fordham, New York. The cause of death was said to be "locomotor ataxia"[12] and stomach cancer.[13] Her obituary mentioned that she had acted opposite John Wilkes Booth.[14]

# 36

# ISABEL SUMNER

After her brief summer affair with John ended in 1864, Isabel went back to Bowdoin High School in the fall and graduated in 1866.[1] Eleven years later, in 1877, she married David Albert Dunbar Jr., a Boston trader.

They had two daughters, Laura born in 1878, a year after they were married, and Sallie (named after Isabel's mother) born in 1888. The family was relatively happy and prosperous until Dunbar's business failed, and they had to move in with Isabel's parents. Dunbar died in 1895. Isabel's father died a short time later. Isabel was left "plagued" with financial worries and having to cope with taking care of two daughters, an aged mother, loneliness, and depression.[2]

With little money left her by her husband and father, she sold the house at 916 Beacon Street, where she had lived most of her life, for $731[3] and moved to a less expensive suburb of Boston. One of the rare times she is mentioned is a scant notice in 1908 about her attending the annual reunion of girls who had gone to Bowdoin High School.[4]

Eventually, her daughter Sallie, who had married into money, moved Isabel into an apartment in the Fairfax Hotel in New York where she died eight years later of stomach cancer on February 23, 1927.[5]

Despite marrying, Isabel had remained faithful to John in at least one way—he had asked her never to show his letters to anyone, and she never did.

After Isabel died, Sallie discovered John's letters, four photographs of John in a variety of poses, and the pearl ring he had given her. One of the photographs was inscribed "J. W. Booth." Sallie kept them secret as well until 1930 when she made them public.

Those letters, discussed in chapter twenty, were acquired by Lincoln ephemera collector Louise Taper and were published along with all other surviving letters John wrote in *"Right or Wrong, God Judge Me:" The Writings of John Wilkes Booth*,[6] a book she co-authored with John Rodehamel.[7]

In 1989, Louise Taper interviewed Isabel's granddaughter, Bobbie Makepiece, about what, if anything, she remembered about her grandmother. All she was able to recall was that Isabel was relatively short, had blue eyes, and never, ever talked about John Wilkes Booth.[8]

# 37

# LOUISE WOOSTER

U nlike many of the women in John's life, when Louise Wooster died she was rich and a legendary figure in her community—a strange honor for a Birmingham, Alabama, madam.

During her "little rehearsals" before the war with John at her Montgomery brothel, John had convinced Lou she could become an actress and then told her he had to leave immediately, promising he would send for her. After waiting in vain, Lou said she tried to become an actress on her own. She gave it up, she said, because of illness. With no other means of support, she went back to prostitution.

In 1871 Lou relocated to Birmingham, Alabama. Iron ore mining and related iron and steel industries were drawing men from all over the South. With so many men and so much money, "Bad Birmingham" was a Mecca for ambitious prostitutes.

By 1873 Birmingham had grown too fast. Public sanitation had been almost totally ignored. Many homes and businesses didn't have clean water. In June, the city had its first case of cholera.

Although thousands of Birmingham's residents fled the city to escape the plague, Louise and many of the city's prostitutes stayed to nurse the sick in brothels-turned-clinics, saving dozens of lives.[1] Somehow none of them came down with cholera themselves.

Lou knew the meaning of "location, location, location." After Birmingham was back on its feet, she bought a two-story home and started her own "high status" bordello. It was directly across the street from City Hall. Three saloons and a livery stable were close by, and it was within shouting distance of the nearby police station (on the payroll, of course) in case a visitor became violent.[2] By 1887, Lou was one of Birmingham's wealthiest citizens. She owned several more buildings, land, elegant furniture, and jewelry and gave generously to Birmingham's charities.[3]

Though Lou's affair with John Wilkes Booth had only lasted a few weeks, it had remained a vivid memory. She was one of many who didn't believe John had died in 1865 and gave numerous interviews to reporters, showing them letters and mementos (but never letting them read or touch them) she claimed John had sent her after his alleged death. Lou also kept a scrapbook of newspaper articles questioning whether it was actually John or another man who died at the Garrett farm.[4]

"The woman's story may or may not be true in every particular," the *Chicago Times* told its readers, "but no one who hears the story from her lips can doubt the sincerity of her belief that Booth is not dead....She believes that Booth still lives—that somewhere in some distant land perhaps he is a homeless wanderer, and that one day the fates may bring them face to face."[5]

The only record of Louise Wooster's affair with John Wilkes Booth is her own *Autobiography of a Magdalen* that she co-wrote with a Birmingham minister in 1911, two years before her death.[6]

The "Magdalen" in the title is a reference to the New Testament's Mary Magdalene, the reviled prostitute who saw the error of her ways and became one of Jesus' most devoted followers. Lou's book is likewise a story of redemption. Since much of it is pure invention (she claimed her father was "old Puritan stock" from New England, that her mother's family were wealthy Southern planters, and that she attended a fashionable boarding school in Mobile), other parts of her narrative, including her affair with John Wilkes Booth, could also have been made up. What wasn't made up was her fixation on the man. That fixation likely came from somewhere, and John had a predilection for prostitutes. It is entirely likely he spent some time "rehearsing" with Lou at "Big Lize's" when he was in Montgomery.

Lou retired in 1901 and died twelve years later in May 1913 of kidney disease. She was buried alongside her sister, who was also a Birmingham madam.[7] Journalists may have been skeptical of what Lou told them about her affair with John Booth, but they knew a good story when they saw it. News articles with titles like "Booth's Sweetheart Dies,"[8] "Assassin's Sweetheart Dead,[9] "Booth's Sweetheart Buried,"[10] appeared simultaneously across the country following her death.

For their part, Birmingham residents cared more about the time Lou cared for their cholera victims than they did about her affair with John Booth. According to local legend, many of Birmingham's prominent gentlemen anonymously sent their drivers in empty carriages to escort her remains to the city's Oak Hill Cemetery as anonymous tokens of respect. The cortege of empty carriages was said to stretch for blocks.[11] Margaret Mitchell, who lived in Birmingham for a time before writing Gone with the Wind, is said to have based Belle Watling, the novel's kind-hearted Atlanta prostitute, on Lou.[12]

In 2004, an opera, Louise: The Story of a Magdalen, based on her life, won an international composition prize for opera.[13] Lou has also been memorialized as the namesake of an award given by the University of Alabama at Birmingham's School of Public Health: the Lou Wooster Public Health Hero Award for exemplary service.[14]

# 38

# CLARA MORRIS

C lara Morris was in Columbus, Ohio, touring with John Ellsler's stock company when she heard about the assassination. She was as horrified as everyone else at the news that President Lincoln had died. She and her roommate, Hattie, were tacking black cotton swatches—bought at triple the usual cost because of the demand—on their outside window when a man passing by told them the assassin had been discovered: the actor Booth!

The girls both laughed. Hattie laughed so hard she almost swallowed the tack she was holding in her mouth. It was a poor joke, Clara told the man, and they both went back inside. A few minutes later they heard a knock on their door. Clara was preoccupied pressing one of her costumes but heard Hattie exclaiming, "Why—why—what!"

Clara turned quickly towards the door. John Ellsler came slowly into the room. He was usually very dark complexioned, but his face was blanched. Even his lips were drained of blood and his eyes were glassy. Clara knew he was devoted to his children. Her first thought from the look on his face was that something dreadful had happened to them.

Ellsler sank down in a chair. Wiping his brow, he looked stupidly at her. Then in a very faint voice, he said, "You—haven't—heard—anything?"

Clara and Hattie turned toward each other at the same instant. Their minds instantly turned to what minutes earlier they thought was a stranger's ill-timed joke. Hattie managed to stammer, "A man—he lied though—said that Wilkes Booth—but he did lie—didn't he?"

"No—no! he did not lie—it's true," Ellsler answered in a faint voice.

Clara and Hattie were both overwhelmed and began sobbing. Ellsler got up and left.

Actress Clara Morris. Clara wrote loving anecdotes about John Wilkes Booth. *Courtesy of Library of Congress.*

Sometime later, Clara saw Ellsler's wife, Euphemia, whom she had never seen shed a tear for any sickness, sorrow, or trouble of her own, break into tears "for the mad boy."

A mass meeting was held in front of the Capitol building to publicly mourn the slain president. Ellsler urged all the actors to stay away, lest their presence arouse ill-feeling. Clara went anyway. The crowd was immense. The police watched for any sign of a riot, periodically glancing anxiously toward the theatre.[1]

Clara was the only one of John's acquaintances to write about her reactions when she first heard about John's killing Lincoln. And that was only because, at the time she wrote, many years had passed since the assassination, and it was safe to mention any possible acquaintance.

Clara had met John in December 1863 when he was the touring star at Ellsler's Academy of Music theatre in Cleveland and she was a teenage ballet girl. Like John, Clara was illegitimate. She was born in Toronto in 1847, the oldest of three children. Her father, Charles La Montagne, a French-Canadian taxi driver, had married her mother, Sarah Jane Proctor, when he was still married to another woman. When Sarah learned about her husband's bigamy, she put her two other children up for adoption and left with three-year-old Clara to Cleveland. Taking her grandmother's maiden name of Morrison, she worked as a housekeeper and cook. Watching her mother being cruelly overworked, Clara jumped at the chance to earn some money when another young boarder told her that the manager of the Academy of Music theatre was looking to hire some ballet girls for an upcoming production.

John Ellsler hardly looked at the fifteen-year-old applying for a ballet job. Ungraciously, he told her he wanted women, not children, for the part. As he turned to leave he noticed Clara's eyes. They had looked blue a moment before. Now they were almost fully dilated and black. "All the father in me shrank under the child's bitter disappointment; all the actor in me thrilled at the power of expression in the girl's face."[2] He told her to come back in a few days. After Clara stepped into a bit part of an older girl who had suffered an attack of stage fright, Ellsler invited her to join the company next season as full-time member.

Clara was earning fifty cents a night as a ballet girl and occasionally playing small parts when John appeared as the Academy of Music's star in 1863. Years later she recalled the moment she fell in love with him. She and two other girls were cast as part of a statue in *The Marble Heart*, a play about a sculptor in love with a woman whose heart was "as cold as marble." In the play they were supposed to stand carefully posed and strongly lighted against a black velvet background. Although draperies covered the girl in the center straight to the floor, the legs of the girls on either side were visible to the audience. During rehearsal John noticed that one of the girls on the side had legs like "broomsticks." "I believe I'll 'advance' you to the center," he said to the girl as he switched their positions. "It was quickly and kindly done," said Clara. The girl was not only spared mortification, in the word "advance" she saw a compliment.[3]

Clara stayed on at the Academy of Music in Cleveland until 1869. Ellsler's was a "family" stock company, which meant he played the male lead and his wife or daughter were always the leading ladies. There was no chance for Clara to go beyond second leading lady if she stayed. Clara decided to leave and take the job of leading lady at Wood's Theatre in Cincinnati. Her big break came at the beginning of the next season when Augustin Daly, famed director of the Fifth Avenue Theatre in New York, hired her as a comedian.

Once again fate stepped in. When Agnes Ethel, Daly's leading lady, refused to play the lead in Daly's opening play of the season, a dramatization of Wilkie Collins's *Man and Wife*, he reluctantly gave the part to Clara. Daly was impressed. He assigned her more roles. Two years later, in 1872, Clara was being hailed as the greatest emotional actress of her day, especially renowned for her role as Camille, a courtesan heroine suffering from tuberculosis. "She has moved to tears more Camilles of real life than ever thronged to the matinees of any other American Actress," wrote an appreciative critic.[4] Watching Clara as Camille, actress

Sarah Bernhardt, who had played the part herself, was astounded. "My God!" she exclaimed, "this woman is not acting, she is suffering!"[5] Clara was not beautiful. She was slim. Her face was ordinary. Her voice was not melodious. What she lacked in aesthetic appeal, she made up for in intensity. "She had no equal in depicting human suffering," said another theatre critic. [6]

A year later Clara had a falling-out with Daly. She felt he was too authoritarian; Daly felt Clara was too defiant. At the end of the season Clara left for the rival Union Square Theatre.

Clara's meteoric career faded by the 1880s. Managers hesitated to hire her because she was often so ill other actresses had to be substituted for her at the last moment. "Clara Morris's engagement in that city [New York] has been even more unsatisfactory than it was here [Chicago]," the *New York Times* told its readers. "It is certain she will never be able to make an engagement here again, unless the house where she appears is guaranteed against financial loss." It wasn't only her illnesses she had to contend with. By then she was addicted to morphine. The usually cited cause was a childhood injury. It was more likely syphilis, "which was epidemic in the theatre world. Many if not all of her recurrent ailments," writes Clara's biographer, "are consistent with manifestations of untreated syphilis or gonorrhea." Clara's career was also in trouble for another reason. The public had lost its taste for the grand gestures of emotional dramas, preferring instead the new trend in realism drama. Stuck with roles that had once made her famous, Clara was now like "an insect trapped in amber."[7]

In retirement, Clara began writing magazine articles on acting and the theatre for *McClure's* and the *Century* magazines, regular pieces for Sunday supplements on topics like "Temptations of the Stage" and "If I Were a Girl Again," novels, and books of her personal reminiscences. An article in the *Boston Herald* and a chapter about John in one of her books was a turning point in the public's impression of the disgraced actor.

Lincoln's wartime secretaries, John Hay and John Nicolay, had written an article in the *Century* magazine characterizing John as an "indifferent" actor who owed what little success he had more to his beauty than any talent.[8] Clara was incensed at what they had written and wrote her own account of what she personally knew of John.[9]

When she had first seen John, she said, "It was impossible to see him and not admire him; it was equally impossible to know him and not love him...He was a gentleman in speech, manner and thought as he was in bearing. He was a great favorite with the men and the women adored him." She wasn't defending him, she said, nor was she apologizing for him. She had no sympathy for what he'd done. But "those who are writing history [meaning Hay and Nicolay] should be fair....he was not a bravado, or a commonplace desperado....as Messr. Nicolay and Hay state." He was ever gentle, considerate, and kind. In condemning him or the fearful crime he committed, there was no need, she said, "to rob him of those gentler qualities which endeared him to his friends" or deny "that ability which made him one of the most promising of the foremost actors of his day."[10]

The article brought her a flood of telegrams thanking her for her courage and sincerity. One of them was from Edwin: "My heartfelt thanks, Clara. I am so glad it was for you to say the first word of compassion for John Wilkes."

Clara was not simply setting the record straight. She had a special affection for John. In *Life on Stage*, her first book about her career, she wrote a long, detailed, and loving chapter devoted to John. Anecdotes from that book are staples in every biography about John—the time another actor cut him during a rehearsal swordfight and instead of lashing out in anger, John told him to fight as hard during the night's performance; when he knocked over a street urchin, picked him up, and used his own handkerchief to wipe the boy's dirty nose; how waitresses fought over who would serve him; how housemaids made and remade his sheets; the letters from women whose signatures he snipped to protect their identity and even then wouldn't let anyone else read them; and how the supporting actresses in her company envied the actress lucky enough to be embraced by John on stage.[11]

By 1910, Clara was totally blind and impoverished.[12] She was unable to pay her $30,000 mortgage. She had bought the home in Yonkers when she was at the height of her career and managed to keep living there by supporting herself from her writing. It was too expensive to keep up solely on her earnings, and she'd had to take out a $25,000 mortgage in 1904 and then a second mortgage for $1,800 in 1908. Other actors pitched in to make the payments at least three times.[13] Inevitably, the house she'd lived in for over thirty-five years was sold in 1914, and she moved to Whitestone in Long Island to live with relatives.

Dubbed in her final years as the "woman of sorrow" because of all her troubles, Clara died in 1925 at age seventy-nine of heart disease.[14] Once hailed as the greatest emotional actress on the American stage, Clara Morris is known today for little else than the chapter she wrote about John in her autobiography, *Life on Stage*.

# 39

# MARTHA MILLS

"Today's [*Chicago*] *Tribune* contains a wretched lie about John Wilkes' family, not one word of truth in it from end to end," Edwin was fuming. "I suspect it is the beginning of a 'blackmail scheme' of which I had some intimation months ago through a Boston lawyer," Edwin wrote his friend Laurence Hutton.

> The widow of this *Tribune* article is only one of the twenty
> that wrote to me after John's death & is the one, I suspect,
> who got all poor Rose's money—some $10,000 from her.
> Rose says all that is ended now & that she will save her
> money—I hope she is not deceiving me.[1]

As early as April 24, 1865, June warned his mother and sister not to have anything to do with "weeping imposters,"[2] but as Edwin said in his letter, after his death several women claimed to be John's widow. Edwin had ignored them all until the *Tribune* article stating that John had not only been married but also was the father of two children. This last alleged widow, Martha Lizola Mills, was not so easily dismissed.

Martha Mills, "the woman claiming to be John's widow." *Courtesy of Schlesinger Library, Radcliffe Institute, Harvard University.*

Martha Lizola Mills was born in 1837 in Stamford, Connecticut, to Abraham Mills, a sailor, and Mary Whitney.[3] Martha's mother died when Martha was young, and her father remarried Caroline Jenks in 1846 when Martha was nine. Her father died a year later, leaving Martha with a stepmother who promptly remarried when Martha was ten years old. Martha was now living with a couple who were not her biological parents and had no parental attachment to the preteen girl. When she ran away to live with family members in Providence, Rhode Island, her step-parents didn't care.

In 1852, Martha, fifteen and unmarried, gave birth to a son (the boy only lived to age four). Three years later, at eighteen, as a single mother living on her own in Boston, she married seaman Charles S. Bellows.

Martha was not a woman who liked to be alone. With Bellows at sea for much of the time, she became involved with a married man, Arthur D'Arcy. A few years later, Ogarita Rosalie was born in 1859.

Martha listed Bellows as Ogarita's father on her birth certificate, but Bellows could not have been the father. At the time of Ogarita's conception, he was five thousand miles away at sea in South America. Since Martha was still involved with D'Arcy at the time, D'Arcy was probably Ogarita's father. But if she named him on the birth certificate, she would have admitted that she and D'Arcy were both adulterers. Listing Bellows as the father was a way to avoid scandal. Sometime later, Martha claimed Ogarita's father was neither Bellows nor D'Arcy. It was the actor, John Wilkes Booth. Ogarita never doubted her mother, and when she became an actress she called herself Rita Booth. Ogarita's daughter, Izola Forrester, would later write a 500-page book claiming her grandmother Martha had been intimate with John.

Martha's affair with D'Arcy ended when he joined the Union army in 1861. A short time later, Martha gave birth to a boy she named Charles Alonzo. Ten years later she married again, this time to John H. Stevenson. Martha listed her name as Martha L. Booth on their marriage certificate.

Charles Bellows, her first husband, was still very much alive when Martha married Stevenson in 1871. Calling herself Martha Booth could have been a way of dodging arrest for bigamy. There were more than twenty Booths in Baltimore,[4] none of them related to the infamous assassin. Despite claiming a Booth surname and despite being married to John Stevenson, Martha applied for a pension as Bellows's widow when he died that same year. Harry Stevenson was born in 1871, the same year she married John Stevenson. Although that marriage eventually went sour, Ogarita and her half-brother Harry remained friends and frequently wrote to one another.

Martha's next husband, Edwin Bates, whom she married while she was still married to John Stevenson, was a farm worker in Burrillville, Rhode Island. The Bates' marriage didn't fare any better than her other marriages. When Martha died at age fifty in 1887, she was buried in Canterbury, Connecticut, not Burrillville.

Martha's daughter, Ogarita, never doubted her mother was telling her the truth that John Wilkes Booth was her father. In 1869, when Ogarita was ten and living in Baltimore, Martha took her and her younger brother, Charles Alonzo, to Bel Air and called on Mrs. Elijah Rogers, the Booth family's one-time neighbor. She introduced them as John's children.[5] Recalling their visit years later, Rogers said Ogarita was "very beautiful" and Alonso was "very much like old Mr. Richard Booth [John's grandfather]."[6]

That brief visit with Mrs. Rogers convinced Ogarita her mother wasn't making it up. When Ogarita began her own acting career at fifteen, she called herself Ogarita Wilkes and continued using that name until 1884 when she began using Rita Booth as her stage name and began wearing a brooch with John's photograph in it. Was claiming to be John's daughter a way to sell her story and bolster her career as a curiosity, or did she really believe her mother's story?[7]

Like her mother, Ogarita was unmarried and a teenager when she had her first child in 1878, at eighteen. She named the girl Izola, after her mother. A year later Ogarita married sixty-four-year-old mill owner William Ross Wilson and left her fledgling stage career to live with him and Izola in Burrillville, Rhode Island. That marriage fell apart and she returned to the stage. In 1884 she married actor Alexander Henderson. A year later she had her second child, Beatrice Rosalie Booth Henderson. Ogarita died of pneumonia in 1891 at age thirty-two. Her death certificate listed her mother as Martha Mills and her father as John Wilkes Booth.[8]

Izola was thirteen when her mother died. She was adopted by journalist George Foster and his wife Harriet and took their family name, but she never forgot the stories her grandmother and mother told her about John Wilkes Booth and that she was his granddaughter. As an adult, Izola was a prolific writer. She published eighteen books, hundreds of magazine articles, and had a brief stint as a screenwriter for silent films, but her real passion was tracking down every rumor to prove her grandfather was John Wilkes Booth. The last years of her life were spent scouring family records and news reports for proof. In 1937, she published what she had found, a book she believed unquestionably proved her genealogy, titling it *This One Mad Act: The Unknown Story of John Wilkes Booth and His Family by His Granddaughter.*[9]

Most historians put little stock in Izola's account of her grandmother's affair with John. The tale is riddled with inaccuracies and contradictions, including an assertion that John did not die at the Garrett farm, that there was an alleged reunion between Martha and John in San Francisco in 1869, and that Martha bore another of his children a year later.[10] Booth expert John O. Hall dismissed Izola's book as a "romantic historical novel."[11]

Two Burrillville, Rhode Island historians, Joyce Knibb and Patricia Mehrtens, are more circumspect. After sifting through all the local legends about Martha and Ogarita in Burrillville and all the related evidence, they wrote their own book, *The Elusive Booths of Burrillville.*[12] They were able to disprove Izola's claim that her grandmother met up with John in California years later and that he fathered another child, but there was circumstantial evidence pointing to a relationship that went beyond the scam June and Edwin worried about.

Martha's visit to Mrs. Rogers could have been a subterfuge to learn enough to convince John's sister Rosalie that they were sisters. But would Martha have been that much of a schemer to deceive her own daughter? Ogarita was convinced. In a letter dated July 6, 1888, to her half-brother Harry Stevenson, she referred to Rosalie as "Aunt Rosalie" and to Joseph Booth as "Uncle."[13] Rosalie in turn was convinced enough to call Ogarita and Harry "her children" and sent them money every spring and fall.[14]

Two other items gave Knibb and Mehrtens pause. One is a book of poems published in 1881 that Rosalie sent to Martha. The inscription on the inside cover in Rosalie's handwriting reads: "Mrs. M. Lizola Bates [Martha's married name] From her ever loving sister Rosalie A. Booth September 11, 1883. Many happy returns of your birthday."[15] The second is a Bible Rosalie sent to Martha. The inscription inside, also in Rosalie's handwriting, reads: "To My Sister Izola, from her affection sister R A. B. God is our Best in time of trouble."[16]

Martha in fact had kept up a regular correspondence with Rosalie and noted the date of each letter she received from her in her diaries. On February 26, 1884, she recorded: "Mother Booth [Mary Ann] fell and hurt her(self)." On October 22, 1885, she recorded: "Mother Booth died today." She also regularly recorded the anniversary of John's death: "J. W. B. has been dead 22 years this morning."

Based on those letters and diary entries, the Burrillville historians said they couldn't conclusively prove or disprove Martha Mills's affair with John Wilkes Booth.[17] Most historians, however, side with Hall for the simple reason that John and Martha were never in Richmond at the same time. At the time of the alleged relationship in December 1859 or early January 1859, John was in Richmond but Martha was in Boston (according to the 1860 census). Even Izola's children were skeptical. There are "tantalizing bits of circumstantial evidence" Izola's son, Richard Merrifield, wrote to his daughter, Gail Merrifield Papp, but all it adds up to is a "moonstruck woman's fatuity over a matinee idol."[18] Yet in the back of his mind, he admitted, "I still think we're all his bastards."[19]

David Taylor, co-author of the *BoothieBarn* blog, like many other historians, dismisses Martha as a fraud. The reason Rosalie gave her any money, he speculates, was because her conscience bothered her about what to do with the money John had given her and felt it best to give the supposedly grief-stricken Martha money to feed John's children. Alternatively, writes Taylor, Rosalie may have wanted to believe Martha because she missed John. Giving Martha his money was a way of preserving the "decent part of their brother's memory."[20]

Was Martha Mills a liar or simply delusional? Ogarita and Harry can't be faulted for believing what she told them. Rosalie believed her despite Edwin and June's admonitions. But since there is no evidence they ever met, what made her sincerely believe that she had had a romantic involvement with John Wilkes Booth?

Martha was not and would not be the first or only person to invent a life or a persona for themselves that confounds reality. Maggie Mitchell was besieged with cranks coming out of the woodwork claiming to be a relative. One woman insisted she was Maggie's mother. A Mr. Baker wrote her several letters about his being her brother and reminded her of the little cottage where they had grown up. A Mrs. John Able, Baker's sister, also said she was Maggie's sister. "I am constantly learning something new," Maggie said after reading about Able in the newspapers, "but I was not prepared to learn...that my name is Baker, and not Mitchell, as my parents and my numerous brothers and sisters have fondly supposed for some years."[21] Maggie said that from all she had read, she felt "the woman is honest in her belief, though how she could deceive herself so I cannot understand." Another woman, calling herself Miss Smith, said she was Maggie's cousin and tried to get money from Maggie.[22]

John St. Helen, a.k.a. David George, wasn't after money. He may honestly have convinced himself he was John Wilkes Booth. He sported the same luxuriant black hair and moustache. He dressed like John in a tailor-made, semi-dark suit and black Stetson derby. He drank heavily and carried a gun. He was very interested in the theatrical news of the days. He often broke into lines from Shakespeare during a conversation. He convinced hundreds of people he was John Wilkes Booth.[23]

If St. Helen/George died believing he was John Wilkes Booth, Martha Mills's belief that she was John Wilkes Booth's lover shouldn't be that astounding. Martha's relationship with John Wilkes Booth may have been all in her mind. For her it was no less real.

# EPILOGUE

John Wilkes Booth is a hard man to make sense of. To some he was kind, gentle, charming, lovable, loyal, generous, always considerate of others, and fond of children. To others he was calculating, callous, moody, depressed, cynical, erratic, manipulative, a liar, and as undisciplined on stage as off it. When he died he had photos of five women in his pocket. Only one of them was his fiancée. Edwin Booth said his brother John "was so peculiar I never seemed to know him."[1]

John had an endless stream of women after him. He didn't have a "type." Many of the women he romanced were beautiful. Others, like Henrietta Irving, Ada Gray, and his fiancée, Lucy Hale, were not particularly good-looking. For John, it was any port in a storm. He fell in love easily—and fell out of love just as easily. His feelings for women, though often genuine, didn't last for long. He was attentive until he seduced them, then he lost interest and went on to the next relationship. His motto, where women were concerned, was "me first." John's only intimacy was with himself.

Nevertheless, the ladies raved over him—especially actresses. "He was very popular with those dramatic ladies...to whom divorce courts are superfluous."[2] Wives and daughters from prominent families were no less immune to his charm and looks. They "flocked to his performances...it was no unusual sight to see numbers standing all over the house" at his matinees.[3] When he left the theatre at night, his adoring fans followed him, each one hoping he would notice her in particular.[4] "Married women waylaid him in every provincial town or city where he played...their motives were various...whether curiosity or worse."[5] They sought introductions. They invited him into their parlors. There wasn't enough space to go into "the millionth catalogue of Booth's intrigues," said an early biographer.[6] Even after he assassinated Lincoln, many women felt a kind of hysterical sympathy and pity and even love for him. It was said that at the very least, one woman would have been at his deathbed if she could get to it. Opera singer Clara Kellogg mused that, given the chance, hundreds of women would have surrounded his deathbed.[7]

John was his family's "golden boy." "I always gave you praise for being the fondest of all my boys," his mother wrote him three weeks before he shot Lincoln.[8] Favoritism in families follows familiar patterns, writes psychologist Ellen Weber Libby. "Sons growing up as the favorite child of one parent are likely to achieve great professional success." They are also more likely, says Libby, to be manipulative and to struggle with issues of intimacy and addiction.[9]

John had more than one reason to have trouble with intimacy. Family life was often unpredictable and chaotic. One day his father might be caring and loving, the next he might be tyrannical. Being the golden boy did not mean he escaped such uncertainty. Growing up in a home with a father who was periodically insane and an alcoholic left deep psychological scars. Adult children of alcoholics are often insecure and take themselves seriously. They crave approval. They are addicted to excitement. They don't feel remorse when they break rules. They are impulsive. They have an animosity toward people in authority. They often become alcoholics themselves. Importantly, they are leery of intimacy because they lack trust and therefore fear commitment.[10] Promiscuity, and especially his penchant for prostitutes, was John's way of sidestepping commitment.[11]

It would have been a miracle if John's lechery didn't result in his contracting a venereal disease. All John's biographers agree that, like their father, Junius's sons (with the possible exception of his youngest, Joseph Adrian, because so little is known of him) were womanizers. We don't know if Junius Sr. or Jr. contracted venereal diseases from their sexual adventurisms, but Edwin did, by his own admission.[12]

Nearly all of the letters John wrote or received were destroyed, so any mention of his having venereal disease no longer exists. John McCullough, one of John's closest friends, was the first actor whose "disease" was tabloid news.[13] McCullough said that John was "a wonderful companion of disease."[14] "Disease" was typical nineteenth-century euphemism for "syphilis."[15] The word was taboo in polite society, shameful to mention because it implied sex outside of marriage. Only fornicators, whores, sodomists, and the like fell prey to it. For moralists, syphilis was their punishment.

John and McCullough often shared a room together. Both were incorrigible womanizers. Both came down with syphilis. Had John lived as long as McCullough (who was sixty-three when he died), he would have experienced the same misery. Despite the social reticence on this issue, John and McCullough were hardly unique in coming down with syphilis. Lincoln's law partner, William Herndon, claimed that, years before he became president, Lincoln told him he had been infected.[16] During the war, more than 73,000 men in the Union army were treated for the disease (another 109,000 were treated for gonorrhea).[17]

The evidence for John's syphilis comes exclusively from the record of his ailments. Individually, they could be due to anything. Cumulatively, his ailments are convincing.

One reason it was so difficult for physicians to be certain someone had syphilis, before the advent of confirming blood tests, is that syphilis is "the Great Imitator." "It apes every disease in any field of medicine [with a] Machiavellian facility in disguise, deceit and malevolence."[18] It has no symptom peculiar to itself. Symptoms can occur on their own or in conjunction with other diseases, and not all of its symptoms are seen in every person. Some of the more common physical ailments are hoarseness, a sudden change from relatively good health to mysterious painful ailments, any lump, erysipelas, pleurisy, insomnia, jaundice, and freckling. Mental symptoms include depression, decreased memory, irritability, emotional overreaction, impulsivity, misanthropy, and grandiosity. When more than a few of these symptoms are seen in the same person, as in John's case, the diagnosis becomes more certain.

Untreated, syphilis usually passes through three stages. In some instances, and for unknown reasons, the infection does not progress any further than the first or second stage. The classic first stage sign is a painless sore called a chancre, typically on the genitals, which heals on its own in a few weeks. Second stage syphilis is associated with a host of physical ailments. Among them are the following: a rash on the palms of the hand and soles of the feet, the episodic bouts of hoarseness John came down with, tumors like the one Dr. Frederick May removed from John's neck, the erysipelas that John came down with while he was staying at Edwin's house in New York, the carbuncles he had lanced when he was staying at Asia's house in Philadelphia, pleurisy that he complained of when William Ferguson invited him to go to Peter Taltavull's Star Saloon for a drink just before the assassination, and the freckling and jaundice that were noticed at John's autopsy.

Unarrested by penicillin or other effective antibiotics, the infection often progresses to the second stage and then the third stage of neurosyphilis when the infection invades the brain and causes personality breakdown and mental derangement.[19]

By late August 1864, just after his bout with erysipelas, people who knew John noticed a personality change typical of syphilis. The change coincided with the sudden breakup with Isabel Sumner, the girl he had seemingly been so passionately in love with.

He'd also lost all interest in money. Three years earlier, he was dickering with the manager of the Boston Museum about salary. In August 1862, he was demanding $80 a night. By September, he was up to $140 a night plus a benefit once a week. By the winter of 1864, he no longer cared about money. His friend Joe Simmonds asked him what had come over him, saying John was "so different from your usual self...[have] you lost all your ambition or what is the matter?"[20]

The matter was that John had lapsed into depression. Invited to join some friends at a saloon, John nodded. "Anything to chase away the blues."[21] He was having trouble sleeping, another common sign of depression. John McCullough, with whom John occasionally shared a room, recalled how he was startled out of his sleep one night by John's tears dropping on his face. "My God," John sighed, "how peacefully you were sleeping. I cannot sleep."[22] His memory had become impaired. He forgot what year it was.[23] Memory loss is common in syphilis.[24]

He was also drinking more than usual. John had always been a steady drinker. Now he was sometimes boozing as much as a quart of brandy in less than two hours. Long-time friend John Deery, owner of a saloon above Grover's Theatre, said that in the days before the assassination John "sometimes drank at my bar as much as a quart of brandy in the space of less than two hours...It was more than a spree, I could see that...Booth was not given to sprees....He seemed to be crazed by some stress of inward feeling."[25]

Friends noted he was no longer "merry and jovial."[26] Instead of the "sweetly dispositioned" actor they had known, he'd become "cold, taciturn, aloof, and at times...almost arrogant."[27] The year before, he had not been far from "high and mighty, like most of the stars...any supernumerary could go to him for advice—and was always sure to get it. Whoever went to him was received with gentle courtesy, and generally came away an ardent admirer."[28] Now he was disdainful about his fellow actors. They were just "mummers." They knew little, thought less, and understood next to nothing.[29]

When a theatre prompter missed giving him his cue, John threw a block of wood at him, just missing his face. During his last appearance on stage, he refused to take a bow, although he was applauded more than anyone else in the play. Gordon Samples, who chronicled John's theatrical career, reflected on "how unlike John Wilkes Booth this was, refusing to acknowledge the overwhelming praise of the audience!"[30] He "never laughed anymore. Smiles crossed his face often, but never anything like a real laugh."

His mother and some of his dearest friends felt he was no longer the same person they had known. "He had changed, and ominous fears in regard to him and his future filled their minds."[31] John's niece, Blanche DeBar, said he had become "morbid."[32] "The first twenty-five years of his life were, or seemed to be, a light-hearted epic which had no connection with the events which brought about his crime and death...It seemed as if there were two distinct John Wilkes Booths," writes historian Kathryn Canavan.[33]

Jim Ferguson, in whose restaurant John and his friends would spend hours drinking and playing cards, couldn't believe what was being said about John. "All the stories about his boasting of his amours," he insisted couldn't be true.[34] He had never heard John brag about the women he seduced. The year before John had torn the signatures from the love letters he received. Even with such anonymity, John wouldn't let anyone read them. After August 1864, he began bragging about his "love ditties" and "hair-breath" scrapes in dark passages with "the most beautiful creatures in the world."[35]

He had also become spiteful. When his friend Samuel Chester wouldn't go along with kidnapping Lincoln, John threatened to implicate him anyways.[36] Although he later apologized, he was clearly not the same man. John told Chester that actor John Mathews, who had also refused to become involved, was a coward "and not fit to live."[37] John and Mathews had been friends since boyhood. John had loafed in Mathews's bedroom at the Petersen Boarding House weeks before. It was the same house and the same room that Lincoln was taken to after John shot him. Even more ironically, John had been lying in the same bed that Lincoln was lain on and died on. John had been incensed that his good friend had turned him down. Mathews had no inkling of John's feeling about him the day of the assassination when he agreed to take a letter that could implicate him in the assassination to the editor of the *Washington National Intelligencer*. When he left, he squeezed Mathews's hand so tightly his nails left marks in Mathews's skin.[38] The kind Jekyll had turned into the malevolent Hyde. He had become an "ego-centered ass."[39] He didn't give a second thought about the fate of the conspirators whom he convinced to be a part of his plot. They were merely tools in his self-indulgent, delusional idea of himself as the South's savior.

The biggest puzzle about John Wilkes Booth is why did he assassinate Lincoln? Depending on who one listens to or reads, he was a typical white Southerner whose political thought predisposed him to killing the Yankee president, a puppet of a broad conspiracy, a lunatic acting on his own, or an ego-centric schemer with an inflated image of his own importance.

The political context is clear. From almost the beginning of the war, John had never tried to hide his sympathies for the South. As the war raged on, he developed a personal hatred for Lincoln, blaming him for instigating the war and overseeing the destruction of the South. What is still debated is whether a high-placed cabal exploited his hatred or whether he acted on his own.

The often-mentioned cabalists include Secretary of War Edwin Stanton, Vice President Andrew Johnson, the Confederate administration, Northern Radical Republicans, the clandestine Knights of the Golden Circle, and International Bankers. An ex-priest claimed the pope was involved, a theory that gained support from John Surratt's brief service in the Vatican guard after the assassination.[40]

There is no hard evidence for any of those conspiracy theories. No one has as yet taken up Booth biographer Michael Kauffman's challenge for anyone who "has ever come across any instance in which Booth's name, his kidnap attempt, his stage appearances in the South, or his murderous deed was ever put to paper by any Confederate of stature" or "any mention by a bigwig Confederate of the names of the alleged conspirators" to send him that information.[41] The same challenge applies to the other conspiracy theorists. Some people simply find it much more psychologically comforting to believe that a president "was the victim of a cause [rather than] a deranged gunman."[42]

Since there is no evidence except innuendo that John was a dupe of some conspiracy, a reasonable alternative is that he was acting on his own.

One explanation for his plot has invoked a variation of the biblical Cain and Abel theme: jealousy of his brother Edwin's greater fame was behind John's killing the president. It was a way to outshine him, a way of putting himself in the limelight.[43]

Whatever rivalry John and Edwin had between them was political, not professional.[44] When someone told John he was a better Hamlet than Edwin, John replied he was wrong. "There's but one Hamlet to my mind," he said, "[and] that's my brother Edwin."[45] Edwin in turn said John had "the genius of my father, and was far more gifted than I."[46] John's photograph was prominently displayed on the wall of Edwin's bedroom.

Other explanations that he was committed to the South because his stage appearances were well received there, or that he killed Lincoln for the fame he believed he would receive, are equally implausible.

John Wilkes Booth was vain and fame had definitely been his ambition. But he already had it; he was not a failed actor. He enjoyed the applause he received when he toured the South, but the applause was just as loud in the North. Although some critics panned his appearances, he was enthusiastically reviewed by many others throughout the country. He consistently drew large audiences and was "widely cheered." John Ellsler, director of the Academy of Music in Cleveland and one-time partner in John's oil field ventures, knew all the theatrical Booths. In his opinion John had "more of the old man's [his father's] power in one performance than [his brother] Edwin can show in a year."[47]

Many of John's contemporaries attributed John's actions to his having inherited, as actress Ann Hartley Gilbert kindly put it, "the family failings."[48] John's brother June mused that "a crack" ran through the male portion of their family.[49] Actor Edwin Forrest was more blunt. In his opinion, "All those Booths are crazy."[50]

But before John murdered Lincoln, none of those who knew him or had any conversations with him thought he was insane. It was only after John killed Lincoln that his sanity was questioned.[51]

Many people took the heredity explanation for granted.[52] Stanley Kimmel, the Booth family biographer, famously titled his book *The Mad Booths of Maryland*. Neither Edwin nor June ever killed anyone. Did the "crack" that ran through the family go deeper in John's brain than in theirs?

Some armchair psychologists contend it was not heredity; it was poor parenting that ultimately put the gun in John's hand. Despite Asia's idealistic portrayal of Junius, at home he was anything but a model father. He was an alcoholic, periodically unbalanced, quick-tempered, and authoritarian. Worst of all, he had caused John and all his siblings to be bastards. In the bad parent explanation, John's hatred for Lincoln was displaced hatred for his own father.[53]

John's animus toward Lincoln had been festering for years. He was politically and racially motivated to kill Lincoln. But so were thousands if not hundreds of thousands of Southerners. Samuel Arnold, Michael O'Laughlen, and John Surratt were willing to kidnap Lincoln but drew the line at killing. John dispatched George Atzerodt to kill Vice President Johnson, but Atzerodt couldn't go through with it. The only one of Booth's gang capable of murder was Lewis Powell.

Did John's syphilis turn him into an assassin? Politics and prejudice can account for John's decision to murder Lincoln but not for his profound personality changes. Before syphilis had begun to affect his behavior, John had toyed with the idea of killing Lincoln, but it was only a passing thought. By April 14, 1865, that idea had become fixated in his mind. He believed his killing Lincoln was God's will, that God had entrusted him as "the instrument of his [Lincoln's] punishment."[54] That kind of grandiose delusion is a hallmark of neurosyphilis.[55]

The fondest of all his mother's children had become "sad, mad, bad, John Wilkes."[56]

# Acknowledgments

This book would not have been possible were it not for the many librarians and curators who located materials for me, often with only scant information. I would like to express my special thanks to the librarians at Wayne State University's Interlibrary Loan Department for their numerous efforts providing me with books and journal articles from other libraries. Special thanks to Abbie Weinberg, research and outreach specialist at the Folger Shakespeare Library in Washington, D.C., who never tired of locating and sending me copies of my many requests. Leah Lefkowtiz at Harvard University's Houghton Library facilitated my research at the Houghton as did the other librarians at the Houghton. Raymond Wemmlinger, librarian and curator of the Hampden-Booth Theatre Library in New York City, provided access to Henrietta Irving's three-page autobiography and letter she wrote and the Booth family letters. Colleen Walter Puterbaugh, research librarian at the Surratt House Museum's James O. Hall Research Center in Clinton, Maryland—a must for any research involving the Booths—was another who tirelessly located materials for me and who kept the library open long past the time she ordinarily would have left to allow me to copy documents. Janet Bloom at the Clements Library at the University of Michigan located relevant items in its inventory. Thanks also to the Surratt Society's Laurie Verge and Joan Chaconas, who opened the library for me when it was normally closed. Similar thanks to Maryanna Skowronski, research director at the Historical Society of Harford County in Bel Air Maryland (home of the Booth family), who allowed me to visit the library when it was normally closed and provided access to its collection of Booth-related materials. Malia Ebel, reference librarian/archivist at the New Hampshire Historical Society in Concord, allowed me access to Lucy Hale's correspondence and her diaries. Dominique Daniel, coordinator of archives and special collections, and Shirley Paquette at the Oakland University Kresge Library in Rochester, Michigan, made the Fred L. Black papers and Booth file clippings available. Alexandra Griffiths at the New York Public Library's Interlibrary and Document Services provided copies of rare newspaper clippings. Janet Bloom, librarian at the University of Michigan's Clements Library, located references to Maggie Mitchell and James Mansfield (the spiritualist Edwin Booth consulted after his wife Mary Devlin died). Special thanks also to Cynthia Van Ness, director of the Buffalo History Museum Library and Archives, for researching possible connections for Henrietta Irving at Buffalo and to Joshua Stabler, Cunningham Memorial Library, Indiana State Library, for searching the library's files for Booth-related photos. Damon Talbot of the Maryland Historical Society's Special Collections Department kindly photocopied and sent me Asia Booth Clarke's invaluable correspondence with Jean Anderson. Scott S. Taylor at Georgetown University's Lauinger Library's Special Collections had the Barbee files waiting for me as soon as I arrived as did Jane Gastineau and Emily Rapoza for the Booth collection at the Allen County Public Library in Fort Wayne, Indiana. Thanks to Laura Anderson for pacing off the distance from the door to box eight in the presidential box to the balustrade over which Lincoln was leaning when he was shot and for allowing me access to Ford Theater's archives. I also thank Kelsy Adelson at the Mount Auburn Cemetery for details about Helen and Lucille Western's burial plot and Terry Alford for details about Booth's engagement to Maggie Mitchell.

A very special thanks to Kathryn Canavan, William L. Richter, Tom Bogar, Joan Chaconas, Dr. Thomas Lowry, and William Binzel, who critiqued various chapters, corrected my factual, textual, and footnote errors, and offered valuable improvements. Any remaining errors are entirely my own.

I also take this opportunity to thank my wife, Barbara Buckley Abel, and Roberta Russ for editing and improving very early drafts. Barbara patiently gave me the time away from family to write this book and finish it by the deadline. She has been my best friend for almost fifty years, my research assistant, my companion on journeys to the libraries we travelled to, my promoter, and my better angel.

Finally, a very special note of thanks to Alex Novak, publisher of Regnery History, for putting up with my numerous revisions, to my outstanding editor Lauren Mann for refining and keeping the text focused, and to Elizabeth Dobak for her diligence in copy-editing the book.

# Abbreviations in Notes

**DRB**    Barbee Papers, Lauringer Library, Georgetown University, Washington, D.C.

**FFP**    Izola Forrester Family Papers, Hutton Collection, Harvard University, Cambridge, Massachusetts

**FSL**    Folger Shakespeare Library, Washington, D.C.

**H-BTL**    Hampden-Booth Theatre Library, New York City, New York

**HL**    Houghton Library, Harvard University, Cambridge, Massachusetts

**HSHC**    Historical Society of Harford County Inc., Bel Air, Maryland

**JOH**        James O. Hall Papers, Hall Research Center,
               Surratt House Museum, Clinton, Maryland

**K-OAK**      Kresge Library, Oakland University, Auburn
               Hills, Michigan

**LOC**        Library of Congress, Washington, D.C.

**MdHS**       Maryland Historical Society, Baltimore,
               Maryland

**NA**         National Archives and Records Services,
               Washington, D.C.

**NHHS**       New Hampshire Historical Society

**O. R.**      The War of the Rebellion: A Compilation of the
               Official Records of the Union and Confederate
               Armies

# Notes

## INTRODUCTION

1. Asia Booth Clarke, *The Unlocked Book. A Memoir of John Wilkes Booth by his Sister Asia Booth Clarke* (New York: G. P. Putnam's Sons, 1938), 56–57.
2. The quote about Macbeth is from G. K. Chesterton's article, "The Murderer as Maniac," in Dale Ahlquist (ed.), *The Soul of Wit. G. K Chesterton on William Shakespeare* (Mineola, NY: Dover Publications, 2012), 67.
3. Stanley Kimmel, *The Mad Booths Of Maryland* (Indianapolis: Bobs-Merrill Co., 1940).
4. The much quoted statement is from Tolstoy's novel, *Anna Karenina*. The idea is not unique.
5. Kingsley Davis, "Illegitimacy and the social structure," *American Journal of Sociology*, 45 (September 1939), 215.
6. James W. Shettel, "J. Wilkes Booth At School. Recollections of a Retired Army Officer Who Knew Him then," *The New York Dramatic Mirror*, (February 26, 1916), 1, 5.
7. Terry Alford, *Fortune's Fool* (New York: Oxford University Press, 2015), 11.

8. Asia Booth Clarke, *Booth Memorials: Passages, Incidents, and Anecdotes in the Life of Junius Brutus Booth* (New York: W. W. Carleton, 1866), viii.

9. Edwin A. Emerson, "The Night That Lincoln Was Shot," *The Theatre*, 17 (1913), 179.

10. *Washington Post*, July 17, 1904, A8.

11. William A. Howell, "Memories of Wilkes Booth," The *Sun* (Baltimore, MD), November 23, 1899, 3.

12. John Deery, "The Last of Wilkes Booth," *New York Sunday Telegram*, May 23, 1909.

13. Clara Morris, *Life on Stage: My Personal Experiences and Recollections* (New York: McClure, Phillips & Co., 1901) 97.

14. John Mathews Testimony, War Department Records (J. A. G.), NA, copy in Barbee papers, Box 4, Folder 2.

15. David Carroll, *The Matinee Idols* (New York: Arbor House, 1972), 31–35.

16. Morris, *Life On Stage*, 97.

17. Quoted by Alford, *Fortune's Fool*, 154.

18. Morris, *Life On Stage*, 97.

19. Ibid. Booth was paraphrasing a line from *The Taming of the Shrew* (Act 2, Scene 1): "everyone knows where a wasp wears its stinger. In its tail."

20. Ibid.

21. Ibid.

22. Ibid.

## 1. SINS OF THE FATHER

1. Born May 1, 1796, Junius was named after Lucius Junius Brutus, the legendary founder of the Roman Republic, a historic figure who reflected his father's anti-authoritarian politics (Stephen M. Archer, *Junius Brutus Booth. Theatrical Prometheus* (Carbondale, IL: Southern Illinois University Press, 1992), 6.

2. Anonymous, *Memoirs Of Junius Brutus Booth, From His Birth To The Present Time* (London: Chapple, Miller, Rowden and E. Wilson, 1817), 11.

3. Junius's mother, Jane Game, died in childbirth when he was four. An undocumented anecdote about the Booth family originating with Izola

Forrester's *This One Mad Act: The Unknown Story of John Wilkes Booth and His Family by His Granddaughter* (Boston: Hale, Cushman & Flint, 1937), 135, claims the Booths were of Spanish Jewish descent, but it has never been corroborated by any independent source.

4. Junius Brutus Booth (JBB) letter, dated May 1, 1839, reprinted in Archer, *Junius Brutus Booth*, 7.

5. William Oxberry (ed.), *Oxberry's Dramatic Biography and Histrionic Anecdotes* (London: G. Virtue, 1826), vol. 1, 445.

6. Anonymous, *Memoirs of Junius Brutus Booth*, 12.

7. Archer, *Junius Brutus Booth*, 283.

8. Hugh Philips, *Mid Georgian London: A Topographical and Social Survey of Central and Western London about 1750* (London: Chandlers, 1964), 142.

9. Kimmel, *Mad Booths*, 18.

10. Anonymous, *Memoirs Of Junius Brutus Booth*, 13.

11. Oxberry, *Dramatic Biography*, 448.

12. F. A. Burr, "Junius Brutus Booth's Wife Adelaide," *New York Press*, (August 9, 1891), 19.

13. JBB to father from Ostend, March 17, 1815, FSL.

14. Burr, "Adelaide," 19.

15. On Kean, see Jeffrey Kahan, *The Cult of Kean* (Hampshire, UK: Ashgate, 1988), 77.

16. William Winters, *Shadows of the Stage* (London: McMillan & Co., 1893), vol. 2, 29; Thomas Ford, *The Actor, A Peep Behind The Curtain. Being Passages In The Lives Of Booth And Some Of His Contemporaries* (New York: Wm. B. Graham, 1846), 9.

17. Ford, *The Actor*, 10.

18. Anonymous, *Memoirs of Junius Brutus Booth*.

19. Archer, *Junius Brutus Booth*, 44.

20. Ford, *The Actor*, 61.

21. Kimmel, *Mad Booths*, 27–28; Titone, *My Thoughts Be Bloody*, 28. All accounts of Mary Ann's being a "flower girl" and their meeting at Covent Garden are based on a newspaper article, "A scandalous Story About the Booth Family," that appeared in the *Cincinnati Commercial* on April 18, 1865, and was widely reprinted. Deidre Barber Kincaid provides a cogent argument they probably met at Mary Ann's father's

flower shop, which was located on Bridge Street not far from where Junius lived on Pratt Street. Deidre Barber Kincaid, "Mary Ann Doolittle? The 'Flower Girl' Myth Of The Booths' Mother," *Surratt Courier*, 19 (March 2004), 3–5; see also Archer, *Junius Brutus Booth*, 66.

22. Kimmel, *Mad Booths*, 27.
23. Archer, *Junius Brutus Booth*, 66.
24. Lisbeth Jane Roman, *The Acting Style and Career Of Junius Brutus Booth* (PhD Thesis, University of Illinois, 1968), 65.
25. Jane Stabler, *The Palgrave Macmillan Burke to Byron, Barbauld to Baillie, 1790-1830* (Baskingstroke, UK: Palgrave Macmillan, 2001), 26.
26. Leslie A. Marchand (ed.), *Lord Byron: Selected Letters and Journals* (Cambridge, MA: Belknap Press, 1982), 329.
27. Asia Booth Clarke, *Personal Recollections Of The Elder Booth* (London: privately printed but not published, 1902), 37–38.
28. Ibid.
29. Asia Booth Clarke, *Booth Memorials*, 64; Asia Booth Clarke, *The Elder and the Younger Booth* (Boston: James E. Osgood & Co., 1882), 52.
30. Archer, *Junius Brutus Booth*, 289–290.
31. Burr, "Adelaide," 19.
32. Archer, *Junius Brutus Booth*, 67.
33. James Winston, *Drury Land Journal: Selections from James Winston's Diaries* (London: The Society For Theatre Research, 1974), 28.

## 2. I'VE BROKEN MY PROMISE

1. Clarke, *Booth Memorials*, 75.
2. Ibid., 77.
3. Kimmel, *Mad Booths*, 30–31.
4. Clarke, *Booth Memorials*, 79; Clarke, *Elder and Younger Booth*, 69.
5. A. O. Kellogg, "Junius Brutus Booth," *The Journal of Mental Science*, 14 (July 1868), 281.
6. *Harford Democrat*, July 6, 1900, 1.
7. Eleanor Ruggles, *Prince of Players. Edwin Booth* (New York: W. W. Norton & Co., 1953), 16–17.
8. Junius letter to Richard, May 9, 1824, reprinted in Kimmel, *Mad Booths*, 339, and Archer, *Junius Brutus Booth*, 93.

9. Julian Mates, *America's Musical Stage: Two Hundred Years of Musical Theatre* (Westport, CT: Greenwood Press, 1985), 24; David Beasley, *McKee Rankin and the Heyday of the American Theatre* (Waterloo, ON: Wilfrid Laurier University Press, 2000), 25.

10. *Philadelphia National Gazette,* June 10, 1824, 1.

11. *Kansas City Star,* January 14, 1886, 3; William W. Clapp Jr., *A Record of the Boston Stage* (Boston and Cambridge: James Munroe and Co., 1853), 278.

12. JBB letter to Francis Wemyss, copy in Archer, *Junius Brutus Booth,* 126.

13. Archer, *Junius Brutus Booth,* 124; *Ohio State Journal,* May 6, 1865, 2; Ella V. Mahoney, *Sketches Of Tudor Hall And The Booth Family* (Baltimore: Franklin Printing Co., 1925), 24–25.

14. Kimmel, *Mad Booths,* 49.

15. The original report of the incident is reprinted in Archer, *Junius Brutus Booth,* 141.

16. James Rush, *Diary,* September 28, 1835, quoted by Archer, *Junius Brutus Booth,* 136–137.

17. Terry Alford, *Fortune's Fool* (New York: Oxford University Press, 2015), 11.

18. Burr, "Adelaide," 19.

19. Ibid.

20. Ibid., 20.

21. Ibid., 19; *Macon (GA) Telegraph,* August 1, 1891, 4.

22. *New York Herald,* July 30, 1891, 5.

23. Burr, "Adelaide," 19.

24. Archer, *Junius Brutus Booth,* 318, n.9.

25. The divorce decree is reprinted in Archer, *Junius Brutus Booth,* 322–324; Kimmel, *Mad Booths,* 340–341, and Roman, *Acting Style,* 51.

26. Clarke, *Booth Memorials,* 48.

27. Archer, *Junius Brutus Booth,* 215.

28. Clarke, *Elder Booth,* 104.

29. *New York Times,* August 1, 1856, 2; Clarke, *Booth Memorials,* 153; *New Orleans Times-Picayune,* August 31, 1888, 2.

30. *Cleveland Leader,* May 6, 1884, 6.

31. The *Sun* (Baltimore, MD), March 11, 1858, 2.

32. Burr, "Adelaide," 12.

## 3. OLD SINS CAST LONG SHADOWS

1. Solangel Maldonado, "Illegitimate Harm: Law, Stigma and Discrimination Against Nonmarital Children," *Florida Law Review*, 63 (2011), 345.
2. Davis, "Illegitimacy and the social structure," 215–233; I. Pinchbeck, "Social Attitudes to the Problem of Illegitimacy," *British Journal of Sociology*, 5 (December 1954), 309–323.
3. *Macon (GA) Telegraph*, August 6, 1891, 4.
4. Clarke, *Unlocked Book*, 59.
5. For the controversy over the location of John's initials on his hand and the speculation that John Wilkes Booth escaped and that someone other than Booth was dragged from the barn who had the initials added to deceive the authorities into believing that the man was Booth, see Constance Head, "J. W. B.: His Initials in India Ink," *The Virginia Magazine of History and Biography*, 90 (July 1982), 359–366.
6. Clarke, *Booth Memorials*, 114.
7. Asia letter to Jean Anderson, June 1855, MdHS.
8. Saturo Saitoh, Peter Steinglass, Marc A. Schuckit, *Alcoholism And the Family* (New York: Brunn/Mazel, Inc., 1992), 277.
9. *Evening Post* (New York), April 9, 1858, 2.
10. *Daily Ohio Statesman* (Columbus), April 15, 1858, 3.
11. Quoted in Arthur W. Bloom, *Edwin Booth: A Biography and Performance History* (Jefferson, NC: McFarland & Co., 2013), 6.
12. Edwin Booth, "Some Words About My Father," in Brander Matthews and Laurence Hutton (eds.), *Actors and Actresses of Great Britain and the United States*, vol. 3 (New York: Cassell & Co., 1886), 102–103.
13. Letter dated April 23, 1876, to Edwina, in *Edwin Booth: Recollections by his daughter, Edwina Booth Grossmann, and Letters to Her and to His Friends* (New York: Century Company, 1894).
14. Bloom, *Edwin Booth*, 6.
15. James Young, "Pictures Of the Booth Family," *New York Times*, July 14, 1896, 12.

16. *New York Daily Tribune*, May 12, 1865, 4. On the Hall family, see Dinah Faber, "Joseph and Ann Hall: Behind the Scenes at Tudor Hall," *Harford Historical Bulletin*, No. 104 (Fall 2006), 3–64.

17. Edwin letter to Nahum Capen, July 28, 1881, in Clarke, *Unlocked Book*, 203.

18. Ella Mahoney, quoted by Alford, *Fortune's Fool*, 14.

19. Kimmel, *Mad Booths*, 66.

20. Alford, *Fortunes Fool*, 17.

21. Clarke, *Unlocked Book*, 45.

22. Kimmel, *Mad Booths*, 70.

23. George Stout, "Knew The Booths in Boyhood Days," *Baltimore American*, July 27, 1903, 13; "Booth's debut," undated clipping, Black papers, Box 8, K-OAK.

24. Blanche DeBar statement in *The World* (New York City), January 11, 1925, 13.

25. John Rhodehamel and Louise Taper (eds.), *"Right or Wrong, God Judge Me": The Writings of John Wilkes Booth* (Urbana, IL: University of Illinois Press, 1997), 37.

26. Ibid., 56.

27. Shettel, "J. Wilkes Booth," 1, 5.

28. George Alfred Townsend, *The Life, Crime, And Capture Of John Wilkes Booth* (New York: Dick & Fitzgerald, 1865), 21.

29. *New York Tribune*, May 5, 1865, 5.

30. Ibid.

31. Clarke, *Unlocked Book*, 99–101.

32. JWB letter to T. William O'Laughlen, August 8, 1854, in Rhodehamel and Taper, *Right or Wrong*, 38.

33. The *Sun* (Baltimore, MD), February 27, 2007, 1G.

34. Rhodehamel and Taper, *Right or Wrong*, 64.

35. *New York Daily Tribune*, May 12, 1865, 4.

36. Adam Badeau, "Dramatic Reminiscences," *St. Paul and Minneapolis Pioneer Press*, February 20, 1887.

37. Rhodehamel and Taper, *Right or Wrong*, 107.

38. Archer, *Junius Brutus Booth*, 224.

39. Asia letter to Jean Anderson, n.d. (estimated 1852) MdHS.

40. Clarke, *Unlocked Book*, 64.

41. Ibid., 92, n.1.
42. Ibid., 91.
43. Ibid., 92.
44. Ibid., 105–106.
45. Ibid., 76–77.
46. Ibid., 74.
47. Ibid., 71.
48. Ibid., 99.
49. JWB letter to O'Laughlen, June 18, 1855, Rhodehamel and Taper, *Right or Wrong*, 41.
50. JWB letter to O'Laughlen, November 8, 1854, Ibid., 40.
51. *St. Louis Post Dispatch*, May 8, 1880, 2.
52. JWB letter to O'Laughlen, April 30, 1854, Ibid., 38.
53. JWB letter to O'Laughlen, June 18, 1855, Ibid., 41.
54. Ibid.

## 4. THEY IDOLIZED HIM

1. Clarke, *Unlocked Book*, 107.
2. The *Sun* (Baltimore, MD), August 14, 1855, 3.
3. Clarke, *Unlocked Book*, 107.
4. Nora Titone, *My Thoughts Be Bloody* (New York: Free Press, 2010), 95–96.
5. Clarke, *Unlocked Book*, 107.
6. Ibid., 104.
7. Ibid.
8. *Southern Aegis*, July 18, 1857, 14; August 8, 1857, 39; August 22, 1857, 55.
9. Townsend, *Life and Crimes*, 21.
10. Gordon Samples, *Lust for Fame: The Stage Career of John Wilkes Booth* (Jefferson, NC: McFarland & Co., 1982), 19; David Beasley, *McKee Rankin, And the Heyday Of The American Theatre* (Waterloo, ON: Wilfred Laurier University Press, 2002), 49.
11. The various stock company roles are described in J. Brander Matthews, "Actors and Actress of New York," *Scribner's Monthly*, 17 (April 1879), 769–784; J. Palgrave Simpson, "The Poor (Walking) Gentleman," *The Theatre: A Monthly Review Of Drama, Music, and the Fine Arts*, 1

(May 1880), 269–273; James A. Herne, "Old Stock Days in the Theatre," *The Arena*, 6 (September 1892), 401–416; Samples, *Lust For Fame*, 52–54; and Thomas A. Bogar, *Backstage At The Lincoln Assassination. The Untold Story Of The Actors and Stagehands At Ford's Theatre* (Washington, D.C.: Regnery, 2013), 24–25, 53–54, 58. The quote about "a good actor" is from Frederick Ware, *Fifty Years of Make Believe* (New York: International Press, 1920), 38.

12. Edwin said he and John had learned fencing from their brother June. Francis Wilson, *Francis Wilson's Life of Himself* (Boston: Houghton Mifflin Co., 1924), 135.
13. Clarke, *Unlocked Book*, 111.
14. Emerson, *Theatre Magazine*, 17 (June 1910), 180.
15. Arthur F. Loux, *John Wilkes Booth: Day by Day* (Jefferson, NC: McFarland & Co., 2014), 18.
16. *Wilkes-Barre (PA) Times*, December 19, 1894, 6.
17. Townsend, *Life and Crimes*, 21.
18. *Washington (WA) Standard*, August 17, 1878, 6.
19. Townsend, *Life and Crimes*, 25.
20. Kimmel, *Mad Booths*, 150.
21. Townsend, *Life and Crimes*, 25.
22. Quoted by Loux, *Booth: Day by Day*, 30.
23. Titone, *My Thoughts Be Bloody*, 168.
24. A. F. Norcross, "A Child's Memory of the Boston Theatre," *Theatre Magazine*, 42 (May 1926), 72.
25. On the Richmond Theatre, see Charles F. Fuller Jr., *Kunkel and Company at the Marshall Theatre, Richmond, Virginia, 1856-1861* (MA Thesis, Ohio University, 1968).
26. Deirdre Barber, "A man of Promise. John Wilkes Booth at Richmond, 1858-1860," *Journal of the South Eastern Theatre Conference*, 2 (1994) 113–129, 114.
27. E. Lawrence Abel, *Singing The New Nation: How Music Shaped the Confederacy, 1861-1865* (Mechanicsburg, PA: Stackpole Books, 2000), 239.
28. John Ford Sollers, *The Theatrical Career of John T. Ford* (PhD Thesis, Stanford University, 1962), 90.
29. Ibid., 85, n. 123.

30. Townsend, *Life and Crimes*, 22.

31. John M. Barron, "An Actor's Memories Of Richmond Befo' the War," The *Sun* (Baltimore), January 20, 1907, 15.

32. Ibid.

33. Edward M. Alfriend, "Assassin Booth," *Sunday Globe* (Washington, D.C.) February 9, 1902.

34. Quincy Kilby, "Some newly collected facts about John Wilkes Booth," n.d. Original typescript in Seymour Collection, Princeton University Library, copy in JOH.

35. JWB letter to Edwin, September 10, 1858, in Rhodehamel and Taper, *Right or Wrong*, 45.

36. *Louisville (KY) Daily Courier*, November 28, 1859, 1.

37. Clarke, *Unlocked Book*, 120.

38. JWB letter to Edwin, September 10, 1858, in Rhodehamel and Taper, *Right or Wrong,* 45.

39. George Crutchfield, Letter to Professor Edward V. Valentine, July 5, 1909, JOH, also in George S. Bryan, *The Great American Myth* (New York: Darrick & Evans, 1940), 86.

40. Ibid.

41. Charles Wallace, "Richmond in by gone days," *Richmond Dispatch*, June 24, 1906, 36.

42. Edward M. Alfriend, "Recollections of John Wilkes Booth," *The Era*, 8 (October 1901), 604.

43. *Daily People* (New York City), December 8, 1901, 3.

44. Alfriend, "Recollections," 604.

45. Among his other honors, he was President of the American Medical Association. *Charleston (SC) Courier*, May 8, 1852, 2.

46. Mary Bella Beale, "Wilkes Booth's Ring," *Atlanta Constitution*, December 31, 1887, 4.

47. Dr. Beale was a third grand master of the Odd Fellows. President James Monroe had once been a guest at their house. *The Times* (Richmond, VA), July 2, 1890, 4.

48. Beale, "Ring," 4.

49. Ibid.

50. J. M. Barron, "The Stage Before the War," The *Sun* (Baltimore, MD), November 4, 1906, 14.

51. JWB letter to Edwin, September 10, 1858, in Rhodehamel and Taper, *Right or Wrong*, 45.

## 5. YOUNG AND PRETTY MAGGIE MITCHELL

1. *Saturday Evening Gazette* (Boston), July 4, 1857, 2.
2. *Richmond Whig*, November 3, 1857, 2; *New York Clipper*, March 27, 1858, 390.
3. *Daily True Delta* (New Orleans), January 17, 1861, 5.
4. Michael Burlingame (ed.), *Lincoln's Journalist: John Hay's Anonymous Writings for the Press, 1860-1864* (Carbondale, IL: Southern Illinois University Press, 2006), 321.
5. *Daily Creole* (New Orleans), December 17, 1856, 2; *Daily Ohio Statesman* (Columbus), June 24, 1856, 3; Ibid., June 25, 1856, 3; Towse, *Sixty Years*, 89.
6. John was a frequent visitor of Maggie's dressing room. *New York Clipper*, December 25, 1915, 8. "From a letter in my possession written by herself I am convinced that a love affair existed between Miss Maggie Mitchell and J. Wilkes Booth and that it is probable she corresponded with him and was in his confidence. She is a rebel & Blanch Booth says Maggie can keep her secrets better than any woman she ever knew." J. H. Baker to Dana, April 24, 1865, NARA RG 107 M473, reel 118, 114. George S. Bryan said that Blanche Chapman Ford told him of a rumored engagement. Bryan, *Great American Myth*, 126. According to John Ford Sollers, the rumor was in fact true. Terry Alford, personal communication.
7. Stated birth year for Maggie's birthdate varies. The 1837 date is based on information found in census data, on www.revolvy.com, and at www.findagrave.com, "Margaret Julia 'Maggie' Mitchell." All that is known of Anna's first husband is that he was a medical doctor (*Trenton Evening Times*, November 20, 1883), that his surname was Lomax, and that he died shortly after he and Anna left England and came to America with their four children. *Brooklyn Daily Eagle*, November 8, 1885, 14. A Wikipedia article asserts Lomax was a bookbinder, but I was unable to locate the cited source.
8. Ibid.

9.  Shirley Burns, "Diminutive Players," *The Green Book Magazine*, 3 (March 1910), 580.

10. On Burton's theater, see D. L. Rinear, *Stage, Page, Scandals and Vandals: William E. Burton and Nineteenth-Century* (Carbondale, IL: Southern Illinois University Press, 2004).

11. *Watertown Daily Times*, December 9, 1891, 13.

12. Ibid.

13. Frederic E. McKay and Charles E. L. Windgate (eds.), Charles R. Thorne Jr., *Famous American Actors of To-day* (New York: Thomas Y. Crowell & Co., 1896), vol. 2, 308–313.

14. *Folio*, 27–28 (December 1885), 220.

15. Advertisement, "Maggie Mitchell Waltz," "At Lucks' Music Store," *Nashville Union and American*, September 9, 1859, 1.

16. Thorne, *Actors*, 313. E.g., "Our Maggie," *Katy O'Sheal*. The latter was her signature play for several years.

17. *Wheeling Daily Intelligencer*, August 30, 1859, 2.

18. *Plain Dealer* (Cleveland), August 5, 1855, 3. After she became famous, the *New York Herald* (March 7, 1889) and several other newspapers reported the brief affair and secret marriage, although some intimated the story was invented by a rejected suitor in Baltimore.

19. *Saturday Evening Gazette*, December 5, 1857, 6.

20. *New York Clipper*, March 27, 1858, 390.

21. The *Sun* (Baltimore, MD), April 2, 1858, 1.

22. *New Orleans Times-Picayune*, April 22, 1858, 1.

23. John M. Barron, "Actors of Days gone by, A Record of Impressions," The *Sun* (Baltimore, MD), November 11, 1906, 15.

24. George Berrell Diary entry quoted in William G. B. Carson, "Bumping over the Road in the 70s," *Educational Theatre Journal*, 10 (October 1958), 203–210, 204.

25. Barron, "Actors of Days gone by."

26. *Charlotte Observer*, February 3, 1924, 16, 19. Alford, *Fortune's Fool*, 57, alters the text leaving the impression that John was taken with Maggie as a performer and that there was no romantic interest at the time.

27. *Richmond Daily Dispatch*, October 17, 1859, 1.

## 6. THIS HARPERS FERRY BUSINESS

1. Clarke, *Unlocked Book*, 110–111.
2. *New York Clipper*, May 7, 1859, 23; *Evening Star* (Washington, D.C.), May 3, 1859.
3. Asia letter to Jean Anderson, n.d. 1860, MdHS.
4. Loux, *Booth: Day By Day*, 47.
5. *New York Clipper*, August 20, 1859, 142.
6. Asia letter to Jean Anderson, June 19, 1859, MdHS.
7. *Richmond Daily Dispatch*, November 21, 1859, 1.
8. Excerpts for the *Charleston Mercury* reprinted in *The Richmond Enquirer*, November 15, 1859.
9. *Richmond Examiner*, November 18, 1859.
10. *New York Clipper*, December 3, 1859, 262.
11. *Richmond Daily Dispatch*, February 2, 1902, 14.
12. Quoted by Deidre Lindsay Kincaid, *Rough Magic: The Theatrical Life of John Wilkes Booth*, (PhD Thesis, University of Hull, 2000), 77.
13. Asia letter to Jean Anderson, n.d. 1859, MdHS.
14. *Richmond Daily Dispatch*, November 21, 1859, 1.
15. George W. Libby, "John Brown and John Wilkes Booth," *Confederate Veteran*, 38 (1930), 138.
16. Ibid., Polly Daffron, "George Libby Recalls Incidents of the War Between the States," *Richmond Times Dispatch*, July 7, 1929, 9. The Richmond Grays' Quartermaster, Major Robert Caskie, told a somewhat different version of how John joined up with his unit ("A reminiscence of John Wilkes Booth," *Texas Siftings* (Austin, TX), August 4, 1883, 5.
17. Crutchfield letter to Valentine, July 5, 1909, JOH.
18. L. Terry Oggel (ed.), *The Letters and Notebooks of Mary Devlin Booth* (Westport, CT: Greenwood Press, 1987) 22.
19. *Richmond Daily Dispatch*, November 21, 1859, 1.
20. Ibid.
21. Libby, "John Brown," 138.
22. *New York Times*, October 31, 1859.
23. Henry G. Tinsley, "Last of John Brown's Harper Ferry Guards," *San Francisco Chronicle*, March 21, 1897, 16.

24. "The Life of Philip Whitlock, Written by himself," www.jewish-history. com/cvilwar/philip_whitlock.html, accessed February 8, 2016.

25. *Richmond Daily Dispatch*, December 5, 1859, 1.

26. John Barron, "John Wilkes Booth, Some Recollections of Him By an Early Virginia Acquaintance," *Daily People* (New York City), December 8, 1901, 3.

27. *Boston Daily Globe*, March 7, 1909, 43.

28. Clarke, *Unlocked Book*, 124.

29. "To Whom it may concern" letter, November 1864, reprinted in Rhodehamel and Taper, *Right or Wrong*, 125.

30. Rhodehamel and Taper, *Right or Wrong*, 6.

31. *Richmond Whig*, December 28, 1859.

32. Ella and her seven siblings and their mother had come from England in 1847. *New York Times*, May 14, 1898, 7.

33. During the war at least two songs, "The Young Volunteer" (Macon, Ga: John C. Schreiner and Son, 1863) and "See At Your Feet A Suppliant One" (Richmond: George Dunn and Co, 1861), carried the caption, "as sung by Miss Ella Wren."

34. The *Sun* (New York City, New York), April 5, 1880, 1.

35. Fred R. Wren, "Edwin Booth," *New Orleans Times Picayune*, July 14, 1907, 10.

36. *Atlanta Constitution*, December 4, 1881, 9.

## 7. THE STAR SISTERS: HELEN AND LUCILLE WESTERN

1. *Overland Monthly and the Out West Magazine*, 1923, 76.

2. Herbert J. Edwards, Julie A. Herne, and James A. Herne, *The Rise of Realism in the American Drama* (Orono, ME: University of Maine Press, 1964), 10.

3. *Boston Herald*, November 18, 1856, 4; December 8, 1856; *Louisville Daily Courier*, November 8, 1858, 4. Brown, *History of the American Stage*, 382.

4. Dale Cockrell, *Demons of Disorder, Early Blackface Minstrels and Their World* (New York: Cambridge University Press, 1997), 69.

5. Ironically, long before the banner of "banned in Boston" became a mantra for puritanical censorship, "the pure and Puritanical city of Boston" (*Detroit Free Press*, May 7, 1859, quoting the *New York*

*Tribune*) did not find *The Three Fast Men* especially objectionable, whereas theatre critics in the west railed at its sexual innuendo and exhibitionism.

6. *New York Clipper*, November, 14, 1863, 241.

7. *Boston Herald*, March 17, 1857, 2.

8. Ibid., March 11, 1857, 2.

9. Ibid., March 18, 1857, 2.

10. Helen and Lucille were the first women to be featured in a minstrel act. Frank Dumont, "The Golden Days of Minstrelsy," *New York Clipper*, December 19, 1914.

11. Brown, *History of the American Stage*, 387; E. Lawrence Abel, *Confederate Sheet Music* (Jefferson, NC: McFarland & Co., 2004), 139.

12. *Boston Herald*, March 13, 1857, 2.

13. Ibid., March 18, 1857, 2.

14. Ibid., March 13, 1857, 2.

15. Ibid., March 24, 1857, 2.

16. Ibid., April 30, 1857, 2.

17. *Louisville Daily Courier*, November 10, 1858, 3.

18. Ibid.; *Boston Herald*, June 16, 1857, 3.

19. *Boston Herald*, June 34, 1857, 2.

20. Ibid., November 10, 1857, 4.

21. Ibid., November 21, 1857, 2.

22. William Dean Howells, *Suburban Sketches* (Boston: James R. Osgood and Co., 1872), 227–230.

23. *New York Times*, April 19, 1858, 4.

24. *New Orleans Times-Picayune*, November 7, 1858, 3; *Louisville Daily Courier*, November 10, 1858, 1; *Pittsburgh Daily Post*, March 17, 1858, 3. The "plump and pretty girls" comment is from an unidentified clipping quoted by Nan Mullenneaux, *Walking Ladies: Mid-nineteenth-century American Actresses' Work, Family and Culture* (Albany, NY: State University of New York Press, 2008), 169–170.

25. The *Spirit of the Times*, 1877, 628.

26. *Boston Herald*, May 24, 1858, 2.

27. *Pittsburgh Daily Post*, October 26, 1858, 4.

28. *Detroit Free Press*, June 12, 1858, 3; *Cincinnati Daily Enquirer*, October 29, 1858, 3; *Louisville Daily Courier*, November 8, 1858, 1; *Chicago Press and Tribune*, December 10, 1858, 9; Robert L. Sherman, *Chicago Stage, Its Record and Achievement* (Chicago: Robert Sherman, 1947), 401.

29. *Sacramento Daily Union*, February 14, 1859, 5. The Bowery Theatre was notorious for its raucous, whistling, caterwauling audiences. Decorum was so rare at The Bowery Theatre that when it occurred, it was newsworthy (Cockrell, *Demons*, 69).

30. *Detroit Free Press*, May 7, 1859, 1.

31. *New York Times*, February 28, 1859, 1.

32. Ibid., April 12, 1859, 1.

33. *New York Clipper*, August 13, 1859; *Sacramento Daily Union*, September 16, 1859.

34. *New York Clipper*, October 22, 1859, 214.

35. *Daily Alta California*, November 1, 1859, 1.

36. *Wheeling (WV) Daily Intelligencer*, October 31, 1859, 3.

37. University of Louisville, "Macauley's Theatre Collection," http://digital. library.louisville.edu/cdm/landingpage/collection/macauley/, accessed 6/7/2015.

## 8. I CANNOT STOOP TO THAT WHICH I DESPISE

1. *Richmond Daily Dispatch*, May 12, 1860, 1.

2. For a description of these pikes see Frank Heywood Hodder, "The John Brown Pikes," *Kansas Historical Quarterly*, 2 (November 1933), 386–390.

3. Clarke, *Unlocked Book*, 113–114.

4. Ibid., 113. Booth also exaggerated his involvement in the Baltimore riots (April 19–21, 1861), claiming he had been one of the rioters and had burned bridges (Michael W. Kauffman, *American Brutus* (New York: Random House, 2005), 424, n. 20) which was not possible since he was in Albany performing as Richard III on April 22 (*Albany Times Union*, November 3, 2014).

5. Titone, *My Thoughts Be Bloody*, 216–217.

6. Clarke, *Elder and Younger Booth*, 152.

7. Lincoln's "taste comment" occurs in a letter he wrote to Lyman Trumbull, April 29, 1860, quoted in David Herbert Donald, *Lincoln* (New York: Simon and Schuster, 1995), 241; John's "taste" in Mary Devlin to Edwin, March 1, 1860, in Oggel (ed.), *Letters and Notebooks*, 44.

8. Bloom, *Edwin Booth*, 43. Nan Mullenneaux, *Walking Ladies: Mid-nineteenth-century American Actresses' Work, Family and Culture* (Albany, NY: State University of New York Press, 2008), 51.

9. Ibid.

10. Letter to Elizabeth Stoddard, March 12, 1863, reprinted in "Life Tragedy of Edwin Booth," *Boston Herald*, November 1, 1903, 402.

11. Quoted in Bloom, *Edwin Booth*, 37.

12. Adam Badeau, "Edwin Booth. On And Off The Stage. Personal Recollections," *McClure's Magazine*, 1 (June–November 1893) 253–267, 26.

13. Badeau, "Edwin Booth," 260–261.

14. Edwin letter to June, October 31, 1858, quoted in Bloom, *Edwin Booth*, 39.

15. Asia letter (n.d. 1859) to Jean Anderson, MdHS.

16. Johnson, "Enter the Harlot," 66.

17. "Edward Freiberger," undated clipping, Black papers, K-OAK.

18. Quoted in Charles F. Jr. Fuller, *Kunkel and Company at the Marshall Theatre, Richmond, Virginia, 1856-1861* (MA Thesis, Ohio University, 1968), 25.

19. Bloom, *Edwin Booth*, 45.

20. Badeau, "Edwin Booth," 361.

21. Asia letter August 21, 1860 to Jean Anderson, MdHS.

22. Mrs. Thomas Bailey Aldrich, *Crowding Memories* (Boston: Houghton Mifflin Co., 1920), 8.

## 9. ALMOST AN EUNUCH

1. *New York Clipper*, June 30, 1860, 87.

2. Ibid., July 14, 1860, 102.

3. Loux, *Booth: Day by Day*, 61.

4. Townsend, *Life and Crimes*, 22.

5. George Alfred Townsend, "How John Wilkes Booth was Started in the Theatrical Profession," *Cincinnati Enquirer*, January 19, 1886, 1.
6. *New York Clipper*, August 6, 1859, 127.
7. *National Republican* (Washington, D.C.), February 16, 1874, 4.
8. Canning paid $45,000 for renovating the Montgomery Theatre in Alabama. *New York Clipper*, June 30, 1860, 87.
9. Mona Rebecca Brooks, *The Development Of American Theatre Management Practices Between 1830 and 1896* (PhD Thesis, Texas Tech University, 1981), 45.
10. Edwin lost money starring his friends Ned Adams and Lawrence Barret as star performers. Both were good stock actors but failed as stars. Ruggles, *Prince of Players*, 232.
11. *Cincinnati Enquirer*, January 19, 1886, 1.
12. Ibid.
13. *Montgomery Advertiser*, September 12, 1860, quoted in Kincaid, *Rough Magic*, 120.
14. Abel, *Singing The New Nation*, 245.
15. Emma Mitchell, another of Maggie's sisters, was a dancer in the troupe. *New York Clipper*, October 20, 1860, 215.
16. *Daily Times* (Columbus, GA), October 5, 1860.
17. *Daily Sun* (Columbus, GA), October 6, 1860.
18. *Daily Gazette and Comet* (Baton Rouge, LA), October, 24, 1860.
19. *Cincinnati Enquirer*, January 19, 1886, 1. Canning's story is improbable, starting with his holding the gun while John scraped away the rust. The second improbability was that the gun was a pistol. It is more likely that it would have been a derringer. Finally, John was known to be a crack shot with a pistol and a rifle; no one was a crack shot with a derringer.
20. *New York Clipper*, November 4, 1860.
21. Kincaid, *Rough Magic*, 125.
22. Abel, *Singing The New Nation*, 246–247.
23. Dear Miss Letter (1860), from the John K. Lattimer Collection, reproduced in Heritage Auctions Catalog (Dallas, TX), November 20, 2008, Lot No. 61201.
24. *Philadelphia Press*, May 18, 1865, 2; Catherine Mary Reignold Winslow, *Yesterdays With Actors* (Boston: Cupples and Hurd, 1887), 141.

25. *New York Dramatic Mirror*, December 31, 1913, 8.
26. *Philadelphia Press*, May 18, 1865, 2.
27. *"Dear Miss" Letter*, Lattimer Collection.

## 18. LITTLE REHEARSALS: LOUISE WOOSTER

1. Louise Wooster, *The Autobiography of a Magdalen* (Birmingham, AL: Birmingham Publishing Co., 1911), 19.
2. Ibid., 7–9.
3. Ibid., 18–19, 29–30.
4. Ibid., 32–33.
5. Ibid., 46–47.
6. Ibid., 48.
7. William Warren Rogers, *Confederate Home Front: Montgomery During the Civil War* (Tuscaloosa, AL: University Alabama Press, 2001), 85; Louise said her name was Jennie Garborough. Thomas P. Lowry gives her name as Jenny Yarborough in his book *Sexual Misbehavior in the Civil War: A Compendium* (e-book, Xlibris Corp., 2006), 13.
8. L. C. W., *Autobiography*, 48.
9. Ibid., 48–49.
10. Lowry, *Sexual Misbehavior*, 13; E. Susan Barber and Charles F. Ritter, "Dangerous Liaisons: Working Women and Sexual Justice in the American Civil War," *European Journal of American Studies*, 10 (2015), 2–19.
11. Lowry, *Sexual Misbehavior*, 56–57.
12. E. Lawrence Abel, *A Finger in Lincoln's Brain* (Santa Barbara, CA: Praeger, 2015), 30.
13. Ibid.
14. Bloom, *Edwin Booth*, 33.
15. Abel, *A Finger In Lincoln's Brain*, 34–44.
16. *New York Daily Graphic*, November 6, 1873, 35.
17. L. C. W., *Autobiography*, 49.
18. Ibid., 50.
19. Ibid.
20. Bloom, *Edwin Booth*, 39.
21. *Montgomery Weekly Advertiser*, December 5, 1860, 3.

22. A printed invitation to the St. Andrews dinner was found among John's personal effects. Edwards and Steers, *Evidence*, 623.ww

23. Ibid.

24. Stanley Kimmel speculates John decided to go as a star under his own name after reading a Montgomery newspaper report that his brother Edwin had received $5,000 as his share of the months profits from a Boston engagement. Kimmel, *Mad Booths*, 157; See also Ruggles, *Prince of Players*, 123, Samples, *Lust For Fame*, 48.

25. *Greencastle (IN) Banner*, November 15, 1860, 2.

26. *New York Times*, November 9, 1860.

27. Ibid., November 20, 1860, from a speech on November 13.

28. Draft of speech, December 1860, in Rhodehamel and Taper, *Right or Wrong*, 58.

29. Effie Ellsler Westen (ed.), *The Stage Memories of John A. Ellsler* (Cleveland: Rofant Club, 1950) reprinted in Rhodehamel and Taper, *Right or Wrong*, 66; Wooster, *Autobiography*, 51–52, 56.

30. Ibid., 52–53.

## 11. THE SOUTHERN MARSEILLAISE

1. Alabama Secession Banner of 1861, http://www.crwflags.com/fotw/flags/us-alsec.html#disc, accessed January 16, 2015. Prior to the adoption of the "Stars and Bars" flag of the Confederacy, various Southern states created their own state secession flags like Alabama's.

2. The "Southern Marseillaise" was adapted to the tune of the revolutionary French national anthem by Armand Blackmar in New Orleans on December 21, 1860, in celebration of South Carolina's secession (George Henry Preble, *Origin and History of the American Flag* (Philadelphia: Nicholas L. Brown, 1917), vol. 2, 498) although Louisiana did not secede until January 26, 1861. It was the South's unofficial anthem until it was replaced by two more popular unofficial anthems, "Dixie" and "The Bonnie Blue Flag."

3. *Daily Graphic* (New York City), June 12, 1875, 11.

4. *Montgomery Weekly Advertiser*, December 19, 1860, 3. Frank P. O'Brien, "Passing of the Old Montgomery Theatre," *Montgomery Advertiser*, November 24, 1907, 6.

5. *Cincinnati Daily Press*, December 24, 1860, 1.

6.  *Springfield (MA) Republican*, Jan 10, 1861, 2.
7.  Abel, *Singing The New Nation,* 237.
8.  *Daily Creole* (New Orleans), December 17, 1856, 2.
9.  *Daily True Delta* (New Orleans), November 18, 1860, 1.
10. On Waldauer, see William Hyde and Howard Louis Conrad (eds.), *Encyclopedia of The History of St Louis: A compendium of History and Biography for Ready Reference* (New York: The Southern History Company, 1899), vol. 4, 2391–2392.
11. *Daily Crescent* (New Orleans), January 24, 1861, 1; *New York Clipper,* March 9, 1861, 375.
12. Ibid., January 24, 1861, 1.
13. *Brooklyn Daily Eagle*, November 8, 1885, 14. An actual count of her Fanchon appearances places the number at around 1,200. Thomas Bogar, personal communication.
14. Alabama seceded on January 11, 1861. Maggie may have left just before since she opened in New Orleans on January 14.
15. *Weekly Post* (Montgomery, AL), February 6, 1861.
16. James P. Jones and William Warren Rogers, "Montgomery as the Confederate Capital; View of a New Nation," *Alabama Historical Quarterly*, 26 (Spring 1964), 1–125; *Weekly Post* (Montgomery, AL), February 13, 1861, 25–26.
17. C. Vann Woodward and Elizabeth Muhlenfeld (eds.), *The Private Mary Chestnut: The Unpublished Civil War Diaries* (New York: Oxford University Press, 1984); *Weekly Post* (Montgomery, AL), February 28, 1861, 16, 18.
18. Lt. Col. John H. Napier, "Martial Montgomery," *Alabama Historical Quarterly*, (Fall–Winter 1967), 107–131, 130; Jones and Rogers, "Montgomery," 67.

## 12. ALL FOR LOVE AND MURDER: HENRIETTA IRVING

1.  *New Orleans Times-Picayune*, January 22, 1865, 4.
2.  Kincaid, *Rough Magic*, 129.
3.  Rochester Union and Advertiser, January, 22, 1861, 3.
4.  *New York Clipper*, December 15, 1860.
5.  Rochester Union and Advertiser, January 26, 1861, quoted by Kincaid, *Rough Magic*, 129.

6. Henrietta wrote a brief autobiography, now housed in the Union Square Theatre Collection, Hampden-Booth Theatre Library (HL). My thanks to Raymond Wemmlinger for making it and other letters available to me.

7. Ibid.

8. Located at the corner of Ninth and Walnut Streets, the Walnut Street Theatre was the first theatre to install gas lighting, air conditioning, and the tradition of the curtain call. Bernard Havard and Mark D. Sylvester, *Walnut Street Theatre* (Charleston, SC: Arcadia Publishing, 2008).

9. Couldock was an England-born émigré, whose acting style was characterized as "old-school" with emotive sentimentalism and great sweeping gestures. *New York Times*, May 12, 1895, 21; John A. Garraty and Mark C. Carnes, *American National Biography* (New York: Oxford University Press, 1999), 581–582.

10. Irving, *Autobiography*, H-BTL.

11. The incident with the diamond was reported in the *Minnesotian* on September 17, 1857, and is also mentioned in Frank M. Whiting, "Theatrical Personalities of Old St. Paul," *Minnesota History*, 23 (December 1942), 313.

12. For Couldock and Henrietta in Chicago, see Sherman, *Chicago Stage*, 405–408.

13. *Rock Island (IL) Argus*, August 19, 1905, 6.

14. *Chicago Press and Tribune*, July 2, 1858, 1.

15. *New York Clipper*, January 29, 1859, 26; February 12, 1859, 342.

16. Ibid., December 3, 1859, 263.

17. Townsend, *Life, Crime and Capture*, 24.

18. *Albany Evening Journal*, February 18, 1861.

19. *New York Tribune*, February 13, 1861; *Albany Atlas & Argus*, February 18, 1861; *New York Clipper*, February 23, 1861; Henry Pitt Phelps, *Players of a Century. A Record of the Albany Stage. Including Notices of Prominent Actors Who Have Appeared in America* (Albany: Joseph McDonough, 1880) 326.

20. C. R. Rosebery, "Actor Checks Into Hotel in Albany," *Albany Times-Union*, April 12, 1965, 18.

21. Ibid.

22. Phelps, *Players*, 324.

23. Ibid., 326.

24. Ibid.

25. Herbert Adams, "John Wilkes Booth Won Hearts in Portland," in Donald W. Beattie, Rodney M. Cole, and Charles G. Waugh (eds.), *A Distant War Comes Home* (Camden, ME: Down East Books, 1991), 36.

26. Clara Morris, *Life on the Stage. My Personal experiences and Recollections* (New York: McClure, Phillips & Co., 1901), 126.

27. The *Albany (NY) Evening Journal* (April 20, 1861, 2) dubbed it "The Baltimore Massacre." The events are described in E. Lawrence Abel, "Cloak and Dagger," *America's Civil War*, 4 (January 1992), 30–37; Daniel Stashower, "Lincoln Must Die," *Smithsonian Magazine*, 43 (February 2013), 74–89.

28. Adams, "John Wilkes Booth," 37.

29. But not in Albany, possibly to avoid the scandal tarnishing the Stanwix Hotel's reputation.

30. *Cincinnati Daily Enquirer*, May 5, 1861, 3.

31. *Louisville Courier-Journal*, May 10, 1861.

32. *Chicago Tribune*, May 14, 1861, 4. The *Chicago Tribune* misreported John's name as J. Edwards Booth. Four years later, the *Albany Atlas & Argus* had an entirely different version. "Quite a pretty sensational story," it said of the previous accounts, "but there is no truth in it." Booth, it went on, "roomed with an actress whose temper was quite as violent as his own." John, it said, was the aggrieved lover: "On returning to his room one night he found his mistress sitting up, and on the table before her two glasses of punch. Thinking she had been entertaining some male friend, he grew jealous, and they quarreled, he finally slapping her face. She subsequently left, and the next night, we believe, having purchased a pistol she sat for some hours on the stairs waiting his coming, with the apparent determination of shooting him; but he didn't come. He perhaps found more agreeable company, and there the affair ended." Reprinted in *New York Daily News*, June 1, 1865.

33. Thomas P. Lowry, "John Wilkes Booth's spurned lover slashed him with a knife and nearly changed the course of history," *America's Civil War*, 20 (November 2007), 23–24.

34. Townsend, "How John Wilkes Booth was Started in the Theatrical Profession," 1.
35. Jim Bishop, *The Day Lincoln Was Shot* (New York: HarperPerennial, 2013 [originally published 1955]), 65.
36. Alford, *Fortune's Fool*, 108.
37. William A. Howell, "Memories of Wilkes Booth," 3.
38. Henrietta Irving, *Autobiography*, HL.
39. *Pomeroy's Democrat* (Chicago, IL), April 29, 1876, 4.

## 13. MY GOOSE HANGS HIGH

1. It was customary at the close of each season for regular patrons to present one or more of the leading stock actors with a gold-headed cane. John received his in Montgomery. *Washington Post*, January 5, 1902, 30.
2. Howell, "Memories of Wilkes Booth," 3.
3. *Washington Post*, January 5, 1902, 30.
4. Howell, "Memories of Wilkes Booth," 3.
5. Ibid.
6. JWB letter to Joseph H. Simmonds, October 9, 1861, in Rhodehamel and Taper, *Right or Wrong*, 72.
7. Ibid.
8. Excerpts taken from Loux, *Booth: Day by Day*, 87–94.
9. *Daily Advertiser* (Newark, NJ), April 26, 1865, 2.
10. Edwin's characterization of John's feelings about secession (Edwin letter to Nahum Capen, July 28, 1881, in Clarke, *Unlocked Book*, 202).
11. Asia letter to Jean Anderson, n.d., MdHS.
12. *Kansas City (MO) Star*, November 8, 1897, 3.
13. Brown, *History of the American Stage*, 510.
14. Clarke, *Unlocked Book*, 115–116.
15. Edwin letter to Nahum Capen, July 28, 1881, in Clarke, *Unlocked Book*, 202.
16. Ibid.
17. Ann Harley Gilbert, *The Stage Reminiscences of Mrs. Gilbert* (New York: Charles Scribner's Sons, 1901), 57–61.

18. Mary Ann letter to JWB, March 26, 1865, Edwards and Steers, *Assassination*, 166. Being a "Roman mother" meant a willingness to sacrifice her child for Rome (i.e., the current war).

19. *Baltimore American*, June 8, 1893, 4.

20. *Daily Advertiser* (Newark, NJ), April 26, 1865, 2.

21. DeBar's sister Clementina was June's one-time wife.

22. Edwards and Steers, *Evidence*, 100 (James H. Baker testimony).

23. Grant M. Herbstruth, *Benedict DeBar and the Grand Opera House in St. Louis, Missouri, from 1855 to 1879* (PhD Thesis, University of Iowa, 1954), 98–99.

24. Edwards and Steers, *Evidence*, 852 (Provost Marshal, Col. H.R. McConnell testimony).

25. *Chicago Tribune*, January 21, 1862.

26. *Evening Journal* (Chicago, IL), February 1, 1862, quoted by Loux, *Booth: Day by* Day, 96.

27. The *Sun* (Baltimore, MD), February 17, 1862.

28. *American and Commercial Advertiser*, quoted by Loux, *Booth: Day by Day*, 98.

29. Herne, "Old Stock Days," 407.

30. Ibid.; Julie Herne, "Biographical note," in James A Herne (ed.), *Shore Acres and Other Plays* (New York: Samuel French, 1928), 11; James A. Perry, *The American Ibsen* (Chicago: Nelson-hall, 1978), 8–13.

31. The *Sun* (Baltimore, MD), February 19, 1862, 2; February 20, 1862, 2.

32. Ibid., March 10, 11, 1862.

33. J. E. Buckingham, *Reminiscences and Souvenirs of the Assassination of Abraham Lincoln* (Washington, D.C.: Rufus H. Darby, 1894), 49. Buckingham was the doorman at Ford's Theatre the night of the assassination.

34. *Boston Post*, reprinted in *Daily Missouri Democrat* (St. Louis, MO), May 21, 1862, 1.

35. Ibid.

36. Winslow, *Yesterdays with Actors*, 142.

37. Ibid.

38. Kincaid, *Rough Magic*, 168.

39. Ibid.

40. Loux, *Booth: Day by Day*, 87.
41. JWB letter to "Dear Miss," April 14, 1864, in Rhodehamel and Taper, *Right or Wrong*, 104.
42. *Daily Courant* (Hartford, CT), April 5, 1862, 3.
43. Edwards and Steers, *Evidence*, 754; Letter dated February 18, 1865.
44. Samples, *Lust*, 92.
45. Kincaid, *Rough Magic*, 172.
46. Booth letter to Edwin Keach, December 8, 1862, in Rhodehamel and Taper, *Right or Wrong*, 83.

## 14. TRUE GRIT
1. Bloom, *Edwin Booth*, 76.
2. Mary Devlin letter to Emma Cushman, January 22, 1863, Mary Devlin letter to Edwin, February, 12, 1863, in Oggel, *Letters and Notebooks*, 101, 105–106.
3. Titone, *My Thoughts Be Bloody*, 278.
4. Townsend, *Life and Crimes*, 21.
5. Asia letter to Jean Anderson, March 3, 1863, MdHS.
6. Ibid.
7. JWB letter to Joseph H. Simmons, March 1, 1863, in Rhodehamel and Taper, *Right or Wrong*, 85.
8. Grover's Theatrical playbill, April 11, 1863, quoted in Rhodehamel and Tapper, *Right or Wrong*, 87, n.2.
9. *Washington National Intelligencer*, April 12, 1863.
10. Charles Wyndham, "John Wilkes Booth. An Interview with the Press with Sir Charles Wyndham," *New York Herald*, June 27, 1909, Magazine Section, 2.
11. *Evening Star* (Washington, D.C.), May 2, 1891, 5.
12. May's account of the operation is in John Frederick May, "Mark of the Scalpel," *Records of the Columbia Historical Society*, 13 (1910), 53, and testimony in Edwards and Steers, *Evidence*, 849–850; Surratt, *Trial of John H. Surratt*, vol. 1, 270. Dr. May would later positively identify John's body by the scar from the operation he performed on John's neck.
13. *Cincinnati Enquirer*, January 18, 1886, 1.
14. JWB Letter to Joe Simmonds, April 19, 1863, in Rhodehamel and Taper, *Right or Wrong*, 88.

15. Edwards and Steers, *Evidence*, 666–667 (Herold statement).
16. May, "Mark of the Scalpel," 53, in Edwards and Steers, *Evidence*, 849; Joseph K. Barnes Testimony, May 20, 1865 in Benjamin Perley Poore (ed.), *The Conspiracy Trial for the Murder of the President* (Boston: J. E. Tilton, 1865), vol. 2, 60; Edward Steers Jr. (ed.), *The Trial. The Assassination of President Lincoln and the Trial of the Conspirators* (Lexington, KY: University of Kentucky Press, 2003), 95.

## 15. EFFIE AND ALICE

1. Emmett C. King, "What Becomes of Old Actors," *Indiana (PA) Democrat*, September 13, 1911, 1; The *Labor World*, April 16, 1904, 5; *New York Clipper*, May 20, 1865, 4.
2. Johnson Briscoe, *The Actors' Birthday Book* (New York: Moffat, Yard & Co., 1907), 155.
3. Jane Germon started her career when she was eight and regularly appeared on stage for more than fifty years. Her father, who worked under the name of Greene Germon, and was the first actor to play the title role of Uncle Tom on stage. *New York Times*, March 7, 1914, 11. He died in 1854 at age thirty-eight when Effie was nine years old. *New York Times*, March 7, 1914, 11.
4. Briscoe, *Actors' Birthday Book,* 155.
5. The *Labor World*, April 16, 1904, 5.
6. *Evening Press* (Providence, RI), August 18, 1859, 2.
7. *Evening Star* (Washington, D.C.), April 14, 1862, 3.
8. Franklin Graham, *Histrionic Montreal: Annals of the Montreal Stage, with Biographical and Critical Notices of the Plays and Players of a Century* (Montreal: John Lovell & Son, 1902), 126.
9. Tidwell, Hall, and Gaddy, *Come Retribution.*
10. *Daily National Republican* (Washington, D.C.), April 14, 1863, 3.
11. *Daily Exchange* (Baltimore, MD), December 19, 1860, 2.
12. The playbill is reproduced in Samples, *Lust for Fame*, 175.
13. United States Census 1850.
14. Graham, *Histrionic Montreal,* 123. An obituary notice mistakenly states she was born in Boston. *New York Times*, October 26, 1890.
15. *Daily Bee* (Boston, MA), January, 24, 1849.

16. *Daily Bee* (Boston, MA), February 25, 1853, 3; March 5, 1853, 3; *Boston Herald*, May 23, 1855, 3; June 14, 1855, 3; February 21, 1856, 3.

17. The ballad about unrequited love was written in 1835 by Mrs. Phillip Millard. *New York Clipper*, November 5, 1859, 23. Alice Gray is the hardest of any of the women Booth was involved with to track down because of the name's popularity in mid and late nineteenth century America and because it was also spelled "Grey." In one instance it was spelled both ways in the same newspaper paragraph, see *Washington National Republican*, November 28, 1874, 4. Besides being a common name among women, it was the name of a racing horse, boats, and even a cow. To complicate researching Alice even more, there was another entertainer named Alice Gray. Although the latter was born twenty years later and was mainly a minstrel player, in late nineteenth century news items it isn't always clear which Alice Gray is meant.

18. *Daily Bee* (Boston, MA), November 28, 1857, 2

19. *States* (Washington, D.C.), September 25, 1858, 2. The *Louisville Daily Courier*, September 27, 1858, 1, reported that the show did go on after Alice burst into tears, "a woman's irresistible appeal."

20. *New York Clipper*, October 2, 1858, 190.

21. Ibid., October 16, 1858, 201.

22. *Buffalo Daily Courier*, September 21, 1858, 3.

23. *Daily Union* (Washington, D.C.), December 3, 1858, 3.

24. *Evening Star* (Washington, D.C.), December 14, 1858, 3.

25. *States* (Washington, D.C.), December 16, 1858, 12.

26. *New York Clipper*, November 5, 1859, 23.

27. Anonymous, "Report of the Committee of the City Council of Charleston," *American Journal of Medical Sciences*, 38 (October 1859), 509–511.

28. *Charleston Mercury*, January 28, 1860.

29. *Daily Exchange* (Baltimore, MD), July 24, 1860, 1.

30. The *Sun* (Baltimore, MD), August 29, 1860, 2.

31. *Baltimore Daily Exchange*, October 19, 1860, 3.

32. *National Intelligencer* (Washington, D.C.), May 4, 1863. 37

33. Ibid.

34. Loux, *Booth: Day by Day*, 129.

## 16. IMAGINE MY HELPING THAT WOUNDED SOLDIER

1. Edwin letter to Adam Badeau, March 3, 1863, in Grossmann, *Edwin Booth,* 142.
2. Bloom, *Edwin Booth,* 65.
3. Edwin letter to Adam Badeau, June 6, 1863, in Grossmann, *Edwin Booth,* 149.
4. Badeau to James Harrison Wilson, September 12, 1863, in Charles H. Shattuck, *The Hamlet of Edwin Booth* (Urbana, IL: University of Illinois Press, 1969), 5.
5. Adam Badeau, "Edwin Booth On and Off the Stage," *McClure's Magazine,* 1 (August 1893), 264.
6. Clarke, *Unlocked Book,* 84.
7. Edwards and Steers, *Evidence,* 767.

## 17. THE MOST BEAUTIFUL WOMAN ON THE AMERICAN STAGE

1. *New York Clipper,* September 20, 1862, 8.
2. Ibid.; *Sacramento Daily Union,* September 4, 1860, 1. Brown, *History of the American Stage,* and his multivolume *A History of the New York Stage from the First Performance in 1732 to 1901* (New York: Dodd Mead, 1902) are standard sources for the plays and actors who ever appeared in New York.
3. *Detroit Free Press,* July 9, 1911, D8.
4. Everett B. Long, *Civil War Day by Day* (New York: Doubleday, 1971), 707.
5. These "card-portraits," Oliver Wendell Holmes wrote, "as everybody knows, have become the social currency, the sentimental 'Green-backs' of civilization." Oliver Wendell Holmes, *Soundings from the Atlantic* (Boston: Ticknor and Fields, 1864), 255.
6. *New York Clipper,* September 20, 1862, 8. Thomas Lowry, the authority on sex during the war, estimates that about 90 percent of all the sexually-related words and pictures in the published letters and diaries of Civil War soldiers have been deleted. Enough has survived, writes Lowry, who moiled for years through those thousands of letters and diaries, to see that those boys and men were no different from the boys and men that lived before the war or after. Thomas P. Lowry, *The*

*Story the Soldier's Wouldn't Tell. Sex in the Civil War* (Mechanicsburg, PA: Stackpole Books, 1994), 5.

7. *New York Clipper*, September 10, 1864, 8.
8. *Daily Bee* (Boston, MA), September 22, 1853, 2.
9. *Boston Herald*, November 18, 1854, 2.
10. *Daily Atlas* (Boston, MA), March 14, 1855, 2.
11. *Boston Herald*, March 15, 1855, 4.
12. *New York Herald*, September 7, 1856, 7.
13. *New York Daily Tribune*, December 8, 1856, 1.
14. William L. Slout, *Burn Cork and Tambourines: A Sourcebook of Negro Minstrelsy* (Rockville, MD: Borgo Press, 2007), 200.
15. Jane Marlin (ed.), *Reminiscences of Morris Steinert* (New York: G. P. Putnam and Sons, 1900), 105.
16. *Saturday Evening Gazette* (Boston, MA), January 31, 1867, 8.
17. *New York Tribune*, February 2, 1857, 8.
18. *Saturday Evening Gazette*, January 31, 1867, 8.
19. *New York Clipper*, September 26, 1891, 9; *Boston Daily Globe*, August 28, 1891, 10.
20. *Sacramento Daily Union*, September 4, 1860, 1.
21. *Daily Crescent* (New Orleans, LA), January 28, 1861, 1; February 19, 1861, 1.
22. *New York Daily Tribune*, October 21, 1861, 7.
23. Rose Eytinge, *The Memories of Rose Eytinge: Being Recollections & Observations of Men Women, and Events, during Half a Century* (New York: Frederick A. Stokes, 1905), 21.
24. *National Republican*, November 11, 1862, 1.
25. *Daily Post* (Pittsburgh, PA), January 19, 1863, 3.
26. Ibid., January 21, 1863, 3.
27. *New York Clipper*, February 3, 1863, 339.
28. *Cincinnati Enquirer*, January 18, 1886, 1.
29. *New York Clipper*, October 17, 1863.
30. *Springfield Republican*, October 13, 1863, 4.
31. *Providence Daily Journal*, October 17, 1863.
32. *Providence Daily Post*, October 19, 1863.
33. *Courant* (Hartford, CT), October 22, 1863.
34. Loux, *Booth: Day by Day*, 136.

35. *Daily Register* (New Haven, CT), October 28, 1863, 259.
36. *New York Clipper*, November 28, 1863; Loux, *Booth: Day by Day*, 136.
37. *Philadelphia Press*, November 9, 1863, 8.
38. *Evening Star* (Washington, D.C.), November 3, 1863, 1.

## 18. STORMING ABOUT THE COUNTRY IS SAD WORK

1. Bloom, *Edwin Booth*, 15. On the rigors of the star system, see Alfred L. Bernheim, *The Business Of The Theatre. An Economic History of the American Theatre, 1750-1932* (New York: Benjamin Blom, 1964), 24–30.
2. Bloom, *Edwin Booth*, 76.
3. *New York Tribune*, February 13, 1861; *New York Clipper*, February 23, 1861; Phelps, *Players of a Century*, 326.
4. Adams, "John Wilkes Booth," 36.
5. *Daily Gazette and Comet* (Baton Rouge, LA), October 24, 1860; *Cincinnati Enquirer*, January 19, 1886, 1.
6. Morris, *Life on Stage*, 97–98.
7. *Boston Herald*, January 5, 1890.
8. Winslow, *Yesterdays With Actors*, 141.
9. Campbell MacCulloch, "This Man Saw Lincoln Shot," *Good Housekeeping* (February 1927), 112, quoting Joseph Hazelton, a program boy at Ford's Theatre who knew Booth.
10. Andrew Cone and Walter R. Johns, *Petrolia* (New York: Appleton, 1870), 10, quoted by Titone, *My Thoughts Be Bloody*, 307.
11. San Joaquin Valley Geology, "How the Oil Industry Saved the Whales," http://www.sjvgeology.org/history/whales.html.
12. Alex Epstein, "Vindicating Standard Oil, 100 Years Later," *The Daily Caller*, May 13, 2011, http://dailycaller.com/2011/05/13/vindicating-standard-oil-100-years-later/. Kerosene was created from petroleum in 1857.
13. Weston, *Stage Memories*, 122–131.
14. Edwards and Steers, *Evidence*, 1154–1155 (Simmonds testimony).
15. Rhodehamel and Taper, *Right or Wrong*, 94, n.1.
16. Loux, *Booth: Day by Day*, 139.

17. Booth letter to Moses Kimball, January 2, 1864, in Rhodehamel and Taper, *Right or Wrong*, 93.
18. Ibid.
19. Ibid.
20. *Morning Herald* (St. Joseph, MO), January 4, 1864, 3.
21. Ibid., January 5, 1864, 2.
22. JWB to John Ellsler, January 23, 1864, in Rhodehamel and Taper, *Right or Wrong*, 96.
23. *Morning Herald*, January 5, 1864, 3.
24. Ibid., January 6, 1864, 2. January 8, the temperature plummeted even further to twenty-nine degrees below zero in the morning. *Morning Herald*, January 8,1864, 3.
25. Ibid., January 8, 1864, 3.
26. Ibid.
27. Ibid., January 9, 1864, 3.
28. Charles A. Krone, "Recollections of an old Actor," *Missouri Historical Society Collections*, 4 (1913), 343, quoted by Loux, *Booth: Day by Day*, 140.
29. JWB to John Ellsler, January 23, 1864, in Rhodehamel and Taper, *Right or Wrong*, 96.
30. Steers and Edwards, *Evidence*, 5 (Edwin Adams letter to Reakert, April 17, 1865).
31. Mrs. McKee Rankin (Kitty Blanchard), "The News Of Lincoln's Death," *The American Magazine*, 67 (January 1909), 261–263.
32. *Louisville Democrat*, January 24, 1864, 2.
33. *Chicago Daily Tribune*, June 8, 1902, 48.
34. *Brooklyn Daily Eagle*, July 6, 1902, 39.
35. Mark, M. Krug (ed.), *Mrs. (Sarah Jane Full) Hill's Journal—Civil War Reminiscences* (Chicago: R. R. Donnelley & Sons, 1980), 225.
36. Charles E. Holding, "John Wilkes Booth Stars in Nashville," *Tennessee Historical Quarterly*, 23 (1964), 73–79.
37. Krug, *Mrs. Hill's Journal*, 231.
38. Angela Seratore, "The Curious Case of Nashville's Frail Sisterhood," *Smithsonian*, July 8, 2013, http://www.smithsonianmag.com/history/the-curious-case-of-nashvilles-frail-sisterhood-7766757/.

39. Hamilton Gay Howard, *Civil War Echoes* (Washington: Howard Publishing Co., 1907), 83.

40. Samples, *Lust for Fame*, 140.

41. Ibid.

42. *Cincinnati Daily Commercial*, February 18,1864, quoted by Loux, *Booth: Day by Day*, 156.

43. Ibid., February 19, 1864

44. Ibid., February 20, 1864.

45. JWB letter to Richard Montgomery Field, February 22, 1864, in Rhodehamel and Taper, *Right or Wrong*, 101.

46. *New Orleans Times-Picayune*, March 20, 1864, 3.

47. Ibid., March 22, 1864, 5.

48. Ibid., March 25, 1864, reprint in Loux, *Booth: Day by Day*, 159.

49. *New Orleans Times-Picayune*, March 26, 1864, 3.

50. JWB letter to Richard Montgomery Field, March 26, 1864, in Rhodehamel and Taper, *Right or Wrong*, 102.

51. *Times-Democrat*, March 29, 1864, 4.

52. *New Orleans Times-Picayune*, April 3, 1864, 3.

53. *Times-Democrat*, April 4, 1864, 5.

54. Kauffman, *American Brutus*, 126.

55. E.g., *New Orleans Times-Picayune*, January 18, 1859, 4.

56. *New Orleans Times-Picayune*, March 24, 1864.

57. Abel, *Singing the New Nation*, 52–57.

58. Ibid.

59. John Smith Kendall, *The Golden Age of the New Orleans Theatre* (Baton Rouge, LA: Louisiana State University Press, 1952), 498.

60. Loux, *Booth: Day by Day*, 160.

61. F. Lauriston Bullard, "Boston's Part in Lincoln's Death," *Boson Herald*, April 11, 1915, 19.

## 19. NOT A SECESH

1. *Milwaukee Sentinel*, April 27, 1861, 1.

2. *Brooklyn Daily Eagle*, April 18, 1862, 1.

3. *New York Times*, May 16, 1886, 4; *Sacramento Daily Union*, December 23, 1861, 47.

4. *Cincinnati Daily Enquirer*, December 1, 1861, 3.

5. Ibid., May 3, 1862, 23.

6. *New York Clipper*, April 12, 1862, 415.

7. *Brooklyn (NY) Daily Eagle*, November 8, 1885, 14.

8. Ibid., April 18, 1862, 1.

9. Burlingame, *Lincoln's Journalist,* 321.

10. *De Bow's Review*, 2 (1862), 543–544.

11. Harry Brown and Frederick D. Williams (ed.), *The Diary of James A Garfield* (Lansing, MI: Michigan State University, 1967), 65, 228.

12. *Evening Public Ledger* (Philadelphia, PA), March 23, 1918, 11.

13. *Daily Evening Transcript*, May 16, 1864, 3.

14. F. Lauriston Bullard, "Boston's Part in Lincoln's Death," *Boson Herald*, April 11, 1915, 19.

15. *Daily Critic* (Washington, D.C.), September 30, 1881, 1.

16. Ibid.

## 28. ISABEL SUMNER

1. Townsend, *Life Crime and Capture*, 24

2. Ibid.

3. Joyce G. Knibb and Patricia A. Mehrtens, *The Elusive Booths of Burrillville. An Investigation of John Wilkes Booth's Alleged Wife and Daughter* (Bowie, MD: Heritage Books, 1991), 168.

4. Bryan, *Great American Myth*, 100.

5. Winslow, *Yesterdays with Actors*, 142.

6. JWB letter to Isabel Sumner, June 7, 1864, in Rhodehamel and Tapper, *Right or Wrong*, 110.

7. Ibid.

8. Ibid.

9. Ibid.

10. JWB to Isabel Sumner, June 17, 1864; ibid., 113–114.

11. JWB to Isabel Sumner, July 14, 1864; ibid., 114–115.

12. JWB to Isabel Sumner, July 24, 1864; ibid., 115–116.

13. Tidwell, Hall, and Gaddy, *Come Retribution*, 263.

14. Ibid.

15. Ibid.

16. A photograph of the ring can be seen at "Under His Hat," http://www.underhishat.org/pearl_ring.html, accessed 3/30/2015.
17. Clarke later related the incident to actor Charles Wyndham, "Recollections of John Wilkes Booth," *New York Herald*, June 27, 1909, Magazine Section, 2.
18. Junius Brutus Booth, *Unpublished Diary*, August 28, 1864, FSL.
19. Abel, *A Finger in Lincoln's Brain*, 36.
20. Asia letter to Jean Anderson, August 15, 1864, MdHS.
21. JWB to Isabel Sumner, August 26, 1864, in Rhodehamel and Tapper, *Right or Wrong*, 116.
22. Ibid.
23. JWB to Isabel Sumner, August 27, 1864; Ibid., 117.
24. Thomas Turner, "Review," *Journal of the Abraham Lincoln Association*, 20 (Summer 1999), 83. Edwin also burned letters and mementos from women that John had kept.
25. Clarke, *Unlocked Book*, 57.
26. Bryn C. Collins, *Emotional Unavailability* (New York: McGraw-Hill, 1997), 8–9, chapters 3–5.

## 21. A GANG OF MISFITS
1. Tidwell et al., *Come Retribution*, 271.
2. Kauffman, *American Brutus*, 128.
3. Quoted in Frank Moore (ed.), *Record of the Year* (New York: G. W. Carleton & Co., 1876), 48.
4. *New York Tribune*, July 22, 1864, 1.
5. Kauffman, *American Brutus*, 129. Kauffman notes that Lincoln addressed his letter "To Whom It May Concern" to avoid any recognition of the Confederacy's existence.
6. Tidwell et al., *Come Retribution*, 264, 273, maintains John's "precise information" about Lincoln's routine is strong indication he was being fed information by the Confederate Secret Service. It's hardly a convincing argument. Lincoln's habits and movements were widely known. If John had relied on information from the Confederate Secret Service alone his adventurism would have landed him in prison. The information he had was that Lincoln did not have a military escort

when he rode to and from his summer home outside Washington. By September, Lincoln had a formidable cavalry guard on those outings.

7. Henry T. Louthan, "A Proposed Abduction Of Lincoln," *Confederate Veteran*, 11 (April 1903), 157. After Confederate defeats at Gettysburg and Vicksburg in July 1863, President Davis and his Secretary of War, James A. Seddon, began receiving offers to assassinate Lincoln. Seddon did his best to discourage all such schemes: "for disposing of those in high office in Washington. . .The Laws of war and morality, as well as Christian principles and sound policy," he said, "forbid the use of such means of punishing even the atrocities of the enemy." O. R. Series IV, vol. 2, 703, 730. Davis was equally unreceptive. J. B. Jones, *A Rebel War Clerk's Diary at the Confederate State Capital* (Philadelphia: J. B. Lippincott, 1866), vol. 2, 24.

8. For a summary of revisionist assessments of Lincoln and his policies, see William L. Richter, *Sic Semper Tyrannis: Why John Wilkes Booth Shot Abraham Lincoln* (Bloomington, IN: IUniverse, 2009), 6–73.

9. Thomas Nelson Conrad, *A Confederate Spy: A Story of the Civil War* (New York: J. S. Ogilvie Pub. Co., 1892), 70; Thomas Nelson Conrad, *The Rebel Scout, A Thrilling History of Scouting Life in the Southern Army* (Washington, D.C.: National Publishing Co., 1904), 119. On Conrad, see Tidwell et al., *Come Retribution*, 282–283.

10. "To Whom It May Concern" letter, November 1864, in Rhodehamel and Taper, *Right or Wrong*, 127. On John's political ideas, see Richter, *Sic Semper Tyrannis*, 6–73, and "'My Policy is to Have No Policy': Abraham Lincoln and the Reconstruction of Our Nation," Surratt Society Conference, March 31–April 2, 2017. John Surratt categorically said that John's abduction plan "was concocted without the knowledge or the assistance of the Confederate government in any shape or form....we never acquainted them with the plan, and they never had anything in the wide world to do with it." In fact, he added, they thought that by carrying it out on their own with no help from the government, they would be seen as even greater heroes in the South. John H. Surratt, "The Rockville Lecture," December 6, 1870, reprinted in Louis J. Weichmann, *A True History Of The Assassination Of Abraham Lincoln And Of The Conspiracy Of 1865* (New York: Alfred A. Knopf, 1975), 429.

11. Tidwell et al., *Come Retribution*, 265.
12. John W. Headly, *Confederate Operations in Canada and New York* (New York: Neale Publishing Co., 1906), 175–185.
13. Edwards and Steers, *Evidence*, 433 (John A. Deveney testimony); Ibid., 179, n.3, 621–622.
14. Martin drowned shortly afterwards when his ship sank in the St. Lawrence with all of John's costumes and other theatrical belongings. Among the various items recovered was a four word note, "one smack little kiss," from a girl signed "N" with a P.S., "Mollie S. was here. Pretty [pray?] also bring with my ring... if you cannot come send me word." *New York Times*, November 15, 1891, 8.
15. Melinda Jayne Squires, *The Controversial Career Of George Nicholas Sanders* (MA Thesis, Western Kentucky University, Bowling Green, Kentucky, 2000), 3.
16. *New York Times*, May 7, 1865, 1. On Nathaniel Beverley Tucker and his duties in Canada, see Ludwell H. Johnson, "Beverley Tucker's Canadian Mission, 1864-1866," *Journal of Southern History*, 29 (February 1963), 88–99. Confederate agent Robert Edwin Coxe likewise said that not only had he never met with John Wilkes Booth in Montreal, he also never heard of him until he read about him in the papers and didn't know anyone else who had. Edwards and Steers, *Evidence*, 398–399 (Coxe testimony). Although he would have undoubtedly lied had he been on trial in the United States, Beverly was in Canada and not facing deportation.
17. *Junius Diary*, November 28, 29, 30, 1864, FSL.
18. King Holmes, Per Anders Mardh, and P. Frederick Sparling (eds.), *Sexually Transmitted Diseases* (New York: McGraw-Hill, 1999), 501.
19. *New York Herald*, November 26, 1864.
20. *Daily National Republican* (Washington, D.C.), April 18, 1865, 2nd edition, 3; *New Berne (NC) Times,* April 28, 1865, 2.
21. Clarke, *Unlocked Book*, 119.
22. Ernest Miller, *John Wilkes Booth Oilman* (New York: Exposition, 1947), 56.
23. Clarke, *Unlocked Book*, 126.
24. Ibid.
25. Ibid., 126–127.

26. *New York Tribune*, July 22, 1861, 1.

27. "To Whom It May Concern," in Rhodehamel and Taper, *Right or Wrong*, 125.

28. Ibid., 126–127. That declaration, coupled with his statement at the end of that letter that he was "a Confederate, at present doing duty upon his own responsibility," written almost six months before the assassination is at odds with any argument that John was working on behalf of the Confederate Secret Service or that the kidnapping plan was a ruse to cover up the Confederate Secret Services' goal of using Booth to assassinate Lincoln. Samuel Arnold was adamant that there never was any connection between John and the Confederate authorities. "I was in Booth's confidence... had anything existed as such he would have made known the fact to me." Samuel Arnold, *Defense and Prison Experience of a Lincoln Conspirator* (Hattiesburg, MS: The Book Farm, 1943), 129. Lewis Powell, another conspirator who would later be enlisted in the kidnapping plot, made a "death bed" confession to Reverend Abraham Gillette. Just before he was hanged, Powell told Reverend Gillette that "until morning of the fatal day (of the assassination), no crime more serious than the abduction had been contemplated." Rev. Dr. Abraham Dunn Gillette, "The Last Days of Payne," reprinted as Appendix H in Betty J. Ownsbey, *Alias "Paine": Lewis Thornton Powell, the Mystery Man of the Lincoln Conspiracy* (Jefferson, NC: McFarland, 1993) 201.

29. JWB letter to Mary Ann Holmes Booth, Rhodehamel and Taper, *Right or Wrong*, 130–131.

30. On Mary Surratt, see Laurie Verge, "Mary Elizabeth Surratt, " in Edward Steers Jr. (ed.), *The Trial. The Assassination of Present Lincoln and the Trial of the Conspirators* (Lexington, KY: University Press of Kentucky, 2003), LII–LIX.

31. Edwards and Steers, *Evidence*, 343 (Chester testimony). Chester was conflating events later associated with the assassination.

32. Ibid. At the trial, Chester denied that John had told him the Confederate government was involved.

33. Ibid.

34. Samuel Arnold, "Confession," April 18, 1865, in Weichmann, *A True History Of The Assassination*, 381.

35. Edwards and Steers, *Evidence*, 458, 619, 1294–1295 (Bryan T. Early, George Grillet, and Mary Van Tyle testimonies).
36. Loux, *Booth: Day by Day*, 200.
37. Abel, *A Finger in Lincoln's Brain*, 34–36.
38. Benn Pitman, *The Assassination of President Lincoln And the Trial Of The Conspirators* (New York: Moore, Wilstach & Baldwin, 1865), 97 (Samuel McKim testimony).
39. John C. Fazio, *Decapitating The Union: Jefferson Davis, Judah Benjamin and the Plot to Assassinate Lincoln* (Jefferson, NC: McFarland & Co., 2015), 80.
40. William E. Doster, *Lincoln and Episodes of the Civil War* (New York: G. P. Putnam's Sons, 1915), 265. Powell's mind, said Doster, "seemed of the lowest order, very little above the brute, And his moral faculties were equally low." For a different opinion, see Betty J. Ownsbey, *Alias "Paine": Lewis Thornton Powell, the Mystery Man of the Lincoln Conspiracy* (Jefferson, NC: McFarland & Co., 1993).
41. Ibid., 5, 106.
42. John De Ferrari, *Historic Restaurants of Washington, D.C.: Capital Eats* (Charleston, SC: American Palate, 2013), 37.
43. Samuel Arnold, "Confession," 382–383.
44. Ibid., 383.
45. Ibid.
46. *Philadelphia Inquirer*, March 18, 1865, 1.
47. Pitman, *Assassination*, 236. By implication, Richmond was not aware of John's intention to kidnap Lincoln.
48. John Simmonds estimates John lost about $6,000 in his oil adventures. Tidwell et al., *Come Retribution*, 265.
49. Edwards and Steers, *Evidence*, 179 (Junius Brutus Booth Jr. statement).
50. John and the "lady" spent the morning walking and then had dinner in the room for the lady, "the excuse being indisposition." Edwards and Steers, *Evidence*, 1163 (Detective Alfred Smith statement).
51. Edwards and Steers, *Evidence*, 345 (Chester testimony). Earlier that month, on February 21, John bought a "brading hair ring" from Tiffany & Co. for $1.50 (Loux, *Booth: Day By Day*, 188, has the cost of he ring at $150, but the receipt clearly shows its cost at $1.50 in Barbee, Box 4, Folder 218). There's no indication of who he bought it

for. Possibly he and Lucy exchanged rings. The braided hair ring would not have been so ostentatious that it would have attracted comment when Lucy wore it.

52. Ibid.
53. Ibid.

## 22. LUCY LAMBERT HALE

1.   Clarke, *Unlocked Book*, 121.
2.   John Wilkes Booth letter to Lucy Hale, Valentine's Day, John Parker Hale Papers, 1926.6, Box 4, NHHS.
3.   The *Sun* (Baltimore, MD), February 26, 1862.
4.   *Weekly Constitution* (Atlanta, GA), December 6, 1881, 1.
5.   Richmond Morcom, "They All Loved Lucy," *American Heritage* (October 1970), 12–15. Morcom purchased Lucy's letters from Jerry Trueson and subsequently donated the letters and photos of Lucy to the New Hampshire Historical Society.
6.   Morcom, "Lucy," 12; Alford, *Fortune's Fool*, 217–218. Morcom's papers, now in the New Hampshire Historical Society, do not describe her. A picture supposedly of a young Lucy looks nothing like her.
7.   Rare photos of Lucy with her dog and with her husband William Chandler in Leon Burr Richardson, *William E Chandler: Republican* (New York: Dodd, Mead & Co., 1940) are reproduced and posted by "Sally" in the Lincoln Discussion Symposium chat room ("New Lucy Lambert Hale pic," July and September 2012, Posts 33 and 162, http://rogerjnorton.com/LincolnDiscussionSymposium/thread-357..html, accessed January 22, 2015) and can also be found at the James O. Hall Library, "Lucy Hale" file, JOH.
8.   Ford testimony, *Trial of John Surratt*, 587t.
9.   John Hay letter to Lucy Hale, August 9, 1869, John P. Hale Papers, 1926.6, Box 6, NHHS.
10.  William Chandler letter to Lucy Hale, Cambridge, July 20, 1858, William Chandler Papers, Box 3, .006, NHHS. Four years later Chandler married Caroline Gilmore, the daughter of the governor of New Hampshire. Years after Booth's death, Lucy married Chandler (by then a widower).
11.  Holmes letter to Lucy, Cambridge, April 24, 1858, NHHS.

12. Ibid., April 30, 1858.

13. W. P. K. letter to Lucy Hale, Cambridge, December 2, 1860, J. P. Hale Papers, Box 4, 1926.6, NHHS.

14. Holmes letter to Lucy, July 29, 1858, NHHS.

15. Frederick Anderson letter to Lucy Hale, Cambridge, April 28, 1864, John P. Hale Papers, Box 4, 1926.6, NHHS.

16. *Cleveland Leader*, January 9, 1874, 3.

17. Ibid.

18. Congressman John Bingham told an interviewer that Lucy obtained the invitation although it was only a rumor. Olney Bluff, "The Presidential Assassins," *Chicago Daily Tribune*, November 23, 1873, 9. Quite possibly the invitation came by way of John Parker Hale Wentworth, Lucy's first cousin who was also John's roommate at the National Hotel at the time. James O. Hall letter to "Mr. Young," July 26, 1998, JOH. Wentworth was an Indian agent from California in Washington for unspecified political reasons. There is no mention whatsoever in the letters, diaries, or photos of Lucy's relationship with John in the voluminous Hale files at the New Hampshire Historical Society.

19. *Chicago Daily Tribune*, December 27, 1874, 2.

20. Gilbert, *Stage Reminiscences*, 58.

21. Mary Ann Booth letter to JWB, March 12, 1865, copy in Barbee, Box 4, Folder 193.

22. For a photo of the envelope and the poems and comments see Dave Taylor, "John Wilkes Booth's Poetic Envelope," https://boothiebarn. com/2015/03/05/john-wilkes-booths-poetic-envelope/, accessed 10/20/2015. For the provenance of the envelop, see James O. Hall, Lucy Hale file, November 15, 1994; December 3, 1994; June 12, 1998, JOH.

23. James O. Hall letter to John Rhodehamel, December 5, 1989, Lucy Hale file, JOH.

24. Dave Taylor, "John Wilkes Booth's Poetic Envelope," https:// boothiebarn.com/2015/03/05/john-wilkes-booths-poetic-envelope/ accessed 8/15/2015.

25. *Chicago Times*, April 17, 1865, 2.

26. *Dayton Daily Empire*, April 21, 1865, 2.

27. Asia letter to Jean Anderson, May 22, 1865, MdHS.

## 23. ANYTHING THAT PLEASES YOU: ELLA STARR

1. *New York Sunday Telegraph*, May 23, 1909.
2. Steers and Edwards, *Evidence*, 1044 (Phillips testimony).
3. Ibid., 1279 (Tracy statement).
4. Thomas T. Eckert, May 30, 1867, quoting Lewis Powell, U.S. Congress. House of Representatives. Judiciary Committee. *Impeachment Investigation*. 39th Cong., 2d sess.; 40th Cong., 1st sess., H. Rep. No. 7, (Washington, D.C. Government Printing Office, 1867), 674.
5. E. A. Emerson, "How John Wilkes Booth's Friend Described His Crime," *Literary Digest*, 8 (March 6, 1926), 58.
6. Ibid.
7. Edwards and Steers, *Evidence*, 687 (Hess statement). Lincoln's son, Tad, was friends with Leonard Grover's son, Bobby, and often watched rehearsals at the theatre; Tad sometimes appeared as an extra in plays. Roger Norton, "What If the Lincolns Had Attended The Play At Grover's Theatre?" *Surratt Courier*, 36 (March 2011), 3–4.
8. Leonard Grover, "Lincoln's Interest in the Theater," *Century Magazine*, 77 (April 1909), 943–949.
9. Ibid.
10. JWB to Mary Ann Holmes Booth, April 14, 1865, in Rhodehamel and Taper, *Right or Wrong*, 144.
11. *New York Tribune*, April 17, 1865, 1; *Daily National Intelligencer* (Washington, D.C.), April 29, 1865.
12. Doster, *Lincoln and Episodes of the War*, 276.
13. *Cincinnati Enquirer*, July 6, 1878, 9.
14. *New York Herald*, April 26, 1864, 4.
15. J. D. Dickey, *Empire Of Mud. The Secret History of Washington, D.C.* (Guilford, CT: Lyons Press, 2014).
16. Margaret Leech, *Reveille in Washington, 1860-1865* (Alexandria, VA: Time-Life Books, 1980), 323.
17. *Evening Star* (Washington, D.C.), April 17, 1865, 3.
18. A hand-drawn map of the area can be seen at https://thelocation. wordpress.com/2012/03/20/hookers-division/. The brothels were closed in 1914 after Congress outlawed prostitution in the District of Columbia. Donna J. Seifert, "Mrs. Starr's Profession," in Charles F. Orser (ed.),

*Images of the Recent Past: Readings in Historical Archeology* (Lanham, MD: AltaMira Press, 1996), 191.

19. The *Oxford English Dictionary* (art. "hooker") cites the earliest known appearance in writing in 1845.
20. Leech, *Reveille in Washington*, 328.
21. Thomas Lowry, *Stories The Soldiers Wouldn't Tell*, 73–74.
22. *New York Sunday Telegraph*, May 23, 1909, quoted by Francis Wilson, *John Wilkes Booth*, 82.
23. *New York Times*, October 5, 1921, 7. When he gave that interview, Deery was destitute and living in an almshouse. In her "confession," Ella said she had known John for three years before coming to Washington and that he had brought her from Baltimore to her mother's bawdy house in Washington
24. Edwards and Steers, *Evidence*, 1192 (Ella Starr note).
25. Ibid.
26. Ibid., 471, Etta letter to J. Wilkes Booth, April 18, 1865.
27. Ibid., 769, John A. Kennedy letter to Col. John A Foster, April 21, 1865.

## 24. ASSASSINATION

1. Kathryn Canavan, *Lincoln's Final Hours. Conspiracy, Terror, and the Assassination of America's Greatest President* (Lexington, KY: University Press of Kentucky, 2015), 11.
2. Edwards and Steers, *Evidence*, 687 (Hess statement).
3. *Daily National Intelligencer*, April 29, 1865, 2. George Townsend, *Life, Crime, and Capture*, 27, said John breakfasted with "Miss Carrie Bean, the daughter of a merchant, and a very respectable young lady."
4. Joseph Hazelton in Campbell MacCulloch, "This Man Saw Lincoln Shot," *Good Housekeeping*, 84 (February 1927), 112.
5. Trial of John H Surratt, I: 495–496 (Charles Wood testimony).
6. M. Helen Palmes Moss, "Lincoln and Wilkes Booth as seen on the day of the Assassination," *Century Magazine*, 77 (April 1909), 951.
7. George Wren, "A shot that wasn't fired," *Boston Weekly Globe*, April 13, 1880, 6.
8. *New York Tribune*, April 17, 1865, 1.
9. *Boston Herald*, December 5, 1881, 2.
10. Edwards and Steers, *Evidence*, 516–517 (Harry Ford statement).

11. *Boston Herald*, December 5, 1881, 2.

12. Weichmann, *True History*, 131.

13. Edwards and Steers, *Evidence*, 833 (Maddox statement). John F. Sleickman, Maddox's assistant, testified that when he went to the saloon between four and five, John was drinking with Maddox, Ned Spangler, a man named Mouldy, and a "boy" from the theatre. Pitman, *Assassination*, 73. The "boy" has variously been identified as "Peanut John" or W. J. Ferguson.

14. W. J. Ferguson, *I Saw Booth Shoot Lincoln* (Boston: Houghton Mifflin, Co., 1930), 46. Pleurisy, a painful inflammation and swelling of the linings surrounding the lungs and chest, is another well-known symptom of syphilis. Diana Coleman, Stephen McPhee, Thomas Ross, and James Naughton, "Secondary syphilis with pulmonary involvement," *Western Journal of Medicine*, 138 (1983), 875–878.

15. The Ford Theatre's presidential box is now about twelve feet above the stage, but the original architectural plans were not available when the theatre was reconstructed. Ford actor Harry Hawk said it was nine feet. Hawk also recalled that just after the shooting, two men bent down to create a platform of their backs so that a doctor (Dr. Charles Taft) at the stage-level seats could climb into the presidential box. "The Killing of Lincoln. The Graphic Story," undated clipping, Black file, K-OAK.

16. Pitman, *Assassination*, 396.

17. Loux, *Booth: Day by Day*, 187; John Surratt letter to Bell Seaman, February 6, 1865, quoted in La Fayette Charles Baker, *The Secret Service In The Late War* (Philadelphia, PA: John E. Potter and Co., 1874), 390.

18. Pitman, *Assassination*, 124 (Lt. John W. Dempsey testimony).

19. John Y. Simon (ed.), *The Personal Memoirs of Julia Dent Grant* (New York: G. P. Putnam's Sons, 1975), 155.

20. Ferguson, *I Saw Booth*, 54.

21. *Daily National Intelligencer* (Washington, D.C.), July 18, 1867, 2. The conversation occurred around 4:00 p.m. The Grants' train left Washington at 4:30 p.m. Bryan, *Great American Myth*, 161.

22. Mary Lincoln letter to Francis Bicknell Carpenter, November 15, 1865, reprinted in Harold Holzer and Sara Vaughn Gabbard (eds.), *1865:*

*American Makes War Harold and Peace in Lincoln's Final Year* (Carbondale, IL: Southern University Press, 2015), 187.

23. Quoted in Isaac N. Arnold, *The Life of Abraham Lincoln* (Chicago: A. C. McClurg & Co., 1909), 430.

24. *Daily Milwaukee News*, April 25, 1865, 2. *Daily National Intelligencer*, April 17, 1865, 1; *Boston Evening Transcript*, April 17, 1865, 4.

25. Trial of John Surratt, 1, 329 (George Bunker testimony).

26. W. Emerson Reck, *A. Lincoln. His Last 24 Hours* (Jefferson, NC: McFarland & Co., 1987), 79.

27. Doster, *Lincoln and Episodes of the Civil War*, 269, 274, 305.

28. Abel, *Finger in Lincoln's Brain*, 59–61. For a different perspective, see Frederick Hatch, *Protecting President Lincoln: The Security Effort, the Thwarted Plots and the Disaster At Ford's Theatre* (Jefferson, NC: McFarland & Co., 2011), 109–117.

29. Frederick W. Seward, *Reminiscences of A War-Time Statesman and Diplomat, 1830-1915* (New York: G. P. Putnam's Sons, 1916), 258–260; T. S. Verdi, "The Assassination Of the Sewards," *Republic: A Monthly Magazine, Devoted to the Dissemination of Political Information*, 1 (July 1873), 291.

30. George Atzerodt, "Lost Confession," in Edward Steers Jr., *The Assassination Of President Lincoln and the Trial of the Conspirators* (Lexington, KY: University Press of Kentucky, 2003), cvi. Townsend, *Life, Crime and Capture*, 76.

31. Jerrod Madonna, *A Threat to the Republic. The Secret of the Lincoln Assassination that Preserved the Union* (Privately published, 2006), 235. If Johnson did in fact issue him a pass, John never used it when he made his escape, and no such pass was found on his body when he died.

32. Ibid, 239.

33. Ibid.

34. Hamilton, *Civil War Echoes*, 84. On duty in the corridors and anterooms of the White House, Johnson's body guard said the goatish Johnson privately entertained many women at the White House when he became president. William H. Crook, *Through Five Administrations: Reminiscences of Colonel William H. Crook* (New York: Harper Bros., 1910), 92. Lincoln, on the other hand, was never suspected of any improper moments in the White House because of Mary's watchful eye.

"I never allow the President to see any woman alone," she angrily told Grant's military secretary, Adam Badeau. Badeau was amazed that "Mary was absolutely jealous of poor ugly Abraham Lincoln." Badeau, *Grant in Peace*, 357.

35. Edwards and Steers, *Evidence*, 1192 (Ella Starr note).
36. Pitman, *Assassination*, 151–152 (Farwell testimony).
37. Buckingham, *Reminiscences*, 13.
38. Edwards and Steers, *Evidence*, 485–486 (Ferguson testimony).
39. On the different medical opinions of the bullet's path, see Abel, *Finger in Lincoln's Brain*, 92–96.
40. Edwards and Steers, *Evidence*, 485–486 (Ferguson testimony).
41. Henry Hawk letter to father, April 16, 1865, in Reck, *Abraham Lincoln*, 109.
42. Si Snider, "Eyewitness of Lincoln's assassination Live Here," *Los Angeles Times*, February 11, 1923, III: 9–10.
43. William Ferguson, "Actor Describes Slaying of Lincoln," The *Sun* (Baltimore, MD), February 12, 1926, 22; "I Saw Lincoln Shot," *Saturday Evening Post*, February 12, 1927, 42.
44. Richard Sloan, "John Wilkes Booth's Other Victim," *American Heritage*, 42 (February–March 1991), 114–116. For more on Withers, see Norman Gasbarro, "William Withers Jr.—Lincoln Assassination Witness," http://civilwar.gratzpa.org/2012/05/william-withers-jr-lincoln-assassination-witness/, accessed September 20, 2015; *Los Angeles Times*, February 16, 1916.
45. Elizabeth C. Mooney, "There's no escaping history on John Wilkes," *Chicago Tribune*, Mary 11, 1984, K20.
46. Joan L. Chaconas, "John H. Surratt Jr.," in Edward Steers Jr., *The Trial. The Assassination of President Lincoln and the Trial of the Conspirators* (Lexington, KY: University Press of Kentucky, 2003), LXI–LXII.

## 25. I HAVE TOO GREAT A SOUL TO DIE LIKE A CRIMINAL

1. Edwards and Steers, *Evidence*, 823; Surratt, *Trial of John H. Surratt*, vol. 2, 1236
2. Edwards and Steers, *Evidence*, 806–807 (Lloyd testimony). Lloyd may have perjured himself to avoid being tried as one of the conspirators. John A. Marshall, *American Bastille: A History Of The Arbitrary*

*Arrests and Imprisonment of American Citizens In the Northern And Border States, On Account Of Their Political Opinions, During the Last Civil War, Together With a Full Report Of the Illegal Trial and Execution Of Mrs. Mary E. Surratt, By a Military Commission, And A Review Of the Testimony, Showing Her Entire Innocence* (Philadelphia: Thomas W. Harley & Co., 1884), 834.

3.  Edwards and Steers, *Evidence*, 939–941 (Mudd statement).
4.  Ibid., 822–823 (Lovett testimony).
5.  Alford, *Fortune's Fool*, 279.
6.  Thomas A. Jones, *John Wilkes Booth* (Chicago: Laird and Lee, 1893), 70–71.
7.  JWB Diary, April 13, 1865, in Rhodehamel and Taper, *Right or Wrong*, 154. For the influence of Shakespeare's Brutus on Booth, see Furtwangler, *Assassin on Stage,* 13–30, 95–116.
8.  Edwards and Steers, *Evidence*, 745–747 (Jett testimony).
9.  Ibid.
10. The U.S. Government had offered $100,000 and three states had each offered $25,000.
11. Ruggles statement in Prentice Ingraham, "Pursuit and Death of John Wilkes Booth," *The Century*, 39 (January 1890), 18–19; Turner Rose, "Rappahannock Ferry," *Washington Post*, May 13, 1918, 138.
12. Jett later testified at the Conspiracy trial and was never charged as a conspirator. Many years later he became insane from untreated syphilis and died in an insane asylum in Virginia in 1884. "Booth's Capture. The Man Who Pointed Out the Refuge of the Assassin Declared Insane," *Chicago Tribune*, September 7, 1882; Eric J. Mink, "Brutus' Judas: Willie Jett," https://npsfrsp.wordpress.com/2011/04/25/brutus%e2%80%99-judas-willie-jett-%e2%80%93-part-3/.
13. *New York Times*, July 30, 1896.
14. JWB Diary, April 21, 1865, in Rhodehamel and Taper, *Right or Wrong*, 155. George Atzerodt, David Herold, Lewis Powell, and Mary Surratt were all hanged. Sam Arnold, Michael O'Laughlen, Dr. Mudd, and Ned Spangler were all sentenced to prison at hard labor.
15. Aldrich, *Crowding Memories*, 72.
16. Pitman, *Assassination*, 93 (Conger testimony).
17. Richter and Smith, *Last Shot*, 132.

18. For arguments for and against Booth shooting himself, see Richter and Smith, *Last Shot*, 122–133.
19. Pitman, *Assassination*, 94–95 (Corbett testimony). For a full length biography about Corbett, see Scott Martel, *The Madman and the Assassin. The strange life of Boston Corbett, the man who killed John Wilkes Booth* (Chicago: Chicago Review Press, 2015). A shorter more succinct examination is Ernest B. Furgurson's, "The Man who shot the man who shot Lincoln," *The American Scholar*, 78 (Spring 2009), 42–51.
20. See Steers, *Lincoln Legends*, 17–202; William Hanchett, "Booth's Diary," *Journal of the Illinois State Historical Society*, 72 (February 1979), 39–56.
21. Edwards and Steers, *Evidence*, 1204 (Conger statement).
22. Ibid.

## 26. ELLA STARR

1. Ella's mother had left the business in charge of Eliza Thomas and retired in Baltimore. Donna J. Seifert, "Mrs. Starr's Profession," in Charles E. Orser (ed.), *Images of the Recent Past: Readings in Historical Archaeology* (Lanham, MD: AltaMira Press, 1966), 190–207. Molly apparently left for New York around the same time. Still in love with John, although he was now much less attentive than before, Ella had stayed on.
2. *Evening Star* (Washington, D.C.), April 15, 1865, 2.
3. Ibid.; *Cincinnati Daily Enquirer*, April 18, 1865, 3; *New York Times*, April 17, 1865.
4. Edwards and Steers, *Evidence*, 1194 (Nellie/Ellen Starr statement).
5. Ibid., 1192 (Ella note to JWB).
6. *Boston Daily Advertiser*, May 30, 1865; *New York Herald*, May 31, 1865.
7. Doster, *Episodes of the War*, 276.
8. Seifert, "Mrs. Starr's Profession," 207. Ella may have been duped by John, but she was a shrewd business woman. She bought a parcel of land on May 16, 1865, for $2,281 that she sold three years later for $5,000 (Starr file, JOH).
9. *Washington Post*, July 15, 1883, 8.

10. *Inter-Ocean*, July 17, 1883, 5. An entirely different description of Molly as the madam "of several fashionable houses" appeared in the *Boston Daily Globe*, July 15, 1883, 1. The Boston paper also mentioned Molly's sister, "Nellie Starr. the mistress of John Wilkes Booth," but said she was deceased.

11. Harry Hawk, "Lincoln Assassination" *Illinois State Register* (Springfield, IL), April 16, 1901, 3.

12. *Richmond Dispatch*, October 5, 1902, 16.

## 27. ASIA AND MARY ANN

1. Colonel Alexander K. McClure, *Recollections of Half a Century* (Salem, MA: Salem Press Co., 1902), 247.

2. Bloom, *Edwin Booth*, 81.

3. Ibid.

4. Edwin to Adam Badeau, April 16, 1865, "Edwin Booth And Lincoln," *The Century Illustrated Monthly Magazine*, 77 (November 1908–April 1909), 919–920.

5. Junius Brutus Booth Jr., *Diary*, April 15, 1865, FSL.

6. Rhodehamel and Taper, *Right or Wrong*, 124–127.

7. The letter was purposely never entered into evidence in the Conspiracy trial. Secretary of War Stanton was trying to prove that John was an agent of the Confederate government and the letter would have cast doubt on his case.

8. Kauffman, *American Brutus*, 284–285. The original letters disappeared and were lost for 130 years until discovered at the National Archives among Attorney General James Speed's letters. Edwards and Steers, *Evidence*, 356, n.2.

9. Clarke, *Unlocked Book*, 131.

10. Ibid., 132–133.

11. Ibid., 131.

12. Ibid., 130.

13. Edwards and Steers, *Evidence*, 116 (Mary Ann to John, March 28, 1865).

14. Aldrich, *Memories*, 72.

15. Ibid.

16. Ibid.

17. Clarke, *Unlocked Book*, 130.
18. Asia letter to Jean Anderson, May 22, 1865, MdHS.
19. Effie Germon letter to Mrs. Clarke, May 3, 1865, in Clarke, *Unlocked Book*, 132.
20. Edwin letter to Emma Cary, May 6, 1865, July 31, 1865, in Grossmann, *Edwin Booth,* 172–173.
21. Asia letter to Jean Anderson, January 15, 1866, MdHS.
22. Bloom, *Edwin Booth,* 85.
23. Ibid., 84 (Asia letter to Edwin, June 3, 1879, 2).
24. Clarke, *Unlocked Book*, 110–111.
25. *New York Clipper*, October 14, 1865, 214.
26. Andrew Davis, *America's Longest Run: A History of the Walnut Street Theatre* (University Park, PA: Pennsylvania State University Press, 2010), 132–134.
27. Asia Letter to Jean Anderson, April 18, 1866, MdHS.
28. Ibid., n.d., 1868.
29. Ibid., March 12, 1868.
30. Edwin Booth letter to General Ulysses S. Grant, September 11, 1867, in John Y. Simon (ed.), *The Papers of Ulysses S. Grant* (Carbondale and Edwardsville: Southern Illinois University Press, 1991), vol. 17, 315–316.
31. *New York Times*, September 19, 1867, 5.
32. *Brooklyn Daily Eagle*, January 14, 1877, 4.
33. Ibid., March 18, 1901, 5.
34. Bloom, *Edwin Booth*, 87.
35. *Poughkeepsie (NY) Eagle-News*, February 8, 1900, 31.
36. Ibid.
37. Mrs. Elijah Rogers letter to Forwood, August 16, 1886; LOC. The letter was discovered by Stanley Kimmel in 1943, three years after his *The Mad Booths of Maryland* was published. The letter was reprinted in the Appendix to Kimmel's 1969, second edition on page 396.
38. *New York Times*, January 7, 1903, 6. Other accounts have Ford or Joseph Booth mentioning the gold tooth. *Hartford Currant*, June 6, 1903, 15; *Detroit Free Press*, March 2, 1911, 5.
39. The *Sun* (Baltimore, MD), January 4, 1903, 12.
40. Ibid.
41. *Cincinnati Courier Journal*, July 1, 1882.

42. Mrs. Elijah Rogers letter to Forwood, August 16, 1886; LOC.
43. *Public Ledger* (Memphis, TN), July 12, 1869, 1.
44. *Coldwater (MI) Sentinel*, February 26, 1869, 2.
45. The body of eleven-year-old Henry Byron, Mary Ann's son who'd died in 1836, was buried in England when Junius had taken the family with him during a European tour in 1836–1837. The burial of the three children on top of John's coffin was one of the reasons Green Mount Cemetery thwarted conspiracy theorists from exhuming John's body in the 1990s to prove it wasn't John Wilkes Booth because doing so would disturb the remains of the three children as well. "So even though Frederick, Mary Ann and Elizabeth never knew their brother John Wilkes," writes blogger David Taylor, "even in death they managed to protect their little brother." https://boothiebarn.com/2014/08/01/the-booth-children-and-mary-anns-acting-career/, accessed 12/5/2014.
46. *New York Times*, July 14, 1896.
47. Mrs. Elijah Rogers letter to Forwood, August 16, 1886; LOC.
48. Asia letter to Jean Anderson, January 28, 1869, MdHS.
49. Ibid., December 6, 1874, MdHS.
50. Asia letter to Edwin, June 3, 1879, 3. Clarke left $20,000 in his will to a Marie Hudsperth of Kingston, England. The *Sun* (Baltimore, MD), November 1, 1899, 9.
51. Asia letter to Edwin, June 3, 1879, H-BTL.
52. Ibid.
53. *The Era Almanack*, 1883, 73.
54. Ruggles, *Prince of Players*, 338.
55. Asia letter to Dollie Clarke Morgan, April 28, 1888, Clarke, *Unlocked Book*, 204.
56. Asia hadn't titled it. She'd only had the initials "J. W. B." tooled in gold in Old English letters on the cover.
57. Farjeon foreword, *Unlocked Book*, 13.
58. *New York Tribune*, September 18, 1928, H12.
59. *Saturday Review of Literature*, October 15, 1938.
60. The *Scotsman*, April 4, 1938, 15.
61. Terry Alford, *John Wilkes Booth: A Sister's Memoir* (Jackson, MS: University Press of Mississippi, 1996).

62. Lyde C. Sizer, "Review," *North Carolina Historical Review*, 74 (July 1997), 349–350.

63. Patria Ann Owens, "Review," *Illinois Historical Journal*, 90 (Winter 1997), 286.

64. *New York Times*, October 23, 1885, 5.

65. Bloom, *Edwin Booth*, 138.

66. Asia letter to Jean Anderson, n.d., 1852, MdHS.

67. Ibid., May 18, 1856.

68. Mary Ann Booth letter to Edwina, 5.

69. Edwin letter to Emma Cary, November 24, 1865, Grossmann, *Edwin Booth*, 74.

70. Edwin letter to Julia Ward Howe, September 24, 1865, quoted in Titone, *My Thoughts Be Bloody*, 93.

71. *Trenton Evening Times*, May 17, 1863, 2.

72. *New York Times*, October 23, 1885, 5.

73. Ibid., October 23, 1885, 3.

74. Edwin letter to Lawrence Barrett, Bloom, *Edwin Booth*, 138.

## 28. "IT CANNOT BE DENIED": LUCY HALE

1. *Cincinnati Daily Enquirer*, April 19, 1865, 2; *Dayton Daily Empire*, April 21, 1865, 2.

2. Statement quoted in the *Evening Argus* (Rock Island, IL), April 27, 1865, 2.

3. *Springfield Republican*, April 21, 1865, 2.

4. *Cincinnati Daily Enquirer*, April 21, 1865, 3; *New York Tribune*, April 26, 1865, 4.

5. Statement quoted in the *Evening Argus* (Rock Island, IL), April 27, 1865, 2.

6. *Washington Post*, September 30, 1881, 3.

7. *Springfield Republican*, April 22, 1865, quoted by John Watson, "Who Leaked Lucy's Name," *Lincoln Assassination Forum*, January 18, 2013. http://lincoln-assassination.com/bboard/index.php?topic=2267.0;wap2.

8. *Dayton (OH) Daily Empire*, May 10, 1865, 2.

9. *Boston Traveller*, May 13, 1865, 4. Even as late as 1929, Francis Wilson in *John Wilkes Booth: Fact and Fiction of Lincoln's Assassination*

(Boston: Houghton Mifflin, 1929), 186, referred to Lucy only as "a Washington Society woman."

10. Alford, *Fortune's Fool*, 398; Edwards and Steers, *Evidence*, 345–346 (Samuel K. Chester statement).

11. Benjamin Perley Poore, *Perley's Reminiscences of Sixty Years In the National Metropolis* (Philadelphia: Hubbard Brothers, 1886), vol. 2, 183–184.

12. Hans L. Trefousse, *Andrew Johnson: A Biography* (New York: W. W. Norton & Co., 1997), 37; William C. Harris, *With Charity for All: Lincoln and the Restoration of the Union* (Lexington, KY: University Press of Kentucky, 1999), 23.

13. Clarke, *Unlocked Book*, 130.

14. Asia Booth Clarke letter to Jean Anderson, May 22, 1865, MdHS.

15. I was unable to find any mention of John Wilkes Booth in the Hale family papers or the Chandler (Lucy's husband) papers at the New Hampshire Historical Society other than a newspaper item with John's initials, JWB, in the corner that Lucy kept. Historians have likewise not found any mention of Booth in Chandler's papers in the Library of Congress or the Dartmouth College Library. Alford, *Fortune's Fool*, 398.

16. Lucy's biographer, Richmond Morcom, commented that Lucy had lots of admirers, "but her heart belonged to daddy." Morcom letter to James O. Hall, Lucy Hale file, JOH.

17. *Washington Evening Star*, December 13, 1873, 3. A few weeks after the *Washington Evening Star*'s report, the item about Lucy's photo was picked up by other newspapers. The *Daily Argus* (Rock Island, IL), December 30, 1873, 4, headlined its piece, "Wilkes Booth's Love." The actual photo was not released until 1929.

18. *Chicago Daily Tribune*, December 27, 1874, 5.

19. *Chicago Daily Inter-Ocean*, June 1878, 4–5.

20. *Brooklyn Daily Eagle,* June 23, 1878, 2.

21. *Chicago Daily Inter-Ocean*, June 1878, 4–5.

22. *Rockford (IL) Daily Register*, June 19, 1878, 2.

23. *Chicago Daily Tribune*, June 21, 1878, 4.

24. *New York Herald*, June 21, 1878, 8.

25. "Lincoln's Assassination," *Philadelphia Inquirer*, June 25, 1878, 1.

26. *New York Tribune*, June 26, 1878, 4. The little that is known about Hunter's personal life can be found in Terry Alford, "Alexander Hunter and the Bessie Hale Story," *Alexandria History*, 8 (1990), 5–15.

27. *New York Tribune*, June 26, 1878, 4; *Chicago Daily Inter-Ocean*, June 29, 1878, 4.

28. E.g., David S. Reynolds, *Walt Whitman's America. A Cultural Biography* (New York: Vintage Books, 1996), 441; Bernie (Julia Burnelle Smade) Babcock's *Booth and the Spirit of Lincoln* (Philadelphia, PA: J. B. Lippincott, 1925) expanded Hunter's article into a full length love story.

29. *Boston Herald*, October 16, 1915, 14.

30. Alford, *Fortune's Fool*, 398.

31. Leon B. Richardson letter to Mrs. Cunningham, October 6, 1944, Barbee, Box 4.

## 29. EFFIE GERMON

1. *Washington Evening Star*, April 14, 1865, 1.

2. *Chicago Tribune*, April 9, 1880, 2.

3. Clarke, *Unlocked Book*, 132.

4. Ibid.

5. E. Mack, *The Effie Germon Waltz* (Philadelphia, PA: Lee & Walker, 1871); S. Hassler, *Effie Germon Galap* (Philadelphia, PA: Lee & Wallker, n.d.).

6. "Strange facts about the Lincoln assassination," http://texags.com/forums/49/topics/1398801, accessed 9/18/2015.

7. *Evening Telegraph* (Philadelphia, PA), February 22, 1866, 3.

8. The *Spirit of the Times*, July 13, 1868.

9. *Sacramento Daily Union*, April 20, 1869, 1.

10. The *Labor World*, April 16, 1904, 5.

11. *New York Times*, September 8, 1870.

12. *New Era* (Valley Falls, KS), November 2, 1878, 4.

13. *Sacramento Daily Record-Union*, May 31, 1882, 2.

14. *Washington Capital*, September 23, 1877, 4.

15. The "Banting diet's" originator was William Banting, a carpenter and undertaker to Britain's rich and famous. Three of his most illustrious internments were King George III and IV and the Duke of Wellington.

In the years between burials, he'd put on a lot of bulk and sought medical help for weight loss from Dr. William Harvey, one of England's prominent doctors. Harvey told him to give up bread, butter, milk, beer, potatoes, and every other starchy food. After losing fifty pounds in six months, Banting wrote a book about his weight loss. His 1863 *Letter on Corpulence*, with recipes for weight loss, became one of the first blockbuster diet books. Barry Groves, "William Banting Father of the Low-Carbohydrate Diet," http://www.westonaprice.org/know-your-fats/william-banting-father-of-the-low-carbohydrate-diet/, accessed April 24, 2016.

16. "Tea Table Gossip," undated 1884 clipping, *Troy (NY) Daily Times*. Fanny Davenport's fifty pound weight loss on the Banting diet almost killed her. *New York World*, reprinted in the *Saint Paul (MN) Globe*, March 27, 1884, 4.
17. The *Sporting Life*, May 16, 1888, 11.
18. *Sacramento Daily Record-Union*, May 31, 1882, 2.
19. *Times* (Reading, PA), October 30, 1884, 3; Franklin Graham, *Histrionic Montreal*, 126.
20. King, "What becomes of Old Actors," 248.
21. *Philadelphia Inquirer*, March 8, 1914, 9; The *Sun* (Baltimore, MD), March 9, 1914, 7.

## 30. ALICE GRAY
1. *Daily National Intelligencer* (Washington, D.C.), May 3, 1864, 1.
2. Ibid., April 7, 1865, 1.
3. *New York Clipper*, July 22, 1865, 118.
4. Ibid., September 16, 1865, 182.
5. Ibid., April 3, 1866, 3.
6. *New Orleans Daily Crescent*, April 23, 1866, 5.
7. *New York Clipper*, July 7, 1866.
8. Ibid., July 28, 1866.
9. *New York Herald*, August 26, 1866, 4.
10. Ibid., September 25, 1866, 7.
11. *Cincinnati Daily Gazette*, April 13, 1867, 2.
12. *New Orleans Times-Picayune*, November 14, 1868, 4.
13. Ibid., March 26, 1870, 1; April 29, 1869, 9.

14. *Register* (Mobile, AL), January 5, 1870, 289.

15. Ibid., January 11, 1870, 3.

16. *New Orleans Times-Picayune*, February 22, 1870, 1; March 8, 1870, 1.

17. Felicia Hardison Londre, *The Enchanted Years of the Stage. Kansas City at the Crossroads of American Theatre, 1870-1930* (Columbia, MI: University of Missouri Press, 2007), 40.

18. Graham, *Histrionic Montreal*, 123.

19. *New York Times*, October 26, 1890, 3.

20. *Commercial Tribune* (Cincinnati, OH), October 26, 1890, 2.

## 31. HELEN WESTERN

1. *New York Clipper*, August 31, 1861, 159.

2. The *Baltimore Daily Exchange*, August 21, 1861, 2.

3. *New York Clipper*, October 5, 1861; November 16, 1861, 247.

4. *New York Clipper*, November 30, 1861, 263; *The United States Biographical Dictionary*, 723.

5. *Cleveland Plain Dealer*, November 30, 1861, 2; *Baltimore Daily Dispatch*, December 9, 1861, 1.

6. *New York Clipper*, January 13, 1877, 334.

7. Quoted in *New York Clipper*, May 9, 1863, 30; July 4, 1863, 94; July 11, 1863, 102.

8. *The Theatre: An Illustrated Weekly Magazine of Drama, Music, Art*, 1 (1886), 321.

9. The *Sun* (Baltimore, MD), November 30, 1863; *New York Clipper*, December 12, 1863, 275; *Toronto Globe*, December 31, 1863, 2.

10. *Brooklyn Daily Eagle*, November 20, 1914, 6; *Life Magazine*, November 19, 1951.

11. *New York Times*, July 12, 1864, 4.

12. *New York Evening Post*, July 12, 1864, 3; July 25, 1864.

13. *New York Clipper*, July 30, 1864, 126.

14. *New York Tribune*, August 4, 1864, 3; *New York Times*, August 5, 1864, 1.

15. *Philadelphia Inquirer*, March 1, 1865, 4.

16. Edwards and Herne, *Herne*, 9. Julie Herne never elaborated on what she meant by "withdraw" other than saying Herne's Catholic upbringing

made him break off his relationship with Lucille. Had that been the case, Herne's Catholic upbringing would never have let him start up with Lucille, a married woman.

17. The *New York Mirror*, 1879, 7.
18. Mayflower, "Letter from Boston," *Sacramento Daily Union*, May 20, 1865, 1; June 2, 1865, 1.
19. Quoted in John Perry, *James A. Herne: the American Ibsen* (Chicago: Nelson-Hall, 1978), 15.
20. Mayflower, "Letter from Boston," *Sacramento Daily Union*, October 10, 1865, 3; "Letter from Boston," December 4, 1865, 1.
21. *San Francisco Chronicle*, July 7, 1866, 1, quoting the *New York Sunday Mercury*.
22. *New York Clipper*, December 1, 1866, 270.
23. *Philadelphia Evening Telegraph*, February 15, 1867, 8.
24. *New York Clipper*, March 16, 1867, 90; *Memphis Public Ledger*, March 21, 1867, 3.
25. *Daily Alta California*, April 29, 1867; *New York Clipper*, June 1, 1867, 62.
26. *Marysville (CA) Daily Appeal*, May 2, 1867.
27. *Daily Alta California*, April 29, 1867, 1.
28. Ibid., August 11, 1867, 1; February 15, 1885, 8.
29. Ibid.
30. *New York Clipper*, June 8, 1867, 70.
31. *Sacramento Daily Union*, June 3, 1867, 1.
32. *Springfield Republican*, June 8, 1867, 4.
33. *San Francisco Chronicle*, July 20, 1867, 1.
34. *New York Clipper*, October 5, 1867, 206; November 30, 1867, 271.
35. Ibid., May 16, 1868, 42.
36. Ibid., August 8, 1868, 142.
37. The *Sun* (New York City, NY), December 12, 1868, 1; *New York Clipper*, December 5, 1868, 278.
38. *Chicago Tribune*, December 25, 1868, 1.
39. *New York Clipper*, December 19, 1868, 294.
40. Ibid., December 5, 1868, 279.
41. *New Orleans Times-Picayune*, December 17, 1868.
42. *Chicago Tribune*, December 25, 1868, 1.

43. *Evening Telegraph* (Philadelphia, PA), December 11, 1868; *Chicago Tribune*, January 11, 1869, 1.

44. *New York Clipper*, December 19, 1868, 294.

45. *Chicago Tribune*, December 25, 1868, 1.

46. Ibid.

47. The *Sun* (New York City, NY), December 12, 1868, 1.

48. *Chicago Tribune*, December 25, 1868, 1.

49. The *Sun* (New York City, NY), December 12, 1868, 1.

50. *Daily Alta California*, December 30, 1868, 1.

51. *Chicago Tribune*, December 25, 1868, 1.

52. *Detroit Free Press*, December 16, 1868, 1.

53. "Lucille Western's Dream," undated clipping, *New York Mirror*, 8.

54. *Sacramento Daily Union*, May 5, 1869, 1; *Corrine Utah Daily Reporter*, April 20, 1869, 1.

55. Beasley, *McKee Rankin*, 74.

56. Eytinge, *Memories*, 307–308.

57. *Chicago Daily Tribune*, January 12, 1877, 5.

58. A year after Lucille died, Herne married Irish born actress Katherine Corcoran and stopped drinking, something the *Detroit Free Press*, November 15, 1882, 2, regarded as especially newsworthy. "James A. Hearne, the former husband of Lucille and Helen Western," it reported with much surprise, "is making an occasional experiment by way of passing a day of sobriety, rather an infrequent thing in his career. Herne did in fact turn over the proverbial new leaf and went on to become a prominent playwright nicknamed the 'American Ibsen' for his realistic plots. He died in New York City, June 2, 1901."

## 32. FANNY BROWN

1. Mick Sinclair, *San Francisco: A Cultural and Literary History* (Oxford, UK: Signal Books, 2014), 64–65.

2. *National Republican* (Washington, D.C.), September 1, 1864, 1.

3. *Boston Post*, January 9, 1865, 2.

4. *New Orleans Times-Picayune*, February 5, 1865, 1.

5. *New York Times*, December 19, 1865.

6. Ibid.

7. *San Francisco Daily Chronicle*, March 7, 1865, 2.

8.  *New York Clipper*, May 6, 1866, 8.
9.  *New York Clipper*, May 20, 1865, 46; *Boston Daily Globe*, August 23, 1897, 10, Carlo.
10. *New York Clipper*, July 1, 1865, 94.
11. Ibid., November 4, 1865, 238.
12. *Argus* (Melbourne, AU), June 7, 1866, 8.
13. The *Press* (Canterbury, NZ), March 12, 1867, 1.
14. Lois M. Foster, *Annals Of The San Francisco Stage, 1850-1880* (San Francisco, CA: Federate Theatre Projects, 1926), 437.
15. *New York Clipper*, February 27, 1869, 374–375.
16. Ibid., October 4, 1879.
17. In 1884, the first journalist to mention the photos said he had seen five cartes de visite, "presumably actresses," implying that at that time they had not been identified. *Denver Rocky Mountain News*, January 13, 1884, 2, reproducing a Cleveland journalist's report. The next journalist's report in the *World*, April 26, 1891, 30, mentioned only four photos and their incorrect identifications. The clerk was noticeably evasive about the identity of one of them. The journalist ventured it was actress Olive Logan. The clerk busied himself to avoid answering. The journalist subsequently learned that it was Lucy Hale's photo, "a daughter of one distinguished Senator from a New England State, and the wife of another now living from the same section." Even then, Lucy's relationship with John was still being hushed. The story of the mistaken naming of the photos and Fanny's eventual identity is also chronicled in BoothieBarn, "Mysterious Beauty," https://boothiebarn.com/2016/01/11/john-wilkes-booths-mysterious-beauty/.
18. *Boston Herald*, October 26, 1885, 4.
19. *Los Angeles Times*, March 1, 1897, 6.
20. *New York Clipper*, September 5, 1891.

## 33. HENRIETTA IRVING

1. *Pomeroy's Democrat* (Chicago, IL), April 29, 1876, 4.
2. *New York Tribune*, September 15, 1863, 7; *New York Herald*, September 29, 1863, 1; *Brooklyn Daily Eagle*, March 25, 1864, 7.
3. *Boston Post*, February 11, 1864, 2.
4. *New York Tribune*, May 26, 1864, 8.

5. "The Irving Polka," Composed Expressly For & Inscribed To Miss Henrietta Irving By Thomas Baker, Musical Director of the Olympic Theatre (New York: Wm. A. Pond & Co., 547 Broadway, 1864).

6. *New Orleans Daily True Delta*, December 15, 1864, 2.

7. On Eddy, see *San Francisco Bulletin*, December 29, 1875, 1.

8. *New York Herald*, January 13, 1865, 4.

9. *New Orleans Daily True Delta*, January 14, 1865, 4.

10. E.g., *Daily Commercial Register* (Sandusky, OH), May 17, 1865, 3; *Evening Press* (Providence RI), May 20, 1865, 2; *Daily Times* (Troy, NY), May 23, 1865, 3; *Milwaukee Sentinel*, May 17, 1865, 2.

11. *Pomeroy's Democrat* (Chicago, IL), April 27, 1876, 4.

12. *New York Tribune*, March 1, 1871, 4.

13. *New York Herald*, February 21, 1871, 7.

14. *New York Clipper*, December 11, 1875; *Albany Daily Evening News*, January 12, 1876.

15. *New York Clipper*, August 1872, 158.

16. *New York Herald*, January 17, 1876, 8; *New York Tribune*, January 17, 1876, 8; *Albany Daily Evening News*, January 12, 1876.

17. Edward Ellis, *An Authentic History Of the Benevolent And Protective Order Of Elks* (Chicago: Charles Ellis, 1910), 294.

18. *Cincinnati Daily Enquirer*, April 26, 1866, 2, reprinting the *Sun* (New York City, NY) article.

19. Ibid.

20. *Pomeroy's Democrat*, April 27, 1876, 4.

21. *Cincinnati Daily Times*, November 11, 1876, 4; *Evansville (IN) Commercial Press*, November 23, 1876, 4. *Detroit Free Press*, September 12, 1877, 3.

22. *Chicago Daily Tribune*, January 14, 1880, 8; June 14, 1880; 8; *New York Clipper*, February 28, 1880, 2.

23. *New York Clipper*, February 28, 1880, 2; Leslie Noelle Sullivan, *On the Western Stage: Theatre in Montana, 1880-1920* (MA Thesis, University of New Mexico, August 1990), 58.

24. E.g., *New York Clipper*, February 17, 1883, 9; *Detroit Free Press*, October 6, 1883, 8; *Brooklyn Daily Union*, May 15, 1884, 1; *New York Clipper*, November 8, 1890, 4; *Detroit Free Press*, October 13, 1891, 4.

25. Henrietta letter to A. M. Palmer, February 12, 1888, Harvard Theatre Collection, copy located in JOH library. Henrietta was not exaggerating about her chances. Henrietta was suffering from uterine fibroids. New York State Death Certificate, November 28, 1905. In the 1880s, the mortality rate for abdominal hysterectomies was seventy percent. Malcolm G. Munro, "The evolution of uterus surgery," *Clinical Obstetrics & Gynecology*, 49 (2006), 713–721.
26. *New York Dramatic Mirror*, January 31, 1891, 6.
27. *Auburn (NY) Bulletin*, May 4, 1895, 2.
28. *New York Clipper*, February 15, 1913, 4.

## 34. MAGGIE MITCHELL

1. Rankin (Kitty Blanchard), "News Of Lincoln's Death," 262.
2. *New York Tribune*, Mary 12, 1865.
3. *Washington Post*, September 30, 1881, 3.
4. Elizabeth F. Loftus and Jacqueline E. Pickrell, "The Formation of False Memories," *Psychiatric Annals*, 25 (1995), 102–113.
5. When John's body was taken from Washington for reburial in Baltimore, Maggie asked Blanche Chapman Ford to clip a lock of his hair to send her. *Washington Post*, September 30, 1881, 3.
6. The trip was advertised as early as January 1867. *Brooklyn Union*, January 25, 1867, 4. Notices appeared in newspapers even as remotely as Pickens Court House, South Carolina. *Kowee Courier*, June 1, 1867, 2; *Montana Post*, September 7, 1867, 5.
7. *Sacramento Daily Union*, December 12, 1867, 4.
8. *Yorkville (SC) Enquirer*, June 27, 1867, 2; *Daily Alta California*, July 28, 1867.
9. Maggie's change of mind set tongues gossiping. According to rumor, Maggie's companion on the voyage (besides her mother) was to have been Robert Henry Hendershot, "the drummer boy of the Rappahannock," who became famous after capturing a Confederate soldier during the Civil War. Alice Fahs, *The Imagined Civil War: Popular Literature of the North & South, 1861–1865* (Chapel Hill, NC: University of North Carolina Press, 2001), 263. Maggie was secretly engaged to Hendershot—so the rumors claimed—but he had abandoned her and eloped with a girl from Poughkeepsie. Allegedly

broken-hearted and humiliated, Maggie was said to have cancelled with Duncan and taken the less publicized voyage on account of Hendershot. (Hendershot would have been no more than twenty years old at the time.)

10. *Washington Post*, July 15, 1883, 3; *Sacramento Daily Union*, March 24, 1869, 2.
11. *Cleveland Plain Dealer*, February 17, 1869, 2.
12. George J. Olszewski, *Restoration Of Ford's Theatre* (Washington, D.C.: U.S. Department of the Interior, 1963), 19. Stock certificates were $500 each, payable "at any time within ten years from date (of purchase).
13. *Daily Alta California*, March 15, 1872, 3.
14. Sharon Hazard, *Long Branch in the Golden Age* (Charleston, SC: History Press, 2007), 90; William L. Slout, *Popular Amusements in Horse and Buggy America* (San Bernardino, CA: Borgo Press, 1995), 52.
15. *Daily Alta California*, December 22, 1878; *Detroit Free Press*, June 12, 1869, 3.
16. *New York Times*, August 25, 1888, 2; *Los Angeles Herald*, September 24, 1888.
17. *New York Dramatic Mirror*, December 1888, 4.
18. *Washington Post*, August 10, 1889, 1.
19. Ibid., July 15, 1883, 3.
20. *Daily Alta California*, April 6, 1889, 5; *New York Times*, March 4, 1889, 5.
21. *New York Times*, December 14, 1889, 2.
22. *Los Angeles Herald*, April 6, 1889, 5.
23. Ibid.
24. *Chicago Daily Tribune*, October 18, 1889, 1.
25. *New York Clipper*, March 27, 1918, 13; *New York Times*, March 23, 1918; The *Sun* (New York City, NY), March 23, 1918, 7. Henry Paddock died in 1896, seven years after their divorce. He remarried but nothing is known about his second wife. He was buried back in Cleveland, his hometown. Abbott remarried after Maggie's death. He died in May 1927.
26. *Duluth (MN) News-Tribune*, October 8, 1907, 5.
27. *Boston Herald*, October 4, 1907, 8.

## 35. ADA GRAY

1. Henry P. Phelps, *Players of a Century*: 346–347.
2. *Brooklyn Daily Eagle*, May 4, 1874, 1.
3. Ibid., July 6, 1902, 39.
4. Ibid., March 4, 1901, 29. The basic plot of *East Lynne* had Lucille's character, Lady Isabel, who is married to Archibald Carlyle, seduced by Sir Francis Levison with whom she runs away, leaving her three children behind. Carlyle divorces Isabel, but Levison doesn't tell her so that she won't pressure him to marry her. Levison also becomes abusive, and she eventually runs away. After a railway accident that disfigures her face, Isabel applies for a job at Carlyle's home as a governess. Carlyle doesn't recognize her and hires her. Just as she is about to die, Carlyle realizes that the governess is Isabel. Before she dies, Isabel begs Carlyle to forgive her. "My sin was great," she gasps, "but, oh, my punishment has been greater." "Oh, dear! Oh, dear!" reflected actress Clara Morris, who knew something about maudlin plays, "the tears that were shed over that dreadful play, and how many I contributed myself!" Morris, *Life on the Stage*, 127.
5. *Washington Post*, September 14, 1883, 2.
6. Ibid., July 10, 1902, 4.
7. *Brooklyn Daily Eagle*, July 6, 1902, 39.
8. Russell Merritt, "Rescued from a Perilous Nest: D. W. Griffith's Escape from Theatre into Film," *Cinema Journal*, 21 (1981), 20.
9. *Brooklyn Daily Eagle*, July 6, 1902, 39; *Chicago Tribune*, June 8, 1902, 48.
10. *Washington Post*, July 10, 1902, 4.
11. Ibid.
12. *Brooklyn Daily Eagle*, August 29, 1902, 5.
13. *Washington Post*, July 10, 1902, 4.
14. Ibid., August 29, 1902, 9.

## 36. ISABEL SUMNER

1. Leah L. Nichols-Wellington, *History of the Bowdoin School* (Manchester, NH: Rumely Press, 1912), 177.
2. Rhodehamel and Taper, *Right or Wrong*, 108.
3. *Boston Herald*, October 14, 1900, 47.

4. Ibid., May 23, 1908, 5.
5. Rhodehamel and Taper, *Right or Wrong*, 108–109.
6. The title is taken from the phrase in John's diary justifying his killing Lincoln. Were it not for those letters, John's affair with Isabel would never have come to light.
7. Rhodehamel is curator of historical manuscripts at the Huntington Library in San Marino, California.
8. Rhodehamel and Taper in *Right or Wrong*, 109, mention one more recollection about Isabel. In her last years she developed an interest in the occult and had two astrological charts created for her and was especially impressed by two passages from them. Rhodehamel and Taper quote the first prognostication about how "the stars revealed that friendships before and after marriage are prone to die in a curious or unexpected manner . . . and ending the career of some person connected with [Isabel Sumner] in discredit and at a sacrifice of character." The second prognostication was that Isabel's "position of Venus does not argue well for domestic and love relations during the earlier part of life. The native born under such relations usually meets with disappointments—separation or some unhappy results."

## 37. LOUISE WOOSTER

1. Terri L. Hicks, *Oak Hill Cemetery: A Reflection of Early Birmingham 1871-1913* (MA Thesis, University of Alabama, Birmingham, Alabama 2013), 14.
2. James L. Baggett (ed.), *A Woman Of the Town* (Birmingham, AL: Birmingham Public Library Press, 2005), 14.
3. Ibid., 16.
4. E.g., *Chicago Times*, April 21, 1890, 2.
5. Ibid.
6. L. C. W. *The Autobiography of a Magdalen* (Birmingham, AL: Birmingham Publishing Co., 1911).
7. "Tourists Dig Birmingham Cemeteries," http://birminghamal.org/2015/10/tourists-dig-birmingham-cemeteries/, accessed December 12, 2015.
8. *Portland (OR) Oregonian*, June 16, 1913, 1.
9. *Washington Herald*, June 16, 1913, 5.

10. *Denver Post,* June 16, 1913, 2.
11. Joseph D. Bryant, "Early Birmingham madam who saved sick will have scrapbook in history center," http://blog.al.com/spotnews/2012/08/early_birmingham_madam_who_sav.html, accessed, 12/13/2015.
12. Ellin Sterne Jimmerson, "Louise Wooster," *Encyclopedia of Alabama,* http://www.encyclopediaofalabama.org/article/h-1862, accessed December 13, 2015.
13. Ibid.
14. "Louise Wooster," wwwsoph.uab.edu/nphw/WoosterAward, accessed December 13, 2015.

## 38. CLARA MORRIS

1. Morris, *Life on Stage,* 104–105.
2. Ibid., 20.
3. Morris, *Life on Stage,* 97–99.
4. Frederic E. McKay and Charles E. L. Wingate, *Famous America Actors of Today* (New York: Thomas Crowell, 1896), vol. 1, 90.
5. *New York Times,* November 19, 1924, 19.
6. Towse, *Sixty Years of the Theatre,* 149–150.
7. Ibid., 228.
8. The *Century,* 39 (January 1890), 433.
9. *Boston Herald,* January 10, 1890, 1.
10. Quoted in Wilson, *John Wilkes Booth,* 234.
11. See this book's preface for these anecdotes.
12. *New York Times,* January 29, 1910, 2.
13. Ibid., September 13, 1910, 9.
14. Ibid., November 21, 1925, 1.

## 39. MARTHA MILLS

1. The article Edwin referred to in the *Chicago Tribune,* December 5, 1885, stated that "it is not generally known that Booth at the time of his death left a widow and two children," and quoted John's alleged widow saying she was among those who saw John's remains before he was finally buried. Edwin's letter to Laurence Hutton is reprinted in Bryan, *Great American Myth,* 363.

2. Junius Brutus Booth to Edwin Booth, April 24, 1865, reprinted in Alford, *Sister's Memoir*, 118.
3. Stamford Historical Society letter, April 16, 1996, FFP.
4. *Wood's Baltimore City Directory* (Baltimore: John Woods, 1870), 70.
5. Mahoney, *Sketches of Tudor Hall*, 45.
6. Rogers letter to Dr. William Stump Forwood, 1886, LOC, manuscripts division. Forwood was working on a biography of John's father and had written to Mrs. Rogers for background information on the family. Either Mrs. Rogers's memory had failed her, or Martha misled her, or she imagined Charles Alonzo, born in 1861, looked like John's grandfather, which was possible but did not mean there was an actual family tie.
7. Gail Merrifield undated letter to Stanley Kimmel, Kimmel Collection, Kelce Library, Tampa, Florida.
8. Harvard University Library, Izola Forrester Family Papers (FFP), Box 12, marriage records.
9. Izola Forrester, *This One Mad Act: The Unknown Story of John Wilkes Booth and His Family by His Granddaughter* (Boston: Hale, Cushman & Flint, 1937).
10. E.g., Bryan, *Great American Myth*.
11. John O. Hall Letter, June 15, 1996, FFP.
12. Knibb and Mehrtens, *Elusive Booths of Burrillville*.
13. Ogarita letter to Harry Stevenson dated July 6, 1888, Box 34, FFP.
14. Rogers letter to Dr. William Stump Forwood, 1886, LOC.
15. Box 34, File 1/1, Donata book inscription, FFP.
16. Ibid. Adding to the skepticism, however, is a handwritten note signed by a Reverend Peleg, stating, "This is to certify on January 9, 1859 I performed a ceremony joining in Holy Matrimony, John Byron Wilkes Booth and Martha Mills D'Arcy at my home in Dingletown Connecticut according to the ordinances of God and the teaching of the Methodist Church." The note was an obvious forgery, more than obvious from the names. John's middle name was not Byron and Martha was never married to D'Arcy. Letter postmarked October 1898 from Brookville, Pennsylvania, allegedly found in a family Bible, FFP.
17. Knibb and Mehrtens, *Elusive Booths of Burrillville*, 162–163, 235.
18. Ibid., Letter to "Dear Gaily, May 16, 1967.
19. Ibid., Letter to "Dear Gaily," November 11, 1867.

20. Dave Taylor, "The Forgotten Daughter—Rosalie Ann Booth," BoothieBarn, https://boothiebarn.com/2013/11/25/the-forgotten-daughter-rosalie-ann-booth/, accessed April 15, 2015.
21. *Trenton Evening Times*, November 15, 1883, 1.
22. The *Brooklyn Magazine*, 2 (April 1885), 39–40.
23. C. Wyatt Evans, *The Legend Of John Wilkes Booth. Myth, Memory, & a Mummy* (Lawrence, KS: University Press of Kansas, 2004).

## EPILOGUE

1. *New York Daily Tribune*, June 7, 1903, 6; Vaughan Shelton, *Mask For Treason. The Lincoln Murder Trial* (Harrisburg, PA: Stackpole Books, 1965), 242.
2. Townsend, *Life, Crime and Capture*, 25.
3. Henry A. Weaver, "NO. 2 Bullfinch Place," *Daily Inter-Ocean* (Chicago, IL), August 27, 1893, 22.
4. Clara Louise Kellogg, *Memoirs of an American Prima Donna* (New York: G. P. Putnam's Sons, 1913), 111.
5. Townsend, *Life Crime and Capture*, 24.
6. Ibid.
7. Kellogg, *Memoirs of an American Prima Donna*, 111.
8. Letter in Shepherd, "They tried to stop Booth," n.p.
9. Libby, "Favorite Child," 19.
10. Kenneth J. Sher, "Psychological Characteristics of Children of Alcoholics," *Alcohol Health & Research World*, 21 (1997), 247–254.
11. Curt R. Bartol and Ann M. Bartol, *Criminal Behavior. A Psychosocial Approach* (New York: Prentice Hall, 1986), 243; Lucy Freeman and Martin Theodores, *The Why Report: A Book of Interviews With Psychiatrists, Psychoanalysts, and Psychologists* (New York: Pocket Books, 1965), 198; Barbara Lerner, "The Killer Narcissists," *National Review*, May 19, 1999, 34–35.
12. Bloom, *Edwin Booth*, 39.
13. Lueger, "Episode of syphilis-shaming," www.slate.com/blogs/the vault/2016/01/08/.
14. *New York Graphic*, November 6, 1873.
15. Deborah Hayden, *Pox: Genius, Madness, And The Mysteries of Syphilis* (New York: Basic Books, 2003), xv; Thomas P. Lowry,

*Venereal Disease and the Lewis and Clark Expedition* (Lincoln, NE: University of Nebraska Press, 2004), 16–17.

16. Emanuel Hertz (ed.), *The Hidden Lincoln, From The Letters and Papers of William H. Herndon* (New York: Viking Press, 1938), 259. During his younger days, Lincoln's neighbors in New Salem and Springfield, Illinois, knew him as a man with "terribly strong passions for women." "He could scarcely keep his hands off them." Judge David Davis, quoted in Douglas L. Wilson and Rodney O. Davis, *Herndon's Informants* (Urbana, IL: University of Illinois Press, 1997), 350. When he was able to afford it, Lincoln regularly paid for sex with prostitutes. A few weeks after one such incident in Beardstown, Lincoln told his new law partner, Billy Herndon, the girl had given him syphilis. Lincoln wrote to a Dr. Drake, Dean of Medicine at the College of Cincinnati, describing his symptoms and asked him to prescribe medicine to treat it. Cincinnati was a long way from Springfield. There were doctors a lot closer, but Lincoln didn't want his "dark secret" to get out in his community. Dr. Drake wrote back to Lincoln saying that he "would not undertake to prescribe for him without a personal interview." William H. Herndon, *Herndon's Life of Lincoln* (New York: World Publishing Company, 1949), 173, n.10. By then the acute phase of the disease had passed, and Lincoln didn't feel the urgency to make the long trip. Lincoln was one of the lucky ones whose syphilis did not progress past the first stage.

17. Lowry, *Story Soldiers Wouldn't Tell*, 104. There were so many cases in Union-occupied Nashville, that the Union authorities established two venereal disease hospitals and mandated that every prostitute in the city had to be licensed, inspected, and treated (if infected). Thomas P. Lowry, *Confederate Heroines* (Baton Rouge, LA: Louisiana State University Press, 2006), 90.

18. Lowry, *Venereal Disease*, 7.

19. Judith O'Donnell and Christopher Emery, "Neurosyphilis," *Current Infectious Disease Reports*, 7 (2005), 277–294; Cheryl Jay, "Treatment of Neurosyphilis," *Current Treatment Options in Neurology*, 8 (2006), 185–192. A previous explanation (Ralph Brooks, "Insane or Ill," *Surratt Courier*, 22 (August 1997), 9) that John's dramatic personality change was due to syphilis met with understandable skepticism since it was predicated on hoarseness, only one of John's symptoms and one not

exclusive to syphilis. Skeptics also maintained that it could not be related to syphilis because, according to the earlier theory, hoarseness was symptomatic of the third stage of syphilis where symptoms are persistent, not episodic. Edward Steers Jr., "Historical Malpractice," *Surratt Courier*, 22 (October 1997), 7. However, hoarseness is symptomatic of a common episodic symptom of second stage syphilis.

20. Quoted in Miller, *Oilman*, 56.
21. Edwards and Steers, *Evidence*, 1279.
22. William Alger, *Life of Edwin Forrest, the American Tragedian* (Philadelphia: Lippincott, 1877), vol. 2, 546.
23. *New York Tribune*, April 17, 1865.
24. Angus Morrison, "Analysis of One Hundred Cases of Neurosyphilis," *American Journal of Syphilis*, 4 (July 1920), 552–559, 556; Lloyd Thompson, *Syphilis* (Philadelphia: Lea & Febiger, 1920), 338.
25. *New York Sunday Telegraph*, May 23, 1909.
26. E. A. Emerson, "How Wilkes' Booth's Friend Described His Crime," *Literary Digest* (March 6, 1926), 58–59, 58.
27. *Los Angeles Times*, February 11, 1928, III, 10, quoting actress Helen Truman.
28. *Washington Post*, July 17, 1904, A8.
29. MacCulloch, "Saw Lincoln Shot," 112, quoting Joseph Hazelton, program boy at Ford's Theatre.
30. Samples, *Lust for Fame*, 176.
31. *Collier's, The National Weekly*, 74 (1924), 12.
32. Edwards and Steers, *Evidence*, 426 (Blanche DeBar testimony).
33. Canavan, *Lincoln's Final Hours*, 30.
34. *Cincinnati Enquirer*, July 6, 1878, 9.
35. Morris, *Life on Stage*, 100; Bloom, *Edwin Booth*, 79.
36. Edwards and Steers, *Assassination*, 340 (Chester testimony).
37. Ibid.
38. Mathews testimony, Surratt, *Trial of John H. Surratt*, vol. 2, 821–822.
39. Chaconas, personal communication, 2017.
40. Hanchett, *Lincoln Murder Conspiracies*; Charles Chiniquy, *Fifty Years in the Church of Rome* (New York: Fleming H. Revell, 1886); Richter, *Sic Semper Tyrannis*, 86–88.

41. Michael Kauffman, "The Confederate Plan to Abduct President Lincoln," *Surratt Courier* (March 1981), 4.

42. Thomas Reed Turner. *Beware the People Weeping. Public Opinion and the Assassination of Abraham Lincoln* (Baton Rouge, LA: Louisiana State University Press, 1991), 252.

43. Titone, *My Thoughts Be Bloody*.

44. Kauffman, *American Brutus*, 127.

45. Morris, *Life On The Stage*, 104.

46. Alfriend, "Recollections of John Wilkes Booth," 604.

47. Quoted in Morris, *Life on Stage*, 103.

48. Gilbert, *Stage Reminiscences*, 57.

49. June letter to Edwin, October 20, 1862, in John C. Brennan, "John Wilkes Booth's Enigmatic Brother Joseph," *Maryland Historical Magazine*, 7 (Spring 1983), 25. Edwin described John as "wild-brained." He was only "insane," Edwin said, on the issue of secession. Edwin Booth, "The Real Edwin Booth," *Literary Digest*, 9 (October 1894), 12.

50. Winter, *Vagrant Memories*, 158.

51. Writers who have weighed in on John's state of mind include James W. Clarke, *American Assassins: the darker side of politics* (Princeton, NJ: Princeton University Press, 1982), 82; R. J. Donovan, *The Assassins* (New York: Harper & Brothers, 1952); D. W. Hastings, "The Psychiatry of Presidential Assassination, Part I: Jackson and Lincoln," *Lancet*, 85 (March 1965), 95–100, "The Psychiatry of Presidential Assassination, Part II: Garfield and Roosevelts," *Lancet*, 85 (April 1965), 157–162; L. Z. Freedman, "Assassination: Psychopathology and Social Pathology," *Postgraduate Medicine*, 37 (June 1965), 650–658; A. E. Weisz and R. L. Taylor, "American Presidential Assassinations," *Diseases of the Nervous System*, 30 (October 1969), 658–659. Dr. Alexander Hamilton said he saw John on stage and devoted several pages of his *Recollections Of An Alienist* to him. John, he said, was "clearly of unsound mind" from his earliest days. "As a boy Wilkes Booth showed many evidence of instability, and was ever subject to moods and fits of melancholy, as well as morbid suspicions and moroseness. ... at one time he ran away from home and joined the pirate oystermen in the Chesapeake Bay." The often-repeated anecdote of John's forgetting his lines about his

character Petruchio Pandolfo was due to "an advance form of brain weakness which in an advanced degree suggests aphasia." Hamilton concluded that John should not be held fully responsible for his crime due to his "constitutional inferiority." Alexander McLane Hamilton, *Recollections Of An Alienist* (New York: George H. Doran Company, 1916), 347–349.

52. *Louisville (KY) Courier-Journal*, December 23, 1902, 4.
53. G. W. Wilson, "John Wilkes Booth: Father Murderer," *The American IMAGO*, 1 (June 1940), 49–60; P. Weissman, "Why Booth Shot Lincoln," *Psychoanalysis and the Social Sciences*, 5 (1958), 99–115.
54. JWB Diary, Rhodehamel and Taper, *Right or Wrong*, 124.
55. Thompson, *Syphilis*, 388.
56. Charles Wyndham, "Recollections of John Wilkes Booth," *New York Herald*, June 27, 1909, magazine section, 2.

# BIBLIOGRAPHY

## BOOKS

Abel, E. Lawrence. *A Finger in Lincoln's Brain*. Santa Barbara, CA: Praeger, 2015.

———. *Confederate Sheet Music*. Jefferson, NC: McFarland & Co., 2004.

———. *Singing The New Nation: How Music Shaped the Confederacy, 1861-1865*. Mechanicsburg, PA: Stackpole Books, 2000.

Abel, E. Lawrence and Buckley, Barbara E. *The Handwriting On The Wall. Toward A Sociology And Psychology of Graffiti*. Westport, CT: Greenwood Press, 1977.

Aldrich, Mrs. Thomas Bailey. *Crowding Memories*. Boston and New York: Houghton Mifflin Co., 1920.

Alford, Terry. *John Wilkes Booth: A Sister's Memoir*. Jackson, MS: University Press of Mississippi, 1996.

———. *Fortune's Fool. The Life Of John Wilkes Booth*. New York: Oxford University Press, 2015.

Alger, William. *Life of Edwin Forrest, the American Tragedian.* Philadelphia: Lippincott, 1877.

Anonymous. *Memoirs Of Junius Brutus Booth, From His Birth To The Present Time: With an Appendix, Containing Original Letters, From Persons of Rank and Celebrity; And Copious Extracts From The Journal Kept By Mr. Booth, During His Theatrical Tour of the Continent.* London: Chapple, Miller, Rowden and E. Wilson, 1817.

Anonymous. *The Empire State: Its Industries and Wealth.* New York: American Publishing and Engraving, 1888.

Archer, Stephen M. *Junius Brutus Booth. Theatrical Prometheus.* Carbondale, IL: Southern University Press, 1992.

Arnold, Isaac N. *The Life of Abraham Lincoln.* Chicago: A. C. McClurg & Co., 1909.

Badeau, Adam. *Grant in Peace, From Appomattox To Mount McGregor.* Hartford, CT: S. S. Scranton & Co., 1887.

Babcock, Bernie (Julia Burnelle Smade). *Booth and the Spirit of Lincoln.* Philadelphia: J. B. Lippincott, 1925.

Baggett, James L. (ed.). *A Woman Of the Town.* Birmingham, AL: Birmingham Public Library Press, 2005.

Baker, La Fayette Charles. *The Secret Service In The Late War.* Philadelphia: John E. Potter and Co., 1874.

Bartol, Curt R. and Barol, Ann M. *Criminal Behavior. A Psychosocial Approach.* New York: Prentice Hall, 1986.

Beasley, David. *McKee Rankin, And the Heyday Of The American Theatre.* Waterloo, ON: Wilfred Laurier University Press, 2002.

Beattie, Donald W., Cole, Rodney M., and Waugh, Charles G. (eds.). *A Distant War Comes Home.* Camden, ME: Down East Books, 1991.

Bernheim, Alfred L. *The Business Of The Theatre. An Economic History of the American Theatre, 1750-1932.* New York: Benjamin Blom, 1964.

Bishop, Jim. *The Day Lincoln was Shot*. New York: HarperPerennial, 2013 [originally published 1955].

Bloom, Arthur W. *Edwin Booth*. Jefferson, NC: McFarland, 2013.

Bogar, Thomas. *Backstage At the Lincoln Assassination. The Untold Story Of The Actors and Stagehands At Ford's Theatre*. Washington, D.C.: Regnery, 2013.

Briscoe, Johnson. *The Actors' Birthday Book*. New York: Moffat, Yard & Co., 1907.

Broadbent, R. J. *Annals of the Liverpool Stage*. Liverpool: Edward Howell, 1908.

Brodie, Janet. *Contraception and Abortion in Nineteen-Century America*. Ithica, NY: Cornell University Press, 1994.

Brown, Thomas Allston. *History of the American Stage; Containing Biographic Sketches of Nearly Every Member of The Profession That Has Appeared On The American Stage, From 1733 to 1870*. New York: Dick & Fitzgerald, 1870.

————. *A History of the New York Stage from the First Performance in 1732 to 1901*. New York: Dodd Mead, 1902.

Brown, Harry and Williams, Frederick D. (eds.). *The Diary of James A Garfield*. Lansing, MI: Michigan State University, 1967.

Bryan, George S. *The Great American Myth*. New York: Darrick & Evans, 1940.

Buckingham, J. E. *Reminiscences and Souvenirs of the Assassination of Abraham Lincoln*. Washington, D.C.: Rufus H. Darby, 1894.

Burlingame, Michael (ed.). *Lincoln's Journalist: John Hay's Editorial Writings for the Press, 1860-1864*. Carbondale, IL: Southern Illinois University Press, 2006.

Canavan, Kathryn. *Lincoln's Final Hours. Conspiracy, Terror, And The Assassination of America's Greatest President*. Lexington, KY: University Press of Kentucky, 2015.

Carroll, David. *The Matinee Idols*. New York: Arbor House, 1972.

Chiniquy, Charles. *Fifty Years in the Church of Rome*. New York: Fleming H. Revell, 1886.

Chinoy, Helen Krich and Henkins, Linda Walsh (eds.). *Women In American Theatre*. New York: Theatre Communications Group, 1987.

Clarke, Asia Booth. *Personal Recollections Of The Elder Booth*. London: privately printed but not published, 1902.

———. *The Elder And The Younger Booth*. Boston: James E. Osgood And Company, 1882.

———. *The Unlocked Book*. New York: G. P. Putnam's Sons, 1938.

Clarke, James W. *American Assassins: the darker side of politics*. Princeton, NJ: Princeton University Press, 1982.

Clapp, William W. Jr. *A Record of the Boston Stage*. Boston and Cambridge: James Munroe and Co., 1853.

Cockrell, Dale. *Demons of Disorder, Early Blackface Minstrels and Their World*. New York: Cambridge University Press, 1997.

Codding, Icabod. *A Republic Manual for the Campaign*. Princeton, IL: Republican Book and Job Printing, 1860.

Collins, Bryn C. *Emotional Unavailability*. New York: McGraw-Hill, 1997.

Cone, Andrew and Johns, Walter R. *Petrolia*. New York: Appleton, 1870.

Conrad, Thomas Nelson. *A Confederate Spy: A Story of the Civil War*. New York: J. S. Ogilvie Pub. Co., 1892.

———. *The Rebel Scout, A Thrilling History of Scouting Life in the Southern Army*. Washington, D.C.: National Publishing Co., 1904.

Crane, William H. *Footprints and Echoes*. New York: E. P. Dutton, 1927.

Crook, William H. *Through Five Administrations: Reminiscences of Colonel William H. Crook*. New York: Harper Bros., 1910.

Dagett, Melissa. *Spiritualism in Nineteenth-Century New Orleans: the Life and Times of Henry Louis Rey*. Jackson, MS: University Press of Mississippi, 2017.

Davis, Andrew. *America's Longest Run: A History of the Walnut Street Theatre*. University Park, PA: Pennsylvania State University Press, 2010.

De Ferrari, John. *Historic Restaurants of Washington, D.C: Capital Eats*. Charleston, SC: American Palate, 2013.

Dickey, J. D. *Empire Of Mud. The Secret History of Washington, D.C*. Guilford, CT: Lyons Press, 2014.

Dickson, Samuel. *San Francisco is Your Home*. Stanford, CA: Stanford University Press, 1948.

Donald, David Herbert. *Lincoln*. New York: Simon and Schuster, 1995.

Donovan, R. J. *The Assassins*. New York: Harper & Brothers, 1952.

Doster, William E. *Lincoln and Episodes of the Civil War*. New York: G. P. Putnam's Sons, 1915.

Edwards, Herbert J. and Herne, Julie A. *James A. Herne. The Rise of Realism in the American Drama*. Orono, ME: University of Maine Press, 1964.

Edwards, William C. and Steers, Edward Jr. (eds.). *The Lincoln Assassination: The Evidence*. Urbana, IL: University of Illinois Press, 2009.

Ellis, Edward. *An Authentic History Of the Benevolent And Protective Order Of Elks*. Chicago: Charles Ellis, 1910.

Ellsler, John A. *Stage Memories*. Cleveland: Rowfant Club, 1950.

Etyinge, Rose. *The Memories of Rose Eytinge. Being Recollections & Observations of Men, Women, and Events, During Half a Century*. New York: Frederick A Stokes Co., 1905.

Evans, C. Wyatt. *The Legend Of John Wilkes Booth. Myth, Memory, & a Mummy*. Lawrence, KS: University Press of Kansas, 2004.

Ezekiel, Herbert T. and Lichtenstein, Gaton. *The History of the Jews of Richmond from 1769 to 1917*. Richmond, VA: Ezekiel, 1917.

Fahs, Alice. *The Imagined Civil War: Popular Literature of the North & South, 1861-1865*. Chapel Hill, NC: University of North Carolina Press, 2001.

Fazio, John C. *Decapitating The Union: Jefferson Davis, Judah Benjamin And the Plot to Assassinate Lincoln*. Jefferson, NC: McFarland & Co., 2015.

Federal Writers Project. *Missouri: A Guide to the "Show Me State."* New York: Duel, Sloan and Pearce, 1941.

Felthous, Alan and Sass, Henning (eds.). *International Handbook on Psychopathic Disorders and the Law*. New York: J. Wiley, 2008.

Ferguson, W. J. *I Saw Booth Shoot Lincoln*. Boston: Houghton Mifflin Co., 1930.

Fields, Armond. *Fred Stone: Circus Performer and Musical Comedy Star*. Jefferson, NC: McFarland & Co., 2002.

Ford, Thomas. *The Actor Or, A Peep Behind the Curtain: Being Passages in the Lives of Booth And Some Of His Contemporaries*. New York: Wm. H. Graham, 1846.

Forrest, William S. *Historical Descriptive Sketches of Norfolk And Vicinity During A period of Two Hundred Years, Also, Sketches of Williamsburg, Hampton, Suffolk, Smithfield, And Other Places, With Descriptions Of Some Of The Principal Objects Of Interest In East Virginia*. Philadelphia: Lindsay and Blakiston, 1853.

Forrester, Izola. *This One Mad Act: The Unknown Story of John Wilkes Booth and His Family by His Granddaughter*. Boston: Hale, Cushman & Flint, 1937.

Forster, John. *The Life of Charles Dickens*. New York: Charles Scribner's Sons, 1899.

Foster, Lois M. *Annals Of The San Francisco Stage, 1850-1880*. San Francisco, CA: Federate Theatre Projects, 1926.

Freeman, Lucy and Theodores, Martin. *The Why Report: A Book of Interviews With Psychiatrists, Psychoanalysts, and Psychologists*. New York: Pocket Books, 1965.

Furtwangler, Albert. *Assassin on Stage. Brutus, Hamlet, and the Death of Lincoln*. Urbana, IL: University of Illinois, 1991.

Galbraith, William and Galbraith, Loretta. *A Lost Heroine of the Confederacy, The Diaries and Letters of Belle Edmondson*. Jackson, MS: University Press of Mississippi, 1990.

Gilbert, Ann Hartley. *The Stage Reminiscences of Mrs. Gilbert*. New York: Charles Scribner's Sons, 1901.

Good, Timothy. *We Saw Lincoln Shot*. Jackson, MS: University Press of Mississippi, 1995.

Graham, Frank. *Histrionic Montreal: Annals of the Montreal Stage with Biographical and Critical Notices of the Plays and Players of a Century*. Montreal: John Lovell & Son, 1902.

Graham, Ian. *Scarlet women: the scandalous lives of courtesans, concubines, and royal Mistresses*. New York: St. Martin's Press, 2016.

Grossman, Barbara Wallace. *A Spectacle of Suffering. Clara Morris on the American Stage*. Carbondale, IL: Southern Illinois Press, 2009.

Grossmann, Edwina Booth. *Edwin Booth. Recollections By His Daughter And Letters To Her And To His Friends*. New York: The Century Co., 1894.

Haley, James L. *Sam Houston*. Norman, OK: University of Oklahoma Press, 2004.

Hamilton, Alexander McLane. *Recollections Of An Alienist*. New York: George H. Doran Company, 1916.

Hanchett, William. *The Lincoln Murder Conspiracies*. Urbana and Chicago, IL: University of Illinois Press, 1986.

Harris, William C. *With Charity for All: Lincoln and the Restoration of the Union*. Lexington, KY: University Press of Kentucky, 1999.

Harwell, Richard Barksdale. *Brief Candle: The Confederate Theatre.* Worcester, MA: American Antiquarian Society, 1971.

Hatch, Frederick. *Protecting President Lincoln. The Security Effort, The Thwarted Plots And the Disaster At Ford's Theatre.* Jefferson, NC: McFarland & Co., 2011.

Havard, Bernard and Sylvester, Mark D. *Walnut Street Theatre.* Charleston, SC: Arcadia Publishing, 2008.

Hazard, Sharon. *Long Branch in the Golden Age.* Charleston, SC: History Press, 2007.

Hayden, Deborah. *Pox: Genius, Madness, And The Mysteries of Syphilis.* New York: Basic Books, 2003.

Headly, John W. *Confederate Operations in Canada and New York.* New York: Neale Publishing Co., 1906.

Henderson, Tony. *Disorderly Women in Eighteenth-Century London: Prostitution and Control in the Metropolis 1730-1830.* New York: Pearson Education, Ltd., 1999.

Herndon, William H. *Herndon's Life of Lincoln.* New York: World Publishing Company, 1949.

Herne, James A. (ed.). *Shore Acres and Other Plays.* New York: Samuel French, 1928.

Hertz, Emanuel (ed.). *The Hidden Lincoln, From The Letters and Papers of William H. Herndon.* New York: Viking Press, 1938.

Herz, Henri. *My Travels in America.* Madison, WI: University of Wisconsin Press, 1963.

Holmes, King, Mardh, per Anders, and Sparling, P. Frederick (eds.). *Sexually Transmitted Diseases.* New York: McGraw-Hill, 1999.

Holmes, Oliver Wendell. *Soundings from the Atlantic.* Boston: Ticknor and Fields, 1864.

Holzer, Harold. *President Lincoln Assassination!: The Firsthand Story of the Murder, Manhunt, Trial, and Mourning.* New York: Library of America, 2015.

Holzer, Harold and Gabbard, Sara Vaughn (eds.). *1865: American Makes War and Peace in Lincoln's Final Year.* Carbondale, IL: Southern University Press, 2015.

Howard, Hamilton Gay. *Civil War Echoes.* Washington, D.C.: Howard Publishing Co., 1907.

Howells, William Dean. *Suburban Sketches.* Boston: James R. Osgood and Co., 1872.

Hubert, Philip G. Jr. *A Sketch of the Actor's Life; its Requirements, Hardships and Rewards.* New York: G. P. Putnam's Sons, 1900.

Hunter, Alexander. *New National Theatre, Washington D.C. A Record of Fifty Years.* Washington, D.C.: R. O. Polkinhorn & Son, 1885.

Hyde, William and Conrad, Howard Louis (eds.). *Encyclopedia of The History of St. Louis: A compendium of History and Biography for Ready Reference.* New York: The Southern History Company, 1899.

Jones, J. B. *A Rebel War Clerk's Diary at the Confederate State Capital.* Philadelphia: J. B. Lippincott, 1866.

Kahan, Jeffrey. *The Cult of Kean.* Hampshire, UK: Ashgate, 1988.

Kauffman, Michael W. *American Brutus.* New York: Random House, 2005.

Kendall, John Smith. *The Golden Age of the New Orleans Theatre.* Baton Rouge, LA: Louisiana State University Press, 1952.

Kellogg, Clara Louise. *Memoirs of an American Prima Donna.* New York: G. P. Putnam's Sons, 1913.

Knibb, Joyce G. and Mehrtens, Patricia A. *The Elusive Booths of Burrillville. An Investigation of John Wilkes Booth's Alleged Wife and Daughter.* Bowie, MD: Heritage Books, 1991.

Krug, Mark M. (ed.). *Mrs. (Sarah Jane Full) Hill's Journal—Civil War Reminiscences*. Chicago: R. R. Donnelley & Sons, 1980.

Leavitt, Michael Bennett. *Fifty Years in Theatrical management*. New York: Broadway Publishing Co., 1912.

Leech, Margaret. *Reveille in Washington, 1860-1865*. Alexandria, VA: Time-Life Books, 1980.

Libby, Ellen Weber. *The Favorite Child*. Amherst, NY: Prometheus Books, 2010.

Linzey, Andrew (ed.). *The Link between Animal Abuse and Human Violence*. Portland, OR: Sussex Academic Press, 2009.

Logan, Olive. *The Mimic World and Public Exhibitions. Their History, Their Morals, and Effects*. Philadelphia: New Word Publishing Co., 1871.

Londre, Felicia Hardison. *The Enchanted Years of the Stage. Kansas City at the Crossroads of American Theatre, 1870-1930*. Columbia, MI: University of Missouri Press, 2007.

Long, Everett B. *Civil War Day by Day*. New York: Doubleday, 1971.

Loux, Arthur F. *John Wilkes Booth: Day by Day*. Jefferson, NC: McFarland & Co., 2014.

Lowry, Thomas P. *Confederate Heroines*. Baton Rouge, LA: Louisiana State University Press, 2006.

———. *Sexual Misbehavior in the Civil War: A Compendium*. e-book, Xlibris Corp., 2006.

———. *The Story the Soldier's Wouldn't Tell. Sex in the Civil War*. Mechanicsburg, PA: Stackpole Books, 1994.

———. *Venereal Disease and the Lewis and Clark Expedition*. Lincoln, NE: University of Nebraska Press, 2004.

Ludlow, Noah. *Dramatic Life as I Found It: A Record of Personal Experience; With an Account of the Rise and Progress of the Drama in the West and South, with Anecdotes and Biographical Sketches of the Principal Actors and Actresses Who Have at Times Appeared upon the*

*Stage in the Mississippi Valley.* New York: Benjamin Blom, 1977 [originally published 1880].

Madonna, Jerrod. *A Threat to the Republic. The Secret of the Lincoln Assassination that Preserved the Union.* Privately published, 2006.

Mahoney, Ella V. *Sketches of Tudor Hall and the Booth Family.* Bel Air, MD: Franklin Printing Co., 1925.

Marchand, Leslie A. (ed.). *Lord Byron: Selected Letters and Journals.* Cambridge, MA: Belknap Press, 1982.

Markel, Howard. *Quarantine: East European Jewish Immigrants and the New York City Epidemics.* Baltimore, MD: Johns Hopkins University Press, 1999.

Marlin, Jane (ed). *Reminiscences of Morris Steinert.* New York: G. P. Putnam and Sons, 1900.

Mates, Julian. *America's Musical Stage: Two Hundred Years of Musical Theatre.* Westport, CT: Greenwood Press, 1985.

Matthews, Brander and Hutton, Laurence (eds.). *Actors and Actresses of Great Britain and the United States.* New York: Cassell & Co., 1886.

McKay, Frederic E. and Windgate, Charles (eds.). *Famous American Actors of To-day.* New York: Thomas Y. Crowell & Co., 1896.

McClure, Colonel Alexander K. *Recollections of Half a Century.* Salem, MA: Salem Press Co., 1902.

McLaurin, John J. *Sketches In Crude Oil. Some Accidents And Incidents Of the Petroleum Development In All Parts Of The Globe.* Franklin, PA: McLaurin, 1902.

Merington, Marguerite (ed.). *The Custer Story: The Life and Intimate Letters of General George A. Custer and His Wife Elizabeth.* Lincoln, NE: University of Nebraska Press, 1987.

Moore, Frank (ed.). *Record of the Year.* New York: G. W. Carleton & Co., 1876.

Morris, Clara. *Life on the Stage. My Personal Experiences and Recollections.* New York: McClure, Phillips & Co., 1901.

Mullenneaux, Nan. *Walking Ladies: Mid-nineteenth-century American Actresses' Work, Family and Culture.* Albany, NY: State University of New York Press, 2008.

Nichols-Wellington, Leah L. *History of the Bowdoin School.* Manchester, NH: Rumely Press, 1912.

Oggel, L. Terry (ed.). *The Letters and Notebooks of Mary Devlin Booth.* Westport, CT: Greenwood Press, 1987.

Olszewski, George J. *Restoration Of Ford's Theatre.* Washington, D.C.: U.S. Department of the Interior, 1963.

Orser, Charles E. (ed.). *Images of the Recent Past: Readings in Historical Archaeology.* Lanham, MD: AltaMira Press, 1966.

Ownsbey, Betty J. *Alias "Paine" Lewis Thornton Powell, the Mystery Man of the Lincoln Conspiracy.* Jefferson, NC: McFarland, 1993.

Oxberry, William (ed.). *Oxberry's Dramatic Biography and Histrionic Anecdotes.* London: G. Virtue, 1826.

Perry, Edwin A. *The Boston Herald and Its History. How, When and Where it was Founded.* Boston, MA: Perry, 1878.

Perry, James A. *The American Ibsen.* Chicago: Nelson-Hall, 1978.

Phelps, Henry Pitt. *Players of a Century. A Record of the Albany Stage. Including Notices of Prominent Actors Who Have Appeared in America.* Albany, NY: Joseph McDonough, 1880.

Philadelphia Daily Inquirer. *The Trial of the Alleged Assassins and Conspirators at Washington City, C.C. May and June, 1865, for the Murder of the President Abraham Lincoln.* Philadelphia: T. B. Peterson & Bros., 1865.

Philips, Hugh. *Mid Georgian London: A Topographical and Social Survey of Central and Western London about 1750.* London: Chandlers, 1964.

Pitman, Benn. *The Assassination of President Lincoln And the Trial Of The Conspirators*. New York: Moore, Wilstach & Baldwin, 1865.

Poore, Benjamin Perley (ed.). *The Conspiracy Trial for the Murder of the President*. Boston: J.E. Tilton, 1865.

———. *Reminiscences of Sixty Years In the National Metropolis*. Philadelphia: Hubbard Brothers, 1886.

Power, Tyrone. *Impressions of America: During the Years 1833, 1834, and 1835*. Philadelphia, PA: Lea & Blanchard, 1836.

Preble, George Henry. *Origin and History of the American Flag*. Philadelphia: Nicholas L. Brown, 1917.

Reck, W. Emerson. *A. Lincoln. His Last 24 Hours*. Jefferson, NC: McFarland & Co. 1987.

Reynolds, David S. *Walt Whitman's America. A Cultural Biography*. New York: Vintage Books, 1996.

Rhodehamel, John and Taper, Louise (eds.). *"Right or Wrong, God Judge Me": The Writings of John Wilkes Booth*. Urbana, IL: University of Illinois Press, 1997.

Rhodes, James Ford. *History of the United States*. New York: Macmillan Company, 1906.

Richter, William L. *Sic Semper Tyrannis. Why John Wilkes Booth Shot Abraham Lincoln*. Bloomington, IN: iUniverse, 2008.

Richter, William L. and Smith, J. E. "Rick" III. *The Last Shot. Essays on Civil War Politics, the Demise of John Wilkes Booth, and the Republican Myth of the Assassinated Lincoln*. Tucson, AZ: Wheatmark, 2016.

Rinear, D. L. *Stage, Page, Scandals and Vandals: William E. Burton and Nineteenth-Century*. Carbondale, IL: Southern Illinois University, 2004.

Rosengarten, Theodore and Rosengarten, Dale (eds.). *A Portion of the People. Three Hundred Years of Southern Jewish Life*. Charleston, SC: University of South Carolina Press, 2002.

Rogers, William Warren. *Confederate Home Front: Montgomery During the Civil War.* Tuscaloosa, AL: University Alabama Press, 2001.

Ruggles, Eleanor. *Prince of Players.* New York: W. W. North & Co., 1953.

Saitoh, Saturo, Steinglass, Peter, and Schuckit, Marc A. (eds.). *Alcoholism And the Family.* New York: Brunn/Mazel, Inc., 1992.

Samples, Gordon. *Lust for Fame: The Stage Career of John Wilkes Booth.* Jefferson, NC: McFarland & Co., 1982.

Sandburg, Carl. *The War Years.* New York: Charles Scribner's Sons, 1940.

Schacter, Daniel L. *Searching for Memory—the brain, the mind, and the past.* New York: Basic Books, 1996.

Schultz, Duane. *The Dahlgren Affair: Terror and Conspiracy in the Civil War.* New York: W. W. Norton & Co., 1998.

Seward, Frederick W. *Reminiscences of A War-Time Statesman and Diplomat, 1830-1915.* New York: G. P. Putnam's Sons, 1916.

Shattuck, Charles H. *The Hamlet of Edwin Booth.* Urbana, IL: University of Illinois Press, 1969.

Sheads, Scott Sumpter and Toomey, Daniel Carroll. *Baltimore During The Civil War.* Linthicum, MD: Toomey Press, 2008.

Shelton, Vaughan. *Mask For Treason. The Lincoln Murder Trial.* Harrisburg, PA: Stackpole Books, 1965.

Sherman, Robert L. *Chicago Stage. Its Records and Achievements.* Chicago: Robert L. Sherman, 1947.

Simon, John Y. (ed.). *The Papers of Ulysses S. Grant.* Carbondale and Edwardsville: Southern Illinois University Press, 1991.

———. *The Personal Memoirs of Julia Dent Grant.* New York: G. P. Putnam's Sons, 1975.

Sinclair, Mick. *San Francisco: A Cultural and Literary History.* Oxford, UK: Signal Books, 2014.

Slout, William L. *Burn Cork and Tambourines: A Sourcebook of Negro Minstrelsy.* Rockville, MD: Borgo Press, 2007.

————. *Olympians of the Sawdust Circle: A Biographic Dictionary of the 19th Century American Circus.* San Bernadino, CA: Borgo Press, 1998.

————. *Popular Amusements in Horse and Buggy America.* San Bernardino, CA: Borgo Press, 1995.

Smith, Gene. *American Gothic. The Story of America's Legendary Theatrical Family—Junius, Edwin, and John Wilkes Booth.* New York: Simon & Schuster, 1992.

Stabler, Jane. *The Palgrave Macmillan Burke to Byron, Barbauld to Baillie, 1790-1830.* Baskingstroke, UK: Palgrave Macmillan, 2001.

Steers, Edward Jr. *Blood On The Moon.* Lexington, KY: University Press of Kentucky, 2001.

————. *Lincoln Legends: Myths, Hoaxes, and Confabulations Associated with Our Greatest President.* Lexington, KY: University of Kentucky Press, 2007.

————. *The Trial. The Assassination of President Lincoln and the Trial of the Conspirators.* Lexington, KY, University of Kentucky Press, 2003.

Stewart, John. *The Acrobat: Arthur Barnes and the Victorian Circus.* Jefferson, NC: McFarland & Co., 2012.

Stone, Henry Dickinson. *Personal Recollections of the Drama: Or Theatrical Reminiscences Embracing Sketches of Prominent Actors and Actresses, Their Chief Characteristics, Original Anecdotes of Them, and Incidents Connected Therewith.* Albany, NY: Charles Van Benthuysen & Sons, 1873.

Surratt, John H. *Trial of John H. Surratt In The Criminal Court for the District of Columbia,* 2 vols. Washington, D.C.: French & Richardson, 1867.

Thompson, Lloyd. *Syphilis.* Philadelphia: Lea & Febiger, 1920.

Tidwell, William A., Hall, James O. and Gaddy, David Winfred. *Come Retribution: The Confederate Secret Service and the Assassination of Lincoln*. Jackson, MS: University of Mississippi Press, 1988.

Tindal William. *Standard History of the City of Washington from a Study of the Original Sources*. Knoxville, TN: H. W. Crew & Co., 1914.

Titone, Nora. *My Thoughts Be Bloody*. New York: Free Press, 2010.

Townsend, George Alfred. *The Life, Crime and Capture of John Wilkes Booth*. New York: Dick & Fitzgerald, 1865.

Towse, John Ranken. *Sixty Years of the Theatre: An Old Critic's Memories*. New York: Funk & Wagnalls, 1916.

Trefousse, Hans L. *Andrew Johnson: A Biography*. New York: W. W. Norton & Co., 1997.

Turner, Thomas Reed. *Beware the People Weeping. Public Opinion and the Assassination of Abraham Lincoln*. Baton Rouge, LA: Louisiana State University Press, 1991.

Vann Woodward, C. and Muhlenfeld, Elizabeth (eds.). *The Private Mary Chestnut: The Unpublished Civil War Diaries*. New York: Oxford University Press, 1984.

Vidal, A. *A Treatise on Venereal Disease*. New York: Samuel S. and William Wood, 1854.

Ware, Frederick. *Fifty Years of Make Believe*. New York: International Press, 1920.

Weichmann, Louis J. *A True History Of The Assassination Of Abraham Lincoln And Of The Conspiracy Of 1865*. New York: Alfred A. Knopf, 1975.

Wemyss, Francis Courtney. *Wemyss' Chronology of the American Stage, from 1752 to 1852*. New York: Wm. Taylor & Co., 1852.

Weston, Effie Ellsler (ed.). *The Stage Memories of John A. Ellsler*. Cleveland: Rowfant Club, 1950.

White, G. Edward. *Justice Oliver Wendell Holmes. Law and the Inner Self.* New York: Oxford University Press, 1993.

Wilson, Dall. *Alice Nielsen and Gayety of Nations: Standing Room Only.* New York: Dall Wilson, 2008.

Wilson, Douglas L. *Honor's Voice: The Transformation of Abraham Lincoln.* New York: Alfred A. Knopf, 1998.

Wilson, Douglas L. and Davis, Rodney O. *Herndon's Informants.* Urbana, IL: University of Illinois Press, 1997.

Wilson, Francis. *Francis Wilson's Life of Himself.* Boston: Houghton Mifflin Co., 1924.

———. *John Wilkes Booth. Fact and Fiction of Lincoln's Assassination.* Boston: Houghton Mifflin, 1929.

Winter, William. *Vagrant Memories. Being Further Recollections Of Other Days.* New York: George H. Doran Co., 1915.

———. *Shadows of the Stage.* London: McMillan & Co., 1893.

Winton, James. *Drury Land Journal: Selections from James Winston's Diaries.* London: The Society For Theatre Research, 1974.

Winslow, Catherine (Kate) Mary Reignolds. *Yesterdays with Actors.* Boston: Cupples and Hurd, 1887.

Witham, Barry B. (ed.). *Theatre in the United States. A Documentary History. 1750-1915. Theatre in the Colonies and the United States.* New York: Cambridge University Press, 2009.

Woo, Celestine. *Romantic Actors and Bardolatry: Performing Shakespeare from Garrick to Kean.* New York: Peter Lang, 2008.

Woods, John W. *Woods' Baltimore City Directory.* Baltimore: John Woods, 1870.

Wooster, Louise C. *The Autobiography of a Magdalen.* Birmingham, AL: Birmingham Publishing Co., 1911.

# CHAPTERS

Adams, Herbert Adams, "John Wilkes Booth Won Hearts in Portland," in: Donald W. Beattie, Rodney M. Cole., and Charles G. Waugh (eds.). *A Distant War Comes Home*. Camden, ME: Down East Books, 1991, 35–38.

Booth, Edwin. "Some Words About My Father," in: Brander Matthews and Laurence Hutton (eds.). *Actors and Actresses of Great Britain and the United States*, vol. 3. New York: Cassell & Co., 1886, 95.

Chaconas, Joan L. "John H. Surratt Jr.," in: Edward Steers Jr. (ed.). *The Trial. The Assassination of President Lincoln and the Trial of the Conspirators*. Lexington, KY: University Press Of Kentucky, 2003, LX–LXV.

Johnson, Claudia D. "Enter the Harlot," in: Helen Krich Chinoy and Linda Walsh Henkins (eds.). *Women In American Theatre*. New York: Theatre Communications Group, 1987, 66–73.

Seifert, Donna J. "Mrs. Starr's Profession," in: Charles F. Orser (ed.). *Images of Archeology the Recent Past: Readings in Historical*. Lanham, MD: AltaMira Press, 1996.

Verge, Laurie. "Mary Elizabeth Surratt," in: Edward Steers Jr. (ed.). *The Trial. The Assassination of Present Lincoln and the Trial of the Conspirators*. Lexington, KY: University Press of Kentucky, 2003, LII–LIX.

# THESES AND DISSERTATIONS

Brooks, Mona Rebecca. *The Development Of American Theatre Management Practices Between 1830 and 1896*. PhD Thesis, Department of Fine Arts, Texas Tech University, 1981.

Fuller, Charles F. Jr. *Kunkel and Company at the Marshall Theatre, Richmond, Virginia, 1856-1861*. MA Thesis, Ohio University, 1968.

Herbstruth, Grant M. *Benedict DeBar and the Grand Opera House in St. Louis, Missouri, from 1855 to 1879*. PhD Thesis, Department of Speech and Drama, University of Iowa, 1954.

Hicks, Terri L. *Oak Hill Cemetery: A Reflection of Early Birmingham 1871-1913*. MA Thesis, University of Alabama, Birmingham, Alabama, 2013.

Kincaid, Deidre Lindsay. *Rough Magic: the theatrical Life of John Wilkes Booth*. PhD Thesis, University of Hull, 2000.

Roman, Lisbeth Jane. *The Acting Style and Career Of Junius Brutus Booth*. PhD Thesis, University of Illinois, 1968.

Sollers, John Ford. *The Theatrical Career of John T. Ford*. PhD Thesis, Department of Speech and Drama, Stanford University, 1962.

Squires, Melinda Jayne. *The Controversial Career Of George Nicholas Sanders*. MA Thesis, Western Kentucky University, Bowling Green, Kentucky, 2000.

Sullivan, Leslie Noelle. *On the Western Stage: Theatre in Montana, 1880-1920*. MA Thesis, University of New Mexico, August, 1990.

# PERIODICALS/ CONFERENCE PRESENTATIONS/ MISCELLANEOUS

Abel, E. Lawrence. "Cloak and Dagger," *America's Civil War*, 4 (January 1992), 30–37.

Alford, Terry. "Alexander Hunter and the Bessie Hale Story," *Alexandria History*, 8 (1990), 5–15.

Alfriend, Edward M. "Assassin Booth," *Washington Sunday Globe*, (February 9, 1902), 2.

———. "Recollections of John Wilkes Booth," *The Era*, 8 (October 1901), 604.

Anonymous. "Report of the Committee of the City Council of Charleston," *American Journal of Medical Sciences*, 38 (October 1859), 509–511.

Badeau, Adam. "Dramatic Reminiscences," *St. Paul and Minneapolis Pioneer Press*, (February 20, 1887), 57.

———. "Edwin Booth. On And Off The Stage. Personal Recollections," *McClure's Magazine*, 1 (June–November 1893), 253–267.

Barber, Deirdre. "A man of Promise. John Wilkes Booth at Richmond, 1858-1860," *Journal of the South Eastern Theatre Conference*, 2 (1994), 113–129, 114.

Barber, Susan and Ritter, Charles F. "Dangerous Liaisons: Working Women and Sexual Justice in the American Civil War," *European Journal of American Studies*, 10 (2015), 2–19.

Barker, Kathleen. "Better than Fiction," *Theatre Research*, 10 (1969), 86–88.

Barron, John M. "An Actor's Memories Of Richmond Befo' the War," The *Sun* (Baltimore, MD), (January 20, 1907), 15.

———. "John Wilkes Booth, Some Recollections of Him By an Early Virginia Acquaintance," *New York Daily People*, (December 8, 1901), 3.

———. "The Stage Before the War," The *Sun* (Baltimore, MD), (November 4, 1906), 14.

Beale, Mary Bella. "Wilkes Booth's Ring," *Atlanta Constitution*, (December 31, 1887), 4.

Bluff, Olney. "The Presidential Assassins," *Chicago Daily Tribune*, (November 23), 9.

Booth, Edwin. "The Real Edwin Booth," *Literary Digest*, 9 (October 1894), 11–12.

Brennan, John C. "John Wilkes Booth's Enigmatic Brother Joseph," *Maryland Historical Magazine*, 7 (Spring 1983), 22–34.

Brooks, Ralph. "Insane or Ill," *Surratt Courier*, 22 (August, 1997), 9.

Burns, Shirley. "Diminutive Players," *The Green Book Magazine*, 3 (March, 1910), 577–582.

Bullard, F. Lauriston. "Boston's Part in Lincoln's Death," *Boson Sunday Herald*, (April 11, 1915), 19.

Burr, F. A. "Junius Brutus Booth's Wife Adelaide," *New York Press*, (August 9, 1891), 19.

Bushman, Brad. J. and Baumeister, Roy F. "Threatened egotism, narcissism, self-esteem, and direct and displaced aggression: Does self-love or self-hate lead to violence?" *Journal of Personality and Social Psychology*, 75 (July 1998), 219–229.

Carson, William G. B. "Bumping over the Road in the 70s," *Educational Theatre Journal*, 10 (October 1958), 203–210.

Caskie, Robert. "A reminiscence of John Wilkes Booth," *Texas Siftings*, (August 4, 1883), 56.

Cather, Willa. "With Plays and Players," (Lincoln) *Nebraska State Journal*, (March 11, 1894), 13.

Coleman, Diana, McPhee, Stephen, Ross, Thomas, and Naughton, James. "Secondary syphilis with pulmonary involvement," *Western Journal of Medicine*, 138 (1983), 875–878.

Daffron, Polly. "George Libby Recalls Incidents of the War Between the States," *Times Dispatch*, (July 7, 1929), 9.

Davis, Kingsley. "Illegitimacy and the social structure," *American Journal of Sociology*, (September 1939), 215–233.

Deery, John. "The Last of Wilkes Booth," *New York Sunday Telegram*, (May 23, 1909).

Duggan, W. Dennis. "The President Is Dead," *Albany County Bar Newsletter*, (February 2010), 5.

Dumont, Frank. "The Golden Days of Minstrelsy," *New York Clipper*, (December 19, 1914).

Emerson, E. A. "How John Wilkes Booth's Friend Described His Crime," *Literary Digest*, 88 (March 6, 1926), 58.

Faber, Dinah. "Joseph and Ann Hall: Behind the Scenes at Tudor Hall," *Harford Historical Bulletin*, No. 104 (Fall 2006), 3–64.

Ferguson, William. "Actor Describes Slaying of Lincoln," The *Sun* (Baltimore, MD), (February 12, 1926), 22.

———. "I saw Lincoln Shot," *Saturday Evening Post*, (February 12, 1927), 42.

Freedman, L. Z. "Assassination: Psychopathology and Social Pathology," *Postgraduate Medicine*, 37 (June 1965), 650–658.

Fox, Dorothy. "Childhood Home of an American Arch Villain," *Civil War Times Illustrated*, 29 (March–April 1990), 11–13.

Grover, Leonard. "Lincoln's Interest in the Theater," *Century Magazine*, 77 (April 1909), 943–949.

Haden, Sara C. and Scarpa, Angela. "Childhood Animal Cruelty: A Review of Research, Assessment, and Therapeutic Issues," *The Forensic Examiner*, 14 (2005), 23–33.

Hawk, Harry, "Lincoln Assassination," *Illinois State Register*, (April 16, 1901), 3.

Hastings, D. W. "The Psychiatry of Presidential Assassination, Part I: Jackson and Lincoln," *Lancet*, 85 (March 1965), 95–100; "The Psychiatry of Presidential Assassination, Part II: Garfield and Roosevelts," *Lancet*, 85 (April 1965): 157–162.

Head, Constance. "The Booth Sisters of Bel Air," *Lincoln Herald*, (Winter 1981), 759–764.

Herne, James A. "Old Stock Days in the Theatre," *The Arena*, 34 (September 1892), 401–416.

H. H. A. "A Society Belle's Fate," *Chicago Tribune*, (March 8, 1885), 12.

Hodder, Frank Heywood. "The John Brown Pikes," *Kansas Historical Quarterly*, 2 (November 1933), 386–390.

Holding, Charles E. "John Wilkes Booth Stars in Nashville," *Tennessee Historical Quarterly*, 23 (1964), 73–79.

Holt, Judge Advocate General. "Mrs. Surratt. Who was Responsible for Her Death," *Chicago Sunday Times*, (August 31, 1873), 4.

Houmes, Blaine V. "Lincoln & Booth: A Love Story?" *Manuscripts, 59* (Winter 2007), 5–11.

———. "Mr. Seward's Orderly," *Surratt Courier*, 39 (February 2014), 3–9.

Howell, William A. "Memories of Wilkes Booth. An Old Associates Recollections of the Trying Days of '60 and '61," The *Sun* (Baltimore, MD), (November 23, 1899), 3.

Jay, Cheryl Jay. "Treatment of Neurosyphilis," *Current Treatment Options in Neurology*, 8 (2006), 185–192.

Johnson, Ludwell H. "Beverley Tucker's Canadian Mission, 1864-1866," *Journal of Southern History*, 29 (February 1963), 88–99.

Jones, James P. and Rogers, William Warren. "Montgomery as the Confederate Capital; View of a New Nation," *Alabama Historical Quarterly*, 26 (Spring 1964), 1–125; (February 13, 1861), 25–26.

Kauffman, Michael. "The Confederate Plan to Abduct President Lincoln," *Surratt Courier*, (March 1981), 1–6.

Kellogg, A. O. "Junius Brutus Booth," *The Journal of Mental Science*, 14 (July 1868), 280–281.

Kincaid, Deidre Barber. "Mary Ann Doolittle? The 'Flower Girl' Myth Of The Booth's Mother," *Surratt Courier*, 19 (March 2004), 3–5.

King, Emmett C. "What Becomes of Old Actors," *Indiana (PA) Democrat*, (September 13, 1911), 1.

Krone, Charles A. "Recollections of an Old Actor," *Missouri Historical Society Collections,* 4 (1913), 323–351.

Levine, Peter. "Draft evasion in the North During the Civil War, 1863-1865," *Journal of American History*, 67 (1981), 816–834.

Lewis, James. "The Representative Comedian—Sketch of his wanderings and Recognition," *New York Daily Graphic*, (June 12, 1875), 11.

Libby, George W. "John Brown and John Wilkes Booth," *Confederate Veteran*, (1930), 138.

Loftus, Elizabeth F. and Pickrell, Jacqueline E. "The Formation of False Memories," *Psychiatric Annals*, 25 (1995), 102–113.

Louthan, Henry T. "A Proposed Abduction Of Lincoln," *Confederate Veteran*, 11 (April 1903), 157.

Lowry, Thomas P. "John Wilkes Booth's spurned lover slashed him with a knife and nearly changed the course of history," *America's Civil War*, 20 (November 2007), 23–24.

MacCulloch, Campbell. "This Man Saw Lincoln Shot," *Good Housekeeping*, 84 (February 1927), 20–21, 112, 115–116, 121–122.

Maldonado, Solangel. "Illegitimate Harm: Law, Stigma and Discrimination Against Nonmarital Children," *Florida Law Review*, 63 (2011), 345.

Matthews, J. Brander, "Actors and Actresses of New York," *Scribner's Monthly*, 17 (April 1879), 769–784.

May, John Frederick. "Mark of the Scalpel," *Records of the Columbia Historical Society*, 13 (1910), 53.

Mayflower. "Letter from Boston," dated April 22, 1865, *Sacramento Daily Union*, May 20, 1865, 1; "Letter from Boston," *Sacramento Daily Union*, June 2, 1865; "Letter from Boston," dated September 16, 1865, *Sacramento Daily Union*, October 10, 1865, 3; "Letter from Boston," dated November 6, 1865, December 4, 1865, 1.

McCann, Walter Edgar. "The Booth Family In Maryland," *The American Magazine*, 17 (January–June 1884), 404–410, 407.

Merritt, Russell. "Rescued from a Perilous Nest: D. W. Griffith's Escape from Theatre into Film," *Cinema Journal*, 21 (1981), 2–30.

Miller, Chuck Miller. "See John Wilkes Booth performing in an Albany Theatre," *Albany Times Union*, (September 21, 2009).

Mooney, Elizabeth C. "There's no escaping history on John Wilkes," *Chicago Tribune*, (May 11, 1984), K20.

Morcom, Richmond. "They All Loved Lucy," *American Heritage*, (October 1970), 12–15.

Morrison, Angus. "Analysis of One Hundred Cases of Neurosyphilis," *American Journal of Syphilis*, 4 (July 1920), 552–559, 556.

Moss, M. Helen Palmes. "Lincoln and Wilkes Booth as seen on the day of the Assassination," *Century Magazine*, 77 (April 1909), 951.

Napier, Lt. Col. John H. "Martial Montgomery," *Alabama Historical Quarterly*, (Fall–Winter 1967), 107–131,

Norcross, A. F. "A Child's Memory of the Boston Theatre," *The Theatre: A Monthly Review Of Drama, Music, and the Fine Arts,* 10 (May 1926), 37–38.

Norton, Roger. "What If the Lincolns Had Attended The Play At Grover's Theatre?" *Surratt Courier*, 36 (March 2011), 3–4.

O'Brien, Frank P. "Passing of the Old Montgomery Theatre," *Montgomery Advertiser*, (November 24, 1907), 6.

O'Donnell, Judith and Emery, Christopher. "Neurosyphilis," *Current Infectious Disease Reports*, 7 (2005), 277–294.

Owens, Patria Ann. "Review," *Illinois Historical Journal*, 90 (Winter 1997), 286.

Pinchbeck, I. "Social Attitudes to the Problem of Illegitimacy," *British Journal of Sociology*, 5 (December 1954), 309–323.

Rankin, Mrs. McKee (Kitty Blanchard). "The News Of Lincoln's Death," *The American Magazine*, 67 (January 1909), 261–263.

Richter, William L. "'My Policy is to Have No Policy': Abraham Lincoln and the Reconstruction of Our Nation," Surratt Society Conference, March 31–April 2, 2017.

Robson, Stuart. "Memories Of Fifty Years," *Everybody's Magazine*, 3 (July 1900), 86–91.

Rosebery, C. R. "Actor Checks Into Hotel in Albany," *Albany Times-Union*, (April 12, 1965), 18.

Sears, Stephen. "Raid on Richmond," *MHQ: The Quarterly Journal of Military History*, 11 (Autumn 1998), 88–96.

Sedly, Henry. "The Booths—Father and Some Personal Reminiscences," *Harper's Weekly*, 37 (November 1893), 1082.

Shepherd, William G. "They tried to Stop Booth," *Collier's, The National Weekly*, (December 27, 1924).

Shettel, James W. "J. Wilkes Booth At School. Recollections of a Retired Army Officer Who Knew Him then," *The New York Dramatic Mirror*, (February 26, 1916), 1, 5.

Sher, Kenneth J. "Psychological Characteristics of Children of Alcoholics," *Alcohol Health & Research World*, 21 (1997), 247–254.

Simpson, J. Palgrave. "The Poor (Walking) Gentleman," *The Theatre: A Monthly Review Of Drama, Music, and the Fine Arts*, 1 (May 1880), 269–273.

Sizer, Lyde C. "Review," *North Carolina Historical Review*, 74 (July 1997), 349–350.

Sloan, Richard. "John Wilkes Booth's Other Victim," *American Heritage*, 42 (February–March 1991), 114–116.

Snider, Si. "Eyewitness of Lincoln's assassination Live Her," *Los Angeles Times*, (February 11, 1923), 9–10.

Stashower, Daniel. "Lincoln Must Die," *Smithsonian Magazine*, 43 (February 2013), 74–89.

Steers, Edward Jr. "Historical Malpractice," *Surratt Courier*, 22 (October 1997), 7.

Stout, George. "Knew The Booths in Boyhood Days," *Baltimore American*, (July 27, 1903), 13 Surratt, John H. "The Rockville Lecture," December 6, 1870, reprinted in: Louis J. Weichmann. *A True History Of The Assassination Of Abraham Lincoln And Of The Conspiracy Of 1865*. New York: Alfred A. Knopf, 1975.

Thomases, Sander, Bushman, Brad J., Stegge, Hedy, and Olthof, Tjeert. "Trumping Shame by Blasts of Noise; Narcissism, Self-esteem, Shame, and Aggression in Young Adolescents," *Child Development*, 79 (November–December 2008), 1792–1801.

Tinsley, Henry G. "Last of John Brown's Harper Ferry Guards." *San Francisco Chronicle*, (March 21, 1897), 16.

Thomas Turner. "Review," *Journal of the Abraham Lincoln Association*, 20 (Summer 1999), 80–89.

Townsend, George Alfred. "How John Wilkes Booth was Started in the Theatrical Profession," *Cincinnati Enquirer*, (January 19, 1886), 1.

U.S. Congress. House of Representatives. Judiciary Committee. *Impeachment Investigation*. 39th Cong., 2d sess.; 40th Cong., 1st sess., H. Rep. No. 7, Washington, D.C. Government Printing Office, 1867.

Verdi, T. S. "The Assassination Of the Sewards," *Republic: A Monthly Magazine, Devoted to the Dissemination of Political Information*, 1 (July 1873), 289 –297.

Wallace, Charles. "Richmond in by gone days," *Richmond Dispatch*, (June 24, 1906), 36.

Weaver, Henry A. "NO. 2 Bullfinch Place," *Chicago Daily Inter-Ocean*, (August 27, 1893), 22.

Weik, Jesse. "A New Story of Lincoln's Assassination. An Unpublished Record of an Eye Witness," *The Century Magazine*, 135 (February 1913), 559–562.

Weisz, A. E. and Taylor, R. L. "American Presidential Assassinations," *Diseases of the Nervous System*, 30 (October 1969), 658–659.

Weissman, P. "Why Booth Shot Lincoln," *Psychoanalysis and the Social Sciences*, 5 (1958), 99–115.

Whiting, Frank M. "Theatrical Personalities of Old St. Paul," *Minnesota History*, 23 (December 1942), 305–315.

Wilson, G. W. "John Wilkes Booth: Father Murderer," *The American IMAGO*, 1 (June 1940), 49–60.

Wolf, Rennold. "The Little Father of the Chorus Girl," *The Green Book Magazine*, 9 (February 1913), 281–291.

Wren, Fred R. "Edwin Booth," *New Orleans Times Picayune*, (July 14, 1907), 10.

Wren, George. "A shot that wasn't fired," *Boston Weekly Globe*, (April 13, 1880), 6.

Wyndham, Charles. "John Wilkes Booth. An Interview with the Press with Sir Charles Wyndham," *New York Herald*, (June 27, 1909), Magazine Section, 2.

Young, James. "Pictures Of the Booth Family," *New York Times*, (July 14, 1896), 12.

# NEWSPAPERS

*Albany County Bar Newsletter*

*Albany Evening Journal*

*Albany Times-Union*

*American and Commercial Advertiser* (Baltimore, MD)

*Argus* (Melbourne, AU)

*Atlanta Constitution*

*Atlas & Argus* (Albany, NY)

*Auburn (NY) Bulletin*

*Baltimore Daily Dispatch*

*Baltimore Daily Exchange*

*Boston Daily Atlas*

*Boston Daily Bee*

*Boston Daily Globe*

*Boston Evening Transcript*

*Boston Herald*

*Boston Post*

*Boston Traveller*

*Brooklyn Daily Eagle*

*Buffalo Daily Courier*

*Cass County Republican*

*Charleston Mercury*

*Chicago Evening Journal*

*Chicago Press and Tribune*

*Chicago Tribune*

*Cincinnati Daily Enquirer*

*Cincinnati Daily Gazette*

*Cincinnati Daily Press*

*Coldwater (MI) Sentinel*

*Columbus (GA) Daily Sun*

*Commercial Tribune* (Cincinnati, OH)

*Courier-Journal* (Louisville, KY)

*Daily Alta California* (San Francisco, CA)

*Daily Argus* (Rock Island, IL)

*Daily Commercial Register* (Sandusky, OH)

*Daily Courier* (Louisville, KY)

*Daily Creole* (New Orleans, LA)

*Daily Crescent* (New Orleans, LA)

*Daily Critic* (Washington, D.C.)

*Daily Dispatch* (Richmond, VA)

*Daily Empire* (Dayton, OH)

*Daily Evening Transcript* (Boston, MA)

*Daily Gazette* (Cincinnati, OH)

*Daily Gazette and Comet* (Baton Rouge, LA)

*Daily Graphic* (New York City, NY)

*Daily Intelligencer* (Wheeling, WV)

*Daily Missouri Democrat* (St. Louis, MO)

*Daily National Intelligencer* (Washington, D.C.)

*Daily Ohio Statesman* (Columbus, OH)

*Daily People* (New York City, NY)

*Daily Register* (New Haven, CT)

*Daily Richmond (VA) Whig*

*Daily Sun* (Columbus, GA)

*Daily True Delta* (New Orleans, LA)

*De Bow's Review* (New Orleans, LA)

*Denver Post*

*Detroit Free Press*

*Enquirer* (Richmond, VA)

*Evening Argus* (Rock Island, IL)

*Evening Public Ledger* (Philadelphia, PA)

*Evening Star* (Washington, D.C.)

*Evening Telegraph* (Philadelphia, PA)

*Evening Times* (Trenton, NJ)

*Greencastle (IN) Banner*

*Hartford (CT) Daily Courant*

*Indiana (PA) Democrat*

*Irish Times and Daily Advertiser*

*Kansas City (MO) Star*

*Kowee Courier* (Pickens Court House, SC)

*Labor World* (Duluth, MN)

*Louisville Daily Courier*

*Madison (IN) Courier*

*Marysville (CA) Daily Appeal*

*Massachusetts Spy* (Worcester, MA)

*Miami Herald*

*Milwaukee Sentinel*

*Minnesotian* (St. Paul, MN)

*Mobile Register and Advertiser*

*Montgomery (AL) Advertiser*

*Morning Herald* (St. Joseph, MO)

*Nebraska State Journal* (Lincoln, NE)

*New Era Valley Falls* (Valley Falls, KS)

*New York Clipper*

*New York Dramatic Mirror*

*New York Herald*

*New York Mirror*

*New York Sunday Mercury*

*New York Times*

*New York Tribune*

*News-Tribune* (Duluth, MN)

*Newark (NJ) Daily Advertiser*

*Plain Dealer* (Cleveland, OH)

*Portland (OR) Oregonian*

*Pomeroy's Democrat* (Chicago, IL)

*Post* (Virginia City, MT)

*Poughkeepsie (NY) Eagle-News*

*Philadelphia Inquirer*

*Pittsburgh Daily Post*

*Press* (Philadelphia, PA)

*Providence (RI) Daily Post*

*Providence (RI) Evening Press*

*Public Ledger* (Philadelphia, PA)

*Raleigh (NC) News*

*Register* (Mobile, AL)

*Richmond (VA) Enquirer*

*Richmond (VA) Whig*

*Rochester (NY) Evening Express*

*Rochester (NY) Union and Advertiser*

*Rock Island (IL) Argus*

*Rockford (IL) Daily Register*

*Sacramento Daily Union*

*San Francisco Bulletin*

*San Francisco Chronicle*

*Saturday Evening Express* (Boston, MA)

*Saturday Evening Gazette* (Boston, MA)

*Siftings* (Austin, TX)

*Southern Aegis* (Bel Air, MD)

*Springfield (MA) Republican*

*States* (Washington, D.C.)

*Sunday Globe* (Washington, D.C.)

The *Brooklyn Magazine*

The *Labor World*

The *Observer* (London, England)

The *Scotsman* (Edinburgh, Scotland)

The *Spirit of the Times*

The *Sporting Life*

The *Sun* (Baltimore, MD)

The *Sun* (New York City, NY)

The *Times* (Washington, D.C.)

The *World* (New York City, NY)

*Times* (Reading, PA)

*Times-Democrat* (New Orleans, LA)

*Times-Picayune* (New Orleans, LA)

*Toronto Globe*

*Troy (NY) Daily Times*

*Utah Daily Reporter* (Corrine, UT)

*Washington (DC) Herald*

*Washington Post*

*Washington (WA) Standard*

*Washington Star*

*Watertown (NY) Daily Times*

*Weekly Post* (Montgomery, AL)

*Wheeling (VA) Daily Intelligencer*

*Wilkes-Barre (PA) Times*

*Wilmington (DE) Journal*

*Yorkville (SC) Enquirer*

# INTERNET SITES

Alabama Secession Banner of 1861, February 10, 2012, http://www.crwflags.com/fotw/flags/us-alsec.html#disc.

Advertisement for *Mazeppa*'s San Francisco Performances, http://bancroft.berkeley.edu/Exhibits/mtwest/sf_admazeppa.html.

BoothieBarn, "Alice Gray: Successful Partnerships," February 9, 2016, https://boothiebarn.com/2016/02/09/alice-gray-successful-partnerships/.

BoothieBarn, "John Wilkes Booth's Poetic Envelope," March 5, 2015, https://boothiebarn.com/2015/03/05/john-wilkes-booths-poetic-envelope/.

BoothieBarn, "John Wilkes Booth's 'Mysterious Beauty'," January 11, 2016, https://boothiebarn.com/2016/01/11/john-wilkes-booths-mysterious-beauty/.

Bryant, Joseph D., "Early Birmingham madam who saved sick will have scrapbook in history center," August 20, 2012, http://blog.al.com/spotnews/2012/08/early_birmingham_madam_who_sav.html.

Gasbarro, Norman, "William Withers Jr.—Lincoln Assassination Witness," May 26, 2012, http://civilwar.gratzpa.org/2012/05/william-withers-jr-lincoln-assassination-witness/.

Greater Birmingham Convention & Visitors Bureau, "Tourists Dig Birmingham Cemeteries," October 27, 2015, http://birminghamal.org/2015/10/tourists-dig-birmingham-cemeteries/.

Groves, Barry, "William Banting Father of the Low-Carbohydrate Diet," April 30, 2003, http://www.westonaprice.org/know-your-fats/william-banting-father-of-the-low-carbohydrate-diet/.

Jimmerson, Ellin Sterne, "Louise Wooster," Encyclopedia of Alabama, November 19, 2008, http://www.encyclopediaofalabama.org/article/h-1862.

Lueger, Michael, "An Episode of Syphilis-Shaming Shows How Cruel Early-20th-Century Celebrity Gossip Could Be," January 8, 2016, http://www.slate.com/blogs/the_vault/2016/01/08/the_cruelty_of_early_20th_century_celebrity_gossip_shown_in_a_record_mocking.html.

Missouri's Union Provost Marshal Papers: 1861-1866, November 9, 11, 1863, www.sos.mo.gov/archives/provost/results.asp?txtName=&txtKeyword=&radSearch=BEG&selCounty=Saint+Louis&offset=1875.

Penski, Ed, "Tudor Hall," http://juniusbooth.org/th.htm.

Sally, "New Lucy Lambert Hale pic," Lincoln Discussion Symposium, December 10, 2012, http://rogerjnorton.com/LincolnDiscussionSymposium/archive/index.php?thread-357-3.html.

Seratore, Angela, "The Curious Case of Nashville's Frail Sisterhood," Smithsonian, July 8, 2013, http://www.smithsonianmag.com/history/the-curious-case-of-nashvilles-frail-sisterhood-7766757/.

Taylor, David, "The Booth Children and Mary Ann's Acting Career," BoothieBarn, August 1, 2014, https://boothiebarn.com/2014/08/01/the-booth-children-and-mary-anns-acting-career/.

Taylor, David, "The Forgotten Daughter—Rosalie Ann Booth," BoothieBarn, November 25, 2013, https://boothiebarn.com/2013/11/25/the-forgotten-daughter-rosalie-ann-booth/.

University of Alabama at Birmingham School of Public Health, "Lou Wooster Public Health Hero Award," www.soph.uab.edu/nphw/WoosterAward.

University of Louisville, "Macauley's Theatre Collection," http://digital.library.louisville.edu/cdm/landingpage/collection/macauley/.

Whitlock, Philip, "The Life of Philip Whitlock, Written by himself," http://www.jewish-history.com/civilwar/philip_whitlock.html.

Watson, John, "Who Leaked Lucy's Name," Lincoln Assassination Forum, Jan 18, 2013, http://lincoln-assassination.com/bboard/index.php?topic=2267.0;wap2.

# INDEX

## A

Abbott, Charles, 289–91
Actor's Fund, 283
Actor's Fund Home, 257
Adams, Edwin, 48
Alabama River, 72
*Aladin and the Wonderful Lamp*,
   88, 186, 194
Albany, NY, 88–91, 93, 95, 97, 134,
   200, 280, 293
Albaugh, John, 69, 285–86
Aldrich, Thomas Baily, 230–31
Alford, Terry, 240, 246, 329
American Revolution, 15
Amsterdam, Netherlands, 5
Anacostia River, 209
Anderson, Frederick, 180
Anderson, Jean, 22, 47, 50, 66–67,
   100, 183, 232, 234, 247, 328

Andrews, Sally, 125, 191
Anglican, 8
*Antony and Cleopatra*, 275
*Apostate, The*, 88–89, 103, 109, 117,
   134, 172
*Apotheosis of Washington, The*, 254
Arch Street Theatre, 32–35, 37, 39,
   69, 95, 110, 234
Army of Northern Virginia, 193
Army of Tennessee, 121
Army of the Potomac River, 123,
   163
Arnold, Samuel Bland, 26, 157, 169,
   171–73, 202, 210, 325
Arriola, Fortunato, 269
Ashby, Turner, 51
*Atlantic*, the, 58
Atzerodt, George, 169, 171–72, 198–
   99, 202, 204–5, 210, 225, 325

Augusta, GA, 11, 115
Australia, 32, 49, 274
*Autobiography of a Magdalen*, 298

# B

Badeau, Adam, 66, 122–25, 228
Bainbridge, A. R., 214–15
Baker, Lafayette C., 218
Baker, Luther, 215–16, 218–19
Baltimore Cemetery, 238
*Baltimore Daily Exchange*, 263, 120
*Baltimore Sun*, 31, 44, 99, 120
Bangor, ME, 55
Barron, John, 37, 40, 44–45
Barrow, Julia Bennet, 125, 131
Barrymore, Ethel, 257
Bateman, Hezekiah, 73
Bateman, Kate, 73
Bates, Edwin, 312
"Battle Hymn of the Republic," 152
Battle of Cold Harbor, 161
Battle of the Wilderness, 161
Beale, Isabella Pallen, 38–39
Beale, James, Dr., 39
Beantown, MD, 210
Beecher, Henry Ward, 287
Bel Air, MD, 11, 13, 18, 24, 238,
    312
Belgium, 2–3
Bellows, Charles S., 311
Benjamin, Judah, 164
Bernhardt, Sarah, 305
Berrel, George, 44
Biddeford, ME, 268
Birch, Jesse, 185
Birmingham, AL, 297–99

Bisham, William, 66
Black Horse Militia, 51
Blackmar, Armand, 142
Blake, Rufus, 87
Blanchard, Kitty, 137, 285
"Bonny Blue Flag, The," 142
Booth, Adelaide Delannoy, 3–6, 8–9,
    16–18, 20, 22, 25
Booth, Blanche DeBar, 49, 54, 322
Booth, Clementina DeBar, 48–49,
    118
Booth, Joseph Adrian, 15, 319
Booth, Richard, 1–3, 12–13
Booth, Richard Junius, 5, 9, 16–18,
    20
Booth, Rosalie Ann, 12
Booth, Sally, 4
Booth, W. D., 234
*BoothieBarn*, 315
Bossieux, Louis, 50
*Boston Daily Advertiser*, 243
*Boston Evening Transcript*, 228
*Boston Herald*, 57–58, 129, 305
Boston Museum, 67, 100, 105, 109,
    117, 129, 138, 140, 149, 152, 321
*Boston Post*, 105, 273, 279
Boston Power Water Company, 110
Boston Theatre, 148
*Boston Traveller*, 245
Bournemouth, England, 239
Bowdoin High School, 295
Bowery Theatre, 42, 59, 118, 280
Braun, Walter, 145–48
Brighton, England, 4
Broadway Theatre, 87, 118, 264, 266
Brockton, MA, 291
*Brooklyn Daily Eagle*, 147, 248
Brooklyn, NY, 131, 279

Brown, Fanny, 127–32, 218, 273–77
Brown, John, 49, 51–53, 63–64, 71, 217
Brown, T. Allston, 127
Brumid, Constantino, 254
Brussels, Belgium, 3
Bryan, William Jennings, 294
Buckingham, John, 206
Buckley, Fred, 129, 274
Buckley's Serenaders, 129
*Buffalo Daily Courier*, 100
Buffalo, NY, 94, 100, 102, 117–18
Bunker, George, 202
Burns, John C., 189
Burrillville, RI, 312–14
Burroughs, Claud, 230
Burton, Walter, 187
Burton, William, 236–37
Burton's Chambers Street Theatre, 42
Burton's New Theatre, 129
Butler, Benjamin "Beast," 142
Byron, George Gordon, Lord, 7–8, 28

C

Cairo, IL, 143
Cambridge, MA, 138
Campbell General Hospital, 172
Canada, 59, 164–65, 210
Canavan, Kathryn, 322
Canning, Matthew W., 69–73, 111–12
Canterbury, CT, 312
Cary, Emma, 233
Catholic, 3, 27

Catholic Church, 3
Catonsville, MD, 26
Cawood, Charles H., 164
*Century*, 305
Chandler, William, 178–79, 248, 250–51
Chapman, Blanche, 236–37
Charles Street Theatre, 31–32
Charles Town, WV, 49–51
*Charleston Mercury*, 49
Charleston, SC, 11, 84, 92, 119
Chattahoochee River, 71
Chesnut, James, 84
Chesnut, Mary, 84
Chester, Samuel Knapp, 69, 169, 174, 182, 246, 322
Chestnut Street Theatre, 132, 266, 269
Chiarini Circus, 274
*Chicago Daily Inter-Ocean*, 248–49
*Chicago Daily Tribune*, 248–50, 291
*Chicago Times*, 298
Christendom, 193
Christmas, 90, 169
*Cincinnati Commercial Tribune*, 261
*Cincinnati Daily Commercial*, 100
*Cincinnati Daily Enquirer*, 93–94, 147, 244
*Cincinnati Daily Gazette*, 59
*Cincinnati Daily Press*, 82
*Cinderella*, 129
Clare, Ada, 130
Clarke, John Sleeper, 31–32, 34, 47, 115, 130, 156–57, 227–29, 231–34, 239, 254

Cleveland, OH, xxiii, 43, 121, 134, 288, 303–4, 324

Clinton, MD, 211

Cobb, Clarence, xx

Cockeysville, MD, xvii, 25

Coleman, Margaret, 204

Collins, Bryn C., 160

Collins, Wilkie, 304

*Columbus Daily Times*, 71–72

Columbus, GA, 71–72, 112, 134, 207

Columbus, OH, 260, 301

Commager, Henry Steel, 240

Concord, NH, 178, 251

Confederate Secret Service, 164

Conger, Everton, 215–18

Conrad, Thomas Nelson, 164

Conscription Act, 123–24

Constitutional Convention, 84

Corbett, Thomas P. "Boston," 217–18

Corbyn, Sheridan, 273–74

*Corsican Brothers, The*, 134

Couldock, Charles Walter, 87

Covent Garden Theatre, 2, 4, 8

Cox, Samuel, 212–13

Coyle, John F., 196–97

Crook, William, 203

Crutchfield, George, 37, 51

Curtis, Ed, 142

Cushman, Charlotte, 67, 112

Cuyler, J. C., 90

**D**

D'Arcy, Arthur, 311

*Daily Alta California*, 269

*Daily Creole*, 82

*Daily True Delta Tribune*, 82

Daly, Augustin, 304–5

Davenport, E. L., 99–100, 172

Davenport, Fanny, 256

Davis, Henry Winter, 28,

Davis, Jefferson, 82, 84, 124, 147, 156, 162, 164, 189

*Dayton Daily Empire*, 244

*De Bow's Review*, 148

Deering House Theatre, 90–92

Deery, John, 185, 187, 190, 321

Dehan, Ann, 117

Delannoy, Agatha, 2–3

*Detroit Free Press*, 59, 100

Detroit, MI, 59

Devlin, Mary, 47, 51, 65–67, 109, 154, 159

Dickens, Charles, 129

"Dixie," 142

Doherty, Edward P., 215–16, 219

Dorchester, MA, 109, 122

Doster, William, 170, 188, 225

Douglas, Clara, 260

Douglas, Stephen, 43, 77–78, 123

Dover, NH, 178, 247–48

Dramatic Oil Company, 135

Drury Theatre, 130

Dry Tortugas, 212

Dunbar, David Albert, Jr., 295

Duncan, Charles C., 287

**E**

*East Lynne*, 293–94

Eddy, Edward, 118, 280–81

Edmonds, Laura, 123

Ellsler, John, 43, 134–35, 301–4, 324

Elmira, NY, 210

*Elusive Booths of Burrillville, The*, 313

Emancipation Proclamation, 122–23, 163

Emerson, Edward, 186

Emerson, Edwin A., 34

England, xx, 3, 5, 7, 12, 16, 20, 42, 73, 102, 163, 194, 234, 239, 240, 254, 264

English Theatre, 5

English, William "Bill" B., 55–57, 90–91, 272

Ethel, Agnes, 304

Etyinge, Rose, 259

*Evening Journal*, 103

F

Faber, J. J., 276

*Fanchon, the Cricket*, 83–84, 103, 148

Farjeon, Eleanor, 240

Farren, Mary Ann, 91

Farwell, Leonard, 205, 223

*Female Robinson Crusoes of America, The*, 56

Ferguson, Jim, 187–88, 190, 200, 208, 322

Field, Richard Montgomery, 140

Fisher, Amelia, 143, 149

Fisher, Kate, 53

Flynn, Ellen, 188

Flynn, Thomas, 5

Ford, John, 35–37, 65, 104, 120, 210, 235–37, 259

Fordham, NY, 283, 294

Ford's Theatre, xxiii, 34, 117, 132, 148, 171–72, 185–86, 194–97, 200–2, 205–6, 210, 237, 253, 259, 286

Forrester, Izola, 311–14

Fort Jefferson, 212

Fort Leavenworth, 135–36

Fort McHenry, 98

Fort Sumter, 84, 92–93

Foster, George, 313

Foster, John A., 191

*Foul Play, The*, 272

France, 163, 255

*Frankenstein*, 7

Franklin, PA, 134–35

Fredericks, William S., 34

*French Spy, The*, 82, 146, 148, 268–69

Front Street Theatre, 11, 104

G

G. P. Putnam's Sons, 240

*Gamester, The*, 118

Garfield, James A., 148

Garrett, Richard H., 214–16

Gayety Theatre, 88

Germany, 289

Germon, Euphemia "Effie," 113, 115–17, 120, 218, 233, 253–57, 260, 276

Germon, Jane Anderson, 115

Gettysburg Address, 122

Gettysburg, PA, 122

Gibbons, Charles F., 255–56
Gilbert, Ann Hartley, 102, 325
Gilbert, Charles, 9
Gillette, Abram, Dr., 170
Godwin, Mary, 7
Gone with the Wind, 299
Good Friday, 193–94
Gorsuch, Edward, 26
Gorsuch, Tom, 26
Gould, Nathan, 91
Gourlay, Jeannie, 209, 259
Grable, Betty, 127
Gramercy Park, 36
Grand Opera House, 272
Grant, Ulysses S., 121, 124, 161–62, 185, 193–94, 196, 199–201, 235
Gray, Ada, 137, 293, 317
Gray, Alice, 110, 113, 117, 120, 218, 259–61, 276
Green Mount Cemetery, 20, 220, 238–39, 242
Griffith, D. W., 294
Grover, Leonard, 186
Grover's Theatre, 110, 113, 117, 169, 186–87, 194–96, 253, 321
Guest, James, 267

# H

Hagan, George, 25
Hale, John Parker, 180–81, 190, 244, 246–47
Hale, Lucy Lambert, 120, 174–76, 178, 187, 190, 195, 218, 243, 246–47, 276, 317
Hall, Ann, 23

Hall, John O., 313–14
Hamblin, Thomas, 42–43
Hamlet, 232
Hanel, Blanche, 233
Hanover, NH, 178–79
Hard Times, 113
Harford County, MD, 11–12, 98
Harlan, James, 249
Harlem, NY, 289
Harpers Ferry, WV, 49
Harris, Clara H., 89–90, 199, 203–4, 207
Harrison, Fannie, 224
Hartford Courant, 131
Harvard University, 179
Haverhill, MA, 261
Hawk, Harry, 207–8, 210, 225
Hay, John, 41, 148, 177, 181, 305
Hazelton, Joseph, 195
Helena, MT, 283
Hemphill, T. J., 231
Henderson, Fannie, 190
Herndon, William, 319
Herne, James "Jim" A., 104, 266–72
Herold, David, 112, 170, 172, 185, 195, 199, 202, 204, 210–12, 214–16
Hess, C. Dwight, 186–87, 194–95, 253
Hess, Julia, 195
Hicks, Thomas Holliday, 93
Hoblitzell, Bill, 263–64
Hoboken, NJ, 67
Holland, 2
Holliday Street Theatre, 11, 13, 17, 35, 65, 98, 104, 110, 113, 120, 236, 260, 263, 266

Holt, Joseph, 218
Home for Incurables, 283, 294
Homes, Oliver Wendell, Jr., 179
Hooker, Joe, 189
Horton, Anne, 191
Howard Atheneum, 99, 131, 267–68
Howell, William "Bill" A., 95, 97–99
Howells, William Dean, 58
Howitzer Corps, 50
Hunter, Alexander, 248–51
Hutton, Laurence, 309

# I

Ides of March, 171
*Indianapolis Daily Journal*, 100
Indianapolis, IN, 107
*Innocents Abroad, The*, 287
Ireland, 264
Irving, Henrietta, xxiii, 85–86, 88, 93–94, 279, 282, 317

# J

Jackson, Thomas Jonathan "Stonewall," 189
Jamaica, 275, 281
Jenks, Caroline, 310
Jenny Lind Theatre, 273
Jesus Christ, 193, 299
Jett, William Storke, 214–15
*John Wilkes Booth: A Sister's Memoir*, 240
John Wilson's Circus Company, 274

Johnson, Andrew, 139, 197–98, 219–20, 223, 235, 246, 270–71, 323
Johnson, Claudia, 66
Johnson, Richard, 101
Johnson, Richard Marshall, 107
Johnston, Joe, 193, 197
Jonas-Penley Company, 2
Jones, Avonia, 169
Jones, Thomas, 213
*Julius Caesar*, xix, 28, 166, 171

# K

Kansas City, KS, 261
Kauffman, Michael, 141, 323
Keach, Edwin F., 106
Kean, Edmund, 4, 6, 12
Keene, Laura, 31, 87, 115, 194, 209–10, 234
Kellogg, Clara, 318
Kennedy, John, 191–92
Key, Francis Scott, 59
Key, Philip Barton, 59
Key West, FL, 212
Kimmel, Stanley, xix, 24, 35, 325
*King Lear*, 119
Kingston, Jamaica, 281
Knibb, Joyce, 152, 313–14
Knights of the Golden Circle, 323
Know-Nothing Party, 28
Kunkel, George, 41, 51–53, 105

# L

*L'Email de Paris*, 288

La Montagne, Charles, 303
*La Petite Fadette*, 83
*Lady of Lyons, The*, 131
Lawrence, William, 274
Lawson, William L., 261
Leavenworth, KS, 135–37, 141
Lee, Robert E., 49, 121, 185, 193
Leslie, Amy, 268
Libby, Ellen Weber, 318
Libby, George, 50–51
*Life on Stage*, 306–7
Lincoln, Mary Todd, 189, 194, 201
Lincoln, Robert, 180, 248–49
Liverpool, England, 264
Lloyd, John, 199, 211, 251
London, England, 1–2, 4–8, 12, 18,
      234, 264, 269
Long Branch, NJ, 288, 291–92
Los Angeles, CA, 277
Lou Wooster Public Health Hero
      Award, 299
*Louise: The Story of a Magdalen*,
      299
*Louisville Daily Courier*, 37
*Louisville Daily Democrat*, 100
Louisville, KY, 59, 137, 139, 285–86
Lumpkin's Alley, 36

# M

*Macbeth*, xix, 5,
*Mad Booths of Maryland, The*, xix,
      325
Maddox, John, 197
Maguire, Tom, 269, 273–75
"Maiden's Prayer, A," 57

Makepiece, Bobbie, 295
Malden, MA, 264
*Man and Wife*, 304
Manhattan, NY, 42
*Marble Heart, The*, 304
Marchant, C. F., 119
Marshall Theatre, 9, 11, 36–37,
      39–41, 43, 45–52, 54, 61, 65, 69,
      109, 177
Martin, Patrick, 165
Mashey, Harry P., 292
Mason-Dixon line, 82
Masons, 20, 281
Mathews, John, xxi–xxii, 200, 250,
      322–323
Matthews, Mary, 280
"Maud Muller," 182
May, Frederick, Dr., 111, 219, 320
Maynadier, George Y., 24
*Mazeppa*, 273–74
McClannin, R. Y., 147–48
McClellan, George, 163
*McClure's*, 305
McCullough, John, xxii, 33–34, 76,
      172, 259, 319, 321
McKim, Samuel, 170
McVicker's Theater, 103
Mead, James Harrison, 61, 91, 266
Meade, George G., 123
Mears, Thomas, 134–35
Meech, Wellington, 86
Mehrtens, Patricia, 152, 313–14
Memphis, TN, 147, 289
Menken, Adah Isaacs, 273–74
Merchants Bank, 100, 110
Merrick, Henry, 196

Metropolitan Theatre, Buffalo, NY, 85, 118, 274

Metropolitan Theatre, Indianapolis, IN, 107

Mexican War, 24

Mexico, 212

Mills, Abraham, 310

Mills, Martha Lizola, 310, 313–16

Millward, William, 229

Milton Boarding School, 25

Milwaukee, WI, 95, 279

Mississippi River, 20, 121, 143

Missouri River, 135–36

Mitchell, Anna, 42–43

Mitchell, Charles, 42

Mitchell, Margaret "Maggie" Julia, 39–45, 67, 77, 81–83, 103–4, 143, 147–48, 152, 238, 244, 285–86, 291, 315

Mitchell, Mary, 71

Mobile, AL, 75–76, 260, 299

*Mobile Register*, 260

*Money*, 260

*Montgomery Advertiser*, 70

Montgomery, AL, 70–73, 75–79, 82, 84–85, 90, 145, 147, 286, 297, 299

Montgomery Guards, 50

Montgomery Theatre, 71, 77–78, 81–82, 147

Montreal, Canada, 59, 116, 164, 264, 267–68

Moore, Andrew, 84

Moore, John, 42

Moore, Minnie, 290

Morris, Clara, xxii–xxiii, 67, 301–7

Mosby, John Singleton, 164

Moss, Helen, 195–96

Mount Auburn Cemetery, 271–72, 328

Mowatt, Anna Cora, 67

Mudd, Samuel, Dr., 165–66, 168, 212

Muzzy, Helen, 207

## N

*Nashville Daily Union*, 139

Nashville, TN, 138–40, 205, 293

*National Republican*, 130

National Theatre, 44, 56–59, 260

Nevins, Allan, 240

New Bedford, NY, 86

New England, 55, 125, 131, 274, 299

New Hall Theatre, 129

*New Orleans Daily Crescent*, 83

New Orleans, LA, 11, 20, 36, 55, 71, 75, 82–84, 130, 140–43, 146, 148, 260–61, 280

*New Orleans Times-Picayune*, 58, 82, 140–41, 261

Newport, RI, 173, 246

New York City Draft Riot, 26, 123

New York City, NY, 123, 166

*New York Clipper*, 43, 50, 56, 60, 70, 118–19, 127, 132, 147, 260, 265, 269–70, 274, 292

*New York Daily Times*, 256

*New York Dramatic Mirror*, 283

*New York Evening Post*, 22

*New York Herald*, 250, 260

*New York Post*, 265

*New York Sun*, 281

*New York Times*, 165, 235, 264, 274, 305

*New York Tribune*, 162, 168, 205, 244, 250, 280
*New York World*, 235
New Zealand, 274
Niagara Falls, 67
Nicolay, John, 305–6
Ninth New York Regiment, 288
Noah, Rachel, xxiii
Norcross, A. F., 36
Norfolk, VA, 11, 63

## O

O'Brien, James, 203
O'Laughlen, Bill, 28–29
O'Laughlen, Michael, 157, 169, 171–72, 195, 210, 325
Oak Hill Cemetery, 299
*Octoroon, The*, 130
Old Arsenal Penitentiary, 220, 235–36
Old Broadway Theatre, 260
Old Capitol Prison, 232
Old Fellow's Hall, 188
*Old Job and Jacob Gray*, 117
*Oliver Twist*, 269
Oregon Trail, 135
Orleans Dramatic Relief Association, 261
Orpheum Theatre, 277
Ostend, Belgium, 3
*Othello*, 2, 140
*Our American Cousin*, xxiii, 115, 194, 206, 233, 259
*Our Baby*, 256

## P

Paddock, Fanchon, 292
Paddock, Henry, 44, 288, 290
Paris, France, 264
Park Theatre, 12, 279
Parker, John, 120, 180, 182, 203, 251
Partisan Rangers, 170
Patti, Carlo, 116, 255
Paunell, George, 134
*People*, xxii
Peoria, IL, 293–94
*Pet of the Petticoats*, 268
Peter Taltavull's Star Saloon, 197, 200–2, 206, 320
Petersburg, VA, 63, 188
Peyton, William, 214
*Philadelphia Inquirer*, 227, 229, 250
Philadelphia, PA, 32–33, 47, 58, 63–64, 69, 87, 95, 110, 115–16, 122, 132, 152, 156–57, 163, 189, 230, 232–34, 254, 260
Phillips, Henry, 185
Phillips, Israel B., 48
Pierls, Nully, 255
Pike's Opera House, 228, 243
*Pittsburgh Daily Post*, 59
Pittsburgh, PA, 130, 270, 292
*Pocahontas*, 130
*Pomeroy's Democrat*, 282
Poore, Benjamin Perley, 246
Pope, Charles, 260–61, 323
Port Conway, 213, 215
Port Hudson, LA, 124
Port Royal, 214–15, 218
Port Tobacco, 169, 211–12
*Portland Advertiser*, 92–93

Portland, ME, 90–93, 134
Portland, OR, 274
Potomac River, 98, 123, 163, 166, 169, 171–72, 212–13
Powell, Lewis Thornton, 170–72, 185, 197, 202, 204, 210, 225, 325
Preston, Noble D., 127
Prince George's County, MD, 209
Proctor, Sarah Jane, 303
Protestants, 3, 28
*Providence Daily Journal*, 131
*Providence Daily Post*, 100
*Providence Evening Press*, 116
Providence, RI, 116, 131, 218, 311

Q

Queen, William, Dr., 165–66

R

Rappahannock River, 214
Rathbone, Henry Reed, 89–90, 199–200, 203–4, 207–8
Reignolds, Kate, 105–6, 134
*Richard III*, 31, 35, 101, 111, 120, 131, 134, 140
Richardson, Leon B., 251
Richmond Blues, 50
*Richmond Dispatch*, 46, 50–52, 226
*Richmond Enquirer*, 67
Richmond Grays, 50–52
Richmond Theatre, 105

Richmond, VA, 9, 11, 14, 35–39, 41, 46–47, 50–52, 54–55, 61, 67, 71, 91, 152, 157, 162, 164–65, 169, 171, 173–74, 183, 188, 191, 202, 314
Ritchie, William, 67
*Robbers, The*, 120
Roberts, Albert, 257
Robey, Franklin, 213
Robinson, James, 43
Robson, Stu, 99
Rochester, NY, 85, 88, 138
*Rockford Daily Register*, 249
Rodehamel, John, 296
Rogers, Elijah, 23, 236, 238, 312
*Romeo and Juliet*, 86, 88, 101, 106, 169
Rose, Frank, 237
Ruggles, M. B., 214–15
Rush, James, Dr., 15

S

Salt Lake City, UT, 272
Samples, Gordon, 322
San Francisco, CA, 19–20, 22, 255, 269–70, 273–75, 313
*San Francisco Chronicle*, 269, 274
Sand, Georges, 83
Sanders, George, 165–66
Savannah, GA, 11, 71, 79
Sawtell Theatre, 283
*School for Scandal*, 118
Scotland, 77, 264
*Scotsman*, the, 240
Scraggs, Sally, 115
Seaman, Belle, 198

Seddon, James, 164

Seward, William H., 195, 197, 202, 204, 211, 223

Seymour, Nelson "Nelse," 254–55

Shakespeare Club, 261

Shakespeare, William, 13, 19, 166, 241, 245, 265, 272, 316

Shelley, Percy Bysshe, 7

Sherman, William Tecumseh, 163, 253, 274, 287

Ship Island, MS, 142

*Sickles*, 59

Sickles, Daniel E., 59

Sickles, Teresa, 59

Simmonds, Joseph "Joe" H., 100, 110, 167, 321

Simonton, John, 276–77

Sixteenth New York Cavalry, 215

Sixth Massachusetts Regiment, 93

*Sketches of India*, 115

*Soldier's Daughter, The*, 42

South America, 274, 311

Southall, John, 50

"Southern Marseillaise," 81, 145–46

Spain, 89, 180, 183, 218, 246–47

Spangler, Ned, 206, 210

*Spirit of the Times*, 254

*Springfield Republican*, 131, 244

St. Charles Theatre, 82, 140, 142, 260, 280

St. Helen, John "David George," 280, 316

St. Joseph, MO, 135–37

*St. Joseph Morning Herald*, 136–37

St. Louis, MO, 60–61, 102–3, 107, 136–37, 139, 143, 189

St. Mary's College, 17

St. Paul, MN, 87

St. Timothy's Hall, 26, 157

Stamford, CT, 310

Stanton, Edwin M., 59, 218, 220, 229, 235, 323

"Star-Spangled Banner, The," 59, 72

Starr, Ella, 183, 185–92, 205, 223–26, 247

Starr, John, 188

Staten Island, NY, 257

Stephens, Alexander, 82

Stevenson, John, 311–12

*Stranger, The*, 177

Stuart, J. E. B., 49

Sullivan, Barry, 118

Sumner, Charles Henry, 152

Sumner, Isabella "Isabel," 151–60, 295–96

Surratt, John, Jr., 168–69, 171–72, 198–200, 210, 323, 325

Surratt, Mary, 168, 198–200, 210–11

Surrattsville, MD, 199, 211

Swann, Oswald, 212


# T

*Taming of the Shrew*, 139

Taper, Louise, 153, 296

Taylor, David, 315

Taylor, Joseph Walker, 162

Taylor, Zachary, 24, 162

Temperance Hall Theatre, 71

*Tempest, The*, 13

Tenth New York Cavalry, 127

Theatre Royal, 267, 274

*This One Mad Act: The Unknown Story of John Wilkes Booth and His Family by His Granddaughter*, 313

Thompson, Lout, 231

*Three Fast Men, The*, 56–58, 60

Tileston, Sally, 152

*Times-Democrat*, 141

Titone, Nora, 64

Tolstoy, Leo, xx

Toombs, Robert, 78, 82

Toronto, Canada, 264, 303

Townsend, George Alfred, 25, 28, 34, 37, 52, 69, 88, 151–52

Treakle, Henry, 188

Tremont Theatre, 14

Trenchard, Asa, 194, 204

*Trenton Evening Times*, 242

Trible Opera House, 293

Trotter, Thomas, 4

Troy, NY, 88, 263

Troy Theatre Company, 88

Truman, Helen, 208

Tucker, Beverley, 165

Tuscaloosa, AL, 75

Twain, Mark, 287

*Two Brothers*, 11

# U

*Uncle Tom's Cabin*, 129

Union Square Theatre, 305

Union Theatre, 135

University of Alabama at Birmingham's School of Public Health, 299

*Unlocked Book: A Memoir of John Wilkes Booth by His Sister Asia Booth Clarke, The*, 23, 48, 240

Urquhart, Charles, Dr., 218

U.S. Congress, 28, 56, 116, 123, 163, 180, 302

U.S. Marines, 49

U.S. Navy, 179, 209, 219

U.S. Senate, 180

USS *Montauk*, 219, 244

*Utah Daily Reporter*, 272

# V

Valentine's Day, 175

Varieties Theatre, 130, 260

Venago County, PA, 135

Vicksburg, MS, 121–22

Virginia Rifles, 50

Vivieux, Fanchon, 83

# W

Waldauer, Augustus, 83–84

Wallack, Henry, 14, 254, 256

Wallack's Lyceum Theater, 254

Walnut Street Theatre, 33, 87, 115, 231, 234, 260

Washington, D.C., xxiii, 44, 89, 93, 104, 110–13, 117–18, 132, 139, 148, 165, 168–69, 171–75, 177, 180–81, 183, 186, 188–90, 193–95, 204–5, 209–11, 217, 219–20, 225, 227–28, 232, 235–36, 244–46, 250–51, 254, 263, 270, 285, 293

*Washington Evening Star*, 224, 229
Washington, Lewis, 63
*Washington National Intelligencer*,
   111, 120, 196, 323
*Washington Post*, 290, 294
Washington Theatre, 113, 117–18,
   120
Watkins, Charles S., 293
Weaver, John H., 235–37
Weichmann, Louis, 198
Western, Helen, 54–61, 63, 91–92,
   218, 263–72, 276
Western, Lucille, 54–61, 63, 91–92,
   263
Wheatley, William, 32
Wheeling, VA, 50, 61
White House, the, xix, 148, 164,
   172, 185, 193–95, 203
White, Mary, 48
White Plains, MD, 210
Whitlock, Philip, 52
Whitney, Mary, 310
Whitter, John Greenleaf, 182
William of Orange, Prince, 5
Wilson, Francis, 277
Wilson, George, 145
Wing, Charles, 270–71
Withers, William "Bill," 259
Wood, Allen H., 289
Wood, Charlie, 195
Wood, Fernando, 123
Wood, George, 137, 139, 260
Woodhull, Jacob, 14
Woodman, Lillian, 67
Wooster, Louise "Lou" Catherine,
   73, 75–79, 297–99
Wooster, Margaret, 75

World War II, 127
Worrell's Olympic Theatre, 274
Wren, Eliza, 48, 53
Wren, Ella, 48, 53
Wren, Fred, 53
Wren, George, 48, 196, 253
Wright, Martin, xxi
Wyndham, Charles, 111

# Y

Yancey, William Lowndes, 77–78,
   82
Yarbourgh, Eliza, 76
Yonkers, NY, 307
Young Guards, 50

# Z

Zekiah Swamp, 212